Shakespeare on the Stage

Shakespeare on the Stage

An illustrated
history of
Shakespearian
performance
by
Robert Speaight

Little, Brown
and Company
Boston and Toronto

This book was designed and produced by
George Rainbird Limited,
Marble Arch House, 44 Edgware Road,
London W2

House Editor: Erica Hunningher
Designer: Judith Allan
Indexer: Myra Clark

First American edition published 1973 by
Little, Brown and Company
34 Beacon Street, Boston,
Massachusetts 02106

Library of Congress Catalog Card
Number: 73-2006

The text was set by
Cranmer Brown (Filmsetters) Ltd, London

Printed and bound by
Jarrold & Sons Limited, Norwich

Color plates printed by
Alabaster Passmore & Sons Ltd, Maidstone

Printed in Great Britain

For Wendy and John Trewin

If people do not trust Shakespeare, I do not see why they bother to produce him at all.

Margaret Webster

The Shakespearian play is composed of a succession of waves through which the spectator moves like a swimmer.

J. Dover Wilson

Contents

Color Plates

Preface

This book takes a very wide view from which much detail is perforce excluded. There is matter in the subject for five volumes as long as this one. Nevertheless to avoid the tedium of a catalogue I have concentrated on those performances and productions which seem to me the most significant and, in the later chapters, on those which I have seen myself. On the continent of Europe I have confined myself to certain countries. The main features of Shakespeare production in England between the reopening of the theatres at the Restoration and the middle of the nineteenth century have been necessarily compressed into a single chapter, but the reader will find them fully chronicled elsewhere. There was no space for a discussion of Scandinavia and the Low Countries where much interesting work has been done; nor, save in a couple of instances, for the flourishing amateur theatre in Britain, Canada, and the United States.

This book is intended for the general playgoer; it will teach little to the theatrical historian. To many of these, however, I am indebted for the personal assistance they have given me. Mr J. C. Trewin has told an important part of the story in *Shakespeare on the British Stage, 1900-1964.* I have relied upon him, while doing my best to escape the accusation of plagiarism from one who has done so much to help me. For the earlier chapters Professor A. C. Sprague has given me some valuable suggestions, and I am most grateful to him. My thanks must also go to Professor Glynne Wickham, Professor Neville Coghill, Sir John Gielgud, Mr Marius Goring, Mr Ivor Brown, Mlle Sylvie Chevalley of the Comédie Française, the Librarian of the Bibliothèque de l'Arsenal, Miss Helen Willard of the Harvard Theatre Collection; and most particularly to Professor Richard Ludwig and the Department of Humanities at Princeton University. They offered me special facilities in the magnificent library at Princeton, and most generously invited me there as their guest to make use of them. My indebtedness to all those who have written about the production of Shakespeare, with a far greater authority than I possess, will be apparent in the following pages, and in the bibliography at the end of the book. Certain passages in the later chapters have already appeared in the *Shakespeare Quarterly*, and I am grateful to the editor of that Journal for allowing their reproduction here.

I must also thank my secretary, Mrs Pat Brayne, for the patience and expertise with which she has typed a complicated MS.

Since the 350th anniversary of the year in which the first folio of Shakespeare's plays was published by two of his fellows coincides with the publication of this book, the story of Shakespeare on the stage has a particular relevance.

R.S.

1 The Wooden O

We cannot say with any certainty when Shakespeare set out over Clopton bridge, with a few necessaries in his saddlebags, plays and poems in his head, and all the world before him. But if we put the date in the autumn of 1586 we shall not be far out. He was twenty-two years old, and leaving behind him a wife – not, it seems, loved to distraction – with three children. He had his living to earn, and perhaps his fortune to make. His ambition, like his genius, knew no bounds, and London would fulfil them both.

Shakespeare could always put his poems on to paper, and before many years had passed Cambridge undergraduates were sleeping with 'Venus and Adonis' under their pillows, in default of better company. Those sensuous stanzas would pleasantly have coloured their dreams. But it was a more difficult matter, then as now, to get a play on to the stage; and Shakespeare was looking for a larger audience than the university wits and the erudite, sophisticated patricians of Southampton House. He was fortunate in his moment. There were now two theatres, standing close to one another, on the northern boundary of the City limits. They represented the transition of play-acting from amateur to professional status, and from provincial vagabondage to metropolitan stability. London was the magnet, as it always has been and always will be. Country squires were no longer permitted to maintain their private companies; licenses for these were given only to peers, and in 1574 Letters Patent were issued to the Earl of Leicester's company to give regular performances in London on weekdays throughout the year. Leicester's wealth, prestige, and intimacy with the Queen lent a particular importance to the enterprise.

Among the members of Leicester's company was James Burbage, a carpenter by trade though an actor by profession. His manual skill designated him for the task of building a theatre and finding a site for it. Now that the actors were settled in the capital they would need a roof over their heads, even if the audience had none over theirs. Burbage chose the fields of St Leonard's parish in Shoreditch for his playhouse, on the edge of the open country, and as far as possible from the jaundiced eyes of the Puritan City Fathers, whose zeal in the making of money was matched by their zeal in preventing other people from spending it. Burbage's 'Theatre' – as it was quite simply called – was opened in 1576, at a cost of six hundred pounds. It was built of wood and probably circular in shape after the model of other public arenas used for bear-baiting and similar entertainments. There is no reason to suppose that Burbage had primarily, and certainly not exclusively, in mind the inn-yards where the company might have acted in the provinces. Evidence suggests that, more often than not, they preferred to play indoors. To declaim within close earshot of the traffic – very noisy over cobbled stones – would have imposed a severe strain on actors and audience alike, and have deprived Mine Host of essential space for parking. When Professor Glynne Wickham tried to reproduce such a performance in the yard of the New Inn at Gloucester, he was forced to abandon the attempt.

Shakespeare: the Chandos portrait

Nor should we think of the Theatre as the primitive and improvised structure that antiquarian fancy has imagined it. A people who could not spend enough on their clothes and country houses, for whom no procession or pageantry could be too splendid, and for whom magnificence ranked among the first duties of man, would hardly have welcomed a 'wooden O' without embellishment. In fact, a preacher at Paul's Cross in 1578 denounced Burbage's playhouse as 'the gorgeous playing-place erected in the fields' – though here Puritan rancour may have coloured the description. No picture or ground-plan of the Theatre has come down to us, but it must have served as a model, variable in detail, for the playhouses that followed it, about which we know considerably more. Of these the Swan (1594), though not the most famous, may be taken as typical; and it is the only one of which we possess an illustration. This was discovered, with a written description in manuscript, in the university library of Utrecht. Both the drawing and description had been copied from an account by John de Witt, who had visited London in or about 1596. We do not know whether de Witt's report was oral or written, nor how accurate was his memory, nor how faithful the transcription of the sketch. This or that detail, perhaps important, may have been omitted or misunderstood. We learn that there were in London at that time 'four theatres of noteworthy beauty' and that of these the 'largest and most distinguished' was the Swan; that it accommodated 3,000 persons, and was 'built of a concrete of flint stones . . . and supported by wooden columns, painted in such excellent imitation of marble that it might deceive even the most cunning'. Other visitors remarked upon the elegance of the London theatres. Both the sketch and the description raise as many questions as they answer; and a great deal of ink has been spilt in answering them.

Interior of the Swan Theatre, Bankside

Shakespeare, as far as we know, had no connection with the Swan; it was at the Theatre, where he was reported to have played after it had come under the patronage of Lord Strange, at the Globe, and later at the roofed-in Blackfriars that he learnt and matured his stagecraft. Nor, if we take de Witt's drawing at its face value, need we assume its identity with all the theatres which preceded or followed it. The Fortune, for example, and several others were rectangular in shape. But we do know that when James Burbage abandoned the Theatre in 1598, to escape the threat of closure, it was rebuilt with the same materials, but now octagonal in form, on the south bank of the river, and rechristened as the Globe. We know, too, that when the first Globe was burnt down in 1613 it was reconstructed exactly as before, only rather more splendidly. There is, then, a general consistency of planning between the theatre which Shakespeare found when he took up his lodgings in Bishopsgate and the theatre which he left on his retirement to Stratford, having made his fortune and earned his immortality. What we must do, therefore, is to collate what we can deduce from de Witt's drawing and description, and what we can conjecture to have been in the mind of James Burbage when he provided London with its first permanent playhouse – the very direct ancestor, be it always remembered, of the theatre in which his son Richard made his name.

Burbage was not starting from scratch. In designing his auditorium he wished to accommodate as many people as could see and hear what was happening on the stage, and in choosing a circular or polygonal shape he was looking back, not only to the bear-baiting arenas, but also to the Roman amphitheatres, rather than forward to the Teatro Olimpico in Vicenza, and other proscenium stages already coming into vogue on the continent. The physical conditions of the theatre for which Shakespeare worked had much more in common with the medieval stage than with the proscenium stage which followed it. No longer amateur and provincial, it was still popular, although in the following reign it would succumb to the pressures, at once more frivolous and refined, of a social and intellectual *élite*. But having built his auditorium for approximately 3,000 spectators, what did Burbage do about his stage? Here he would have had two prototypes in mind – the booth stages easily erected and taken down in a courtyard or town hall, and the great chamber of a nobleman's house or inn of court where plays used frequently to be given. These would have a panelled screen, with two doors, at one end, leading into a fairly narrow passage, and a musicians' gallery above it. The reconstructed hall of Grays Inn and the dining-hall at Magdalene College, Cambridge, although this has only a single door, are among several examples to be seen today.

It will be evident that de Witt's drawing incorporates the essential features of both prototypes. His stage is apparently fixed, though it need not have been so if it were of lighter construction, and if the whole space of the arena were required for other forms of entertainment. Whether it was fixed at the Theatre we do not know; it was certainly permanent at the Globe. Bear-baiting, and less respectable amusement, were catered for near by. The two doors and gallery at the back reproduce the two entrances, screen, and gallery of a Tudor Hall, where a stage could be built out in front of them. When the indoor theatre at Blackfriars was opened in 1608 this was the formula in use, so that a company performing a play at the Globe in summer could repeat the performance at the Blackfriars in winter with minimal changes in production – and both theatres were licensed to the King's Men, with Richard and Cuthbert Burbage in command. There is thus no conflict between what de Witt presumably saw at the Swan and James Burbage presumably built at the Theatre. And if the story is true that Shakespeare looked after the horses of more privileged playgoers while they were attending the performance, it was probably at the entrance of the Theatre that he held the bridles. We may assume that he did not hold them for very long.

The Globe

With an auditorium for 3,000 spectators, and a stage forty-three feet wide and twenty-seven feet in depth, cherished notions of Elizabethan 'intimacy' rather go by the board. They are more pertinent to the Blackfriars with its seating for 700. The larger public playhouses suggest a disconcerting parallel with the multi-purpose auditoriums in America, and more particularly in Canada, whose wretched acoustics drive actors and audience to despair. But whatever the size of the Elizabethan theatres, their shape ensured that the actors should have space to perform in, and that no one in the audience should be too far away from them. With the gallants sitting on the stage and the groundlings swarming below it, there was little risk of the actor losing touch with an audience which surrounded him on three sides. And there is yet another cherished notion which de Witt's drawing lays by the heels – and that is the hypothesis of an inner stage. Volumes have been written on how this feature, for which there is no evidence whatsoever, was employed in the production of Shakespeare's plays. It has served for Juliet's bed-chamber, and Juliet's tomb, and Friar Lawrence's cell; for Gertrude's closet and Brutus' tent; for any domestic interior where two or three persons are gathered together. The productions of entire plays have been reconstructed with neat alternations between the inner and the outer stage – perhaps because the imaginary archway giving entrance to this imaginary alcove seemed happily to foreshadow the proscenium, behind which we are all supposed to feel more comfortable.

One is grateful to scholars like Mr Hosley and Professor Glynne Wickham for ridding us of this incubus; for no one had asked themselves how a scene could be played in a recess where the actors would be invisible and inaudible to large sections of the audience, and which would in itself be necessarily too shallow to accommodate dramatic movement. Moreover the space it was supposed to occupy would be needed for the stacking of properties required for the play in performance. If there had been an inner stage at the Swan, it is incredible that de Witt should not have recorded it. Since a curtained-off space was often required in plays of the period, this was provided for by hangings suspended from the front of the balcony. These could be drawn back to reveal one of the back openings, about seven feet wide and nine feet high – a space, not for drama, but discovery. So we can imagine the 'discovery' of the caskets in *The Merchant of Venice*, with the suitors taking them up and advancing down stage to meditate and discourse upon their choice; of Ferdinand and Miranda playing chess in *The Tempest*; of Falstaff asleep in *Henry IV, Part One*; perhaps of Hermione in the last scene of *The Winter's Tale*, although here the supposed statue is so central to the denouement of the play that a more strategic and advanced position was probably found for it. The argument that an 'inner stage' would have lent 'intimacy' to interior scenes is refuted by the unoccupied length of bare boards yawning between semi-audible and semi-visible actors, confined in a space no wider than a passage, and an audience trying to make out what was going on there. A spectator in the third gallery of the Swan seated just underneath the man displaying a flag in de Witt's drawing was likely to have asked for his money back if he were expected to follow a scene being played on the 'inner stage' upon which so much unsupported theory has been lavished.

So we are now in a position to reconstruct, from external and internal evidence, the structural framework within which Shakespeare's plays were produced at the Theatre or the Globe. A wide projecting platform, raised about five feet six inches from the ground, set in a round or polygonal arena, the rear portion of the stage covered by a roof, either supported by pillars or extending like a pent-house. A wall at the back with two entrances and a gallery above it, divided – in the case of the Swan – by short pillars, and perhaps above this a third gallery for musicians. The tiring house, or actors' dressing-rooms, was behind – probably, in the case of the Globe, built flush with the walls of the arena. There was a trapdoor in the middle of the platform. The convenience of *two* doors at the back will be evident, since this enabled the actors to exit by one of them at the end of a scene, and the characters in the following scene to enter by the other. Only in one place, in all the thirty-eight plays of the Shakespearian canon, do the same characters finish one scene and begin the next. Let us see then how this might have worked in a given context.

We must imagine Macbeth going out by one door (A) on his way to Duncan's bedchamber, and Lady Macbeth immediately entering at (B). Macbeth naturally returns at (A) and Lady Macbeth exits from it to replace the daggers beside the sleeping grooms. When the knocking of Macduff is heard, the guilty pair will go out at (B), since (A) is far too closely associated in their minds, and in that of the audience as well, with the crime they have just committed. The stage is now empty; the knocking continues; and we have the stage direction – 'Enter a Porter'. If he enters at (B) he will presumably have collided with his master and mistress on their way out. If he enters at (A) he will appear to be coming *either*

[1] I am indebted for this suggestion to Mr Michael Macowan
[2] Lecture to the Shakespeare Conference at Stratford-upon-Avon, 1972

from Duncan's bedchamber, *or* from the main entrance of the castle which he is presently to open. I suggest – and here the comic and macabre effect of his entrance makes its impact – that he comes up *through the trapdoor*.[1] Even to an audience familiar with the play, this will be surprising; to an audience seeing the play for the first time it would have been even more so. But since the Elizabethan stage was *essentially* unlocalized, the porter will be able to fetch Macduff and Lennox from (A), without anyone thinking that this leads *only* to Duncan's room; Macbeth and his lady can return from (B); and Macduff can exit, unsuspecting, at (A) on his mission to awaken the King. The Elizabethan stage had the advantage of being anywhere one wanted at any particular moment; it could remind one of locality, and as easily allow one to forget it.

Professor Coghill, basing himself on the text, has very persuasively argued[2] that the Witches made their exits and their entrances on wires; and that these 'hoverings' could easily have been contrived by the skilled mechanics of the day. He has also demonstrated that Malcolm's army *must* have made its entrance from the auditorium, since it could not otherwise have seen the branches of Birnam Wood – hung, supposedly, from the balcony – which were to serve for its camouflage. He applied the same reasoning to the entrance of Portia and Nerissa in the last act of *The Merchant of Venice*. 'That light we see is burning in my hall' could only have been spoken from a similar distance.

Other uses for the trapdoor will spring to mind. It will certainly serve for Ophelia's grave, and perhaps for Malvolio's prison. Equally clear is the convenience of the upper stage. Here is Antony's rostrum, Juliet's and Brabantio's balcony, Cleopatra's monument, Christopher Sly's stage box, and the battlements of Angiers. We must imagine Antony starting his oration above, with Caesar's corpse below, and then coming down (by an inner staircase) for its conclusion, the dialogue of the citizens covering his descent.

Visscher's view of London

But there is one detail of de Witt's drawing that puzzles us. Who are all these people looking on from the balcony? If they are privileged spectators of a play which could dispense with the upper stage – *Love's Labour Lost* and *As You Like It* are examples – they would spend a great deal of the afternoon contemplating the backs of the performers. It has been plausibly suggested that they are other actors, watching not a performance but a rehearsal and waiting for their cues. They would be in the natural position for taking them up with the least delay, and for knowing when to do so.

You will often hear it argued that Shakespeare would have welcomed the scene designer as his ally, and have exploited to the full the amenities and mechanism of the modern stage. Others have claimed that the absence of scenic embellishment was the very condition of his art. The latter beg what can no longer be described as a question at all. Was it likely, in the first place, that audiences accustomed to three-dimensional 'mansions' in performances at Court – a convention inherited from the medieval stage – should have been content with bare boards, poetry, and passion in their public theatres? Why should their tastes suddenly have acquired the austerity of their Puritan opponents? Even if Shakespeare had disposed of a lighting panel capable of flooding his stage with moonlight, is it probable that the greatest poet in the language would have absolved himself from writing 'How sweet the moonlight sleeps upon this bank'? What audience complains today that the effect of the poetry is diminished by its visual counterpart? It is no argument that the Elizabethan audience was more able than we are to 'piece out our imperfections with your thoughts' and 'to cram within this wooden O the very casques that did affright the air at Agincourt'. They were only too pleased when the necessity for doing so was spared them.

Travelling players visit a manor, 1610

The amateur company of 'rude mechanicals' who presented *Pyramus and Thisbe* at Duke Theseus' court felt the need of a moon, a brake, a wall, and a lion if their tragedy were to be suitably performed. They managed as well as they could, but others would have managed better. If Philostrate had been in charge, and the reunited lovers performing the play, the case would have been substantially altered. The lion would have looked like a lion; the wall would have borne some resemblance to masonry; the brake would have been manifestly in leaf; and who knows but a moon might not have been let down from the ceiling? None of these visual aids would have taxed unduly the office of the Master of Revels, under whose authority they were procured. The Lord Chamberlain's – later the King's – Men had the status of Court officials; they were known as Grooms of the Royal Chamber and wore a special robe when they attended a Coronation – and the Court was not likely to starve their property room. Costumes and scenic elements used in an elaborate Masque would be handed on to the public theatres, not much the worse for wear. What was good enough for Henslowe at the Fortune would not be too good for Burbage at the Globe; and Henslowe's inventory has come down to us in considerable detail.

The development of scenic furnishing in the theatre was a progress from emblem to illusion. Whatever constructions were accommodated on the stage of the Globe *stood* for something; once Inigo Jones had his way, and the roofed in theatres ousted the open theatres in patrician favour, they *simulated* something. It may well have happened that leading actors disliked playing important scenes from the gallery, since this removed them so far from the audience; and we know that it was the custom to let down a throne from the roof, so that it came into place well forward, more or less over the trap-door. From here it could as easily be raised to clear a space for the following scene. Other elements could be brought in from the doors at the back; these were wide enough to allow the passage of Imogen's or Desdemona's bed. It appears certain that for the last act of *Richard III* the tents of Richard and Richmond faced each other across the forestage; and is it fanciful to imagine Hecate's cauldron rising up through the trap-door, or descending from the roof, as the paraphernalia of the banquet scene is quickly cleared away? Did the Apparitions stalk across the balcony, or did they, too, arise from the trap-door? It depended, maybe, on how important Burbage, or another, thought it that the audience should see his face. We know that trees were among the properties in use. Did Orlando nail his verses to one of them, or did he make do with one of the forward pillars? Did the Globe possess these pillars? In the later plays, when Shakespeare had retired to Stratford, the stage directions are more explicit. Ariel in *The Tempest,* dressed as a 'harpy', evidently flies down from the roof, and the banquet which vanishes 'with a quaint device' presumably disappears through the trap. And in *Cymbeline* Jupiter descends, astride an eagle and launching a thunderbolt. Quaint devices for us, but fairly sophisticated for the 'wooden O'. In the main, however, stagecraft at the Globe is matter for conjecture, and we shall be kept guessing in default of further evidence. But, starting from the premiss that any audience likes to see and hear as clearly as possible what is happening on the stage, I think we may assume that scenic accessories were used not only to flatter the eye but to assist the understanding, and to translate to the forefront of the stage what, in their absence, would have taken place at the back.

2

When all is said, however, this was an actor's and a dramatist's theatre; those who craved for pageantry could find plenty of it elsewhere. Shakespeare was himself an actor, and according to Aubrey, whose gossip should not be taken for gospel, 'did act exceeding well'. He would have started as a Hired Man at ten shillings a week, playing and doubling small parts and shifting furniture, until in 1594 he had a part share in the enterprise of the Lord Chamberlain's Men. This was quick advancement. He continued to act, in his own plays and Ben Jonson's, until 1603; and he may have done so until he had made enough money to retire to Stratford. Adam in *As You Like It* and the Ghost in *Hamlet* are among the parts he is reported to have played. This denotes him as a 'character' man; and such subsidiary rôles would have enabled him to keep an eye on what Burbage or Will Kempe were doing with his text. He may well have discharged the function of 'guider' – which was Dekker's word for a stage director. But in whatever way he was employed, Hamlet is speaking from Shakespeare's experience when he gives his views on acting. The famous speech is not quite the irrelevance it appears, since Hamlet is desperately anxious that the players – a respectable company, we must suppose – shall do justice to the *Murder of Gonzago.* It tells us all we want to know about what good judges considered good acting to be at the turn of the century, when the Globe had earned the right to Ben Jonson's encomium of 'the glory of the Bank'.

Just as Shakespeare was moulding his verse, with no loss of imagery and incandescence, to the rhythms of colloquial speech, and turning his back on rhetoric – the difference between a relaxed and a coiled spring – so the style of

acting appropriate to Alleyn as Tamberlaine or Burbage as Richard III was no
longer suited to Hamlet, and still less to Leontes and Prospero. Probably the
Fortune was still in competition with the more naturalistic methods of the Globe,
if these were developing in line with Hamlet's advice to the players. But even
the Globe with its 3,000 spectators invited a broader style than a performance at
Court or the Blackfriars, where there were no groundlings with ears to be tickled.
Shakespeare's own preferences are not in doubt. He enjoined the actors to speak
'trippingly' and not to encumber their speech with useless and inflated
gestures; not to confuse restraint with insipidity; to preserve a certain smoothness even in the height of passion; always to have something in reserve; to 'hold
as t'were the mirror up to nature'. The comedians were still a problem. Evidently
Will Kempe had taken the bit between his teeth, and his gags had set the
auditorium on a roar. But Shakespeare would have none of this, and Kempe
took his talents elsewhere. The censure of a single connoisseur mattered more
than the plaudits of the pit. No dramatic critic or stage director has bettered the
instruction given to the players at Elsinore.

Even if we add another sixty minutes to the 'two hours traffic of the stage', the
Elizabethan actor must have possessed a secret of flexible, rapid, and musical
delivery which his successors have largely lost. We simply do not know what an
Elizabethan performance sounded like, but we may assume that a voice suitable
for rhetoric was also cultivated for the stage. This was described as 'that
pleasant and delicate well ordered song'. Mr Bertram Joseph[1] defines it as a
'sustained tone', reaching without effort to the furthest seats in the theatre,
combining melody and meaning, and producing the effect of nature with the
maximum of art. We should also remember how volatile, demonstrative, and
uninhibited were Englishmen of that time. It was the Puritans who fathered the
stiff upper lip. Lips were free when Erasmus visited the Court of Henry VIII;
Englishmen, he noted, were for ever kissing one another. There is no need to
read ambivalence into Antonio's affection for Bassanio; for the Elizabethans all
affection was physical in one way or another. Shakespeare does, it is true, voice a
momentary discontent when it comes to staging a major campaign, but he does
not complain of a boy as Juliet, or even as Cleopatra. To judge from a performance of *Othello* at Oxford in 1610, he would have had no need to complain of

The Children of the Chapel Royal

his Desdemona who 'in her death moved us specially, when, as she lay in her
bed, her face alone implored the pity of the audience'. Genius can always turn
convention to commodity, and Shakespeare left the sophisticates of a later time
to puzzle out the Freudian complications of a Duke who fancies himself in love
with a great lady, but is really in love with a girl dressed up as a boy (actually a boy
pretending to be a girl dressed up as a boy), and the great lady falling in love with
the same girl, but happily contenting herself with her twin brother, and the girl
falling in love with the Duke, whose suit she is presenting to the great lady. The
brain turns Pirandellian cartwheels when it troubles to explore the shimmering
depths of *Twelfth Night*; and should we be tempted to wonder what Shakespeare
would have done with his love scenes if he had had actresses to play them, we
have only to remember what happened to love in the theatre when the actresses
eventually came into their inheritance. The mind boggles at the notion of Nell
Gwynne, or another, 'hopping forty paces through the public street'; but the
picture of an athletic boy Cleopatra, whose voice had not yet descended a
'chopine', behaving so gamesomely, is both seductive and plausible. It was just
because there were certain things that Shakespeare could not ask his boy actors

so do that they were able to suggest them so convincingly. 'The iron tongue of midnight has told twelve; lovers to bed.' Who wants a bedroom scene after a line like that?

The boy actors of the Elizabethan and Jacobean stage were divided into two categories – the choristers who were pressed, ruthlessly on occasion, into the service of the cathedrals and the religious foundations, and formed acting companies of their own; and the juvenile recruits to the professional theatre who often graduated into regular members of the company, playing mature, and masculine, parts when they were old enough to do so. The two were in hot competition. During the eighteen years before James Burbage opened his Theatre the Court had ordered forty-six performances from the children's companies and only thirty-two from the professionals; and Burbage was asking for trouble in converting a room at the Blackfriars Priory into a theatre with the Children of the Chapel Royal already established on the premises. His son Richard was equally rash in leasing the Blackfriars Theatre to those who had the Children under their management. Neither Rosencrantz, nor Hamlet himself, questioned the Children's competence; they merely agreed that the 'boys carry it away'. A discussion quite irrelevant to the play, and now nearly always cut in its performance, would have had a topical relevance for the audience at the Globe.

Richard Burbage

We know from the First Folio the names of the principal actors among the Lord Chamberlain's men. Of these the most famous was Richard Burbage; his brother Cuthbert seems to have been occupied in administration. Between them they held half of the shares in the Globe playhouse. It was a cooperative enterprise; in this sense all the profit-sharing actors were actor-managers. Richard was born in, or about, 1568, and died in 1619. We know several parts that he played, and others we can easily surmise. We also know from the portrait in the Dulwich Gallery what he looked like. The features are broad, with high forehead and commanding eyes; a face that would carry, though it is inexpressive here. Since he was a painter, we may deduce that Sir Thomas Overbury took him for his model of 'An Excellent Actor' – which appeared in the sixth edition of the *Characters*.

Whatsoever is commendable in the grave Orator, is most exquisitely perfect in him; for by a full and significant action of body, he charms our attention. . . . He doth not strive to make nature monstrous, she is often seen in the same scene with him, but neither on stilts nor Crutches; and for his voice 'tis not lower than the prompter, nor louder than the Foil and Target.

If, as seems likely, this tribute was paid to Burbage, it is easy to conclude that Burbage practised what Hamlet preached. When he died one of his admirers could find no better epitaph than 'Exit Burbage'; and we have Flecknoe's lines for corroboration:

> He is gone and with him what a world are dead,
> Which he revived, to be revived so,
> No more young Hamlet, old Hieronymo,[2]
> King Lear, the grieved Moor, and more beside
> That lived in him, have now for ever died.
> Oft have I seen him leap into the grave,
> Suiting the person which he seemed to have
> Of a sad lover with so true an eye,

[1] *The Tragic Actor* (1959)
[2] *The Spanish Tragedy*

> That there I would have sworn he meant to die.
> Oft have I seen him play this part in jest,
> So lively that spectators and the rest
> Of his sad crew, whilst he but seem'd to bleed,
> Amaz'd, thought even then he died indeed.

Although Shakespeare heads the list of principal players in the First Folio, this was no doubt a compliment to the dramatist rather than the actor. Following Burbage come Phillips, Heminge, Pope, Condell, Sly and Kempe. It is a sobering thought that if Heminge and Condell had not kept their prompt-books we might have lost the whole of Shakespeare's works, except for a few *Quartos*, many of them imperfect. Heminge – a rotund, asthmatic actor, remembered for his Falstaff – was also a competent man of business. Fellow players entrusted him with the care of their orphans and their estates, and for a time he acted as agent for all the London companies in their negotiations with the Master of Revels. His authority enabled him to get hold of the prompt-books, for after Burbage's death the following couplet was in circulation:

William Sly

Kemps nine daies vvonder.

Performed in a daunce from
London to Norwich.

Containing the pleaſure, paines and kinde entertainment
of *William Kemp* betweene *London* and that Citty
in his late Morrice.

Wherein is ſomewhat ſet downe worth note; to reprooue
the ſlaunders ſpred of him: many things merry,
nothing hurtfull.

Written by himſelfe to ſatisfie his friends.

William Kempe: title page to
Kemps nine daies wonder

LONDON
Printed by *E. A.* for *Nicholas Ling*, and are to be
ſolde at his ſhop at the weſt doore of Saint
Paules Church. 1600.

Then fear not, Burbage, heaven's angry rod
When thy fellows are angels and old Heminge is God.

William Sly must have run him close as Falstaff; humour and animation shine out from a face which is a mask for comedy. But apart from Burbage, we know little for certain of what parts were played by which actors. One thinks there may have been a Welshman, and certainly a good Welsh accent, in the company; Sir Hugh Evans, Fluellen, Owen Glendower. Certain types, infinitely varied, run through the plays; Berowne, Benedick, Petruchio, Hotspur, Falconbridge, and ultimately Enobarbus. Someone not unlike Sir Ralph Richardson may have given breath and body to them all. Rosalind, Viola, and Imogen called for the talents of one boy actor; Beatrice, Portia, and Desdemona for another; Cordelia, Marina, and Miranda for a third. One of the boys, Dicky Robinson, the only one to be mentioned in the Folio, developed as a popular comedian; and Kempe succeeded Tarleton as the leading 'clown'. He was impudent and idolized, playing Dogberry in *Much Ado,* and Peter in *Romeo and Juliet* – for want of anything meatier to chew. He ranked third in the company until he suddenly sold his shares in February 1599, and then executed his famous solo dance from London to Norwich. These players were athletes as well as actors; the stuff from which Benson formed his company three centuries later; roguish, no doubt, when the humour took them, but no longer vagabonds. One or two of them even became churchwardens. John Lowin joined the company in 1603, and with Taylor took over some of Burbage's parts, and also some of his shares, after the great tragedian's death. Again judging from his portrait, Lowin was a heavily built man and excelled in heavy rôles – Falstaff and Henry VIII among them. He outlived the demolition of the Globe in 1644, and looks every inch a king of the theatrical establishment – indeed rather more established than theatrical, in his sober Caroline attire.

John Lowin

The absence of dramatic criticism at the time – and the theatre got along very well without it – leaves us in the dark about much that we should like to know. What, for example, were the uses of soliloquy? Did the actor begin by talking to the audience, and then, as Shakespeare's art matured, did he increasingly talk to himself? May we not detect a difference of perspective between Richard III telling us frankly that he is going to 'play the villain', Viola wondering why Olivia has sent Malvolio after her with the ring, Edmund arguing the natural rights of bastardy, or Iago trying to justify his machinations – and Hamlet in the contemplation of suicide, or Macbeth in the meditation of murder? The perspective would shift easily for the same character in the same play. Hamlet, in his first soliloquy, could inform the audience in urgent, loquitive verse that he is burnt up inside because of his mother's marriage; and, in his last, ask no one but himself 'what is a man, if the chief good and market of his time be but to sleep and feed?' Richard III's soliloquy on the eve of Bosworth and Richard II's in the cell at Pomfret both invite introspection, even if they do not positively demand it. So does Claudius' 'O my offence is rank, it smells to Heaven'. It was easy to share one's most secret thoughts with the audience under that open sky and in that octagonal arena, or in the candle-lit interior of the Blackfriars. Whether they were spoken *to* the audience or *with* them was a matter of theatrical discretion.

We can speak with more certainty about the use of music. The golden age of lyric and dramatic verse in England was also a time of high musical accomplishment; and here, as in so many other respects, Shakespeare took advantage of the moment with which fortune had favoured him. The Court was musically minded. Henry VIII was himself a composer; Edward VI played the lute, and Mary and Elizabeth the virginals. The publication of *Musica Transalpina*, a selection of Italian madrigals with English words, in 1588, inspired the English school of madrigalists. The passion for music even invaded the barbers' shops. Men waiting to be shaved would cool their impatience by strumming on the lute – an instrument with only four strings and easy to master. Music, for Shakespeare, was an analogue of the harmony which should reign on earth, and certainly reigned in Heaven.

> The man that hath no music in his soul
> Nor is moved by concord of sweet sounds
> Is fit for treasons, stratagems, and spoils . . .
> Let no such man be trusted.

It is to the sound of music that Lear wakens to sanity, and the statue of Hermione stirs to life. When Henry IV is dying, Warwick calls for 'music in the other room'; Cerimon in *Pericles* revives Thaisa to the 'still and woeful music' of the viol; and Orsino in *Twelfth Night* calls for music which is 'the food of love'. These accompaniments on strings would have been played by musicians, visible or hidden as required, in the gallery. In the case of the mysterious hautboys heard by the soldiers in *Antony and Cleopatra* it would have come from beneath the stage. In whatever context music was employed, it reinforced dramatic meaning and very often illustrated human character – generally by a song. Here Shakespeare could draw upon the boys' voices, and there were certainly adult players in the company who could sing. One of them would be called upon for Amiens in *As You Like It* and Balthazar in *Much Ado*. Robert Arnim would have been heard as Feste, Autolycus, and the Fool in *Lear*. From the boys who played Desdemona, Glendower's daughter, Ariel, and the fairies in *A Midsummer Night's Dream*, something more than competence was called for. On the other hand, Ophelia could get through her significant snatches with less than professional skill. The songs were accompanied, or otherwise, as the character or scene dictated. Feste would not have brought an instrument to Toby's drinking bout, nor even to Orsino's court. Iago could break spontaneously into 'Let me the canakin clink' at another drinking bout, which had more serious consequences than Toby's defiance of the licensing laws in Olivia's household. On the other hand Ophelia is described as entering with a lute for her mad scene, although this stage direction is now more generally honoured in the breach than the observance. Brutus alludes three times to the instrument on which Lucius accompanies his song; Queen Katharine in *Henry VIII* commands her maid of honour to 'take thy lute, wench'; and Pandarus in *Troilus and Cressida* asks for an instrument before he embarks upon the song which distils the heated eroticism of the play.

The musicians disposed of whatever instruments were best adapted to their dramatic use – strings for magic and mystery and reconciliation, trumpets and drum for a battle, a military parley, or a royal entrance. Edgar, when he replies to Edmund's challenge in the last act of *Lear*, enters 'armed, with a trumpet before him'. In *Hamlet* there is talk of the recorders which presumably accompanied the Dumb Show; and in *A Midsummer Night's Dream* the huntsmen are commanded to awake the sleeping lovers with their horns. The demand for music is more explicit in the later plays; *Coriolanus* and *Henry VIII* both call for wood-wind, brass and drums, and *Henry VIII* for 'four Quiristers singing'. The private theatres gave larger scope for musicians, and we know that here they played during the intervals. A consort of viols, echoing thinly at the Globe, would have made its appropriate effect under the rafters of the Blackfriars. To a certain extent Shakespeare's use of music was following the theatre in the direction of masque – which was also, implicitly, the direction of opera. He wrested it, as he wrested everything else, to his purposes; and these were the development of tragedy into what has been called romance, where tragedy and comedy were reconciled. To the achievement of this harmony music made its natural contribution.

II The Eminent Tragedians

A long, illustrious line, they stretch from the reopening of the theatres at the Restoration, and make of our story a study in comparative histrionics. Of production, as we understand the word today, there was very little. The proscenium had been quick to impose an orthodoxy, gleefully accepted by actors and audiences alike. Scenery had been edging its way in before the twilight of the Commonwealth, and when this was lifted we should not exaggerate the difference. The stage still thrust out several feet beyond the proscenium arch; the lights in the auditorium were left on during the performance; and the actors' soliloquies or asides were given conversationally to the stage boxes and beyond. The hangings of the pre-Restoration theatre were replaced by painted flats, and the action of the play was to that extent more precisely localized. There was now a curtain, but since this was not lowered once the play had started the flats were changed in full view of audience and actors alike. People already accustomed to scenery in the Masque, which demanded it, now clamoured for it in plays which did not. They would clamour for it in Shakespeare for a good long time to come. The proscenium was a frame, and the frame asked for its picture. Tentatively at first, and presently in full sail, the actresses swept on to the boards. The King took note of them.

The sorry tale of Shakespearian adaptation now began. He must be refined (or coarsened) in tune with contemporary taste, and it is among the ironies of history that the London of Charles II should have considered itself refined. In *The Law against Lovers* – Davenant's version of *Measure for Measure* – the scenes and characters of low life were omitted, and Angelo was turned into a respectable prig, testing the virtue of Isabella before he risked a proposal of marriage. In *Macbeth*

> The devil damn thee black, thou cream-fac'd loon,
> Where got's thou that goose look?

became 'Now friend, what means thy change of countenance?' Shakespeare's blank verse was made blanker in a different understanding of the epithet, when it was not replaced by rhymed couplets. *The Tempest*, in which Davenant collaborated with Dryden, was probably acted in 1667 and published in 1670. Here Miranda was given a sister, Dorinda, and Prospero a young protégé, Hippolito, who had never set eyes on a woman, as the sisters had never set eyes on a man. When Ferdinand arrived on the island, long past the age of innocence, the ensuing comedy not only lengthened the play considerably but quite overwhelmed the central Shakespearian theme – although the original text, with Caliban's speeches all turned into prose, reappeared here and there. With Trinculo as the Boatswain, and Stephano as the Master of the ship, there was small wonder it foundered.

Now that Dryden was in the field, lesser talents could hardly be blamed for following him. Otway transferred Verona to classical Rome, and allowed Juliet to wake up before Romeo had swallowed the apothecary's poison – a

Frontispiece to the Rowe edition of *The Tempest*, 1709

happy ending which was retained for more than a century. Nahum Tate omitted the Fool in *King Lear*, gave Edgar as a husband to Cordelia, and saved both Lear and Gloucester for a further lease of miserable existence. He changed *Coriolanus* into *The Ingratitude of a Commonwealth*, but not even this topical allusion could turn the piece into a popular success. Another adapter, Crowne, also appealed to public sentiment when he christened the second part of *Henry VI*, aptly enough, *The Misery of Civil War*; and D'Urfey flattered a different aspect of public taste when he staged an attempted rape in *Cymbeline*. The most respectable of these adaptations were Colley Cibber's *King Richard III*, and Betterton's version of *A Midsummer Night's Dream*, which became *The Fairie Queene* with music by Purcell. Cibber's play was produced at Drury Lane in 1700 and held the stage as first-class 'Elephant and Castle' melodrama for nearly two hundred years. Richard's 'Off with his head – so much for Buckingham' was a gag which star performers of the part were long reluctant to discard. *The Fairie Queene* was given at the Dorset Garden house in 1692. If this foreshadowed Benjamin Britten, that was all in its favour. Nevertheless Pepys thought it 'the most insipid ridiculous play that I ever saw in my life'. Lord Lansdowne's version of *The Merchant of Venice* began with the ghosts of Shakespeare and Dryden rising crowned with laurels, and a masque of 'Peleus and Thetis'. A banquet followed at which Shylock sat alone, drinking a toast to money. By the end of the seventeenth century, and well beyond it, Shakespeare had become a man for all seasonings.

Several young players who had made their name as 'actresses' now matured as actors in their own right: of the boys in Davenant's company Kynaston developed from 'the loveliest lady' admired by Pepys into the man who at sixty, according to Cibber, had 'his teeth all sound, white, and even as one would wish to see in a reigning toast of twenty'; whose gravity was due 'to the stately step he had been so early confined to in a female decency'. Yet in women's parts critics discussed 'whether any woman that succeeded him so sensibly touched the audience as he'. Equally popular was Robert Nokes, whose Nurse in Otway's travesty of *Romeo and Juliet* delighted the town. Cibber describes how 'The ridiculous solemnity of his features were enough to have set a whole bench of bishops into a titter, could he have been honoured . . . with such grave and right reverend auditors.'

Such then was the theatre on which Thomas Betterton (*c*. 1635-1710) as Hamlet set the stamp of genius in December 1661. In a bookshop near Charing Cross he had listened as a boy to John Rhodes's reminiscences of the great days – for Rhodes had been prompter and wardrobe master at the Blackfriars. Scarcely had the handsome presence made its first effect, and the low, modulated voice come to the end of ''Tis not alone my inky cloak, good mother' than Pepys whispered to his neighbour 'It's beyond imagination' – and was told to keep his comments to himself. Pepys saw Betterton at the beginning of his career, Pope at the end of it – and Pope's opinion was the same. Betterton's version of *Hamlet* anticipated many that were to follow it. Voltimand and Cornelius were dispensed with; so was Polonius' advice to Laertes – not yet become as familiar as Kipling's *If* – and 'How all occasions do inform against me'. But Fortinbras was allowed his last entrance, and the play its martial close – a permission rarely accorded thereafter until Forbes-Robertson restored them. Elsewhere Restoration 'refinement' had been at work. The Kettle drum and trumpet 'proclaimed'; they did not 'bray out'. 'Now might I do it pat, now he is praying' became

Frontispiece to the Rowe edition of *Hamlet*, 1709

'Where is this murderer, he kneels and prays'; treason dared not 'reach', rather than 'peep', at what it would; 'mourning cloak' was preferred to 'inky'; and Claudius had 'stept' in between the election and Hamlet's hopes. 'Popp'd in' was evidently considered impolite. Betterton did no more than speak the words set down for him, only wondering, maybe, what Taylor would have thought of them.

Barton Booth, who was playing the Ghost, declared of Betterton that 'instead of my awing him, he terrified me. But divinity hung round that man'. The time was to come presently when a few wisps of divinity would seem to hang around Booth; so his tribute is not to be despised. In the closet scene a spectator remembered how Betterton's 'countenance (which was naturally ruddy and sanguine)' would 'turn instantly on the sight of his father's spirit, as pale as his neckcloth' – an effect that reminds one, inversely, of Duse's famous blush in *Magda*. The single flaw in Betterton's Hamlet was that he went on playing it for too long. His physique – a large head sitting on a short neck, and a body now grown corpulent and clumsy – no longer served him. His voice had dropped an octave or two, but he could still 'tune it by an artful climax, which enforced universal attention, even from the fops and orange girls'. And Cibber remarked how 'in all his soliloquies of moment, the strong intelligence of his attitude and aspect drew you into such an impatient gaze and eager expectation, that you almost imbibed the sentiment with your eye before the ear could reach it'. His versatility was remarkable. As Richard Steele stood with the crowd in Westminster Abbey for Betterton's funeral, he remembered the 'moving and graceful energy' with which Othello had addressed the Senate, and the 'wonderful agony' of his suspicion when he learnt that Desdemona had lost the handkerchief; 'the fierce and flashing fire' of Hotspur; 'the dignity and contempt' with which Brutus answered Cassius' heedless accusations; and even the 'young man of great expectation, vivacity and enterprise' which, for this discerning critic, was not always beyond an old man of seventy clinging to his favourite part.

Barton Booth

2

An event, hardly noticed at the time, was to have momentous consequences. James Rich, the manager of Drury Lane, cut off a slice of his forestage to make room for extra seating. It was on to this stage, slightly but significantly curtailed, that Barton Booth (1681-1733) entered as leading tragedian only six months before the death of Betterton. People soon began to speak of his 'silver tongue', but until the death of Betterton he lived, as Cibber had it, 'only in the promise' of his reputation. He was quickly to fulfil it. Some complained that he sacrificed the total line of a part to its salient 'points', but when he was playing at his best 'the Blind might have seen him in his voice, and the Deaf have heard him in his viasage'.[1] There was more virility than bluster in his Hotspur, more grief than thunder in his Lear. He followed Hamlet's advice to 'use all gently' – if we give a fairly wide latitude to gentleness – and in *Othello* 'when he wept, his tears broke from him perforce. He never whimpered, whined or blubbered; in his rage he never mouthed or ranted'.[2] The impression is still of harmony a shade too undisturbed, of grace a shade too unruffled, of classical balance and proportion. This was the Betterton inheritance, shorn – one feels – of just a little of its power.

[1] Aaron Hill
[2] Theophilus Cibber

A convention in the acting of tragedy was now crystallizing. Speech was inflated into declamation, and the right attitude was freezing into the rhetorical pose. The actors who followed Betterton seemed too often to drag 'the sentiment along like a dead weight, with a long-toned voice and absent eye, as if they had fairly forgot what they were about'. One sees what Cibber meant; they were listening to the sound of their own voices – the deadliest of theatrical sins. Of the women only Mrs Barry, who played Lady Macbeth with Betterton, and Mrs Porter who was contemporary with Booth, qualified as eminent tragediennes. Mrs Barry was so habituated to blank verse that she rose in delirium on her death bed to chant it. Mrs Porter did not always avoid a 'musical monotony',[1] but at best she escaped it. Johnson admired her in 'the vehemence of rage', and Davies describes how as Queen Katharine in *Henry VIII*, 'the suppression of her tears when she reproached the Cardinal, bespoke the tumultuous conflict in her mind, before she burst into the manifestation of the indignity she felt in being obliged to answer so unworthy an interrogator'.[2]

The interim between the early retirement of Booth and the meteoric emergence of Garrick was filled by the burly figure of Quin (1693-1766). He was big enough to dominate the stage when he was on it, but not to leave a very large footprint after he had gone. He had dignity and presence and a lively sense of character, and probably the makings of a great comedian. His Falstaff was memorable, and he drew upon it somewhat for his Henry VIII. It is small wonder that his Lear fell flat, since he had asked for twenty rehearsals and only turned up for two of them! Quin always recited; as the rhyme had it:

> Mark one who tragical struts up and down
> And rolls the words as Sisiphus his stone

and since he had the deaths of two actors to his discredit, one can understand the observation of Smollett that he was a man 'whose wit was apt to degenerate into extreme coarseness, and manner into extreme arrogance'.

3

David Garrick was born at Hereford in 1717, the son of a Captain in the Army and the grandson of a Huguenot refugee. The French blood did not count for nothing. In the summer of 1741 his passion for the stage took him to Ipswich, where he acted under the name of Lyddal. It was a short, though versatile, apprenticeship. On 19 October of the same year, Giffard, the manager of Goodman's Fields Theatre, who had already engaged him for the season at Ipswich, now presented him under his own name as Richard III. Goodman's Fields was an unfashionable playhouse in the East End, although fashion was soon to flock to it. The announcement that Richard would be acted 'by a gentleman who never appeared on any stage', though not quite accurate, was true enough for purposes of publicity. The shock was electric; such acting had not been seen since Betterton. Garrick had chosen Richard for his London début, because the character did not quarrel with his own athletic, but small, physique. Very high heels gave him a few inches that he lacked. From the triumphant chuckle of 'So much for Buckingham!' to the volley of rage on

> Cold friends to me! What do they in the North
> When they should serve their sovereign in the West?

[1] A. M. Taylor *Next to Shakespeare* (1950)
[2] *Dramatic Miscellany* 1 p.385

the desperate courage of 'Give me another horse' and the agony of 'Bind up my wounds', he held a rather small, and not particularly expectant, audience in the hollow of his hand. No trace, here, of Quin's *recitative* or Cibber's melodious mouthing; nature in her many moods and quicksilver transitions had shattered the neo-classical façade of theatrical orthodoxy.

It was a week before London woke up to what had happened. Then the young Pope drove up from Twickenham, and 'the coaches of the nobility', we are told, 'filled up the space between Temple Bar and Whitechapel'. Pope thought that 'young man never had his equal as an actor, and will never have a rival'. In the following year, with Peg Woffington as his mistress, he conquered Dublin, drawing such crowds in the hot weather that many people died of what became known as the 'Garrick fever'. Thomas Gray and Horace Walpole were among the rare dissentient voices; and George III found him 'a great fidget'. Quin, too, remained in the opposition; 'If this young man is right' he observed 'then we have all been wrong'. Moreover, it was the force of Garrick's personal genius which brought into compelling focus tendencies already astir. According to Steele, the chief originality in his delivery of 'To be or not to be' was the preservation of a level mean between *piano* and *forte*. Thomas Morris, on the other hand, refers to his 'awkward hobble' – which meant that he rode rough-

David Garrick as King Lear: the storm scene

shod over metre when passion had the priority: but here John Hill is probably a safer guide than Morris.

> He delivers an equal number of syllables in two succeeding lines in very unequal time; and while he gives a more than common force to such passages as will bear it, he delivers others of more familiar import with a naked simplicity, which, tho' the very reverse of that pomp we generally expect in tragedy, is not less just or affecting.

Johnson declared that Garrick was 'no declaimer; there was not one of his own scene-shifters who could not have spoken "To be or not to be" better than he did; yet he was the only actor I ever saw whom I could call a master, both in tragedy and comedy, though I liked him in comedy best'. Professor Sprague has suggested that Garrick not only deflated declamation, but substituted for it a pantomimic style. One has the impression of a light and lithe masculinity, which one hardly associates with Betterton, and certainly not with Booth or Quin. The suppleness of voice was translated to the whole of that small and vibrant physique. When Boswell asked Johnson: 'Would not you, sir, start as Garrick does if you saw a ghost?' Johnson replied: 'I hope not; if I did, I should frighten the ghost.' Garrick's playing in this scene evidently *contained* the Ghost, just as his playing of the storm scene in *Lear* contained the storm. The Ghost was dressed in steel-blue drapery which gave the impression of transparent armour.

Garrick was especially notable as Hamlet, Macbeth, Richard III, and Lear. *Macbeth* was billed 'as written by Shakespeare'; yet Davenant's singing witches were still up to their time-honoured tricks. The 'dagger' speech was always a *tour de force,* and terrified a French audience when they heard it. It was said that when Garrick told the First Murderer 'there's blood upon thy face', the observation had such urgency that the actor in question involuntarily replied: 'Is there, by God?' In *Lear* he played with the idea of restoring the Fool, but concluded that this was more than the Age of Elegance would stand. When he acted Lear for the last time, some people pleaded with him to restore the original ending. But if the death of Cordelia was too much for Johnson, it would certainly have made the less judicious grieve.

Garrick used his slight physique to suggest a weak, amiable, and complacent old man. He had discarded the powdered wig, which had inappropriately served for Macbeth, in favour of a few wisps of grey hair standing up from his forehead, and he walked with a stick – 'his very stick acted', we are told – throwing it away as he knelt to call down the curse on Goneril 'with a broken, inward, struggling utterance'. All the actors in the company were 'judiciously habited in old English dresses'. This was an important innovation. The storm was re-enacted not only in Garrick's voice, but in 'his distracted looks' as he came down stage with 'his hands expanded, and his whole frame actuated by a dreadful solemnity'.[1] The first unmistakable sign of madness was a laugh that seemed 'without any connection with the soul; an involuntary emotion of the muscles'.[2] He resisted the sudden effect and the sharp transition just where these were most inviting.

> His movements were slow and feeble; misery was depicted in his countenance; he moved his head in the most deliberate manner; his eyes were fixed, or, if they turned to anyone near him, he made a pause, and fixed his look on the person after much delay; his features at the same time telling the audience what he was going to say, before he uttered a word.[3]

[1] *General View of the Stage* p.234
[2] Aaron Hill *London Daily Advertiser*
[3] Aaron Hill

In the scene of reconciliation with Cordelia he put his finger to her cheek, and then looked at it before the words: 'Be your tears wet?' Even in the botched-up happy ending his sudden 'Did I not, fellow?' was compared, many years later, to similar effects of startling spontaneity by Sarah Siddons.

In *Romeo and Juliet* he met the competition of Spranger Barry's silver tongue and seductive charm. The difference was expressed by the actress who played Juliet with them both. Garrick, she said, was so impetuous that she thought he would leap up on to the balcony, Barry so alluring that she felt like leaping down from it. One did not look to Garrick for the delights of pure lyricism, although Smollett was to remember 'the sweetness and variety of his tones' as well as 'the fire and vivacity of his action'. It was on lines such as 'Then I defy you, stars!' that he showed his mettle. He surrounded himself with the best actors he could find, and tried to discipline them in the style which he had developed for himself. 'I have seen you' wrote Kitty Clive '*endeavouring* to beat your ideas into the heads of creatures who had none of their own. I have seen you, with lamb-like patience, endeavouring to make them comprehend you, and I have seen you when that could not be done – I have seen your lamb turned into a lion.' Kitty Clive knew what she was talking about. Standing in the wings one night and watching Garrick, she turned on her pretty heel and exclaimed: 'Damn him, he could act a *gridiron*!'

But the picture of Garrick as the friend of Johnson and Sheridan, turning out his prologues with a pretty wit, should not lead us to overrate his aesthetic

Spranger Barry as Romeo and
Mrs Rossiter as Juliet: the balcony
scene, 1759

Mrs Pritchard as Hermione in
The Winter's Tale, Drury Lane
Theatre 1756

Opposite above: David Garrick as
Richard III

Sarah Siddons as Lady Macbeth and
J. P. Kemble as Macbeth: the dagger
scene, 1738 (below)

Overleaf: 'The shower of gold':
scene for Charles Kean's *Henry V*,
Princess' Theatre, 1859

[1] W. Whitehead

discretion. Even Shakespeare was a mine to be exploited, not a dramatist to be served; like everything else, he was grist to Garrick's mill. Flattered by French applause, he excised the gravediggers in *Hamlet* to please Voltaire, and introduced a new death scene for *Macbeth*; it was *lèse-majesté* for an actor-manager to 'go off fighting' with Macduff. Moreover, the eighteenth-century audience could be as indiscreet as the actors they applauded. Peg Woffington played the entire part of Cordelia clasped round the waist by an amorous spectator, and Mrs Cibber's Juliet had been forced to share the tomb with her admirers.

Of the actresses who played with Garrick the most talented were Mrs Cibber and Mrs Pritchard. Johnson thought Mrs Cibber 'got more reputation than she deserved, as she had a great sameness; though her expression was undoubtedly very fine'. Her 'demi-chant' was a legacy of the old school, and it seems that not even Garrick could completely cure her of it. Mrs Pritchard was a powerful, uneducated, and purely instinctive actress. A great Lady Macbeth, Garrick only complained that she was 'apt to blubber her sorrows'. Johnson commented that

> her playing was quite mechanical. It is wonderful how little mind she had. Sir, she had never read the tragedy of *Macbeth* through. She no more thought of the play out of which her part was taken, than a shoemaker thinks of the skin out of which the piece of leather of which he is making a pair of shoes is cut.

Mrs Siddons, who regarded Mrs Pritchard as 'the greatest of all the Lady Macbeths', found this incredible until a man who had supped with Mrs Pritchard confirmed it. Thomas Davies agreed with Garrick that 'her few defects in tragedy proceeded from a too loud and profuse expression of grief and want of grace in her manner'. Dibdin maintained that she was 'everywhere great, everywhere impressive, and everywhere feminine', and that her *forte*, in contrast to Mrs Cibber, was 'unceasing variety'. Rosalind and Beatrice gave ample scope for it.

> Her comic vein had every charm to please
> 'Twas Nature's dictates breath'd with Nature's ease.
> Even when her powers sustained the tragic load,
> Full, clear and just the harmonious accents flow'd.
> And the big passions of the feeling heart
> Burst freely forth and shamed the tragic art.[1]

The 'tragic load' was soon to be carried by an even greater actress, in whom the 'comic vein' would not be conspicuous, and in whom tragedy would certainly not be shamed.

4

When Garrick saw young John Henderson as Shylock, he remarked that the role of Tubal was very creditably performed. The observation did less than justice to Henderson, a careful character actor, noted for his subtle handling of soliloquy, speaking *over* the pit, not *to* it. Thus far had the proscenium imposed its convention. But the relationship between actor and audience was still much closer to what it had been at the Globe than to what it was later to become. The proscenium doors stood on the audience's side of the arch, and were so high

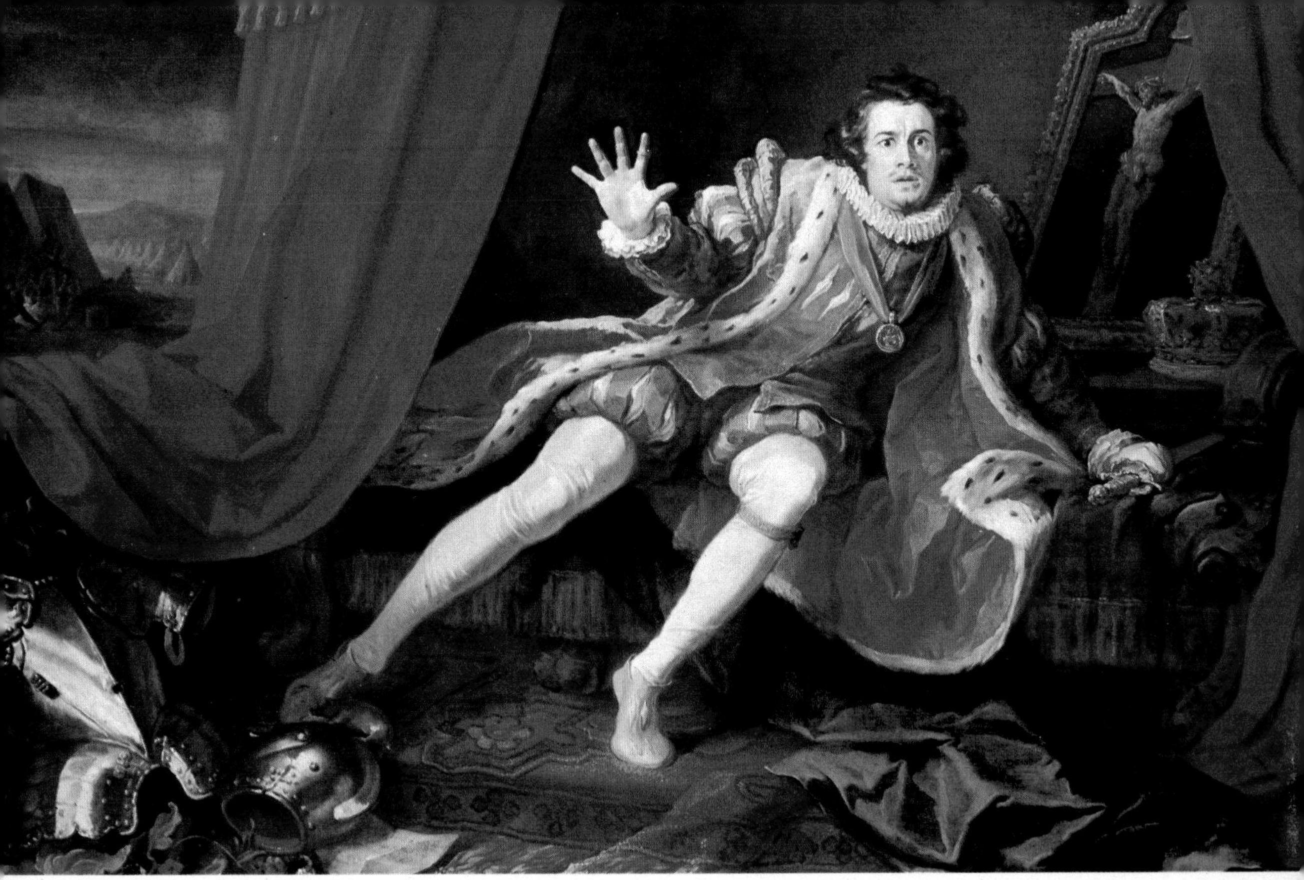

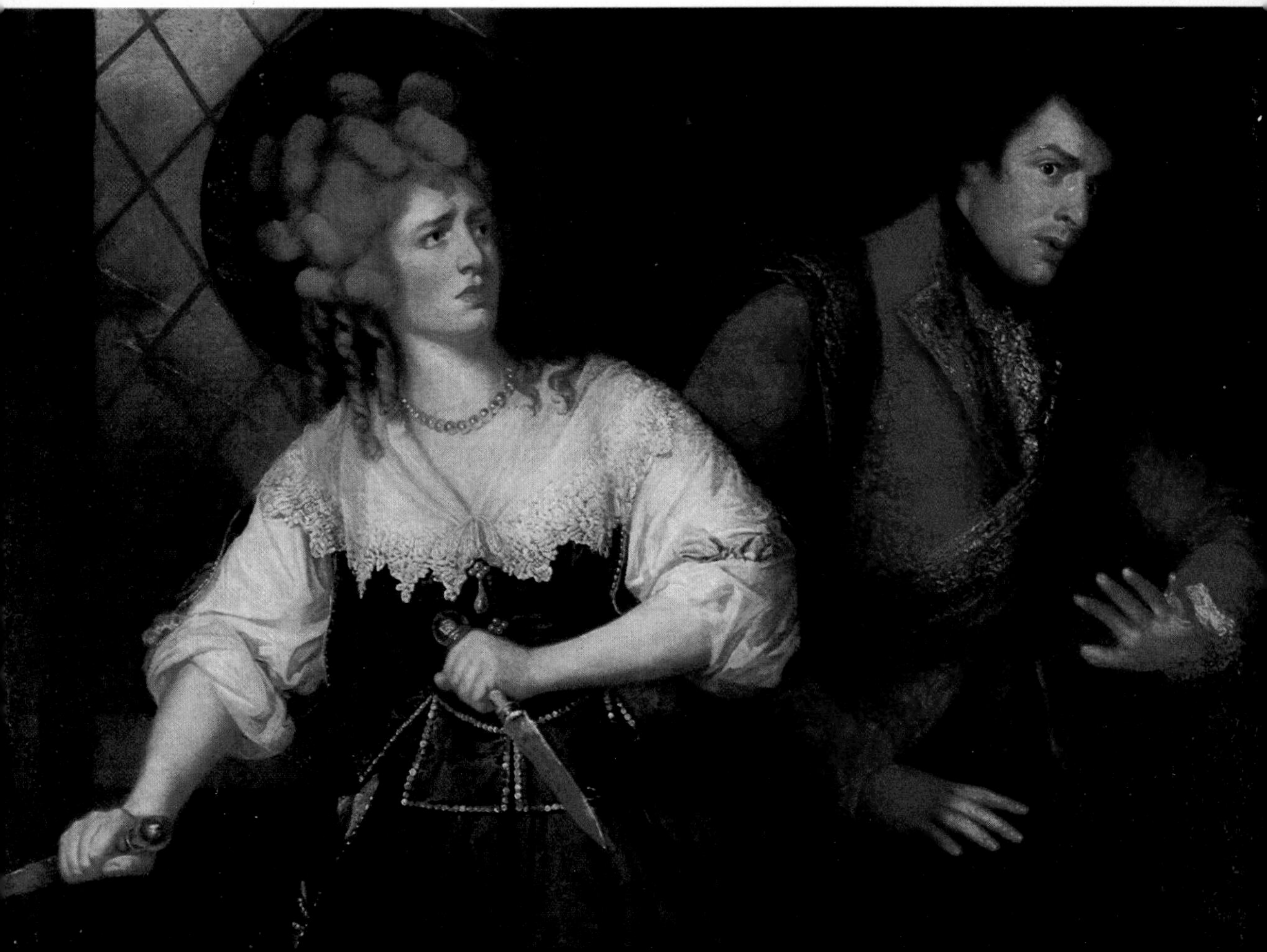

valued that when the new Drury Lane was rebuilt without them in 1812, the actors successfully agitated for their restoration. The lights were left on in the auditorium, and if a balcony were required for the action of the play the stage-boxes filled the need. The actors continued to perform well down upon the apron; and although the scenery was richly pictorial it remained a background, not an enclosure. There were footlights and an orchestra pit, but the actors were in touch with their public as they are not in many modern theatres which have neither. From the beginning of the nineteenth century on into our own times theatres were to get bigger and bigger, and progressively worse adapted for the performance of Shakespeare's plays. 'Large theatres' said Joanna Baillie, the dramatist and friend of Sir Walter Scott, 'are a bane and a pest to the drama.' Unfortunately they have generally proved a boon to the managers.

Henderson's Falstaff was so good that even Munden, on whose malleable features comedy could write what it chose, declined an attempt to better it. So, less surprisingly, did John Philip Kemble (1757-1823). Verse and brush have combined to implant an image of Kemble which it is not easy to dislodge. The Lawrence portrait shows a Hamlet who not only thinks before he acts, but seems doubtfully capable of acting at all – whereas Hamlet all too often acts before he thinks. The soubriquet of 'stately John' is borne out by Campbell's 'Valedictory Stanzas':

J. P. Kemble as Hamlet by
Sir Thomas Lawrence

Opposite: Mrs Jordan as Viola

> Fair as some classic dome
>   Robust and richly graced,
> Your Kemble's spirit was the home
>   Of genius and of taste;
> Taste, like the silent dial's power,
>   That, when supernal light is given,
> Can measure inspiration's hour
>   And tell its height in heaven.
> At once ennobled and correct
>   His mind surveyed the classic page,
> And what the actor could effect
>   The scholar could presage.

This seems a fair summary if we allow to 'genius' – a doubtful admission – its equivalence with taste. For Scott, who knew him well and often saw him act, 'J.K. is, I think greater than himself, and that is twenty times greater than any actor I ever saw.'[1] Kemble was a scholar and a gentleman. He read widely, and his instinct never led him where his intellect refused to follow. Boaden, his biographer, described him as 'an abstraction of the characteristics of tragedy', and admitted that his deportment was 'too scrupulously graceful'. Kemble might have stepped out of Corneille, as his sister – Sarah Siddons – might have stepped into Racine. This is not to say that he was dull, although now and again in *Macbeth* he was said to 'nod'; and where Garrick had paused for the sake of an effect, Kemble paused because nothing would make him get a move on. His Hamlet was described as 'lad-like' – some years away from the Lawrence portrait – and to an American, who saw him nearer the time when Lawrence painted him, he appeared 'sweet' and 'graceful' and 'gentlemanly'. The beauty of his performance lay in 'its retrospective air – its intensity and abstraction'.

Fine as the voice may have been, it was always subject to the asthma which increasingly, as he grew older, threatened to cripple Kemble's power of speech.

[1] To Lady Abercorn (23 March 1813)

There were new readings in plenty: 'Did *you* not speak to it?' addressed to
Horatio, more likely as a graduate of Wittenberg to have ventured a question to
the Ghost; 'and for my soul what *can* it do to *that*?', where Garrick's quicker
instinct had leaped on to the last, essential word. For the first of these Kemble
had Johnson's imprimatur: 'To be sure, Sir; *you* should be strongly marked. I
told Garrick so, long since, but Davy could never see it.' As for the second, Sir
Walter Scott, in whose company Kemble could always shed a little of his
romanità, admitted that 'by giving a peculiar emphasis to every word of the
sentence [he] lost the effect which to be vehement should be instant and un-
divided'. No doubt the slowness and stateliness grew upon him, for an actor's
natural style easily develops into mannerism. For Scott, who saw him in *Macbeth*,
his entrance had nothing of the breathless warrior who had won his spurs – and
his earldom – at Forres; it was merely 'the stately step of Kemble as he descended
on the stage'. Yet even as Macbeth, the sudden simplicity of 'If I stand here, I
saw him', and the despairing sigh of 'She should have died hereafter' were to be
remembered. When he played the part with Mrs Siddons in 1816, Hazlitt, who
had described his Hamlet as 'a man in armour', was unsparing in his praise,
even though 'his tones had occasionally . . . a learned quaintness, like the

Drury Lane Theatre 1773 (left) and
Sadlers Wells Theatre 1809

colouring of Poussin.' *The Times* had compared him to 'the ruin of a magnificent temple, in which the divinity still resides'. Hazlitt denied this. 'The temple is unimpaired; but the divinity is sometimes from home.'[1]

There must have been something more to Kemble than formal splendour, and here Byron had the word for it. Kemble, he said, was 'the most supernatural of actors'. He meant, I think, not only that in person and style he was a little more than life size; but that he had a quality almost angelic. Mr Bertram Joseph has written that

> Kemble was classic, not in the sense that he concentrated on the outward appearance of calm grandeur, formal dignity and comparative stiffness, but because he worked from within outwards, from a classical tragic conception to the details of the acting in which it was embodied. And for him the tragic conception was essentially one of consistent intensity; the character must be developed undeviatingly in one straight line of progressive intensity; everything must point to the same end.[2]

In the light of this acute summary it is easy to pick out the parts in which he was successful. He could be an impassioned Hotspur – albeit with no trace of Northumbria in his accent – because Hotspur is a character, conceived in

[1] *The Examiner* (16 June 1816)
[2] *The Tragic Actor* (1959) p.187

monochrome, who rides roughshod over every obstacle, looking neither to right nor left. Scott admired Kemble in the 'confusion of mangled recollections', fumbling for his words, and darting forward into his abuse of Bolingbroke 'like a greyhound slipped – like a rocket lighted – like a bolt from a crossbow'. At his best Kemble certainly did not lack animation. But one suspects that his high watermark was Coriolanus. Here again was a rôle asking precisely for that 'straight line of progressive intensity' which Mr Joseph singles out as Kemble's *forte*, and inconsistent neither with 'splendid formality' nor with 'supernatural' dimensions. When Sarah Siddons as Volumnia knelt to her brother as Coriolanus the Shakespearian stage must have known one of its finest hours.

As the years went on and his vocal infirmity grew worse, we can sympathize with Kemble's comment that no other member of his family knew the misery of 'drawing on their own chest and finding the cheque dishonoured'. He reigned for long periods both at Covent Garden and Drury Lane, and did much to bring Shakespeare production into line with the periods in which the action of the plays was set – drawing his inspiration from paintings and engravings, and setting a pattern which others were to follow for the next hundred years. Elderly playgoers could still remember 'the miserable pairs of flats that used to clap together on even the stage trod by Mr Garrick; architecture without selection or propriety; a hall, a castle, or a chamber, or a cut wood of which all the verdure seemed to have been washed away.'[1] After his farewell performance on 23 June 1817, he retired to Lausanne where he was happy with his garden and his books. He died there in February 1823 – always, he used to say, 'rather jealous of Mont Blanc'.

5

According to Byron, 'of actors Cooke was the most natural, Kemble the most supernatural, Kean the medium between the two. But Mrs Siddons was worth them all put together.' Like John Philip, Sarah Siddons (1755-1831) could descend from the majestic to the familiar. Her easy converse with Virgilia and Valeria in *Coriolanus*, and her courteous dismissal of the guests in the banquet scene from *Macbeth* was compared to her brother's by-play with Mamillius in *The Winter's Tale*. She also had John Philip's scholarly thoroughness, picking up a hint from the Egyptian statues in Landsowne House for the right attitude – arms held close to the side and hands clenched – to express intensity of feeling. Volumnia, predictably, was among her greatest parts. The rôle invites – and imposes – a dignity and decorum which emotion may be expected to colour but not disturb. And yet how far from Kemble's 'stately step' was his sister's greeting of Coriolanus when he returns victorious from the wars! It will be noted from the following description that at the 'Lane' or the 'Garden' there was no lack of 'supers'.

> No fewer than two hundred and forty persons marched in stately procession across the stage. In this procession Mrs Siddons had to walk. . . . But at the time – as she so often did – she forgot her identity; she was no longer Sarah Siddons, tied down to the directions of the prompter's book: she broke through old traditions; she recollected that she was Volumnia, the proud mother of a proud son, and conquering hero. . . . She towered above all around her, and yet became so true to nature, so picturesque, and so descriptive, that pit and gallery sprang to their feet electrified by the transcendent execution of the conception.[2]

Sarah Siddons as Lady Macbeth: the letter scene (left) and the sleep-walking scene

Tradition had dictated that, in the sleep-walking scene from *Macbeth*, Lady Macbeth should hold the candle throughout, but rumour got around that Mrs Siddons was planning to put it down, thus freeing her hands for a scene in which they would be fully occupied. This was regarded as an impermissible innovation; and what was the result?

> She laded the water from the imaginary ewer over her hands – bent her body to listen to the sounds presented to her fancy, and hurried to resume the taper where she had left it, that she might with all speed drag her pallid husband to their chamber.[3]

The actress had understood that Lady Macbeth would have been seriously embarrassed by a taper in the scene where the murder was committed, and no less so in the scene where it was re-enacted. Asked to describe the effect of her playing here, Sheridan Knowles replied: 'Well, sir, I smelt blood! I swear that I smelt blood.' She had hesitated to attempt the part because her own physique so flatly contradicted her conception of it. She imagined the character as a fragile and delicate blonde; subduing Macbeth by the dual exercise of intellect and beauty, moved by the memory of her father and the babe to whom she had 'given suck'; needing all the aid the 'spirits that tend on mortal thoughts' could give her for the accomplishment of a fearful crime; stronger than Macbeth in one way and weaker in another, since it is she who finally breaks under the burden of remorse. All this she achieved in a legendary performance; only the blonde fragility was beyond her.

Much of the detail and emphasis has come down to us. The long pause – and Mrs Siddons could pause as long as Kemble, though with better reason – on 'made themselves——air'; the sudden energy on '*shalt be* what thou art promised'; the association of '*my* spirits in your ear' with the spirits she has just invoked; the downward and decisive inflection on 'We *fail*'; the triumph in her voice on 'Great Glamis! Worthy Cawdor', and its supernatural timbre, with the staring eyes and hollowed hands, as she called upon the 'sightless substances' that 'wait on nature's mischief'; the sharp significance of 'Tomorrow – as he *purposes*'; the slow insinuation of 'be the serpent under't'; the tenderness of 'I have given suck' transformed into the fiendish cruelty of 'plucked my nipple from its boneless gums'; the deadly whispering of the colloquy following the murder; the authority of 'Give *me* the daggers', which caused more than one member of the audience to start out of their seat. 'Not all the perfumes of Arabia' came like the whispered echo from a hollow grave; and the final 'Oh, oh, oh' was a shudder rather than a sigh, with an undertone of imbecility, at once pathetic and horrifying. When a man from the gallery in Glasgow exclaimed 'She's a fallen angel!' he was saying more in five words than many dramatic critics had said in fifty. He was also underlining the quality which Byron had recognized in her and her brother alike.

As Katharine in *Henry VIII* – a part that Dr Johnson had recommended to her – she so terrified the Duke of Buckingham's surveyor with 'You were the Duke's Confessor, and lost your office on the complaint of the tenants' that the actor in question declared that not for the world would he face her again before the footlights. But there was little left of this authority by the time the divorced Queen had come to sicken and eventually to die, with a realism that broke all the rules of 'splendid, formal' acting. Just as Charles Young had seen her as Volumnia 'rolling from side to side' in that triumphal march, so as Katharine

Quoted by Alan S. Downer *The Eminent Tragedian: William Charles Macready* (1966) p.21

J. C. Young *Life of Charles Mayne Young* (1871)

J. Boaden *Memoirs of Mrs Siddons* (1827) p.262

she omitted no symptom of physical decline. In comedy she was not successful. 'How *could* such a countenance be arch?' exclaimed Charles Young – forgetting that archness is the Goodwin Sands on which so many Shakespearian comédiennes are wrecked. But it seems that Mrs Siddons, for whom femininity ranked as a virtue in itself, took unkindly to male disguise. After she had gone into retirement in 1812, a number of her admirers subscribed to an appeal begging her to return. When she did so, three years later, to play Lady Macbeth for the benefit of Princess Charlotte, disuse had somewhat staled her infinite variety; her speech was slower and her pauses more prolonged. But Hazlitt, while he regretted her reappearance, pushed down the loud pedal of his prose to convey the picture of her ascendancy. She was perhaps the only pure tragédienne to have given her services to Shakespeare, combining as she did the romantic freedom and the classic form. There has never been anybody like her.

6

Eliza O'Neill as Juliet

Eliza O'Neill (1791-1872), a charming actress from Dublin, made the nearest bid for the vacant throne, conquering the town with the best Juliet since some ravishing chorister had played the part under Burbage. Yet Byron refused to see her for fear of disturbing his memory of Mrs Siddons, and another critic replying to those who held Miss O'Neill to be the more natural of the two distinguished between the verisimilitude of a waxwork and the Apollo Belvedere. There was all the difference between 'an *exact* representation and an *ennobled* one'.[1] Miss O'Neill did, however, win the unbounded admiration of Talma; and this must be weighed in the balance against more grudging comparisons. He maintained that no actress on the French stage could equal her for sensibility, tenderness and pathos. She could both draw tears and shed them – 'buckets full' as she boasted to Fanny Kemble – and do so without disfigurement.

The Kembles had shown that there was nothing irreconcilable between the theatre and the Establishment; indeed they were an Establishment in themselves, walking with poets and princes, and never losing their hold upon the pit. But now a phenomenon was trudging the provinces, ready to prove that a great actor could be disestablished, and yet make and lose a fortune, send his son to Eton, and his wife down Piccadilly in a coach and four. We are not concerned with the vagrancy and vagaries of Edmund Kean (1790-1833); all that matters here are the 'flashes of lightning' – in Coleridge's phrase – that he brought to the interpretation of Shakespeare. Where Sarah Siddons was the sublime apotheosis of a great school, Kean inherited nothing and bequeathed nothing. He was a school unto himself.

Mrs Siddons had seen him in Belfast; thought he played 'well, *very* well; but there was too little of him to make a great actor.' At the Haymarket he was considered too small for Rosencrantz; in some provincial towns his Harlequin was preferred to his Hamlet; and although Stephen Kemble told him in Birmingham that he was better as Hotspur and Henry IV than John Philip himself, Birmingham was still a tidy distance from Drury Lane. If Arnold, stage manager at the 'Lane', had not happened to be in a box at Dorchester, and if the finances of the 'Lane' had not been in such low water, negotiations for Kean's appearance there would not have been under way before he and Arnold parted for the night. Arnold wished him to play Richard III, but Kean – fearing that the trunk and hose necessary for Richard would expose his lack of inches – insisted upon playing Shylock. The smallest actor gains an inch or two in a gaberdine.

The 26 January 1814 was an evening of snow and fog. The house was not more than a quarter full, and only two critics were in front. Among the sparse audience was Dr Drury, the headmaster of Harrow, and when the new Shylock – only twenty-four years old, in a black beard and wig, leaning on his crutched stick and looking already, as Douglas Jerrold put it, 'like a chapter in *Genesis*' – had opened with 'Three thousand ducats' – thoughtful pause – 'well?', Dr Drury whispered to his neighbour: 'He is safe.' True in one sense; untrue in another. Just as Kean took every risk in his acting and usually justified it, so his public took a risk whenever they saw him perform – since he might be drunk or not even appear at all. But for that historic evening he was safe as houses. The sarcasm – spoken with the burning eyes as well as with the slightly hoarse voice – of 'and for these courtesies I'll lend you thus much moneys'; the tenderness of his 'good-night' to Jessica, which had an almost musical charm; the racial pride and pathos of his scene with Salanio and Salarino; the anguish and ferocity of his regard as Gratiano taunted him – the look 'of a man who asserts his claim to suffer as one of a race of sufferers'[2] – all this, with the recovered dignity of his exit, warranted his manager's admission that he had saved the house from ruin.

His Richard III confirmed Hazlitt's earlier impressions:

Edmund Kean as Richard III

> We cannot imagine any character represented with greater directness and precision, more perfectly *articulated* in every part. Perhaps, indeed, there is too much of this; for we sometimes thought he failed, even from an exuberance of talent, and dissipated the impression of the character by the variety of his resources.

But in one 'who *dares* so much' Hazlitt found little to blame. In the wooing of Lady Anne, Kean appeared 'like the first tempter, to approach his prey, certain of the event, and as if success had smoothed the way before him'. And 'his attitude in leaning against the side of the stage' before he came forward was 'one of the most graceful and striking' the critic remembered to have seen. 'It would serve a Titian, Raphael, or Salvator Rosa as a model.' Very effective also was the quiet 'Good-night' to his friends on the eve of Bosworth, 'pausing with the point of his sword, drawn slowly backward and forward on the ground, before he retires to his tent'. At the end, Kean 'fought like one drunk with wounds; and the attitude in which he stands with his hands stretched out, after his sword is taken from him, had a preternatural and terrific grandeur, as if his will could not be disarmed, and the very phantoms of his despair had a withering power.'[3]

Byron was moved to ecstasy after seeing Kean as Richard: 'By Jove, he is a soul! Life, nature, truth, without exaggeration or diminution. Kemble's Hamlet is perfect; but Hamlet is not nature. Richard is a man; and Kean is Richard.'[4] Mrs Trench was reminded 'constantly of Bonaparte – that restless quickness, that Catiline inquietitude, that fearful somewhat resembling the impatience of a lion in its cage'.[5] Kean's power to express the 'groundswell troubling the deeps' was described by George Henry Lewes: 'In watching Kean's quivering muscles and altered tones you felt the subsidence of passion. The voice might be calm, but there was a tremor in it; the face might be quiet, but there were the vanishing traces of recent agitation.'[6]

[1] Mrs. Trench
[2] *The Morning Chronicle* (15 February 1814)
[3] *Dramatic Essays* (1895) pp.6-7
[4] *Representative Actors* p.341
[5] Ibid p.342
[6] *On Actors and the Art of Acting* (1875) p.133

In a judgment which is often quoted Lewes maintained that 'the greatest artist is he who is the greatest in the highest reaches of his art, even although he may lack the qualities necessary for the adequate execution of some minor details'. Judged by these standards Lewes considered Edmund Kean 'incomparably the greatest actor' he had ever seen, and it was mainly on the strength of his Othello that he awarded him the palm. Kean had the voice and features, but far less than the required stature, for the part. Even his temperament did not always help him – for, as Kemble acutely pointed out, 'Othello is a *slow man*'. Although it would be rash to conclude with Kemble that 'the whole thing was a mistake', Hazlitt agreed that the character was misconceived. 'Othello is tall, but that is nothing; he was black, but that is nothing. But he was not fierce, and that is everything.' Kean had no doubt adopted the light Moorish tan, because the facial play on which he relied for so much of his effect would thereby be more visible.

In the first two acts he was not remarkable, although Keats was impressed by the authority of 'Keep up your bright swords, or the dew will rust them.' Here it seemed as if 'his throat had commanded where swords were as thick as reeds. From eternal risk, he speaks as though his body were unassailable.'[1] It was an effective drop from this into the colloquial 'Were it my cue to fight, I should have known it/Without a prompter.' But the speech to the Senate went for little; Lewes described it as 'very bad ... this long simple narrative was the kind of speech he could not manage at all'. Kean was impatient for the sardonic effect – a quite wrong effect – he had up his sleeve for 'This only is the witchcraft I have used' followed by the too casual greeting to Desdemona: 'Here comes the lady: let her witness it.' Kean's reading of these two lines demonstrated the weakness of his intellectual grasp. The smiling deprecation of the first, and the rapturous heart-lift of the second, equally escaped him. Opinion differed about his greeting of Desdemona in Cyprus. One critic complained that he spoke here 'in the sepulchral accent, and solemn utterance, of a penitent grateful for his salvation; or a shipwrecked mariner returning thanks for his deliverance'; but another caught an overtone of the misery to come in 'if it were now to die/T'were now to be most happy.'

The change came in the third act, which is perhaps the greatest challenge to an actor's powers that the theatre can throw out. Iago's description of the 'green-eyed monster' stung him into a sudden fury, and the assumed composure of 'not a jot, not a jot' was belied by his voice and deportment, as he clung to the scenery striving to keep back his tears. Lewes describes him, after Iago's first exit, standing at the back of the stage with his 'joined uplifted hands, the palms being upwards ... lowered upon his head, as if to keep his poor brain from bursting'. The sheer vigour of the performance varied a little from night to night, but the expression was the same: the pathos of 'O, the pity of it, Iago', the desolation of the 'Farewells', spoken, according to Leigh Hunt, with divided syllables 'in long, lingering tones, like the sound of a parting knell', and reminding Junius Brutus Booth of 'cathedral chimes'; the fury of 'Blood, blood, blood', where Keats saw the 'very words stained and gory'. The final scenes – shockingly abridged – left an impression of all passion spent, and only resolution firm. Kean literally died standing, so that it was no longer Othello himself but his body, empty of the passion which had consumed it, that fell heavily to the ground.

His undersized and graceless physique did not matter when imagination

Edmund Kean as Othello

possessed it; seizing Macready by the throat on 'Villain, be sure thou prove my love a whore', he 'seemed to swell into a stature which made Macready appear small'. No doubt he mixed his lights and shadows with a 'Caravaggio force of unreality',[2] and what you remembered in his performances were the 'flashes of lightning' rather than the firmness and consistency of structure. But the flashes of lightning were hits, not misses; Kean knew exactly what he wanted to do and did it, whether or not it was the right thing to have done.

He died, broken and bankrupt, in 1833, after collapsing as Othello into the arms of his son, Charles, who was, literally, supporting him as Iago. What Kenneth Tynan said of another actor – that he was 'a flawed piece of masonry' – might be said of Edmund Kean. The deep cracks in the monument had at last brought it to ruin. There were no funeral trappings at the Abbey; Kean was buried at Richmond. But Fanny Kemble spoke for the great school which he had superseded, and which it was not in the nature of his genius to replace.

> an eye like an orb of light, a voice exquisitely touching and melodious in its tenderness, and in the harsh dissonance of passion terribly true . . . to these he adds the intellectual ones of vigour, intensity, amazing power of concentrating effect – these give him an entire mastery over his audience in all striking, sudden, impassioned passages, in fulfilling which he has contented himself, leaving unheeded what he could not compass – the unity of conception, the refinement of detail, and evenness of execution. . . . If he was irregular and unartist-like in his performance, so is Niagara compared with the waterworks of Versailles.

7

Mr and Mrs Charles Kean as Macbeth and Lady Macbeth, Princess' Theatre 1858

Charles Kean (1811-68) was not a great actor; George Henry Lewes wrote of his 'perpetual blank look and open mouth'.[3] He followed, naturally enough, in his father's footsteps, but where the greatest performance of Edmund Kean was his Othello, Charles's best part was Ford in *The Merry Wives*. A comparison between the jealousy of Othello and the jealousy of Ford illustrates the disparity of talent. If Charles had been the great actor that he perhaps imagined himself to be, an Eton education might have been a handicap; in the event it was a help, giving him literary and antiquarian tastes and a desire – easy to understand in his circumstances – for official patronage and social respectability. He must at least be given credit for presenting Shakespeare's plays with an eye to total effect, and for establishing a pictorial tradition which held the stage until Granville-Barker and William Poel rose to challenge it. That we should now consider many of the pictures unnecessary and distracting is not here to the point. From 1851 to 1859 Charles Kean's productions at the Princess' Theatre were always splendid and often, in the convention of the time, imaginative.

His aim was to reconstruct with a pedantic accuracy of detail the architecture, costumes, and properties of the period in which the action of the plays were set. It never occurred to him, or to anyone else, to relate them to the period in which the plays were written. His diligent research did not enquire into the conditions of the stage on which they were originally performed. He met, at every point, the contemporary demand for the picturesque – natural in a city whose grace and beauty were being progressively destroyed. He satisfied the Victorian thirst for sheer accumulation. There could not be too many supers, banners, coats of arms, fairies, dancing girls, heralds, and halberdiers. But the quantity was not devoid of quality. If Shakespeare had indicated 'another part of the

[1] *The Champion* (21 December 1817)
[2] G. H. Lewes *On Actors and the Art of Acting* (1875)
[3] John Forster and George Henry Lewes *Dramatic Essays* (1896) p.177

forest', then another part of the forest there had to be. Forres would not do service for Dunsinane, nor one sentry beat on the battlements of Elsinore for another. Every castle had its quota of ante-rooms, banqueting hall, council chamber, and corridors. Everything was stated; nothing was suggested; and no expense was spared.

As one by one the great painted cloths came down, the actors took second place to the scenery. Nevertheless, pictorially speaking, each production was a coherent vision of the play; it had the courage of Kean's convictions, his showman's instinct and his scholar's care. For *A Midsummer Night's Dream* he went to Herculaneum and Pompeii; in *The Tempest* Ariel sped to liberty from a galleon in full sail on a perfectly calm sea, with bright red oars assisting the reluctant breeze, while the goddesses appeared with the Temple of Eleusis in the background, and enough sheaves of corn to furnish a Harvest Festival in Westminster Abbey. *The Winter's Tale* gave one a view of Minerva's Temple at Syracuse, and the 'Ear of Dionysus' for Hermione's prison. The gardens of Leontes bristled with pergolas and pavilions, and Time – impersonated by a woman – sat on 'the great globe itself', Luna and Phoebus in support with their oxen and horses. Kean had competent artists to help him – Grieve, Cuthbert, Days, Lloyds, Telbin, and Gordon – and sometimes two or more of them collaborated on the same play. Gordon went to Turner for a 'country near Dover' in *Lear*; Lloyds showed Swinsted Abbey by moonlight for *King John*; Cuthbert had the castle of Forres rising out of a deep glen for *Macbeth*. In *Richard II* Traitor's Gate had its attendant barge; and no eye could doubt the rafters of Westminster Hall. The caparisoned horses of Bolingbroke and Norfolk faced each other at Coventry before the pink benches of a grandstand that might have housed some heavy bets on the Gold Cup. John of Gaunt would have been hard to distinguish against the kaleidoscopic heraldry of his counterpane; ships rode at anchor in Milford Haven; there were views of the Dee estuary from Flint, and of the Vale of Evesham from the 'wilds of Glostershire'. Nor was this all; Bolingbroke must be shown in an 'Historical Episode', riding through the London streets on horseback to the acclamations of the crowd.

In *Henry V* Kean disdained any appeal to 'piece out our imperfections with your thoughts'. A further 'Historical Episode' sent Henry in triumphant procession along the South bank with old London Bridge in the background, maidens dressed up as angels rattling their tambourines to the fore, and ships, flaunting their pennons, moored at the quayside. The choruses, spoken by a woman, standing in a small circular Gothic temple, were illustrated by the English camp at sunset and the French camp at sunrise – the French gathered round a table, and one of them drinking on the ground, the English hearing Mass celebrated by three bearded priests. There was evidently no lack of padres in an army supposed to be fighting against desperate odds. In *Henry VIII* Wolsey's banquet and masque displayed a rich perspective of gold plate and Gothic candelabra; and in the King's Council Chamber the dull pink of throne, seats, and stools stood out against the blue and gold of the walls. One passed from the King's closet to the King's stairs, and from Old Palace Yard to the interior of Grey Friars Church at Greenwich for the christening of Princess Elizabeth. It was all magnificent and, in this instance, not altogether misplaced.

One or two playgoers, however, may have agreed with George Henry Lewes:

Those who, like myself, care a great deal about acting and very little about splendid

[1] *On Actors and the Art of Acting* (1875) p.22
[2] *Dramatic Reminiscences* p.234
[3] Richard Findlater *Six Great Actors* (1957) p.120
[4] John Forster
[5] *Shakespearian Players and Performances* (1954)

dresses, must nevertheless confess that what Charles Kean professed to do in the way of scenic illustration, he did splendidly and successfully.[1]

And the criticism of others, still waiting in the wings of the nineteenth century, was forestalled by George Vandenhoff, an actor of exceptional talent and intelligence: 'If the public taste has become so pampered by indulgence, that it can only be tempted by show and glare, then I say give it *spectacle pure and simple*.'[2]

The spectacles of Charles Kean were certainly pure, as purity was understood by the Victorians; but they were anything but simple, and it must often have happened that one could not see the scene for the scenery.

8

Vandenhoff tells us a good deal about William Charles Macready (1793–1873) who had risen into competition when Edmund Kean was still a name to conjure with, and into hardly challenged eminence when Kean had died. Indeed he was always known as the 'eminent tragedian'. The epithet is chilling; it seems to fight shy of genius. Vandenhoff describes Macready's style as 'an amalgam of John Kemble and Edmund Kean. He tried to combine the classic art of the one with the impulsive intensity of the other; and he overlaid both with an outer plating of his own, highly artificial, elaborately formal . . . He was a Narcissus in love with his own form-alities.' This reads suspiciously like theatrical pastiche. Kean's experience as Harlequin had given him a physical agility for which, in the case of Macready, the playing fields of Rugby were a poor substitute. He moved with a rolling gait and an alternate thrusting forward of the shoulders, and his eyes slept in their sockets. His voice, beautiful in itself, had a remarkable range, but its over-accented staccato was destructive of Shakespearian verse. He restored as much of the text as suited him; discarded Nahum Tate's ending to *King Lear*; and in *Coriolanus* allowed the plebs a liberty he generally refused to the actors playing beside him. The Volscian army, we are told, 'with battering rams and towers seemed to spread over the stage in their thousands',[3] opening up for the procession of Roman women – 'one long sable line of monotonous misery'.[4]

Macready was a splendid Cassius – '*impiger, iracundus, inexorabilis, acer*' – but his Brutus was merely Cassius with a different make-up. It is curious that so clinical an introvert should have failed in introspection on the stage. His Hamlet was 'lachrymose and fretful', and even an admiring critic compared his Othello to 'an elderly negress of evil repute, going to a fancy ball'. Morbidly conscientious in private life, he gave all the waverings of conscience in *Macbeth*, even though the heroic dimensions of the character escaped him; and for George Henry Lewes he failed to load the stage with preternatural terrors. But the performance was rich in memorable touches. The imperious command to the witches – 'Stay and speak'; the desperate recoil from Banquo's ghost; the dropping of his truncheon on hearing that Lady Macbeth is dead; the half-drawn sword over the messenger who announces the approach of Birnam Wood; the energy of the fight in which he died, contrary to Shakespeare's instructions, on the stage – did all this add up to a great performance? Professor Sprague, who has so ably reconstructed it,[5] returns an open verdict – valid, I think, for Macready's acting as a whole. His last performance was as Macbeth, after which he retired to Cheltenham, and the long winter of his discontent.

William Charles Macready as Brutus

Dora Jordan (1762–1816) was a worthier bedmate for Charles II than for William IV by whom, nevertheless, she had ten children. It was the most virtuous, as it was the most fruitful, of theatrical liaisons. Hazlitt described how she 'rioted in her fine animal spirits' as Rosalind, and Sir Joshua Reynolds how she did 'as much by the music of her melancholy as the music of her laugh'. She did the same as Viola. Charles Lamb recalled how

> when she had declared her sister's history to be a 'blank' and that she 'never told her love', there was a pause, as if the story had ended – and then the 'worm in the bud' came up as a new suggestion – and the heightened image of 'Patience' still followed after that, as by some growing (and not mechanical process), thought springing up after thought, I would almost say, as they were watered by her tears.[1]

There were other delights in that production; Bensley's Malvolio throwing 'over the part an air of Spanish loftiness', and Dodd's Aguecheek where

> you could see the first dawn of an idea stealing slowly over his countenance, climbing up little by little, with a painful process, till it cleared up at last to the fulness of a twilight conception – its highest meridian. . . . A glimmer of understanding would appear in a corner of his eye, and for lack of fuel go out again. A part of his forehead would catch a little intelligence, and be a long time in communicating it to the remainder.[2]

These were all players of an earlier generation. Among the actresses of the mid-nineteenth century Helen Faucit (1817–98) was for many years Macready's leading lady, and would have liked to be something more. Her attachment added a further complication to that already burdened conscience. She had Macready's earnestness without his egotism, and spoke Shakespeare's verse with a more natural simplicity. Hermione's agony of separation in *The Winter's Tale*, and Imogen's death of the heart in *Cymbeline* – when she hears the false news of Posthumus' infidelity – were movingly within her range. A softer Sarah Siddons, she was reluctant to play Lady Macbeth because the character conflicted so sharply with her own. Yet a fellow-actor declared that he had only learnt from Helen Faucit 'what a delicate and refined fiend Lady Macbeth could be'. And so we are brought to Charles Fechter (1824–79) a French actor, whose foreign emphasis was more worrying than his foreign accent. He was a distinguished Hamlet, 'lymphatic, delicate, handsome, and with his long flaxen curls, quivering sensitive nostrils, fine eye and sympathetic voice, perfectly representing the graceful prince'.[3] Hamlet's royalty of nature had not yet been challenged by the heresy that all men are equal, and Hamlet rather less equal than the others. Fechter's Othello was ruined by a misplaced realism; the 'lounging on tables and lolling against chairs' which Lewes compared to placing 'the "Sleeping Faun" of Phidias on a comfortable feather-bed'; a confusion between the natural and the familiar as foolish as an 'attempt to heighten the reality of the Apollo [Belvedere] by flinging a paletot over his naked shoulders'.

Samuel Phelps (1804–78) was a man with a mission – to bring Shakespeare to Islington, as Lilian Baylis was to bring him to the New Cut. Working for a balanced ensemble within a limited budget, he restored to the stage in their original text *Richard III*, *Antony and Cleopatra*, and *Timon of Athens*, and removed the last vestiges of adaptation from *King Lear*, *Romeo and Juliet*, and *Macbeth*. As an actor, he may have lacked something of sheer personality. A 'careful and judicious' Richard III does not set the pulses beating, and one

Charles Fechter as Hamlet

Below: Johnston Forbes-Robertson's portrait of Samuel Phelps as Wolsey

raises the eyebrows a little at a 'chastely executed' Macbeth. But when his
critics referred to the 'chastity' of Phelps's performances, they were probably
commending his absence of trickery and mannerism, and his perfect elocution –
only to be equalled by Forbes-Robertson who played with him as a young man.
He was imposing within the limits of an innate modesty; a splendid Duke in
Measure for Measure, an eloquent Prospero, and a passionate Coriolanus. If one
thinks of him as a little pedestrian, a contemporary impression of his final taunt
to Aufidius gives one pause. On 'fluttered the dovecotes in Corioli', he paused
before 'fluttered', spoken with a natural break in the voice and a rising inflection; and then 'lifting his arm to its full height above his head, he shook his
head to and fro, as in the act of startling a flock of doves'.[4] This sealed the
tragedy as firmly as Olivier's spectacular fall from the ramparts.

Barry Sullivan (1824-91) was an Irish tragedian of what already seemed like
the old school in 1852, so that Gordon Bottomley who saw him in 1886 could
describe him as 'the last of Betterton's heirs and line'. He stormed the barns to
great effect as Richard III, and in his earlier days excited the admiration of
Bernard Shaw. Shaw's admiration was perhaps the most important thing about
him, for he had given the 'Perfect Wagnerite' an example of almost operatic
elocution which a greater than Sullivan would obstinately refuse to follow.

Design for Charles Fechter's *Hamlet*:
Elsinore, the platform before the castle,
1864

[1] *On Some of the old Actors*
[2] Ibid
[3] G. H. Lewes *On Actors and the Art of
Acting* (1875) p.22
[4] Shirley S. Allen *Samuel Phelps and
Sadlers Wells Theatre* (1971)

II Lyceum Nights

If you wanted to recapture, however faintly, the gaslit grandeur of the old Lyceum, and to obtain an introduction to its presiding deity, you would naturally turn to Gordon Craig's study of Henry Irving[1] (1838-1905). With a wayward and wilful charm, and a passionate partiality, Craig evokes for us his ideal *übermarionette*. The 'white angel', that Laurence Irving complained had been foisted on to his grandfather's memory, is here replaced by a semi-sanctified demiurge, with something of St Michael and a good deal more of Milton's Lucifer. Then you turn to the table of illustrations, and you notice that not one of them shows Irving in a Shakespearian part. There is Irving as Lesurques in *The Lyons Mail*, and Irving as Mephistopheles, and several variations on Irving as himself. You come to the conclusion, everywhere confirmed by Gordon Craig, that what mattered at the Lyceum was Irving. We know from Ellen Terry that he regarded success in Shakespeare as essential to an actor's reputation, but the thought crosses our mind that he was just as happy when Shakespeare was out of the way. He liked to describe himself as the obedient servant of his audience; he would never have described himself as the obedient servant of William Shakespeare. He served no one but himself, although in doing so he served the English theatre as no one had ever served it before.

There was nothing petty in this sublime selfishness, for Irving identified himself completely with the work in hand. He did not despise his audience like Kean or, still less, his fellow-actors like Macready. He was generous because *largesse* was part of his nature; just and considerate because he had been tempered by injustice; patient because he had waited a long time for recognition. He was proud and sensitive, but he was not vain. He could criticize himself, and accept criticism from other people. 'Never again' he said sadly, as he put away his costume after a disastrous Othello. Ellen Terry had learnt from Mrs Charles Kean that 'God' should not be pronounced like 'Gud', and she passed on the advice to Irving. When she told him that he dragged his leg, he dragged it much less thereafter. Sarah Bernhardt described him as a 'great artist rather than a great actor'; and for Coquelin – prince of professionals and the perfect illustration of Diderot's famous *paradoxe* – he was 'a kind of methodical Mounet-Sully, setting great store by the exterior of his part'. In a prolonged controversy with Coquelin Irving argued that 'it matters little whether the player sheds tears or not; but if tears can be summoned at his will and subject to his control, it is true art to utilize such a power'. Coquelin, for his part, failed to understand 'why he plays Mephisto with the voice of Romeo'. Others were to wonder why he played Romeo with the voice of Mephisto. But when Chaliapin was seen to doff his hat before Irving's statue, a greater than Coquelin had paid the tribute which Paris had withheld.

Irving's patience with supporting players was unwearied; they might not get it right, but little by little they would get it better. As Laurence Irving has written, the 'method had its dangers, for it tended to produce a number of

Interior of the Lyceum Theatre 1847

[1] *Henry Irving* (1930)

Opposite: Henry Irving as Benedick
1882

Overleaf: Henry Irving as Benedick
and Ellen Terry as Beatrice in
Johnston Forbes-Robertson's painting
of the cathedral scene in
Much Ado about Nothing

weak imitations of himself; its virtue lay in the unity of conception and execution in his productions for which he took full responsibility and was ready to accept the praise or blame which they incurred'.[1] Sometimes he had an inspired clue. Gordon Craig, in a dither what to do with Oswald in *King Lear*, murmured something about the part being 'barbaric'. Irving hummed and hawed, then came the flash of insight: 'Malvolio'. Whatever you thought of his performances, he gave you, as Craig put it, 'the stateliness of happenings and the majesty of the appearance of things . . . and a reverence for *l'esprit*, as opposed to the higgledy-piggledy, go as you please, loose-limbed, loose-lipped, racketty stuff'.[2]

Bernard Shaw recognized the originality of Irving, and understood it better than a good many of Irving's critics or admirers. Having quickly discarded the stock in trade technique acquired in provincial repertory, he had patiently constructed the mask of the *übermarionette*. This was not exactly Irving's personality; it was Irving's *persona*, and he applied it to every part he played. For Bernard Shaw Shakespeare was music drama – or sometimes not even that. Mercutio's 'Queen Mab' and Juliet's 'Gallop apace' were arias, pure and simple; the balcony scene was a duet, or it was nothing. As Shakespeare's art deepened, his music became more complicated and more interesting – that was all. Shaw was looking for what he found in Salvini – a newer and better, a more human and sophisticated, Barry Sullivan. He acknowledged that Irving's mission 'was to re-establish on the stage the touching, appealing nobility of sentiment and affection – the dignity which asserts itself when it is wounded'. Thus he was able to switch the 'nunnery' scene in *Hamlet* from brutality to pathos, and to turn the implacable 'Jew that Shakespeare drew' into an offended patriarch. But his formal training, like his formal education, was minimal. He had seen and admired Phelps, but he had not taken from Phelps the most precious thing that Phelps had to give him – a perfect and unmannered elocution. Indeed it may be doubted whether Irving the actor took anything from anyone. Henry James was to write of 'the strange tissue of arbitrary pronunciations which floats in the thankless medium of Mr Irving's harsh, monotonous voice'.[3] This led to incoherence in scenes of cumulative passion. Significant detail and an almost sacerdotal dignity were his *forte*; the grand rhythmical sweep was generally beyond him. Only the strict and prolonged discipline of a school like the Comédie Française, with different physical endowments, could have made of him the instrument that Shaw was asking for. Irving's performances were variations on a self that could never be mistaken; but he wore his self with a difference. In reply to the question whether he was tall, Graham Robertson – that fastidious theatrical connoisseur – explained that he was 'tall when he wanted to be'.

W. B. Yeats used to say that 'intellectual pride' was Irving's strongest point, but here there was more pride than intellect. Irving was nothing of an intellectual; if he had been, he would have seized upon Ibsen like the 'famished wolf' to which Ellen Terry compared him in *Macbeth*. He read only what was relevant to the work in hand; he had little sense of poetry; and no ear for music, although he was a shrewd judge of what music would be theatrically effective. It was the same with painting; here he relied upon Ellen Terry, who had been married to an artist and lived with an architect. But, as Gordon Craig points out, he had absorbed a good deal from Gustave Doré's saturnine romanticism, which was closely akin to his own. An illustration from Doré's Don Quixote

[1] *Henry Irving, the Actor and his World*
(1951) p.338
[2] *Theatre Arts Monthly* (January 1938)
[3] *The Scenic Art* (1949)

gave him the picture for the apothecary scene in *Romeo and Juliet*. Ellen Terry
had the interesting idea of wearing black for Ophelia's mad scene, since she
was then in mourning for Polonius. But Irving persuaded her, with infinite
tact, to wear white. Nobody but Hamlet could wear black in *Hamlet*, even when
Hamlet was not on the stage. In production, as in performance, it was the
theatrical effect that mattered; and Shakespeare was useful or dispensable in
so far as he lent himself to the effects of which Irving was a master.

Shaw did not mount his batteries against the Lyceum until 1895, when
Irving was already past his best in the greater Shakespearian rôles. The Lyceum
had long since become a national institution, as respectable as the Royal
Academy. People went to see Irving at the Lyceum as they went to see W. G.
Grace at Lords. If Irving was miscast, as he was as Romeo, or miscalculated as
he did in *Lear*, or if Grace was out for a duck, they did not ask for their money
back. Each was an eminent Victorian, perfectly attuned to the age in which
he lived. Nevertheless Irving, as Henry James put it, was 'a bone of contention
in London society second only in magnitude to the rights of the Turks and the
wrongs of the Bulgarians'; and James, while admitting his flair for the picturesque, compared him to a painter who 'goes in for colour when he cannot
depend upon his drawing'.[1] William Archer wrote of those who had made
Irving 'a law unto himself'; of the heretics who remained 'not perhaps to pray,
but at least to reflect and qualify their unbelief'; and of others who complained
that he 'could neither walk nor talk'. An American critic, H. A. Clapp, found
that 'everywhere, in the best English society, to admire him without reserve is
held eccentric to the verge of affectation'. Indeed, caught as we are between the
idolatry of Craig, the exasperation of Shaw, the gushing of Clement Scott and
William Winter, and the pernickety criticism of Henry James, it is Clapp who
gives us the surest basis for appreciating the art of Henry Irving, and for guessing how far it served the interpretation of Shakespearian rôles. Clapp admitted
that Irving could 'never be quite trusted with his legs, his shoulders, or his
tongue for five consecutive minutes'; that his speech suggested 'Cornwall,
Devonshire, and occasionally northern Vermont . . . an Irving *patois* developed
out of his own throat and brain through the operation of the familiar law of the
survival of the unfittest'; that he lacked 'that temperamental solidity and force
out of which alone the actor's most potent lightning can be forged'; that his
style was 'staccato' with 'no sweeps or long strokes in it – everything accomplished by a series of light, disconnected touches or dabs, the total effect of
which, when the subject is not too lofty, is agreeable and harmonious . . . the
flight not of the storm-defying eagle, but of the short-winged, often-resting
domestic fowl'. Here one is tempted to protest that if Irving could not fly like
an eagle, he could easily look like one. Clapp noted 'the monotonous repetition
of the rhythmic nod of the head, the dull stamp of the foot, and the queer
clutch of the breast in exciting passages'; but he emphasized Irving's refinement and his charm 'which a formal training might have destroyed with his
mannerisms'. He remembered him as 'a crisper of the nerves and a pleaser or
tingler of the retina'; and his face as 'without exception the most fascinating I
have seen upon the stage'.[2] But Irving still loomed, challenged but indes-
tructible, above praise or denigration. The accolade had tapped the portico of
the Lyceum long before that morning in the summer of 1895 when its high
priest took the train to Windsor.

And there was Ellen Terry. Irving's reign at the Lyceum (1876-1902), and

Photo of Ellen Terry by
Mrs Julia Margaret Cameron

Opposite: Ellen Terry as
Lady Macbeth 1888

[1] Ibid
[2] 'Reminiscences of a Dramatic Critic'
Atlantic Monthly (1902)

his partnership with Ellen Terry (1878-1903) were each the longest in English theatrical history. Of course the Lyceum was Irving's personal creation. There was no detail which he had not designed or supervised, unless it were the potatoes which prompter Allen baked, surreptitiously, every night, in his corner. But the Lyceum audience, and a vital part of its productions, were also the creation of Ellen Terry. She provided the chequered sunshine to Irving's chiaroscuro. With less genius, she had a more acute intelligence. Where he conquered his audience, she charmed them. Henry James found, a little grudgingly, that she belonged properly 'to a period which takes a strong interest in aesthetic furniture, archaeological attire, and blue china'. She had 'charm, a great deal of a certain amateurish, angular grace, a total want of what the French call *chic*, and a countenance very happily adapted to the expression of pathetic emotion'.[1] If in the eyes of the public the two stars shone equally, they did not shine equally behind the stage. Irving always did what he wanted, and Ellen Terry generally did as she was told. She was Irving's most faithful ally, most devoted friend, most ardent admirer, and most discerning critic. Seeing him as she did year after year at the closest quarters, in good times and bad, she enables us to see him too, and more clearly than any critic watching him from the stalls; much more clearly than George Bernard Shaw, who wanted her to leave Lyceum Shakespeare altogether and get down to serious business with Ibsen. In telling us about Irving, she also tells us a great deal about herself.[2]

She saw the point of Irving without claiming that he was perfect. He was only selfish as a general is selfish on the eve of a great battle. He surrounded himself with the best officers, non-commissioned officers, and foot-slogging infantry he could find, but he was his own Chief-of-Staff and his own Paymaster-General. There were veterans who had played with Macready; young men like Martin Harvey and Johnston Forbes-Robertson, who were each to do the stage some service, and win their accolades in the course of time. Forbes-Robertson was an exquisitely spoken Buckingham in *Henry VIII*; and in *Much Ado about Nothing* – of which we catch a glimpse from the painting he did of the church scene – went further than anyone in persuading an audience that Claudio was not irredeemably a cad. Irving, let it be confessed, did not deserve the prominence that Forbes-Robertson had given him in that picture. The scene ends with Benedick's 'Go, comfort your cousin; I must say she is dead, and so farewell' – the kind of practical conclusion that Shakespeare generally preferred in a theatre where there was no curtain to ring down. For this, Irving substituted the following, for which W. G. Wills might have blushed:

> *Beatrice*: Benedick, kill him – kill him, if you can.
> *Benedick*: As sure as I'm alive, I will.

For an actress who had already electrified the house with 'Kill Claudio' this was theatrically redundant, as well as impertinent in the last degree. But in spite of Ellen Terry's tears, and in defiance of her sure taste, Irving remained obdurate. Shakespeare's ending to the scene had often earned seven or eight curtain calls, but these were not enough. Irving had large ideas about what was meant by 'bringing down the house'.

The temptation, however, was one to which he did not always succumb. His first Shakespearian part at the Lyceum was Hamlet – before Ellen Terry joined the company – and after seeing him she never wanted to see another. He 'did not go out to the audience. He made them come to him'. Very pale – beautiful when you saw him close, but haggard from a more distant view, and seeming older than his years, his hair 'blue-black, like the plumage of a crow, the eyes burning – two fires veiled as yet by melancholy' – he 'kept three things going at the same time – the antic madness, the sanity, the sense of the theatre'. Clapp admired the mental quality of a performance in which the actor was able

> to show the superfine sanity which constantly characterizes his wildest utterances, and yet to indicate his dangerous nearness to that madness with which 'great wit ever is allied'; and finally to exhibit a character that, in spite of all the contradictions with which the master-poet has chosen to fill it shall yet be human, lovable, and reasonably comprehensible.

The same critic – who saw the performance in New York – found the soliloquies, though poor in elocution, genuinely 'thought aloud'; and throughout there was 'an unerring sense of the relation of each speech to every other, to every personage, and the whole play'.[3]

Irving entered, trailing his cloak, at the end of a long procession, with the lights dimmed. His instruction to the players had the ease and certainty of a royal command. Courtesy, humour, and swiftness in repartee marked his performance throughout, and his sparring with Polonius stopped short of downright rudeness. Where a great effect was called for, he was ready with it, writing the first lines of his speech for *The Murder of Gonzago* frantically against a pillar. But throughout the first two acts of the play the audience were uncertainly with him, so delicate was his brushwork on the portrait he was gradually building up. It was not until the climax of the 'nunnery' scene, when he caught sight of Polonius and the King, that his emotion burst the dykes which had hitherto contained it. This was described as 'Irving's Marengo'; and Edward Russell saw the originality of his Hamlet in 'the trick of fostering and aggravating his own excitements'.

An example of his attention to detail was shown in the play scene. He began by toying with a peacock feather at Ophelia's feet and then, after rushing to the throne on the King's exit, threw it away on the words 'a very – very – *peacock*!' Without getting himself bogged down in Oedipan quicksands, he did not burke the realism of his reproaches to Gertrude, although 'I'll lug the guts into the neighbour room' was more than a nineteenth-century audience could have been expected to stand from a Hamlet who had done so much to win their sympathies. Had he won them too easily? Bernard Shaw certainly thought so; perhaps we should think so too. Most Hamlets of the time, and later, would seem too mature for a modern taste; but except for this, none have satisfied more perfectly than Irving the *optique du théâtre*. The permissive society, however, has different *optiques*. 'The glass of fashion and the mould of form' are the least of its requirements, and the last thing it expects of Hamlet – or of anyone else – is that he should 'prove most royally.' In later productions Ellen Terry was the Ophelia; 'a somewhat angular maiden of the Gothic ages', as she appeared to Henry James 'with her hair cropped short like a boy's, and a straight and clinging robe wrought over with contemporary needlework', and achieving pathos with 'the curious, husky monotony of her voice'.[4]

Richard III followed in 1877. Irving achieved his limp by wearing a heel upon one shoe and not upon the other, and gave the play as Shakespeare wrote it. The performance confirmed his reputation, although it failed to convert Henry

Ibid
The Story of my Life (1908)
'Reminiscences of a Dramatic Critic'
Atlantic Monthly (1902)
The Scenic Art (1949) p.143

Ellen Terry as Portia 1879

James; he noted the 'livid complexion and Gothic angularity', but missed 'the
rapidity, the intensity and *entrain*'. He was also, as we shall see, moving with the
times when he wrote of Shakespeare production in general that 'the more it is
painted and dressed, the more it is lighted and furnished and solidified, the less
it corresponds or coincides, the less it squares with our imaginative habits. The
more Shakespeare is "built in" the more we are built out.'[1] As often happened
on an opening night, Irving's voice gave out before the end; but a critic,[2]
writing many years later, did not forget 'the dark, misshapen tragic figure . . .
standing with outstretched arms against the lovely background of the peaceful
heavens . . . The figure of the King became in that moment a thousand times
more tragic than it had been before.' There was no rivalry between Richard's
tent and Richmond's; the former occupied the entire stage with a table and
red lamp at the back, where the last of the Plantagenets brooded over his plans
for the battle. *Richard III* is a melodrama which turns into a tragedy; Irving,
equal to both, was perfectly equipped to operate the transition.

When he travelled he did so with a purpose, and in 1879, on a yachting cruise in the Mediterranean, he put in at Venice with vague ideas of *Othello* or Otway's *Venice Preserved* at the back of his mind. Here, and elsewhere, the appearance and characteristics of the Levantine Jew had suggested a new conception of Shylock. In Tunis, we are told, he had seen a Jew 'beside himself over some transaction, tear his hair and his clothes, fling himself upon the sand writhing with rage, and a few minutes later become self-possessed, fawning and full of genuine gratitude for a trifling gift of money. Picturesque in his fury, having regained his composure, the Jew had stalked away with kingly dignity behind his mule team.'[3] The picture stayed with Irving. If this was not 'the Jew that Shakespeare drew', he might have drawn it – or had he drawn it, after all? Was the bond conceived in fun, and only claimed in fury? If nobody raised an eyebrow at Jessica's elopement, and if she was on such easy terms with Portia, might not that suggest an elder of the synagogue and a man respected, even if he were resented, on the Rialto?

Irving produced *The Merchant of Venice* in a text to which some, though by no means all, of its rightful belongings had been restored. The Prince of Aragon; Jessica's talk with Lorenzo which suggested a very different Shylock; the scene between Portia and Nerissa before they set out for Mantua – all this was omitted. Bassanio's casket scene was cut by a third, and as the successful run of the play proceeded the fifth act was dropped completely, a one-acter by Wills being put in its place. It is almost incredible that the loveliest Portia of her time submitted to such treatment, although others were quick to protest. Her by-play during the comedy of the rings had sent the play dancing to its moonlit conclusion. This, however, was the last thing that Irving wanted, and he was not the first actor to decide that Shylock must have the last word. So far was Shakespeare from being properly understood at a time when the world of art and letters, of rank and fashion, was flocking to the Lyceum to see him.

Nevertheless, with Ellen Terry as Portia the famous partnership was seen at its best, and most evenly balanced. Prepared for a turbulent Shylock, she had conceived a very quiet treatment of the trial scene, but when she found that Irving was going to be quiet too, she was forced to be commanding. His opening was slow and meditative, and a blind man in the audience complained that he could not hear the money-lender in 'Three thousand ducats – well'. Irving took the point and made him more audible. He came over the Rialto bridge, neatly and soberly dressed, wearing a black cap and a wisp of grey beard; a Shylock in the later fifties, with nothing to obscure the play of feature with which, in default of vocal range, he could always magnetize an audience. In proposing the bond, second thoughts seem to have prevailed; there was no doubt from his expression that this 'merry jest' was no laughing matter. After Jessica's elopement the curtain fell, and then went up again on a bare stage. Shylock, returning over the bridge, knocked three times on the door of the empty house before the curtain was again lowered. One only wonders why it had been thought necessary to lower it before. A pause, and a change of lighting, would have sufficiently indicated the passing of a few hours.

In the scene with Tubal, Salanio and Salarino, the weakness of Irving's voice again betrayed him; but in the trial scene many thought he gave the finest performance of his life. Matter and manner, method and conception, were here perfectly matched. He played throughout with a menacing and self-confident quiet, except when he rushed forward on Portia's 'Bid me tear the

Henry Irving as Shylock 1879

bond', and again, with a vindictive shriek of triumph, on 'A sentence – come, prepare'. He triumphed once again as he returned Gratiano's boorish jibes with a glance of pitiless contempt; seemed about to fall as he reached the door; drew himself up to the proud fulness of his height; and stalked slowly out. A similar effect of collapse and recovery was achieved by Olivier nearly a hundred years later. Who that heard that wail of agony from outside the court could doubt that, however eminent, Irving was not the last of a mighty line?

He slyly admitted later that he had wrenched Shylock to a pathos not wholly justified by the text. Henry James found the performance 'rigid and frigid, and above all painfully behind the stroke of the clock'; where Edmund Kean had been 'hissing hot' in the scene with Tubal, Irving missed its points by drawing it out. But then a certain diabolical *froideur* was Irving's *forte*; and H. A. Clapp wrote of 'the great passion only hinted at through the grim reserve of the latter half of the trial scene'. Ellen Terry, also, disappointed Henry James, giggling too much, 'too free and familiar, too osculatory, in her relations with Bassanio', patting and stroking him when he had chosen the right casket. For Henry James Ellen Terry always had 'too much nature'; he would have liked 'a little more art'. *The Merchant of Venice* ran for more than two hundred consecutive nights. The long run – often to the disadvantage of the actor's performance, though not to his manager's purse – had come to stay.

In the autumn of 1880 Edwin Booth (1833–93) came to London for a season at the Princess' Theatre. His Hamlet was received with appreciation which stopped short of enthusiasm. If he was put a little out of his normal stride by the prestige of Irving not far away, Irving was anxious only to play the host to a great American actor. When he proposed that he and Booth should alternate the parts of Othello and Iago, Booth gladly accepted. It was not a happy arrangement, since Booth was less than outstanding as Othello, and Irving failed in it altogether. According to Ellen Terry, 'he screamed, he ranted, and he raved – lost his voice, was slow where he should have been swift, incoherent where he should have been strong . . . yet night after night he achieved in his speech to the Senate one of the most superb and beautiful bits of acting in his life'. As Iago, however, he may well have given his most definitive performance of a Shakespearian rôle. He had everything in his favour – sardonic humour, the *diable au corps*, only the most colloquial verse, and a costume which he had himself designed. He perfectly combined the Machiavellian and the *fausse bonhomie* – an 'Englishman Italianate', as A. B. Walkley happily phrased it. Ellen Terry remembered him eating grapes and spitting out the pips, as he wove his conspiracy. Booth's method seemed old-fashioned beside the novelty of Irving's technique; for Booth still retained the habit of delivering all his lines four-square to the audience. A contributor to *Macmillan's* magazine drew a succinct comparison between the two performances:

> The American Iago, clear, cool, and precise, admirably thought out, never deviating a hair's breadth from the preconceived plan, design and execution marching hand in hand with ordered steps from the first scene to the last; a performance of marvellous balance and regularity, polished to the very finger-nails. The Englishman's startling, picturesque, irregular, brilliant – sometimes less brilliant than bizarre – but always fresh and suggestive, always bearing that peculiar stamp of personality which has so often saved the actor in his sorest straits.[1]

When Irving rolled up his costume for Othello with such relief, he also

[1] Quoted by Laurence Irving, ibid p. 375
[2] *The Scenic Art* (1949) p.162
[3] *Henry Irving, the Actor and his World* (1951) p.388

rolled up his Iago. He never played the part again – understandably perhaps, for there was not on the English-speaking stage an Othello in sight to partner him.

He was now tempted, unwisely, to *Romeo and Juliet*, with a thought no doubt of what Hawes Craven might do with Verona. At forty-four, he knew that he was too old for Romeo – had he indeed ever been theatrically young? – and that Mercutio, in spite of an early death, was the part for him. But if he played Mercutio, there was no Romeo available. With hindsight they might have picked on Forbes-Robertson, but he was still thought of primarily as a painter, and when Ellen Terry had seen him act she advised him to stick to his easel. In spite of these misgivings *Romeo and Juliet* was decided upon. The result was one of Irving's worst performances and most beautiful productions. As Henry James wrote: 'Mr Irving is not a Romeo; Miss Terry is not a Juliet; and no one else, save Mrs Stirling [the Nurse] is anything in particular. The play is not acted; it is costumed.'[2] Irving restored the prologue and the Rosaline passages, for which his moodiness and melancholy were well adapted. Hawes Craven and Telbin led the eye from the sun-baked market-place of Verona to the tomb of the Capulets, dank with intimations of mortality. The Meininger company had been showing a new way with a crowd in their *Julius Caesar* at Drury Lane, and the supers at the Lyceum followed – and occasionally worsened – their instruction. When Irving came down to see how they were getting on under his stage-manager's direction, he told them 'not to fidget'. Nevertheless the production was remarkable for its realism, anticipating Zeffirelli's *mafia* at the Old Vic eighty years later. Combining beauty and terror, love and hate, poetry and discord, it 'clothed the Loop of Chicago in the lush opulence of the Italian Renaissance'.[3]

But this was not enough. If Irving – as well as his critics – knew that he was miscast, Ellen Terry was also below her best. When Henry Labouchere reproached Irving for attempting what all his friends 'would have told you was

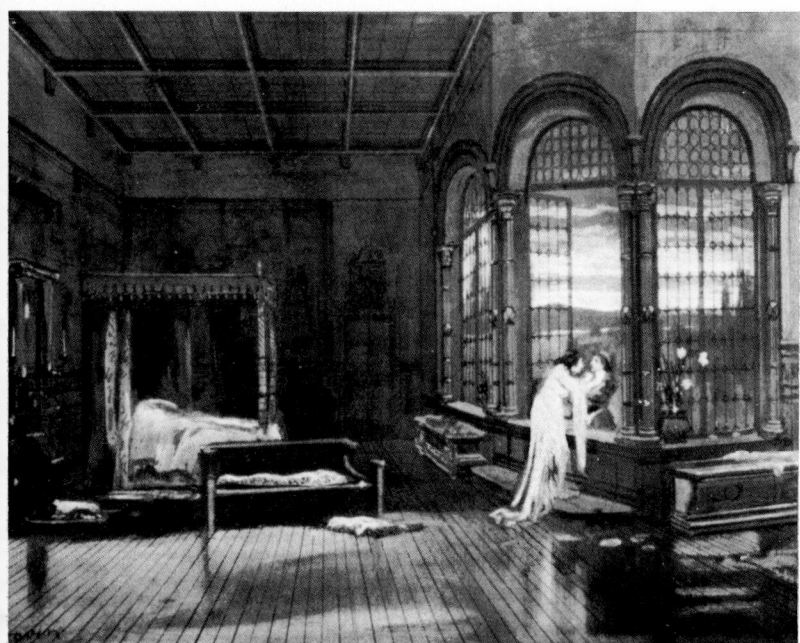

Set design for *Romeo and Juliet*,
Lyceum Theatre 1895

a physical impossibility', she retorted 'that the worst thing Henry Irving could do, would be better than the worst of anyone else'. She was remembering the calm desperation of his scene with the Apothecary, and the haunted figure breaking into the tomb. He had his moments, the poetry of attitude making up, to some extent, for the poverty of speech; so had she – notably in the scene where the Nurse, played deliciously by the veteran Mrs Stirling, comes back from her meeting with Romeo. This she insisted on acting with the serious impatience of a girl five fathom deep in love. The visual beauty of the production compensated for the deficiencies of its 'star-crossed lovers', and carried it to crowded houses for twenty-four weeks. But Irving's Romeo was rolled away with his Iago; and it could be better spared. Of all the Lyceum productions of Shakespeare, *Much Ado about Nothing*, which followed, may well have been the truest to its author. A serious melodrama as well as a comedy of manners, the play will always stand up to solid treatment. Decoration helps it; fantastication destroys it altogether. Irving, who never condescended even to rubbish, gave it all the drama and décor it deserved. The illustrations from a book on Italian Ceremonies – picked up for a casual £80! – suggested Telbin's wonderful set for the church scene 'with its real built-out round pillars thirty feet high, its canopied roof of crimson plush from which hung the golden lamps universally used in Italian cathedrals, its painted canopy overhanging the altar, its great iron-work gates, its altar with cases of flowers, and flaming candles rising to a height of eighteen feet, its stained-glass windows and statues of saints'.[1] All this was put up during an act interval of fifteen minutes. Most of the other scenes were suggested by painted front cloths, so skilfully lit that the eye was cheated into giving them the depth and dimension required. For a

[1] Ibid p.402

moment Irving was tempted to substitute electricity for the softer gaslight, but Ellen Terry persuaded him to let well alone.

Benedick made comparatively light demands upon him, but he met them with the dry humour – the tang of a patrician *amontillado* – which he always had at his command. The switch from banter and self-mockery to the defence of injured innocence had a military crispness. Ellen Terry's Beatrice sparkled like the star she was born under – the most radiant of all her Shakespearian creations. Only Dogberry and his patrol seem to have been ineffective, for high comedy suited Irving better than low. This was shown in *Twelfth Night* which misfired completely. Irving had taken over Bensley's Malvolio, as Charles Lamb had handed it down to him, with the result that his detractors applauded him and his admirers were bewildered. But Toby, on whom the weight of the comedy really falls, went for nothing, and on the opening night Ellen Terry's Viola was hampered by a poisoned finger and one arm in a sling.

After a glance at *As You Like It* and rejecting Jaques, and the realization that even if an actor-manager wanted to play Brutus, he could not do so in face of Mark Antony and the Forum, Irving returned to the hardest test of all – *Macbeth*. He had played it before under Bateman's management, and relatively failed. Now he had Ellen Terry at the height of her powers and popularity. She was not the obvious casting for a public brought up on the legend of Sarah Siddons, but she knew that what Mrs Siddons thought about the part was very different from what she had done with it. Perhaps she, Ellen Terry, might realize Mrs Siddon's original conception of an intensely feminine woman distorting her nature in the service of her husband's ambition, and out of a woman's love for him. 'I cannot understand why Mrs Siddons shd write *down one* set of

Preliminary study for *Macbeth* (left) and the banquet scene (right), Lyceum Theatre 1888

ideas upon the subject and carry out a totally different plan. Why? . . . because
one way is well within her methods and physical presentation.' Might not the
other way be well within her own?

Some people thought it was – notably Joseph Chamberlain, who admired
the power as well as the delicacy of her performance. But opinion was sharply
divided, both about herself and Irving. Shaw, for once, thought him fine, and
Irving himself regarded Macbeth as his best part. Henry James found him 'a
very superior amateur, ingenious, intelligent, fanciful, with a decided sense of
the picturesque'; the voice without charm, and the diction without subtlety;
'grappling in a deliberate and conscientious manner with a series of great tragic
points'. There was warrant for making Macbeth 'so spiritless a plotter before
the crime and so arrant a coward afterwards'.[1] The performance had much in
common with Booth, but James found more genius in Booth – perhaps because
he also found more art. For H. A. Clapp Irving's Macbeth was 'admirably consistent, briefly pathetic or fantastically impressive', with little evidence of
physical courage or moral scruple. The character became 'softer of fibre as the
play went on, more hysterical and spasmodic, more inordinate in grimace and
snarl. "Ere the bat hath flown" and "Light thickens" were so delivered as
darkly to haunt the secret places of the memory as some sombre winged things
haunt the recesses of caves.'[2]

Irving looked the Highland chieftain to the life, and now conveyed more
surely than before the conflict of a sensitive conscience with a criminal resolution. On a visit to the morgue in Paris, not only had he been struck by the sight
of one of the corpses, but had fancied from the behaviour of another visitor that
he had identified the murderer! How this macabre expedition assisted his performance of Macbeth is rather difficult to fathom. The earlier scenes of introspection were grist to his mill, but the brutalizing of the character as the play
moved towards its climax taxed his physical resources – for Macbeth is never
more energetic than when he is at bay. Moreover this is both the shortest and
the swiftest of Shakespeare's tragedies, and although Irving could be swift as
a hawk in the expression of his thought – people sometimes compared him to
Disraeli – his tendency was to be slow in speech and movement. A dash of
Barry Sullivan would have assisted the bustle of the final scenes, where the
making of points should be subordinate to the making of pace.

The production was as pictorial as Irving himself in the accepted Caledonian
convention. Alice Comyns Carr's dress for Ellen Terry was immortalized by
Sargent, but Irving appropriated the red cloak which she had proposed to wear
over it. He could not resist so 'fine a splash of colour'. Laurence Irving suggests
that the total effect was rather too crepuscular. The single moment of sunlight
in the play – Duncan's entrance into Dunsinane – was contradicted by torches
flaring in the darkness. Only on the arrival of Birnam Wood was the sun permitted to shine. Arthur Sullivan composed the music, which was not quite
what Irving wanted. By dint of a few tuneless ti-tum-ti-tums he suggested the
effect he was after, and Sullivan agreed with him.

A few more challenges remained – Wolsey and Lear, Iachimo and Coriolanus.
The production of *Henry VIII* was the most sumptuous ever seen at the Lyceum.
The play is an invitation to pageantry, and Irving accepted it with an open purse.
Alma Tadema, with Hawes Craven and his assistants, reconstructed a Tudor
England, while Alice Comyns Carr and Seymour Lucas went to Holbein for
the costumes. Irving sent his *cappa magna* to be dyed in Rome, but a slightly

Left: Ellen Terry as Queen Katharine in *Henry VIII*, Lyceum Theatre 1892

Henry Irving as Wolsey 1892

[1] *The Scenic Art* (1949) pp.36-9
[2] 'Reminiscences of a Dramatic Critic' *Atlantic Monthly* (1902)
[3] *Henry Irving, the Actor and his World* (1951) p.544
[4] John Doran *Blackwood's Magazine*

rosier red was eventually produced in England. His success as Wolsey was unqualified; here, *in excelsis*, was the 'plume of pride' of which Yeats was afterwards to write. And the pride was matched by the pathos. There was a reminiscence of Manning in the ascetic features, and we are told that 'several unbelievers of long standing' were induced 'to conversion and penitence' by the performance.[3] Irving reminded Sir Robert Peel of Wilberforce's description of Manning as 'the incarnation of evil'; this was to out-Strachey Strachey, and what people took away from Irving's Wolsey was not only – perhaps not chiefly – the pride, but the fall that followed it.

Lear in 1892 was a total failure. Irving, in disregard of Ellen Terry's warning, had assumed a voice for the part with the result that he was virtually inaudible from start to finish. Henry Arthur Jones, who admired him with reservations, wrote of his performance on the opening night that he was 'slow, laboured, un-inspired, screechy, forcibly feeble, failing chiefly where all representations of Lear fail'. Returning a few nights later, Graham Robertson found a Lear as 'magnificent and terrible in its pathos' as it had always been magnificent in appearance. But the failure was irretrievable. Irving seems to have been follow-ing, however haltingly, in the footsteps of Kean for whom the 'warmest bursts of passion never removed him beyond the weakness of age'.[4] It is worth noting that the successful Lears of modern times – Donald Wolfit, John Gielgud, Michael Redgrave – have played for power, enfeebled only by the nemesis of its abuse. In a letter to Ellen Terry Shaw suggests what had gone wrong with Irving's performance, and was always liable to spoil other parts as well:

> Swift brute force, concentrated self-assertion, and the power of letting the electricity discharge itself in the meaning of the line, instead of in the look and tone of the stage figure, are all just what he has not got. His slowness, his growing habit of overdoing his part and slipping in an imaginative conception of his own *between* the lines (which made such a frightful wreck of Lear), all of which are part of his extraordinary insensibility to literature, are all reasons why he should avoid me, though his feeling for fine execution, and his dignity and depth of sentiment, are reasons why I should *not* avoid him.[1]

The settings for *Lear* were inspired by the sketches[2] of Ford Madox Brown (1844). These incorporated the imagery of the *Pelican Daughter*, and a theme from the Bayeux Tapestry for Lear's awakening to sanity. The figure of the King as a clown was reproduced on the back of his throne. The period suggested was after the departure of the Romans, and before the Norse invasions.

Cymbeline was tempting Providence, since the play was little known and little liked, and the scissors would need to be busily at work if Iachimo were to be made into an actor-managerial part. But Imogen was also a temptation to Ellen Terry, and to anyone who knew her worth to the Box Office. She may have felt herself to be 'fat and fifty', but the English stage would have had the right to go into mourning if she had never been given her chance as Imogen. Her epistolary relations with Shaw were now close and constant, and she sent him the acting edition of the play, with her own careful annotations. *Cymbeline* is a perplexing muddle of sentiment and melodrama, and Granville-Barker was the first to make theatrical sense of it. Shaw considered Irving's cuts 'stupid to the last extremity'. They were also prudish and insensitive. 'Disloyal' had to make do for 'adultery', and much else was sacrificed 'to please the curates for whom the Lyceum seems chiefly to exist'. Imogen was not allowed to pray for 'as small a drop of pity as a wren's eye', and Irving had jettisoned his own description of Imogen's eyelids as 'white and azure, laced with heaven's own tinct'. Ellen Terry managed to restore 'How of adultery?' and the 'wren's eye', but the whole balance of the play was disturbed by the paring down of the other parts in order to make Iachimo more prominent than Posthumus – an unnecessary operation since Iachimo will always be the more interesting of the two. Ellen Terry was plagued with letters telling her what Mrs Siddons, or another, had done with Imogen, and before the opening night she described herself as '*all earth* instantly I get on the stage . . . No inspiration, no softness, no sadness even, tight, mechanical, *hidebound*. I feel nothing.' Shaw, though prepared to 'slaughter' the production – for the play, in any case, was no favourite of his – bade her go ahead as she felt. Mrs Siddons's Imogen in 1896 would be as absurd as Duse's Magda in 1815.

When it came to performance he derided the play, and laid his customary bouquet at the feet of Ellen Terry. His admiration for Irving was for once unqualified; 'no vulgar bagful of points, but a true impersonation, unbroken in its life current from end to end, varied on the surface with the finest comedy and without a single lapse in the sustained beauty of its execution'. Even Henry James admitted 'a duskiness of romance, an eccentricity of distinction'; and in the 'indulgently impressionistic' setting the kind of success that was 'stamped with the *coup de pouce* of Mr Tadema and the great scenic art of Mr Irving'.[3]

Before his notice was in print Shaw pursued Ellen Terry with advice, which was always to the point.

> In playing Shakespear, play *to* the lines, *through* the lines, *on* the lines, but never between the lines. There simply isn't time for it. You would not stick a five bars rest into a Beethoven symphony to pick up your drumsticks; and similarly you must not stop the Shakespear orchestra for business. Nothing short of a procession or a fight should make anything so extraordinary as a silence during a Shakespearian performance.[4]

The young Granville-Barker was already coming to these conclusions, and fifteen years later he would act upon them. Meanwhile the play ran for as long as it was expected to, and Ellen Terry no longer felt like 'earth' when she stepped on the stage as Imogen. 'I never *feel* like myself when I am acting, but someone else, so nice, and so young and so happy, and always in-the-air, light and bodyless.' Fat she certainly was not; fifty she may have been; but in these words to Shaw she had given her performance in a phrase, as she gave it every night to her audience in the last but one of her Shakespearian rôles at the Lyceum.

Realizing that he was now too old for Richard II – which in his younger days he might have played beautifully – Irving next decided on *Coriolanus*. It ran for only thirty-three performances. Volumnia's steel was not in Ellen Terry's armoury, and Irving's 'plume of pride' was not enough to sustain the most extrovert of Shakespeare's protagonists. Coriolanus must always be up and doing; Irving was happiest when he could be up and thinking, or when thought and feeling were at one. He was further handicapped by an inappropriate beard which, as in Lear, obscured his facial play. Indeed it would be difficult to find a part to which he was less suited. And so the great Lyceum story drew towards its end with the century, and the reign, to which it belonged. A younger generation was knocking at the door, and one or two of them were threatening to break it down. Forbes-Robertson's Hamlet had come to challenge Irving's; Mrs Patrick Campbell was rivalling Ellen Terry in beauty and talent, although she was never to approach her in Shakespeare; Frank Benson had mustered his company, and was taking to the road. Of all this we shall treat in a later chapter. But when they carried Irving's coffin, with its pall of laurel wreaths, into Westminster Abbey, the curtain had been rung down on the greatest and the longest reign the English theatre had known; a triumph, not unbroken, of art, of personality, of perseverance. If a question mark remains against Irving as a Shakespearian interpreter, we may call two writers into the witness box – one a critic, the other a dramatist. For Arthur Symons Irving's art was 'wholly rhetoric, that is to say, wholly external; his emotion moves to slow music, crystallises into an attitude, dies upon a long drawn out word'. For Henry Arthur Jones 'he could not untwist the chains that tie the hidden soul of harmony . . . It would be difficult to recall any one sustained passage of Shakespeare's verse that was spoken by Irving in such a way as to delight or even to satisfy the ear as well as the mind.' Nevertheless his 'peculiar dignity of manner could not have belonged to one who had been at an English public school', and – most importantly – 'contempt of wealth, contempt of death – Irving had them'.[5]

As for Ellen Terry, thousands would have echoed the declaration of Bernard Shaw that her name rang 'like a chime through the last quarter of the nineteenth century'.

Ellen Terry and Bernard Shaw (1931) p.44
Now in the Whitworth Gallery, Manchester
The Scenic Art (1949) pp.282-5
Ellen Terry and Bernard Shaw (1931) p.66
The Shadow of Henry Irving (1931)

IV In America

Oscar Wilde's rather cheap aphorism that Britain and the United States are two countries divided by a common language – whatever grain of truth may be allowed to it in other contexts – has no relevance to the theatre. Here the story is one of reciprocal hospitality and fruitful exchange. In the nature of things the American theatre began as an immigrant theatre, and for a long time continued to be so. It is among the marks of a settled society that it will ask for entertainment, and in 1750 we find Walter Murray and Thomas Kean – no relation to his namesakes – bringing up their trunks from the West Indies, and playing *Richard III* at the Nassau Street theatre in New York. Green curtains hung from the ceiling, and a pair of paper screens stood right and left. Six wax candles lit the front of the stage, and six more shone from a chandelier made out of the hoop of a barrel. In the following year Robert Upton produced *Othello* at the same theatre. His production was given at Williamsburg on the occasion of renewing a treaty with the Cherokee Indians, and here the Emperor and Empress of the tribe sent their attendants to stop the killing on the stage. Producing *Othello* before the Indians was always an occupational risk. A ... later, during the Seminole war, they captured a company ... play and proceeded to dance in their clothes.

... States, where race is a live issue, *Othello* has always been ... rly as 1821 a group of negro actors in New York, with James ... ir head, performed *Othello* and *Richard III* in an improvised ... e corner of Bleeker and Mercer Streets. Hewlett's Richard was ... pressive, but the venture was short-lived. The players were ... a magistrate, who, from fear of civic disturbances, exacted from ... never to act Shakespeare again. Near by was the African Free ... d in 1787, and out of this – according to popular report – came ... e most famous figure in negro theatre history. The grandson of ... ieftain, he was born about 1807, either in New York or Maryland, ... the University of Glasgow to complete his education. Starting ... areer as a call-boy, he was soon acting in London, touring the ... playing Othello in Dublin. Here he was seen by Edmund Kean, ... m for a part which he had made so memorably his own. Together, ... Iago, they played in England and on the Continent for many ... r natural a negro Othello seems to us – and the text gives him ... nt – it was a novelty to nineteenth-century audiences, for whom ... a Berber chieftain went virtually unchallenged.

... Park Theatre was opened in New York where Charles Ciceri and ... scenery for *As You Like It*, and later for *Hamlet*, *Henry VIII* ... Their productions were said to have 'surpassed, for elegance ... rything of the kind heretofore seen in America'. But a respect ... e was no part of the baggage brought over in the *Mayflower*. ... rformance of *Hamlet* was stopped as immoral, and a cock fight ... Nevertheless in, or around, 1850 Burton's theatre was opened

in New York with Burton himself as an impressive Bottom and Falstaff; and in 1863 Brougham, a member of Burton's company, opened the Lyceum – without proscenium doors. But in 1844 Benjamin Webster, catching a whiff of the *avant-garde* from Tieck in Germany, had given *The Taming of the Shrew* between two screens and against changing curtains. In October 1863 Davenport and Wallack opened Grover's new theatre with a performance of *Othello* before Lincoln and his cabinet.

Steadily the stars of the British stage – Kean, Vandenhoff, Macready – had been making their way across the Atlantic. Most important of these for the future of the American theatre was Junius Brutus Booth (1796-1852). He was born in St Pancras; began his career in 1813; and four years later was playing Richard III at Covent Garden, and Iago to Edmund Kean's Othello at Drury Lane. In 1820 he was Lear at Covent Garden. Then he emigrated to America, where his first appearance was as Richard III at Richmond, Virginia. With his blue-grey eyes, Roman head, massive physique, magnificent voice, and wonderful elocution, he could strike an audience cold with terror, and plausibly evoke the presence of supernatural powers. Richard's 'What do they in the north when they should serve their sovereign in the west?' was among the remembered moments of the nineteenth-century theatre. Booth was also quite unpredictable, fetching a sword from the prompter in full view of the house for the fight in *Macbeth*, tiptoeing on to the stage as Cassius in the last act of *Julius Caesar*, removing the ham from the sandwiches he was proposing to eat before playing Shylock, and as Richard III appearing indifferently in a dressing-gown or a royal robe. Walt Whitman observed that 'no actor so well understood the value of a stage wait' – and those were days when actors were prepared to wait for a very long time. As a character he was both convivial and misanthropic, retiring for long periods to his farm in Maryland, where he might be seen, a phantom figure, riding through the country at midnight in the costume of Hamlet or Richard. Constance Rourke, in *The Roots of American Culture* (1942), described him as 'an acutely edged individual; he was also an archetype. No one was quite like him, yet he comprised the sum of many men.' This was putting it mildly.

Junius Brutus Booth died on the steamship *J. S. Chenowith* as it was cruising down the Mississippi. He had two sons. One was the assassin of President Lincoln, the other was the greatest actor America has yet produced. In each case a strange heredity counted for much. With John Wilkes we are not concerned, except in so far as his crime deepened the natural melancholy of his brother. Edwin, while still a boy, acted as dresser to his father and was familiar with his moods. Later his own negro attendant said of him: 'Dat chile sure is born lucky – he done gifted to see ghosts'; and Otis Skinner confirmed that 'Edwin Booth saw ghosts always – he lived with them – ghosts of great achievements, great ideals, great tragedies, overwhelming adulation, great plans, great calamities, great joys, and great sympathies'. In other words, Booth was a dreamer – and a mixture of good dreams and bad was the right psychological terrain for a Hamlet that was arguably the finest of the century. 'You look like Hamlet' his father said to him one day, as he stood dressed in black velvet to go on as Jaffier in *Venice Preserved*; and a man who was described, not without reason, as 'the darling of misfortune' was type casting for the part. Both looks and manner assisted him. 'There was an air of melancholy about me' he explained to William Winter 'that made me seem more serious than I really was.'

Edwin Booth as Iago

Nevertheless he was too serious for the comedy of love. 'This fellow Benedick is a lover, and I hate the whole tribe of them' he confessed to Otis Skinner; and he only narrowly scraped through Benedick and Petruchio thanks to vivacity, fire, and mental alertness, distinction of behaviour and speech. When he opened Booth's theatre in 1869 with *Romeo and Juliet* he was seen to be disastrously miscast; indeed you will not find many players who have succeeded equally as Hamlet and as Romeo.

He was often compared with Irving and, as we have seen, they played together in *Othello*. Booth had little of Irving's sheer revelry in mischief, which lent itself to certain kinds of eccentric comedy, but as Iago he could send a sudden shiver down the spine on 'How quiet is this town tonight!' As the performance developed there was a steady darkening of tint and texture until the gay Machiavellian schemer came to assume a leopard's grace and menace. In the soliloquies anguish gave an extra intensity to hate. What Booth did, and failed to do, with the part is shown by his own prescription for it:

> Don't *act* the villain, don't *look* it or *speak* it (by scowling and growling, I mean) but *think* it all the time. Be genial, sometimes jovial, always gentlemanly. Quick in motion as in thought; lithe and sinuous as a snake. A certain bluffness (which my temperament does not afford) should be added to preserve the military flavour of the character; in this particular I fail utterly, my Iago lacks the soldierly quality.[1]

But in many respects the performance remained unchanged. Lucia Calhoun tells us that 'if Othello had suddenly turned upon him, at any moment in their interview, he would have seen only the grave, sympathetic, respectful, troubled face that was composed for him to see'.[2] Dutton Cook could 'remember no Iago at once so natural and plausible, so intellectual and so terrible'; and we learn from another witness that his 'most pernicious lies' were 'administered in the most deceptive form, that of an involuntary confidence'.[3] The mask was debonair, but whenever it was dropped evil incarnate was visible behind it – 'radiant with devilish beauty'.[4] The sly vigilance with which he observed Desdemona's quasi-flirtation with Cassio; his unspoken hatred of Emilia; the cold, tranquil assurance of 'But I'll set down the pegs that make this music'; the half-audible 'I like not that' at the beginning of the temptation scene; the aim, deliberately indirect, of 'Good name in man and woman, dear my lord'; the grinding of the teeth on 'From this time forth I never will speak word' – all these points are brought out in Professor Sprague's reconstruction of Booth's Iago in the work already referred to.[5]

William Winter, writing in 1902, spoke of elocution as a 'lost art' and of Booth's 'purity of enunciation, exquisite adjustments and proportion of emphasis, absolute mastery of the music and meaning of Shakespeare's verse'. Booth would say that he had no ear for music, but that any mistake in the speaking of blank verse jarred on him like a false note. As a boy he was never allowed to watch his father act. Junius Brutus made him listen from the dressing-room: 'I want' he said 'your ear to be educated first.' Otis Skinner confirms that he was 'not a noisy actor at any time. He was a man of grace, sensibility, poetic imagination, and naturally expressive moods. Towards the end his work became laboured and set, but never stilted. He was singularly without mannerism.'[6] The contrast between a classical and a romantic actor, between an inspired individualist and the superb exponent of a secure tradition, between a player who kept the rules and one who broke them – not always with impunity – is clear in any comparison between Booth and Irving.

[1] Furness Variorum *Othello* p.214
[2] *The Galaxy* (January 1869)
[3] Towse *Sixty Years at the Theater* (1916) pp.190-1
[4] Otis Skinner *Footlights and Spotlights* (1924) p.93
[5] *Shakespearian Players and Performances* pp.121-35
[6] *Theatre Arts Monthly* (June 1926)

Booth's Othello – only lightly bronzed by the desert sun – pleaded his love for Desdemona with an Arthurian chivalry, but he was too slight in physique, and in temperament too intellectual to compass the emotion of the rôle. The sensuality was missing, and the execution, according to Winter, 'kept the smoothness of a bird's flight'. His interpretation of Shylock varied a good deal; sometimes he was like a shabby, money-grubbing dealer in old clothes; sometimes he mixed the calculations of high finance with the prescriptions of the mosaic law; sometimes he held to a mean between these two extremes, with grizzled hair, red cap, gaberdine, and pointed red shoes. He salted the trial scene with diabolical humour, cut the fifth act altogether, and omitted a good deal elsewhere. As Macbeth, sure-footed as the stag and with a face hardly less ruddy than his wig, he was described by Charlotte Cushman as 'the great ancestor of all the Bowery ruffians'. Here again his interpretation varied, with alternating stress on the martial and the imaginative. His speaking of 'After life's fitful fever he sleeps well' was like an adagio lament; and at the end of the banquet scene, where the Ghost was only imagined, he was left holding in his hand the crown which had been so dearly purchased.

In Lear, as in Othello, the physique was not equal to the voice. He made a great effect with 'the terrors of the earth', and the reconciliation with Cordelia was deeply affecting; but in general, for want of physical exuberance – in so far as this is demanded of Lear – he depended on a ground-swell of emotion which was rarely released into claps of thunder or flashes of lightning. From the first he showed an innate sovereignty already threatened with decay. He began by giving the play in Nahum Tate's travesty, modified by Kemble; then he laid it aside, and in 1878 produced a version of his own. He also used Cibber's version of *Richard III*, but restored Shakespeare's text in 1876. Here, we are told, he plunged 'like a viper' into the fight with Richmond, and combined the devious charm of the diplomat with the blunt *bonhomie* of the man at arms. His Richard II was a companion portrait to his Hamlet; the one underlined the other. People compared Richard's 'Terrible hell make war upon their spotted souls' to Hamlet's 'Is it the King?'; heard the tolling of despair in 'Of comfort no man speak'; caught the indulgent self-pity in 'I'll be buried in the King's highway'; and were electrified by 'Fiend, thou torment'st me ere I come to hell'. In *Julius Caesar* Booth, at different times, played Brutus, Cassius and Antony. His Cassius was generally considered inferior to Lawrence Barrett's; less electrical, less flexible and free, and the biting envy was missing. In Antony the darker shades of the character were hardly stressed, but as Brutus he was perfect. The moral fervour and ascetic mind were comfortably within his range, and he copied his father's business with the corpse of Henry VI in *Richard III* by striding across the head of the murdered Caesar.

Booth's Hamlet was compared to 'Indian summer sunshine'. Whether or not this was the colour of his performance, it was certainly the colour of his personality. More than most actors of his calibre, he was acquainted with grief. His first, and adored, wife Mary Devlin had died in 1883; his second went insane; in 1867 his entire theatrical property was destroyed by fire; the assassination of Lincoln brought obloquy upon his name, and his management of the theatre which bore it lasted only four years. His energy was sapped by indolence, and for a time he took refuge from his worries in drink. When Otis Skinner asked him how far he was influenced by his father, he replied: 'I think I am a little quieter.' His Hamlet was patrician, poetic, dreamy, and intensely spiritual,

Edwin Booth as Hamlet

standing midway between the realism of Fechter, which he regarded as frivolous, and the rhodomontade of Forrest which was already old-fashioned. It was not enough, he insisted, that 'an actor should make known the fact that Hamlet's soul is haunted by supernatural powers; he must also make it felt that Hamlet possesses a soul such as is possible for supernatural powers to haunt'. The *pietàs* far outweighed the panic as he followed his father's shade with the sword held out like a cross in front of him, and the effect of the scene was prolonged in the way he afterwards looked and spoke. As a result of it he was visibly a man separated from the rest of the world – very much as Helena Modjeska described him sitting out alone on the observation car, smoking a cigar, while the special train, with its actors, properties, and scenery, rolled out over the endless plains.

He showed Hamlet as substantially sane; delirious only when he stabbed Polonius through the arras and fought with Laertes over the grave; no longer in love with Ophelia – although here he was never able to carry the audience with him – but treating her with a tenderness to which certain remarks in the play scene – if they had been spoken – would have given the lie. There were few startling new readings, or flashy pieces of business. At first he threw away the recorders after requesting Rosencrantz and Guildenstern to play upon them, but then realized that this was the last thing Hamlet would have done. It was just as surely the last thing that Booth would have done. In the 'nunnery' scene

Hamlet, McVickers Theatre, Chicago, 1873

he caught sight of Polonius and the King much earlier than was then usual, and evidently played the rest of it for their benefit – thus mitigating the harshness of his speeches to Ophelia. In the graveyard scene Yorick's skull still wore a mouldy fool's cap. Charles Clark described Booth's Hamlet in 1870 as 'a man of first class intellect and second class will'. The 'Indian summer' aspect of the performance became more marked as time went on. Now in his early fifties, with hair turned prematurely grey, he was 'less active, less agonized, more meditative and stoical, less "tragic", and more obviously a subject for moral admiration'.[1] Seen in 1884 he appeared as 'the good man enduring' or 'the passive suffering centre'. Yet his sheer intellectuality could still electrify, and as Kitty Molony – his Ophelia – put it, his energy sometimes made one feel 'as if Jove's lightning bolts had been turned loose and were striking all about one'.[2] Booth stated Hamlet for his generation as Forbes-Robertson, Barrymore, and Gielgud were to state it for theirs. He would not have stated it for ours. As a perceptive critic of his later interpretation observed: 'The psychological Hamlet is yet to arise.'[3] Charles Shattuck's verdict may stand that the art of Edwin Booth, 'framed in Victorian plush and ormolu, would be precious to us if we could see it again – beautiful in itself, a lesson in high dedication, a reliving of things long gone'.[4]

Nor as a manager was Booth in advance of his time; indeed he was not always abreast of it. Here the comparison is all in favour of Irving. Booth's company was often less than mediocre; the clichés of the star system were enshrined among the canons of that 'Standard Theatre' which he believed it was his mission to establish. He did, it is true, introduce 'walled' scenery for his *Hamlet* of 1870, and his *Winter's Tale* was strongly influenced by Charles Kean's – the court scene being identical in both. He was generally appreciated by that educated opinion which Edwin Forrest – a *monstre sacré* if ever there was one – was unable to touch. Born in 1806 of mixed Scots and German parentage, Forrest made his début in 1820 and was soon fighting a duel in New Orleans. Five years later he was playing Iago to Kean's Othello in Albany. Described as 'a gay and dashing blade', he gambled all through the night, won all the takings, threw the cards in the fire and the money on the floor, and never gambled again. At the age of only twenty, he astonished New York as Othello with his rough realism, animal vigour, and resounding voice. Standing five feet ten in height, he was endowed with a vibrant physique, extravagant muscularity, and chunky lower limbs. *Harper's* magazine spoke of his 'brawny art', his 'biceps aesthetics', and his 'tragic calves'; of his 'pant, roar, and rigmarole'. But there was more to Forrest than sound and fury, muscle and megalomania. He may have represented the vital and crude Americanism of his age, but Longfellow thought his Lear as close to nature as any performance he had ever seen. His voice could roar like Niagara, but it could also sigh like a zephyr. For William Winter he lacked imagination and spirituality or, at the best, stood like 'a landmark on the border-line between physical and spiritual power'.

Edwin Forrest as Othello

He was like a rugged old tower that stood out on the landscape. The architecture may not be admired, but the building is distinctly seen and known. He was tremendously real. He had a grand body and a glorious voice, and in moments of simple passion he affected the senses like the blare of trumpets and clash of cymbals, or like the ponderous, slow-moving, crashing, and thundering surges of the sea.

So the similes gather, and are repeated by one witness after another.

Winter was a squeamish critic, and while he could admire the eyes of Forrest, which flashed like Kean's, his 'certainty of touch, profound assurance, and solid symmetry', he was less amenable to the 'snorts and grunts, the brays and belches, the gaspings and gurglings, the protracted pauses, the lolling tongue, and the stentorian roar'. It was said by one spectator that if Forrest 'spoke out loud he'd be heard down at the Battery'; by another that 'if his pauses get much longer, the audience will have time to stroll in the lobbies between the sentences'; and a third remarked to his neighbour, 'Wake me up when Forrest dies.' Lear and a bearded Coriolanus were his best parts; Winter described his Hamlet as 'a bull in a china shop'. Yet he was not an uncalculating or undisciplined actor. If he could unloose the whirlwind, he was also master of a monolithic repose. He played Lear over a space of forty years and, with his compulsive urge to capture a new reading, always spent the day with the text before acting the part at night. He was as constant in study as he was inconstant in behaviour. When a young man observed to him: 'How wonderfully you acted King Lear!' Forrest replied: 'Acted! I may act Spartacus, I may act Metamora, but by God, sir, I *am* King Lear.' On that occasion he had been inspired by the rage of Henry Clay at the proposal to annex the state of Texas. Forrest himself was a native of Pennsylvania, but he had something of a Texan temperament. 'A vast animal bewildered by a grain of genius' would appear to sum up his meteoric flash across the stage.

If one looks more closely at contemporary records of Forrest, the animality is more evident than the genius. Of intelligence, or delicate imagination, there is no trace whatever. His vice was not only to make excessive points, but almost invariably to make the wrong ones. In *Othello* – 'Were it my cue – to *fight*! – I should have *known* it without a *prompter*!'; the lachrymose inflection on 'And often did beguile her of her *tears*'; the substitution of sound for sense whenever there was an excuse for making a noise, and frequently when there was not; the sudden 'demi-volte of a fencer up the stage' as he saw Desdemona approach in the middle of the temptation scene; 'your *napkin* – is – too *little*!'; 'If thou dost slander *her*,' with barbaric fury, 'and *torture me*', with a drivelling self-pity; and the ludicrous gesture of wiping a tear off his arm in the final speech on 'albeit unused to the melting mood'. His Macbeth, according to Forster, was 'no more than Richard III disguised in tartan'. To emerge from Duncan's death-chamber with his eyes still riveted on what he would already give anything to forget, and to stalk about the stage rattling his truncheon on 'Tomorrow and Tomorrow', was perfectly calculated to make the judicious grieve. It may well have been true that 'the noise of artillery could scarcely be more stunning' than Forrest's voice; but, all in all, one is inclined to write him down as a 'poor man's' Edmund Kean.[5]

Among the other leading actors of the nineteenth century James Henry Hackett (1800-71) was remembered for his Falstaff. In the *Merry Wives* the scene that follows the ducking in the Thames was exorbitantly funny because it was played so seriously. Richard Mansfield (1857-1907) deserves more detailed notice. Arthur Ruhl described him as 'a granite personality . . . under whatever mask he wore was a felt force, a certain all-thereness close to genius. With these he wore the polished insolence of Beau Brummel as if it were a glove, rose to his full height in parts calling for decision and aggressive masculinity.' This chimes with Bernard Shaw's reference to 'the solitary despotism of his temperament'.

[1] Charles Shattuck *The Hamlet of Edwin Booth* (1969)
[2] Ibid p.xvii
[3] O. B. Bunce
[4] *The Hamlet of Edwin Booth* (1969) p.xvii
[5] See *Dramatic Essays* John Forster and George Henry Lewes, edited by William Archer and Robert W. Lowe, (1896) pp.17-41

Richard Mansfield as Richard III

Richard Mansfield as Henry V

Initially a friend of Irving, with whom he liked to smoke a good cigar, he attributed – quite unjustly – his later failures to Irving's influence with society and the Press. Coquelin criticized his style as 'metallic and staccato', but Mansfield held that no actor was interesting without mannerism. He struck oil so to speak, with his Richard III at the Globe theatre in London on 16 March 1889. The play was given with Cibber's scenario and Shakespeare's text, sets by Telbin, and music by Edward German. No innovation here – but in Boston, later in the year, Mansfield developed a new conception of the part. Starting a little slowly, he tried to indicate the progress of evil over the passage of time and showed his fear of Divine retribution before he heard that the young princes had been murdered. He opened the play with the murder of Henry VI – killed with a mordant smile – and the following scenes were acted with a cold malignant levity of manner and tone. These became deeper with Richard's accumulating guilt. The throne was bathed in blood-red light, and there was an indication that Tyrell was murdered after reporting on his mission to the Tower. By the end of the play fear had so seized upon Mansfield's Richard that he mistook Catesby for one of the ghosts; and after waking from his nightmare he leaped from his couch, waved his unsheathed sword above his head, and stumbled to his knees as if in combat with imaginary foes. His 'have mercy Jesu!' lingered in the memory of playgoers.

Nevertheless, one cannot escape the conclusion that Mansfield, for all his prestige, was a tasteless actor; a slightly cheaper version of Beerbohm Tree without quite the courage of Tree's convictions or the flair to give them form and substance. It was a little late, in 1889, to return to Cibber. In 1893 he appeared as Shylock, moved by jealousy of Irving as much as anything else. The performance was spoiled by illustrative business – spitting on 'your worship was the last man in our mouths', a gesture to the canal on 'to bait fish withal' – and of the casket scenes only the last was retained. Mansfield introduced the fifth act with a dance of muscular young women pretending to be fairies, and he commissioned William Winter to write a song for Jessica's elopement. Both these impertinences were later discarded. *Julius Caesar* followed in 1902. Mansfield, with his pale face and sunken cheeks, gave to Brutus the fanaticism that more properly belongs to Cassius. He moved through the part not like a man who is painfully making up his mind, but as one fatally predestined to assassinate his friend. The blow, when it was struck, was perfunctory, and he recoiled from it with an expression on his face as of a man insane. By a rare stroke of discretion, Caesar's ghost was heard but not seen. Henry V appears to have been among the best of Mansfield's parts. The *camaraderie* was touched with sarcasm, when this was called for, and the performance, in spite of careless elocution and a certain sluggishness of movement, had an attractive simplicity. Mansfield had an adequate command of French, evident even when he was supposed to be speaking it badly, and in the wooing of Katharine he registered – in more senses than one – an easy victory.

2

On the distaff side Charlotte Cushman (1816-76) was the only player to bequeath a legend comparable to Edwin Booth's. The imagination quails before an actress who won acclaim as Wolsey as well as Katharine, Romeo and Hamlet as well as Lady Macbeth. What, one cannot help asking, was the

ineteenth century thinking about? We read of her tall, thin, and lanky
physique; her stately and peculiar genius; the strange and brilliant vitality of her
presence; of her strong chin, firm tight lips, and sweeping brow; of her Shakespearian creations which were compared to 'white marble suffused with fire'.
Sheridan Knowles placed her Romeo beside Kean's Othello, and cited the
'banishment' scene with the Friar as an exhibition 'of topmost passion . . . my
blood ran hot and cold'. We read of her courage in the fight against the cancer
from which she died; of the fortune – $500,000 – which she left behind her; of
her celibate life and total lack of sex appeal; of her fondness for children. Her
monument stands in Mount Vernon cemetery at Boston. If she had not died in
her virginity, we should be tempted to describe her as the last, and not the least,
of the Pilgrim Mothers.

She began her career as an opera singer, but broke her voice by misusing it.
She was not to misuse it again. As Katharine in *Henry VIII* there was a
startling contrast between the deference with which she listened to Campeggio
and the scorn with which she drew herself up to her full height and rounded
upon Wolsey. At the end of the same scene, when Griffith advised her that she
was called back into the court, her retort: 'When *you* are called, return' was
given with an excoriating mixture of petulance and contempt. In the subsequent
interview with the two Cardinals, and again in the death scene, she indicated
that Katharine was gradually wasting away from consumption. Here she had
the halting speech of an invalid, showed pity for Wolsey, indignation with the
messenger, a poignant affection for Henry, and a deep longing for Paradise. She
had a pause after 'Say', and then 'his long trouble' was breathed out in a kind
of sob. Her voice thickened towards the end, and there was a proud majesty in
her last command.

Her Lady Macbeth was imperious from the start, greeting Duncan as an
equal, snatching the daggers from her husband with contemptuous authority,
and practically lifting him off the stage. In the sleep-walking scene she achieved
a memorable effect with the wringing of her hands on 'Nought's had, all's
spent'. As Portia and Rosalind she was altogether too heavy-handed, for although
she could assume a masculine vigour, a feminine charm was beyond her. One
inclines to the opinion that the only thing wrong with Charlotte Cushman as an
actress was that she ought to have been a man. She retired from the stage in
1852, but two years later she was reading *Henry VIII* to the Duke of Devonshire
and his guests at Brighton. Like Mrs Siddons she found it difficult to make a
positively last appearance'.

Charlotte and Susan Cushman as
Romeo and Juliet

Although Helena Modjeska (1840-1909) was born in Poland, much of her
career belongs to the American theatre. It was in Posen that she made her name
as Juliet, rehearsing the balcony scene in a wood and the tomb scene in a
cemetery. When it came to the performance she plucked a rose from her hair
and threw it down to Romeo on 'I would kill you with much cherishing'. There
was a single, narrow bed for the nuptial parting. Juliet was not dishevelled; the
bed showed no sign of having been slept in; and Romeo had no cause to lace up
his jerkin. Indeed the conventions of the time made any other treatment of the
scene impossible; the hot blood was allowed to stir everywhere but where it
stirred most hotly. Modjeska had rather outgrown her Juliet by the time she
came to play it in America, but people remembered her resort to the dagger on
'Vile earth to earth resign', and again on 'myself have power to die'; her grief,
alternately real and affected, as she wheedled the Nurse; and the way she

cowered in a big chair at the thought of Tybalt's ghost. Her Rosalind lacked colour and her Viola definition; she was too much of a woman to find it easy to impersonate a man. Her Queen Katharine lacked weight, and as Lady Macbeth she tried to realize the conception of the part which Sarah Siddons had set forth in print but never executed. She was deeply impressive only in the sleep-walking. Her Desdemona had great charm, and her Portia was rated by some as inferior only to Ellen Terry's. She played Ophelia as a mature and passionate woman – a very unusual conception to which her brilliant treatment of the mad scene did not, however, quite seem to belong. Isabella in *Measure for Measure* may well have been the finest of her Shakespearian parts; here the youth was missing, and the articulation not always clear, but the right intention shone through. Nineteenth-century audiences did not look for youth in their Shakespeare heroines. Modjeska had considerable beauty, and she quickly acquired a mastery of English, speaking it with only a slight and rather attractive accent. For some years she played leading parts with Booth, whom she warmly admired. She used to recall how he had criticized her – rightly, one feels – for putting her arm on Shylock during the 'quality of mercy' speech; and she remembered Otis Skinner as Macduff with his legs made up to reproduce the scars of battle. She took much pride in her costumes; a Greek tunic falling just below the knee for Viola, black plush with jet and real lace for Katharine. When she had retired she liked to take them out of their cupboard for the admiration of her visitors, and to recall the days when she had worn them. She died at her home in California, where Bastien-Lapage's portrait of Irving hung in the library, and her body was brought back to Poland for burial.

Ada Rehan (1860–1916) was born in Limerick – and to the grand manner with a dimple in it. Her personality is eloquent in Sargent's portrait, where there is a strong hint of Meredithian comedy – the wit and the *hauteur*. Equally well, one feels, she might have come down to us as a Romney or a Gainsborough *grande dame*. With her brown hair, grey-blue eyes, and mercurial temperament, she captivated England, America, and Bernard Shaw.

Helena Modjeska as Ophelia

> I cannot judge from Miss Rehan's enchanting Rosalind whether she is a great Shakespearian actress or not; there is even a sense in which I cannot tell whether she can act at all or not. So far I have never seen her create a character; she has always practised the same adorable arts on me, by whatever name the playbill has called her. I have never complained; the drama with all its heroines levelled up to a universal Ada Rehan has seemed no such dreary prospect to me; she is irresistible.

Rosalind was perhaps her best part; it inspired Justin Huntly McArthy's couplet:

> Oh, happy generation that can see
> The dearest daughter of Melpomene

Audiences remembered her gypsy quality, and her dash through the trees (Augustin Daly's unmistakable trees), snatching Orlando's verses from a bough, and throwing herself, hands trembling, at the foot of a great elm. The words, as she repeated them, 'fell from her lips like drops of liquid silver, the exquisite music of her speech seemed to die away in one soft sigh of pleasure'. The same voice in *The Taming of the Shrew* could cut like a knife or ring like a bell as she was swayed by 'regal whirlwinds of temper', or suddenly soften on 'Now, if you love me, stay'. In the church scene from *Much Ado about Nothing* she whipped

Sargent's portrait of Ada Rehan

up the rippling waters of the play into a storm of passionate indignation; and her native exuberance carried her with a combination of east wind and sunshine through Mistress Ford. A life-long addiction to Thackeray and Balzac, as well as to Shakespeare, had given her a ripe and balanced appreciation of the *comédie humaine*. She paid eight visits to Europe, and it was said in Paris – where they care for art as well as for nature – that she 'combined the charm of Mlle Reichenburg and the piquancy of Mlle Réjane'. There was a marked reminiscence of Réjane in that uptilted nose. In October 1891 she laid the foundation stone of Daly's theatre in London, and opened it as Katharina in the *Shrew* two years later. Daly's Shakespeare productions were the most lavish that America had seen, and Ada Rehan with John Drew starred in all of them. His *Merchant of Venice* in 1898 had Shylock bargaining with Antonio beside the pillar with the lion of St Mark, and the Salute church in the background. In Belmont ornate furniture, heavy coffered ceilings and carved woodwork failed to overpower a Portia who was not too graceful to be gay. Ada Rehan kept a house in the north of England; here, with her bull-dog and spaniel she might be seen striding along the Cumbrian shore. Chips, the monkey, she presumably left at home. Ada Rehan's fondness for animals was the natural corollary to her love of life in all its healthier manifestations, and it was this that she communicated from the stage. Tragedy she wisely left alone.

Adelaide Neilson as Juliet

You may search the annals of the English theatre for a really satisfactory Juliet until Peggy Ashcroft came to give scepticism the lie. In America, however, there were three, at least, that demand a place in the story. Adelaide Neilson (1846-80) was born in Leeds, the illegitimate daughter of unknown parents. She started life as a nursemaid, worked in various factories, and then took to the stage. In 1865 she was playing Juliet in Margate, and continued to play it in America for many years afterwards. William Winter, who saw the performance in Boston in 1880, speaks of her 'face just sufficiently unsymmetrical to be brimful of character'. 'I haven't a *feacher*, I know', she used to say; yet her beauty irradiated the scene. Winter compared her Juliet to 'golden fire in a porcelain vase'. She reminded him now of a picture by Murillo, and now of a poem by Heine; and she was remarkable for what she did *not* do. There was no initial hostility on 'Art thou not Romeo and a Montague?'; no terror on 'The

Mary Anderson

orchard walls are high and hard to climb'; no temper to the Nurse on 'bye and bye I come'; no rushing on from 'Dost thou love me' to 'I know thou wilt say ay'; no fear when Friar Lawrence describes how the potion will work. The style was large, and the transitions easy and natural.

She was excellent, too, in other parts. Rosalind's 'Sir you have wrestled well, and overthrown more than your enemy' was said with no trace of coquetry. Imogen's 'False to his bed!' was a cry of honest indignation, without rant or self-consciousness. Her Viola appeared as 'a slip of a girl' stranded on the shore, distantly but surely related to some fugitive ideal of beauty which she was forever trying to catch.

Mary Anderson (1859-1940) first played Juliet in Louisville, Kentucky, on 25 November 1875, and from 1883 to 1888 was seen in three seasons at the Lyceum (London) both as Juliet and Hermione. She was sometimes criticized as cold. The keynote of her Juliet was Romeo's premonition: 'My mind misgives/ Some consequence yet hanging in the stars.' This was evident as she stood alone in the darkening hall when the last guest had gone; in her frenzy at the climax of the potion speech; in the calm despair following her final interview with the Nurse; in the reckless misery of suicide. Her Rosalind was essentially serious beneath the swagger, 'Sir you have wrestled well' being spoken to Orlando, and the rest of the sentence as an aside. But a backward look at Orlando followed it.

She allowed herself a furtive caress during the forest wooing, and wrung a plausible pathos from the swoon when shown the napkin dyed in Orlando's blood. In *The Winter's Tale* she doubled Hermione and Perdita, the latter's single speech in the final scene being conveniently cut. She was generally preferred as Perdita, where she really did succeed in dancing like 'a wave of the sea'. The play ran for 166 consecutive nights at the Lyceum. In 1889 Mary Anderson retired from the theatre, and in the following year she married Antonio de Navarro. They settled in Broadway, but the proximity of Stratford-upon-Avon did not tempt her back upon the stage.

Julia Marlow (1867-1933) was born in Cumberland, and after her family had emigrated to the United States was educated in Kansas City and Cincinnati. She applied herself from an early age to the study of Shakespeare. Her voice had a coloratura flexibility; and a certain gypsy quality, a boyish, hoydenish grace, reminded people of Herrick's 'a sweet confusion in the dress'. She was almost too ready for Juliet when she came to it, for, in contrast to Adelaide Neilson, her personality was a shade too predominant, and she had a maturity beyond her years. She was Juliet as Juliet might have become if she had lived on into

Julia Marlow as Cleopatra,
New Theatre, 1909

Right: Maude Adams as Viola in
Twelfth Night, Sanders Theatre,
Cambridge, 1909

womanhood. But here the evidence of Arthur Symons commands respect.

I thought there was rhetoric in the play as well as the natural poetry of drama. But I see that it only needs to be acted with genius and intelligence, and the poetry consumes the rhetoric . . . this mysterious tragic child, whom love has made wise in making her a woman, is unknown to us outside Shakespeare.

Where Julia Marlow as Juliet was 'ripe humanity', as Ophelia she was

that same humanity broken down from within. As Viola she is the woman let loose to be bewitching in spite of herself . . . serious, with a calm and even simplicity, to which everything is a kind of child's play, putting no unnecessary pathos into a matter destined to come right in the end. Duse is the soul made flesh, Réjane the flesh made Parisian, Bernhardt the flesh and the devil; but Julia Marlow is the joy of life, the plentitude of sap in the tree.

These were high comparisons from a critic qualified to make them.

Julia Marlow played for many years with E. H. Sothern (1859-1933) and eventually married him. They were an ill-matched pair. As Arthur Ruhl put it:

Miss Marlow seems destined by nature for the older, loftier style. There is a noble simplicity in her face and shape and movement, a mellowness and richness which seem part of an earlier, less nervous time. Mr Sothern, on the other hand, strikes one as a contemporary who prefers to be an ancient.

John Mason Brown compared his Shylock to a 'sort of early broker, mourning his losses, who had just voted for Landon'.[1] He did, however, brilliantly succeed as Malvolio; here again Symons pays his tribute:

It is an elaborate travesty, done in a disguise like the solemn dandy's head of Disraeli. He acts with his eyelids which move when all the rest of the face is motionless; with his pursed, reticent mouth, with his prim and pompous gestures; with that self-consciousness which brings all Malvolio's troubles upon him. It is a fantastic, tragically comic thing, done with rare calculation, and it has its formal, almost cruel share in the immense gaiety of the piece.

Until the turn of the century, and well beyond it, the story continued to be one of stellar performances and productions with Shakespeare squeezed in, never very comfortably, between the stars and the scenery. Less conspicuously, however, stock companies in Boston and Philadelphia, with straitened means and stars in short supply, were illustrating the virtues of simplicity. In Boston, more particularly, William Warren was as fine an actor as many who made their name on Broadway. It was in Cambridge, Massachusetts, that George Lyman Kittredge was appointed to the chair of English literature at Harvard in 1894. 'Kitty', as he was known to many generations of students, took them through six plays of Shakespeare every year, word for word and line for line. We are told that he 'feared general ideas and destroyed them', declaring 'war to the death on gushing Mrs Jamesons, moralizing clergymen, and fantastic Teutonic metaphysicians'. With his silver white hair and beard and quick stride he was a familiar figure in Cambridge. The traffic would stop in Harvard Square when he raised his cane. In 1904, with George Pierce Baker (1866-1935), he built a temporary Elizabethan stage within Sanders Theatre at Harvard. Here Forbes-Robertson played Hamlet, and Maude Adams appeared in *Twelfth Night*. In America, as in England, the revolution was under way.

[1] F. D. Roosevelt's Republican opponent in the 1936 election

V France and Italy

Paul Valéry defined poetry as 'that which is lost in translation'; and for a long time Shakespeare in France was 'translated' in the sense that Quince used the word of Bottom. For Frenchmen the problem was how to tidy up that tangled and teeming undergrowth into a logical *parterre*. Shakespeare – they had been told by Voltaire – was a barbarian of genius; how could he be civilized?

Jean-François Ducis (1733-1816) described his version of *Hamlet* as 'a new tragedy imitated from the English'. It was certainly new, and the imitation was a curious form of flattery. Fortinbras, Laertes, Cornelius, Rosencrantz, Guildenstern, Osric, Marcellus, Bernardo, Francesco, the Players, the Gravediggers and the Ghost were all omitted from the *dramatis personae*. Hamlet's father was poisoned by Claudius in conspiracy with Gertrude – and Claudius was not his brother but merely an ambitious prince. At the beginning of the play the guilty pair were not yet married. Ophelia was the daughter of Claudius, and did not go mad. When the rebellion, fomented not by Claudius but by Laertes, broke out, Hamlet mastered it; Claudius committed suicide; Gertrude stabbed herself to death after begging Ophelia to marry Hamlet; and Hamlet succeeded to the throne.

Ducis excused himself in a letter to Garrick for 'having been obliged in some respects to write a new play . . . all I have tried to do is to turn a parricidal queen into an interesting part and to create a model of filial tenderness out of Hamlet's pure and melancholy soul'. After much hesitation this travesty was performed by the Comédie Française at the Salle des Fossés Saint-Germain-des-Prés on the 30 September 1769. Diderot was among the critics who were irritated by an invisible Ghost in the closet scene – and indeed Ducis himself regretted its absence. For the next thirty years he continued to revise the text until in 1803 Talma assumed the principal part.

François Joseph Talma (1763-1826) was the greatest French actor of his time, and perhaps of all time. He was also a richly cultivated man, a philosopher of the art he practised. 'The intelligence comes into play only in the wake of the sensibility; it judges, chooses, and sets in order the impressions that our sensibility registers upon us.' Or again: acting is 'the sphere in which a magnetic personality exercises a power of sympathy which cannot be resisted or defined. That is great acting: but though it is inborn and cannot be taught, it can be brought forth only when the actor is master of his craft.' He maintained that it took at least twenty years to bring this mastery to perfection. Moreover Talma had a good knowledge of English, and a certain acquaintance with the English theatre. He was more sensitive than Ducis to the values of the original text, and Ducis made considerable alterations to the last act of *Hamlet* in order to provide him with a worthier vehicle for his powers. Madame de Stael wrote to him from Lyon in 1809: 'your talent in the rôle of Hamlet seemed to me like the genius of Shakespeare . . . it was a poetry of looks, of gestures and intonations'. She did not object to an invisible Ghost: 'It is all there in the face of Talma, and certainly no less effective for that.' Others wrote of his 'distorted face, his haggard eyes,

François Joseph Talma

his voice, his sombre and melancholy accent, his taut muscles, his trembling and convulsions'.

English reactions were no less enthusiastic. After noting the extraordinary beauty of his voice, his capacity to express the *impatience* of suffering, and his total absorption in soliloquy, a contemporary goes on to explain and to justify a certain reticence of facial expression:

> On the English stage, it appears commonly to be the object of the actors to give every sentiment the whole effect of which the words of the part will admit, as fully as if that sentiment were the only one which could occupy the mind of the character at the time. . . . In the character of Hamlet, in particular, there are several passages in which it is the custom to express minor and passing sentiments with a keenness little suitable to the profound grief in which Hamlet ought to be absorbed at the commencement of the play, and which can be natural only when the mind is free from other more powerful emotions. It appears to us that the consistency of character is much more judiciously and naturally preserved in the acting of Talma.

Talma was much influenced by David, and when he appeared as a Roman in toga and sandals, the great Mlle Clairon exclaimed 'O, how ugly! He looks exactly like an ancient statue' – which was of course precisely the intention. For the first production of Ducis' *Hamlet* the actors were dressed in Nordic style, but Talma wore a suit of black silk, a kind of short black overcoat edged with brown fur, and black leather boots.

Ducis attacked *King Lear* with some trepidation, since it was tempting both Providence and the police to exhibit on the French stage a king who had gone out of his mind. In Ducis' version Goneril was mentioned but did not appear; and it was Regan alone who persuaded her father that Cordelia was plotting against him with the King of France. Edmund and Edgar were alike the virtuous and legitimate sons of the Duke of Kent; Gloucester and the Fool were omitted; and the fortunes of war were reversed at the last moment by the eloquence of Edgar who was given in marriage to Cordelia, and restored Lear to the throne. The play was acted before the Court at Versailles, and afterwards in Paris – at the Salle du Faubourg St Germain – in January 1783. Brizard – whom Ducis described as 'l'acteur de la nature' – made a deep impression as Lear, clean shaven and with streaming white hair framing his expressive features. Brunetti's décor represented the castle of Cornwall in the first two acts, and for the rest of the play a forest bristling with rocks and an immemorial oak tree standing by a cave in the background.

In his *Macbeth* Ducis omitted the characters of Donalbain, Banquo, Fleance, Lady Macduff and her son, Hecate and the three Witches. Macduff, Lennox, Ross, Menteith and Caithness were doubled up into two characters – Loclin and Seyton. Duncan's voice was heard, but he did not appear. It was now Lady Macbeth who had heard the Witches' prophecy, and it was both at her instigation and inspired by a dream that Macbeth committed the murder. Old Siward, who had brought up the young Malcolm as his son, suggests to Macbeth that he shall be placed on the throne. When Macbeth accidentally reveals this plan to his wife, she has Siward and Malcolm arrested. Macbeth is about to stab Siward when the sight of a scarf daubed with the dead king's blood excites him to frenzy. Siward overwhelms him with reproaches, and when Lady Macbeth raises her knife against the young prince, Macbeth protects him. He then orders his wife to be imprisoned, and subsequently commits suicide in expiation of his crime – dying with the hope of heaven instead of the certainty of hell.

Ducis' second version (1790) bore only a slender resemblance to his first. Duncan now appeared with a confidant, and a sibyl was introduced to moralize in the manner of a Greek chorus – but this intruder survived only a single performance. Lady Macbeth was allowed her sleep-walking – and also a family. In the final scene – still apparently somnambulist – she murdered both Macbeth and her children. By 1798 the play had been revised six times. Talma took over the title rôle in 1792 with Marie Vestris as a remarkable Lady Macbeth; and here again Madame de Stael brings him before us.

> You should see Talma trying to give a touch of the vulgar and the bizarre to the accent of the witches, and still preserve in his imitation all the dignity that our theatre demands. . . . The actor's low and mysterious voice speaking the verse; the way he puts his finger to his lips, like the statue of silence; his look which changed to express a horrible and repulsive memory – everything combined to depict a fresh marvel on our stage.[1]

Stendhal, who saw the production in 1804, described Ducis' version as 'a detestable travesty of Shakespeare's magnificent play. It is worth not one pipe of tobacco; although the apparition of Mlle Raucourt, clad in white and lighting up her murderous figure with an immense and smoky torch would doubtless have prostrated me with terror had it been decently presented'.

Kneeling before a print of Corneille, Ducis demanded inspiration for his improvement of *Romeo and Juliet*. Here the following characters were omitted: Lady Montague and Lady Capulet, Paris, Mercutio, Benvolio, Tybalt, Friar Lawrence, Friar John, Balthasar, Sampson, Gregory, Peter, Abraham, and the Apothecary. Mercutio and Benvolio were amalgamated into a person called Alberic. The Prince of Verona and Tybalt were both mentioned; the first as a suitor for Juliet's hand, and the second as her brother. The balcony scene, the nuptial parting, the potion soliloquy, and the fights were all cut out. The play, according to the *Mercure de France,* had been 'embellished by the French poet, who had managed to avoid the faults of his model, to give it fresh beauties, and to be original even in the process of imitation'. Other critics blamed Ducis for including the speeches in justification of suicide, and were surprised that the censor had permitted them. At the first performance Romeo and Juliet died among the tombs, the one by the sword, the other by poison, and their families were reconciled in consequence. For the second he wrote a new fifth act in which the reconciliation was sealed by the marriage of Romeo and Juliet, notwithstanding the fact that Romeo had killed Capulet's son. But Ducis' principal innovation was to have turned Montague into a leading part, having already lost two sons through the family feud, and now engaging Romeo to assassinate both Capulet and Juliet. As Romeo pleads for reconciliation, Montague – borrowing his lines from Macduff – exclaims: 'He had no children' – when it was clear to the simplest spectator that, after all, Capulet had a daughter! The play was accepted unanimously by the Comédie Française and first performed in 1776. The extraordinary elevation of Montague was due to Ducis' friendship for Brizard who acted the part with memorable effect. It was later destined for Talma, but the death of the great tragedian spared him an embarrassing epilogue to his triumphs.

In the same year (1793) Ducis tackled *Othello*. Emilia was among several characters dispensed with and there was no move to Cyprus. The action passed

Revue d'Histoire du Théâtre (January-March 1965) p.20

either in the Senate chamber, Othello's Venetian palace, or Desdemona's
bedroom. The handkerchief became a diamond bracelet. The rôle of Brabantio
was enlarged, and that of Iago diminshed. Desdemona died by stabbing; to
put a pillow to criminal use was an affront to French propriety. Even so, the
play was a hazardous challenge; and at the climax of the fifth act a voice was
heard from the audience. 'It's a Moor who has done that; it's not a Frenchman.'
At later performances Ducis bowed to popular demand. Brabantio and the
Doge arrived in time to stay Othello's avenging arm, and the play ended happily.
Not until 1800 was the original ending restored. This was largely due to Talma
who declared: 'I *will* kill her; if the pit won't stand for it, I'll make them'. He
took some pride in getting his way, and reported on it to his English friends.
But there was some fainting in the audience.

Talma's Othello set the seal on his reputation, and he chose it for his farewell
performance. On 31 October 1793 – the day when the Girondins, among whom
he had many friends, were executed – he noted in his diary: 'One plays better
when one is unhappy. I was really inspired, and the public understood the
reason very well. I felt all the fury of the part.' Talma had also insisted that Iago
should be given his proper dimension of evil, but it was inconceivable that
Ducis' adaptations should hold the stage once the fever and the freedom of
romanticism had taken possession of public taste. Théophile Gautier deplored
the blindness of French actors who would 'admit Shakespeare only in very
small doses'; and preferred Ducis' 'laughable' version of *Othello* to Alfred de
Vigny's 'accurate and dramatic translation'.

Alexandre Dumas' first theatrical experience was a performance of Ducis'
Hamlet given by pupils of the Conservatoire at Villers-Cotterêts; later, in
1827, he saw Charles Kemble in the part, with Harriet Smithson as Ophelia,
at the Odéon. 'It was only then that I realized what the theatre was; it was the
first time that I saw real passion on the stage, stirring men and women of flesh
and blood. I knew my *Hamlet* so well that I had no need to buy the libretto.'[1]
This libretto was a prose translation of the acting version. It may not have been
Ducis' Hamlet; it was less than Shakespeare's. Fortinbras and the Norwegian
wars, certain of Ophelia's songs, Horatio and the sailors, 'O what a rogue',
Claudius' effort at repentance, and the end of the closet scene, with a good deal
of dialogue, had been omitted. Nevertheless it was an acceptable text for its
time, and Dumas was bowled over – *bouleversé* – by the scenes with the Ghost
and in the graveyard, and by Kemble's 'business' in watching Claudius and
Gertrude during the play scene through Ophelia's fan. In 1840 he conceived
the idea of translating *Hamlet* in collaboration with Paul Meurice.

The first performance of this version in 1846 was gilded with all the luxury
of the *belle époque*. Dumas, who was living at St Germain-en-Laye, hired the
small local theatre for the occasion. 'On a beautiful evening, after dinner, I led
my guests to the performance. All the boxes and galleries had been reserved
for them. I had *Hamlet* played for their benefit, and then I entertained them to
supper with the actors. I sent them all back at three o'clock in the morning by a
special train.'[2] The play was given fifteen times at St Germain-en-Laye with a
loss to Dumas of only 3,000 frances. On 15 December 1847 it was produced at the
Théâtre Historique with Philibert Rouvière in the principal part. Gautier
approved:

Rouvière, with all his exaggerations, is still the most comprehensive Hamlet one
could find; he has in some ways the English style of Kemble and Macready, and is

Delacroix's lithograph of *Hamlet*: the play scene

very effective. Strange and unpredictable, with a certain bitter incisiveness. Perhaps he is too nervous and disordered, too mad, and his playing too constantly spasmodic; more nobility and dreaminess in the meditative moments would give relief to the moments of impetuosity.[3]

Rouvière was also an artist, continually torn between the stage and the studio. He designed the costumes himself under the inspiration of Delacroix, whose lithographs of *Hamlet* had been published in 1834. The portrait of him in the part by Manet, executed in the year before his death, was modelled on a painting by Velasquez – presumably of an actor of the time – and now hangs in the National Gallery at Washington. Rouvière played Hamlet in Paris, the provinces, and abroad; and in 1861 his passionate interpretation had not changed:

I can see him still with his thin legs in the black tights, the pale mask of his face, the rictus which revealed his ferocious teeth, his phosphorescent eyes, agitated and febrile, striding up and down the stage with a lost look, leaping on to a table, laughing bitterly at Yorick's skull. And when he killed Polonius! He rushed forward like a madman, as he cried 'A rat! a rat!'; disappeared behind the curtain concealing the

Revue d'Histoire du Théâtre (October–December 1964) p.407
Ibid p.409
Ibid

old man; one heard the noise of a heavy fall, and Hamlet slowly emerged walking backwards. In a moment he turned round, and then one saw him grasping the thin rapier which he shook three times to let drop the blood of his victim, and looking at it with so fixed and fearful an expression that the whole audience shivered with fright.[1]

There were certain differences between the Dumas/Meurice version of 1847 and that of 1864 published under Meurice's name alone. This was much closer to the original. The first ghost scene was restored, and Laertes was charged with the mission to Norway on which he reports to the King. Claudius' prayer was put back in its proper place with the scenes, previously omitted, that follow the death of Polonius. The only difference was that Hamlet left for England of his own accord. The meeting with Fortinbras and the Captain now took place in the cemetery, just before the scene with the gravediggers, and the ending was as Shakespeare wrote it. One had come a long way since Ducis; but much of what Meurice had restored was amputated before the play could be given at the Comédie Française in 1886 with Mounet-Sully in the title rôle. The actor playing Laertes insisted that the character should be whitewashed out of all recognition, and it was not until 1896 that Mounet-Sully obtained the restoration of Fortinbras.

Mounet (1841-1916) was the only French actor of the nineteenth century to be mentioned in the same breath with Talma, and we know much more about his Hamlet. He had studied it through the eyes of Goethe in *Wilhelm Meister*; then in the accurate, though literary, translation of François-Victor Hugo; and finally he collated the translations with the English original. Everything at once became clear to him. Mallarmé had the impression of a performance governed by intelligence, the ideal Hamlet of a romantic century whose romanticism was beginning to wear thin:

At once thinker and mime, the tragedian interprets Hamlet with a sovereign mastery of the mental and plastic requirements of his art; above all as Hamlet exists, by hereditary right, in the minds of the *fin de siècle*. It was appropriate that for once, after the agonizing romantic vigil, we should see the beautiful demon summed up in our own time, and in a way that perhaps would not be understood tomorrow.[2]

The popularity of Wagner had counted for something in opening a breach in the Chinese Wall of French classicism. The criteria of taste had changed, and if Shakespeare was a 'barbarian' that was no longer to be counted against him. For Jules Lemaitre Mounet fulfilled to the letter the Hamlet of *Wilhelm Meister*; he only criticized a plaintive tone too reminiscent of a sick child, and he admired the 'involuntary staginess of his simulated madness, and his violent outbursts; the effort he made to act being such as to make him incapable of self-control when he did act'.[3] It seems that in certain passages – notably over the corpse of Polonius – the brutality of the character was considerably muted. The notes Mounet appended to François-Victor Hugo's translation analysed Hamlet's irresolution as follows:

The role [of simulated madness] so tires, kills, and degrades him in his own eyes that the moment comes when he asks himself whether the struggle to go on living is worth while. 'To be or not to be.' But in the instant of giving effect to his thought, his nimble brain comes to the rescue of his idle arm, and provides his natural cowardice with an excellent reason for living. 'Perchance to dream.' He is the very epitome of mental and physical irresolution.[4]

Mounet-Sully as Hamlet

Mounet was rare among the great actors of his generation in seeing the play as a whole. For this reason he regretted the omissions and infidelities of the Dumas/Meurice version on which he was forced to work in the theatre. He saw the necessity of Fortinbras as a symbol of political health and vigour.

> All through the performance of this play . . . I want the public to be given the feeling of the carelessness, disorder, and continous orgy in which the king and queen and the whole court are living, barely two months after the death of Hamlet's father, who was a good king, a gallant soul, and a fine warrior.[5]

Mounet realized, of course, that *Hamlet* required shortening, and he studied the cuts in Irving's acting version of 1878, without necessarily adopting them. Irving, like Booth, had quite failed to see the point of Fortinbras. Moreover Mounet had a prophetic sense of what was wrong with current methods of producing Shakespeare:

> The quick changes of décor have the priceless advantage, in a work as long as this one where the length forces one to make cuts, of making these cuts less important. And the introduction of simple curtains at the back, or even in the foreground . . . has the advantage, equally great, of allowing the stage-hands to continue their work [in silence?], and prepare a big scene, or a series of scene changes, behind the curtains without interrupting the action. The interval as we have it in France, with all the consequent chatter, is the death of theatrical illusion.[6]

As far as he was able to Mounet put these principles into effect. In the 1886 production a single décor sufficed for the second and fourth acts; in the third a mobile oratory for Claudius allowed the three scenes to follow each other

[1] Ibid p.410 '*Nos Hamlets*'
[2] *Revue Indépendante* (1 November 1886)
[3] *Revue d'Histoire du Théâtre* (October-December 1964) p.420
[4] Ibid p.424
[5] Ibid p.427
[6] Ibid

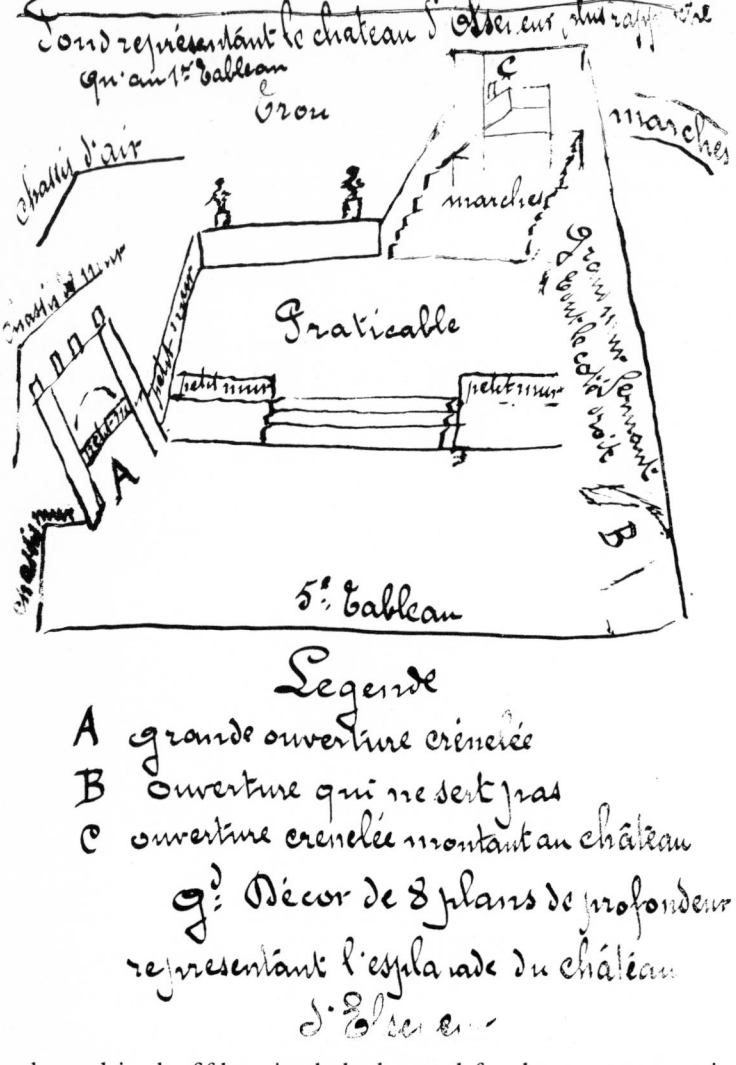

Plan for *Hamlet*, Comédie Française
1886

closely; and in the fifth a simple background for the armoury permitted a quick transition from the cemetery. Only the intermissions remained sacrosanct.

Mallarmé's admiration did not extend to the other actors, whom he found too detailed in their naturalism, or to the décor which remained too sumptuous for his taste in spite of its relative mobility. No doubt the poet who tried to reduce poetry to a blank page would have liked to reduce drama to a blank stage. He also criticized – wrongly, as we should think today – the elaborate Renaissance costumes; these removed the play from the never-never land of legend where his symbolist imagination confined it. The production had in fact been mounted with the greatest care. Fifteen days of rehearsal had been given up to the duel under the supervision of Vigeant who was not only an expert fencing master but also, according to Francisque Sarcey, 'an artist and a philosopher'. The designer had been sent to Nuremberg to copy the spades which the gravediggers might be supposed to have used. This pedantry did not save Sarcey from boredom during a scene which he quite failed to understand. Even Mounet's performance bewildered him. He described it as 'Brutus pretending to be mad', but admitted that this was 'the Hamlet of Eugène Delacroix – princely from head to foot'.

Many details of that performance have come down to us. How Mounet shed real tears on 'Seems, madam, nay I know not seems'; how he touched his arm and body on 'O that this too too solid flesh would melt', and drew from his breast the miniature of his father on 'Three months dead, nay not so much, not two'; how the outcry 'Angels and ministers of grace' was followed by a long drawn out sigh on 'defend us', and how the subsequent invocations, timid at first, became imperative; the wild laugh on 'O my prophetic soul, my uncle?' and the religious horror of 'Most horrible'; the arms stretched out in agonized entreaty as the Ghost goes out, and the faint that followed. Mounet did not believe that Ophelia was the *ingenue* of stage tradition, and he tried, without success, to restore such passages as put her innocence in doubt. In the closet scene he struck the armchair to draw the attention of Gertrude to the presence of the Ghost which he could see and she could not; and she struck it herself on 'all that is I see'. Mounet was particularly sensitive to the dramatic evolution of the graveyard scene; the contrast between the ambience of death – he wiped his hands after fondling Yorick's skull, as he had wiped them earlier in the play after

Hamlet and the Ghost,
Comédie Française 1886

Sarah Bernhardt as Portia

Opposite: Philibert Rouvière as Hamlet

[1] How Shakespeare envisaged Othello is indicated by the description of the Prince of Morocco in *The Merchant of Venice*: 'a tawnie Moor all in white'
[2] Laura Lovat *Maurice Baring* (1947) p.37
[3] *Theatre* (1954) p.155
[4] Joanna Richardson *Sarah Bernhardt* (1959) p.142

shaking hands with Rosencrantz and Guildenstern – and the *young* person who had died, leading up to Hamlet's desperate and public avowal of his love. From the moment of his return from England Mounet's Hamlet was no longer divided between duty and irresolution. He regarded himself as the instrument of Providence, resigned to whatever fate had in store for him. . . . .

In 1899 Mounet was a bearded Othello, with Sarah Bernhardt as his Desdemona. He was more negroid than was then usual, and this incurred Gautier's disapproval.

Why turn the Moor of Venice into a negro? The very title of Shakespeare's tragedy contradicts it. The Moors are not black. Their skin has a dark olive tan, like Cordova leather or Florentine bronze, not like English boot black. There was nothing surprising about a young Venetian girl falling in love with a handsome Moor with regular features, blazing eyes, and imposing stature, even if his features had a light layer of liquorice juice. Most of the young patricians painted by Vecelli, Giorgione or Tintoretto have the complexion of deep carnation, the tawny shades of an orange skin, not far removed from the most intense African sunburn.[1]

In the same year as Mounet's Othello, Sarah Bernhardt (1844-1923) appeared as Hamlet at the Théâtre de la Renaissance. She had already been seen in Hamlet's costume, breakfasting in the Boulevard Pereire. Catulle Mendès fought a duel to defend her right to play the part; and since Mounet saw the performance ten times and Maurice Baring described it as 'the ultimate triumph of intelligence',[2] her impertinent challenge cannot be written off as a bad joke. She was already fifty-four – and no relation whatever to Wilhelm Meister. Colette described her face as 'sculpted in white powder'; a boyish and practical Hamlet, remarkable for its consistency and infinite variety of expression. In Hamlet's reply to Polonius – 'words, words, words' – the first was spoken with an absent-minded indifference, the second with a sudden attention to what he was saying, and the third with 'something between a smile and a smothered sigh', as if words only echoed the universal emptiness of things. Desmond MacCarthy recalled how Sarah stood tiptoe 'like a great black exclamation mark, her sword glittering above her head'[3] as she cried 'C'est le roi!' after the killing of Polonius. In the summer of 1899 she brought the production to London. *The Times* was respectful, and Clement Scott, in *The Daily Telegraph*, laid at her feet such laurels as he had not already laid at the feet of Irving. He noted the advice to the players given from the miniature stage on which *The Murder of Gonzago* was to be performed, and Sarah's gesture in kissing Gertrude's hair after she was dead. Max Beerbohm, however, in an article entitled *The Princess of Denmark*, suggested that her doublet and hose should have been confiscated by the customs officials at Charing Cross. The translation was by Eugène Morand and Marcel Schwob. As one of Sarah's biographers has written: 'When Hamlet's "Wormwood! wormwood!" was turned into "Absinthe! Absinthe!", a strange air of the Boul' Mich' hung over Elsinore'.[4]

Sarah's only other Shakespearian rôle was Lady Macbeth, although she appeared in the costume of Portia to recite 'the quality of mercy'. Lady Macbeth she played at the Odéon in 1889. Sarcey described her voice in the banquet scene as 'delicious music . . . low, vibrant, and imperious' as she exclaimed 'Enfantillage pure!' to her terrified husband; even her reproaches had the softness of a caress. Mme Weber was playing the part at the same time, and here the great critic thought it a mistake to imitate the breathing of a sleepwalker. Where Sarah Bernhardt was instinctive, Madame Weber was theoretical.

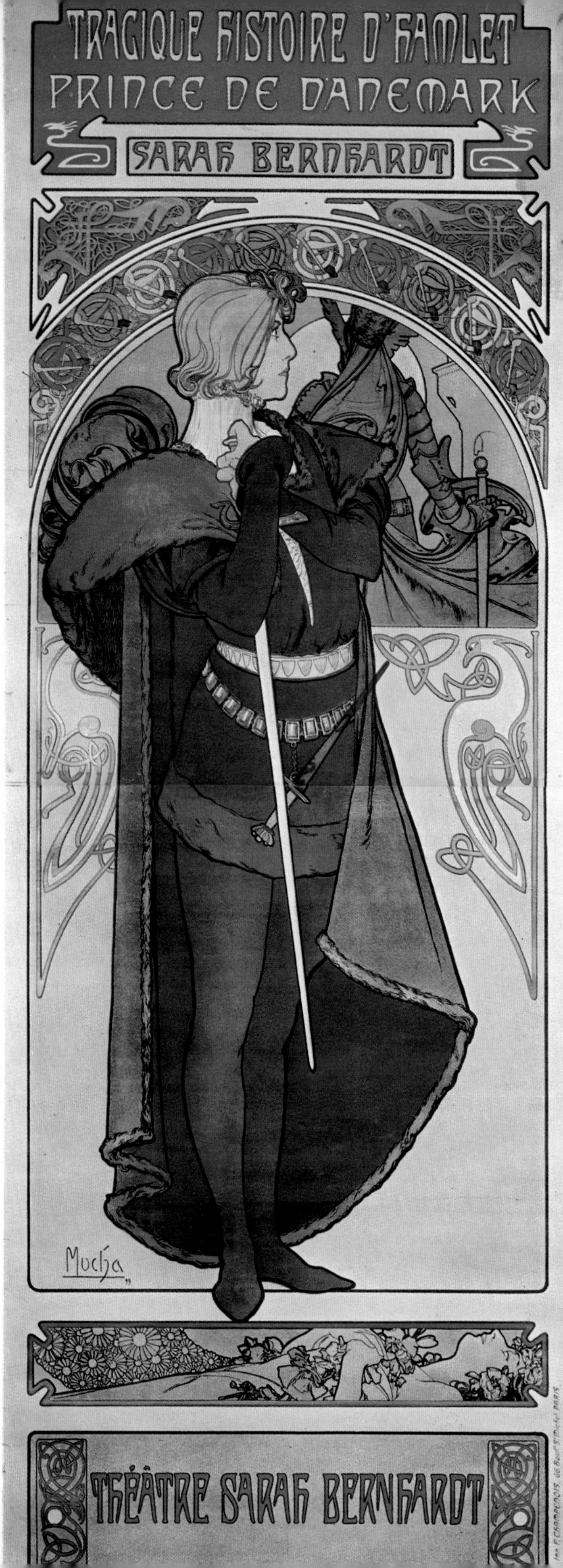
TRAGIQUE HISTOIRE D'HAMLET
PRINCE DE DANEMARK
SARAH BERNHARDT
Mucha
THÉATRE SARAH BERNHARDT

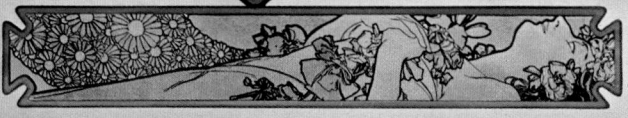

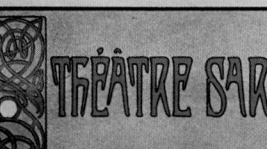

The Odéon had seen a number of Shakespeare productions. In 1886 a
sumptuous *Midsummer Night's Dream,* with Mendelssohn's music encored
during the interval, a female Puck, and Mounet-Sully's Oberon – 'grave and
solemn like the Tiresias of the ancient tragedy'[1] – failed to attract the public.
The opening scene reminded Sarcey of a picture by Watteau, although he
admitted to a 'holy horror' for spectacle carried to excess. A year later, in a
review of *Much Ado about Nothing,* he was writing of Benedick and Beatrice
exchanging 'their Italian conceits and gongorisms, mixed up with horrible
coarse jests, like a couple of tennis players'. Sarcey's sense of classical propriety
was outraged by the exuberance of Shakespeare's genius, but he could not deny
his mastery of stagecraft. 'This Shakespeare is a great magician. He goes after
his effect against the winds and tides, and always gets it.' Sarcey did not realize
that the 'winds and tides' were the conventions of a theatre for which Shakespeare had not written.

Sarah Bernhardt as Hamlet

Opposite: Alphonse Mucha's poster for
Hamlet, with Sarah Bernhardt in the
title rôle

2

The story of Shakespeare in Italy is one of a few players competing for a few
great parts. Eleanora Duse (1858-1924) was over thirty when she tackled Juliet,
looking, as she waited in the wings, even more than her age. But as soon as she
began to act she became a naive and smiling child with a young voice and
girlish gestures. She wisely left Lady Macbeth alone and as Cleopatra, we are
told, 'her peculiar force seemed to fade away into air'[2]; but in view of her success
in Goldoni she might well have been tempted to Rosalind. Adelaide Ristori
(1821-1906) was by many thought the equal of Rachel, although George Henry
Lewes, who had admired her as Medea, was disappointed by her Lady Macbeth.
In describing her as a 'conventional actress' he meant that 'with great art she
employs the traditional conventions of the stage, and reproduces the effects
which others have produced, but does not deeply move us, because not herself
greatly moved. Take away her beauty, grace and voice, and she is an ordinary
comedian.'[3] Ristori could succeed in *Medea* because the part belongs to a
simplified and ideal drama, where convention will carry the player a long way.
Lady Macbeth is an individual, and to be greatly acted demands original
treatment.

With the actors we find one man of outstanding talent, and one of genius,
competing in a limited number of tragic rôles. Ernesto Rossi (1827-96)
produced *Julius Caesar* in his own translation, which may not have been much
worse than the others in vogue. As Macbeth he was a superb figure, but
spoiled his performance by exaggerated pantomime, and the ventriloquy with
which he imitated the sleeping grooms. At the end of the banquet scene he
tumbled over his long cloak, tripped, fell, and rolled over with his heels in the
air. He then lay crouching and trembling on the floor in expectation of some
further shock. As Romeo, to which he was less physically suited, he staggered
away from the tomb, the poison already working in him, and stood with his
back to Juliet as she revived. He then turned, and seeing that the tomb was
empty, and Juliet standing close by, he slowly threw up his arms, standing on
tiptoe to the fullness of his height, and fell to the ground so that the lovers died
in each other's arms. As Henry James observed: 'the superiority of his pantomime
to his delivery seems to me to fix him, in spite of his great talent, in the second
line of actors'.[4] Nevertheless his fellow-countryman Salvini much admired his

[1] Sarcey
[2] Maurice Baring *Punch and Judy* (1924)
p.303
[3] *On Actors and the Art of Acting* (1875)
p.170
[4] *The Scenic Art* (1949) pp.53-5

Hamlet. 'I do not believe' Salvini wrote 'that there ever was an artist who could pronounce the words "I love you" as Ernesto Rossi said them'.

Othello has always been popular in Italy, and James Agate used to maintain that the average Italian hairdresser had more of the Othello temperament than the most accomplished virtuosi of the north. The advantage, however, is not necessarily with a Latin approach. Henry James had little praise for Rossi's

> Italian conception of the part . . . how crude it was, how little it expressed the hero's moral side, his depth, his dignity, anything more than his being a creature terrible in mere tantrums; e.g. knocking Iago's head half a dozen times on the floor, and then flinging him twenty yards away . . . Rossi gloats in his tenderness and bellows in his pain.[1]

The particular qualities of Italian Othellos were defined by the American critic, Stark Young, in writing of Giovanni Grasso, the Sicilian actor, in whom a primitive animality was as marked as it was in Rossi: his playing

> exercises us not by refining on our reflections and adding nuances to our inner experiences; but by putting into play those more universal faculties of the heart and mind that make us a part of all human experience everywhere. Such art has not the subtlety of mists and shadows and visionary depths; but for all that it may have a subtlety of its own, the subtle and infinite simplicities of light on a wall or of the sky at noon.

It is difficult for an Italian actor to present an Othello 'not easily jealous', but the synthesis between a southern temperament and the character as Shakespeare created it was achieved by Tommaso Salvini (1829-1915) in a performance which stands among the classics of the stage. For Henry James this was still 'the portrait of an African by an Italian'. He noted the 'quick suspicion and passionate rage', but also the 'frank tenderness', the 'easy expenditure of force', the 'passion beginning in noble repose and spending itself in black insanity', the 'visible and audible beauty beyond praise'. He noted Salvini's 'tiger-like spring to reach Iago from his kneeling posture by Desdemona', but he emphasized that for all its 'tremendous force' the performance was 'magnificently quiet, and from beginning to end had not a touch of rant or crudity'.[2] Salvini's Othello faced a severer test when, in 1875, it came under the exacting scrutiny of George Henry Lewes – for Lewes had a vivid recollection of Edmund Kean. He 'came away with the impression that, although in certain passages manifestly inferior to Kean, the representation as a whole was of more sustained excellence', and declared that 'in the three great elements of musical expression, tone, timbre, and rhythm'[3] Salvini was the greatest speaker he had heard.

Tommaso Salvini as Othello

Salvini was a man of powerful physique, and unusual physical strength. He could lift a man out of a chair with one arm and put him on a table. He was also a champion billiards player and one of the best horsemen in Italy. He took musical lessons at sixteen, and lowered his naturally bass voice to baritone. Helena Modjeska compared him to a masterpiece by Michelangelo. He modelled his Othello on a Moor he had seen in Gibraltar with a majestic walk, Roman face, slightly projecting lower lip, slender moustache, and a copper to coffee complexion. Salvini added a little hair to his chin. We have a minute record of his performance.[4] An easy authority marked it from the start, with a smile in response to Iago's 'Are you fast married?'; a commanding 'Keep up your bright swords'; a smile again on 'or the dew will rust them'; and a smile, now

[1] Ibid p. 175
[2] Ibid p.175, 189
[3] *On Actors and the Art of Acting* p.278
[4] Tuckerman Mason *The Othello of Tommaso Salvini* (1890)

disdainful, in reply to Brabantio's accusations, which turned to a slight expression of disgust when they were repeated before the Senate. The smile persisted faintly through 'Rude am I in my speech', where the tone was one of mingled sadness, weariness, indignation and scorn. There was a quiet intensity on 'Send for the lady to the sagittary'; a meaningful glance at Brabantio for 'Her father loved me'; deprecation for the opening lines of the 'wooing' speech, descriptive gestures for 'antres vast and deserts idle', exultation for 'Upon this hint I spake', haughty self-assertion for 'This only is the witchcraft I have used', and a great simplicity for 'Here comes the lady; let her answer it.' Othello's confidence in Iago was demonstrated throughout the scene, which ended with a threatening gesture to Brabantio on 'My life upon her faith' and a rapturous embrace for Desdemona.

In the second act 'O my fair warrior' was impetuous and exultant. A momentary shortness of breath was indicated on 'It stops me here', and a kiss was exchanged during Iago's 'O you are well tuned now'. In the cashiering of Cassio, Othello's concern for Desdemona was shown as the main excuse for his anger. Salvini sat at a table, very playful and affectionate, through Desdemona's subsequent entreaties, and seemed about to embrace her on 'I will deny thee nothing' when Iago and Emilia came in. The great temptation scene was planned with infinite mutations of mood. There was grave anxiety on Iago's 'Think, my Lord?', and Salvini – still seated at the table – threw down his pen, crossed to Iago on 'too hideous to be shown', and shook him warmly by the hand on 'My lord, you know I love you'. To Iago's next speeches he listened with sympathetic interest, but seemed impatient with his reticence. He showed no personal feeling on 'O misery', and laughed incredulously with a shrug of the shoulders on Iago's 'I speak not yet for certain'. 'Look to your wife' found him gravely attentive, but 'Observe her well with Cassio' was answered with an angry headshake. 'Dost thou say so' was low and anxious; 'and so she did' was scarcely audible; and the voice faltered on 'I am bound to thee for ever'.

At this point Salvini went up to the window, returned, and leaned on the back of a chair during Iago's next speech. On 'Foh! one may smell in such a will most rank' his hand went to his sword; and on 'Farewell, farewell', he seated himself again at the table, trying vainly to write when Iago had gone out, dashing his pen on the table and striking it with his fist on 'O curse of marriage'. His voice remained faint and low during the short exchange with Desdemona; was still deeply sad on 'False to me?'; and the rage began to reverberate only with 'Avaunt, begone' when Iago re-entered. He started the 'farewell' speech leaning on the chair; sank into it on 'Farewell, content'; and threw himself back in it, his outstretched arms on the table and his head resting upon them, as he broke out into passionate weeping on 'Othello's occupation's gone'. From a low and threatening 'Villain, be sure thou prove my love a whore' the voice increased in volume until he rushed upon Iago, forcing him to his knees and raising a foot to stamp out his life. Restraining himself with difficulty he staggered to a couch up stage. 'Death and damnation' sounded like the cry of a wounded beast; and Salvini's lips curled into a horrible smile as 'O monstrous, monstrous' came in a low, sibilant murmur. 'I'll tear her all to pieces', for all its ferocity, was still not loud; and then came the ultimate cry of anguish on 'Now do I see 'tis true'.

Salvini's interrogation of Desdemona over the loss of the handkerchief was rapid, grave, and quiet, although he repelled her embrace with some violence.

Again there was rapid, horrible exultation when he grasped at Iago's suggestion that she should be smothered in her bed. He received the letter relieving him of his command without emotion, and when he struck Desdemona across the face with it, the blow seemed to be involuntary and at once regretted – as if this were the kind of thing a gentleman did not do. He bade her 'out of my sight' in a stern whisper. Just as Salvini used a colloquial tone whenever he was able to, some of his most tragic effects were achieved through smiles and laughter – as when he dashed the purse at Emilia's feet after treating her as the madam of a bawdy house. In the last scene he entered with bowed head, only just audible for 'It is the cause, my soul'; threw his cloak on a chair; drew his sword; and partly opened the curtains enclosing Desdemona's bed. On 'Yet I'll not shed her blood' he laid the sword on the table, and spoke 'I'll smell it on the tree' from behind the curtains. Thunder was heard and lightning seen through the window as the broken voice came into the room with 'Thou dost almost persuade justice to break her sword'. It was only when Desdemona exclaimed 'Alas! he is betrayed', on hearing of Cassio's supposed death, that it rose into wild, headlong fury. Salvini then dragged her to her feet, and forced her back through the curtains which were then closed. When Emilia entered he put his head through them, and played the following scene pacing up and down between the alcove and the door. The lights came up at the general entrance, and 'Are there no stones in Heaven but what serve for the thunder' was given with full voice. Salvini's aspect at this moment was described as Titanic. He wounded Iago with Montano's sword, and then relapsed into a chair, rising slowly for his final speech. 'I have done the state some service' was a proud boast, followed very quietly with 'and they know it'. The voice was broken during the next lines, and the body relaxed. Then, catching sight of the curved scimitar on the table, which he struck with the palm of his right hand, and leaning against it, he snatched up the sword and moved to the centre of the stage. On 'and smote him thus' he held the imaginary Turk in his left hand and the sword in his right; took a pace or two backward; and seizing the point of the scimitar with his left hand, grasped the blade just below the hilt with his right, and drew it violently across his throat. Facing the audience he staggered backward and died, convulsively, before he could reach the alcove.

Such, then, was the Othello of Tommaso Salvini. George Henry Lewes missed the 'deep, manly, and *impersonal* pathos' of Kean's 'Farewell, the tranquil mind', and the 'groundswell of subsiding passion' in the fourth act. The fifth he criticized as 'underfelt and overacted'. Henry Austin Clapp, who saw the performance in America with Booth as Iago – each actor playing in his own language! – found it 'orientalised and supersensualised, at the cost of some of the Master's conception, and of much of the Poet's beautiful thought – a tawny barbarian'. But these were small cavils within the chorus of international acclaim. Whether you agreed with Salvini's Othello or not, there was never any doubt that here was a tragic actor of the first rank. He went on playing the part till he was seventy, stooping in the wings like the old man that he had now become, and growing taller and younger as he entered to face the Doge and the Magnificoes.

At first sight Salvini's physique would have seemed to disqualify him for Hamlet, but here opinions sharply differ. He had been attracted to the part by seeing Irving, whose vocal and physical defects he admitted, while admiring his scenes with Ophelia, Rosencrantz and Guildenstern, and the players. No doubt William Winter's fidelity to Irving was too absolute for him to appreciate Salvini on any level – for he remained impervious even to the splendour of his Othello.

> He had the aspect and apparent muscularity of a bull . . . would have tossed Uncle Claudius into the sea; slain Rosencrantz and Guildenstern by the simple method of smashing their heads together; placed Mother Gertrude in a nunnery; married Ophelia off-hand; spanked Brother Laertes, and kicked Fortinbras down the castle stairway – and would have attended to all that business before breakfast.

Looking at pictures of Salvini one is inclined to take Winter at his word; but Lewes – an incomparably finer critic – held that of all the Hamlets he had seen Salvini's had the 'greatest excellences'. He thought that in the ghost scene there should be less physical terror and more metaphysical awe, but he admired the quiet handling of the soliloquies; the tender treatment both of Ophelia and Gertrude; and the climax of the play scene 'as he wildly flings into the air the leaves of the manuscript he has been biting a moment before, and falls exhausted on Horatio's neck'. Lewes was no sentimentalist, and when he describes his emotion at Salvini's 'dying close', the tribute cannot be disregarded.

> No more pathetic death has been seen on the stage. Among its many fine touches there was the subtle invention of making the dying Hamlet draw down the head of Horatio to kiss him before sinking into silence; which reminds one of the 'Kiss me, Hardy', of the dying Nelson. And this affecting motive was represented by an action as novel as it was truthful – namely, the uncertain hand blindly searching for the dear head, and then faintly closing on it with a sort of final adieu.[1]

William Poel, who had held a spear for Salvini when he came to London, confirms Lewes to the letter: 'I myself have never failed to uphold that Salvini's impersonation of Hamlet was the only perfect one that has been given within living memory.'

It is arguable that if a man looks like a bull he has no business to be playing Hamlet; but whether or not Salvini looked like a bull, it is clear that he did not behave like one. That London visit was a crowning triumph. At the instance of Robert Browning he was made a guest member of the Athenaeum, and given a reception by the Arts Club and the Garrick. Browning had written to him:

> I do not know whether what you say to me is true about the chords of tenderness that you lacked, or which failed to respond to the touch in your first representation of Hamlet. But this I know, that during your play on Friday the entire lyre of tragedy responded magnificently.

An incidental, but not unimportant, aspect of Salvini's success was to have married a young orphan girl while he was in the city.

He went on to play a Macbeth, described by Henry James as 'rich and grave . . . whom we deeply pity and whose delusions and crimes we understand and almost forgive . . . sombre enough, but wonderfully frank and transparent . . . a fair-haired, sturdy Northern warrior' with 'eyes distractedly blue', and giving 'a strange sense of being honest through it all'.[2] When he spoke of his 'hangman's hands' he seemed to Robert Louis Stevenson to have 'blood in his utterance'. Nor, in *Lear*, did James forget how on 'Ay, every inch a king' Salvini had torn off the twig of a tree and turned it into a sceptre. There were moments, after all, when realistic scenery had its uses.

[1] *On Actors and the Art of Acting* p.277
[2] *The Scenic Art* (1949) pp.175-6

VI Germany and Russia

Whatever one may think of the heresy that Shakespeare should have written his plays in German, there can be no question that German has an easy advantage over French as a vehicle for translating them. Neither Germany nor Austria had a *grand siècle* to impose its 'classical moment' on the development of drama; and the sage of Weimar, for all the Hellenic hankerings of his later years, was open to Shakespeare in a way that the stage of Ferney was not. In the fifth book of *Wilhelm Meister* – published in 1795 – seven chapters are devoted to a presentation of *Hamlet*, and from 1791 to 1817 Goethe was in charge of the Court Theatre at Weimar. He wrote the plays, directed the productions, attended to the Box Office, and even painted the sets. Weimar was the tiny capital of a state that counted no more than 106,000 inhabitants, and the potential audience of a theatre with 500 seats was about 2,000. It had already seen a number of Shakespeare's plays – and *A Midsummer Night's Dream* and *The Tempest* had also been given in musical adaptations. Goethe was divided between his admiration for Shakespeare as a poet and his distress that he was not a different kind of dramatist. His work for the Duke of Saxe-Weimar may be described as a bridge between the romantic and the classical approach – and the bridge sometimes broke down.

The repertoire had necessarily to appeal both to aristocratic and to bourgeois taste. Actors who mumbled their lines in domestic comedy or farce on Monday were liable to massacre Shakespeare's verse on Tuesday, and Goethe had to bring them to heel with a conductor's baton. His preference was for tragedy because tragedy was more easily grasped by his public. Yet here again his admiration for Shakespeare was divided. '*Macbeth*' he told Eckermann 'is Shakespeare's best acting play, the one in which he shows most understanding of the stage. But would you see his mind unfettered, read *Troilus and Cressida*.' At the beginning Goethe tried to give Shakespeare, if not exactly as the plays were written, at least without extensive cuts. This intention must not be taken too literally. In *King John*, we are told, 'we have suppressed or modified only such allusions as have no meaning for us today, certain rather free expressions, and here and there a secondary rôle'. Goethe was not alone in forgetting that in belonging 'to all ages' Shakespeare also belonged to his own. He telescoped the two parts of *Henry IV* into a single play – always a perilous proceeding – and after the death of Schiller – 'the dramaturgic motor of Weimar', as he was called – in 1805, Goethe gradually lost his taste for seeing Shakespeare acted or for producing him. He preferred to hear him read aloud. Schiller's versions of *Lear*, *Julius Caesar*, *Othello*, and *Macbeth* were all given at Weimar. Of these *Macbeth* at the Hofttheater in 1800 was the most successful, no doubt because it was the most 'sublime'. The porter's speech was replaced by a morning hymn, and the 'midnight hags' transformed into respectable Eumenides. Lady Macbeth became a 'super-sorceress', in Goethe's phrase, exercising her magic on a weak and contemplative partner. August Wilhelm Schlegel who, with Ludwig Tieck, had proved that a faithful translation of Shakespeare could also be effective, was indignant at Schiller's misplaced 'sublimity'.

Goethe, with Schiller at his elbow, introduced a style of acting and production to suit the neo-classical Shakespeare of their adaptations. Speech became closer to music, movement to dance, and grouping to symmetrical composition. *Romeo and Juliet* was so altered, with no brawls and consequently no reconciliation between Capulets and Montagues, that Goethe was afraid to publish the amended text. As Tieck was to complain: 'only a little of the original remained, and what was left appeared in a totally different light, and was so oddly changed, that its true meaning was lost'. In so far as Goethe was thinking in theatrical terms at all, it was in terms of the total synthesis that Wagner was later to realize. 'Shakespeare' he said 'belongs essentially to the history of poetry, not of the theatre, where he appears only by accident'. For Goethe, Shakespeare was too universal for the stage and too great to comply with its demands.

Nevertheless both Goethe and Tieck understood, though perhaps without quite knowing it, the direction that Shakespearian production was to take. When Goethe declared: 'Nothing is truly theatrical that is not symbolic to the eye' he was anticipating Appia and Craig and Robert Edmund Jones. The sketch exists for a unit stage intended for a production of *A Midsummer Night's Dream* at Weimar. This is as classical as anyone could wish, but it is also perfectly adapted to Shakespeare. A double flight of steps led up to a platform with openings above and below, and only within these could a change of scene be indicated. Goethe's idea – intended, no doubt, to unify what appeared so disparate – was carried further by Karl Immermann at Dusseldorf in 1840, where the steps were eliminated and a classical architrave replaced the upper stage. Meanwhile in 1817 – the year when Goethe finally abandoned the theatrical for the literary Shakespeare – Tieck saw the forestage in the theatre at Windsor Castle. There was much virtue, he realized, in that forestage. 'If we want to play Shakespeare genuinely', he wrote in 1836, 'we must begin with a theatre which is similar to his'; and in the same year, assisted by Gottfried Semper, he made a reconstruction of Henslowe's Fortune. In 1843 – now aged seventy – he was invited by the King of Prussia to produce a Shakespeare play in the new palace at Potsdam. Here he built a stage on two levels; the upper platform, reached by off-stage steps, had a background of columns and architrave – an adroit compromise between Goethe's sketch for the *Dream* and what Immermann had

Set design by Karl Immermann for *Twelfth Night*, Dusseldorf 1840

Jocza Savits' *King Lear*, Royal Theatre, Munich, 1889

done in Dusseldorf. Classical form and Elizabethan utility were cleverly combined.

> It seems quite possible to me to build a stage approximating architecturally to the older English stage, without banishing painting and decoration altogether. It could, in fact, undoubtedly be built so that the illusion to which we have become accustomed would be even more magical and more varied as well as more purposeful and theatrical, so that it would enhance the effect of the play instead of weakening or wrecking it as so often happens now.[1]

These ideas – revolutionary for their time – were to bear important fruit. In 1889 Baron von Perfall, intendant of the Royal Theatre in Münich, resented the publicity and prestige attaching to the spectacular Shakespeare productions then being given by the Meininger players – presently to be discussed. He therefore requested Herr Savits, director of the theatre, to prepare a production of *King Lear* according to Elizabethan methods. Savits directed twelve different plays of Shakespeare within six months. William Poel attended a performance

[1] *Dramaturgischen Blattern* No. 711

of *Lear*, and thought it 'the best cast and the most stimulating performance of the tragedy I have ever seen'.[1] Four years later he founded the Elizabethan Stage Society, and in Paris Antoine had also taken the hint. A number of good minds were now thinking alike in the matter of Shakespeare production, but in Germany they had gone further than anywhere else towards putting their theories to the test.

2

The company directed by Herr Kronegk, and fed with the Duke of Saxe-Meiningen's silver spoon, performed forty-one plays – several of them by Shakespeare – in thirty-eight European cities. Berlin saw them in 1874, London in 1881. Their productions were notable for disciplined ensemble; for this reason William Poel was impressed by them, although they were the reverse of Elizabethan. The actors, more often than not, were chosen for their strong physique in order to show off their splendid costumes. Principals were required to walk on as supers. Kronegk aimed at an extreme realism. The players were forbidden to look into the audience, and the most important scenes were acted upstage. Nevertheless the Meininger *Julius Caesar* made theatrical history, if only as a proof that the militarism of the barrack square could effectively be translated to the boards. The Forum was reproduced with pedantic accuracy, down to an exact copy of Pompey's statue, and Caesar's poor performance was unredeemed by his resemblance to Caesar's bust. The weather was as changeable as stage machinery could make it. In the last act soldiers descended from the mountains into a narrow gorge, and then into a small wood. The stage was strewn with dead and dying. Kronegk taught his actors like parrots, and moved them about at rehearsals on a floor marked out with chalk into squares and numbers. He went to actual life for characteristic intonations; insisted on complicated make-up; and introduced the cyclorama. When the company visited Russia, Ostrovsky found the performance of *Julius Caesar* –

> a pleasure not much different from that which we derive from well co-ordinated movements of disciplined troops on parade, or from a well trained corps de ballet. We see in them not art, but skill . . . neither Caesar nor Shakespeare, but an excellently disciplined company of mediocre actors and disgustingly wailing actresses make a display of themselves . . . everywhere one sees the stage director. The leading player acts by command according to pattern. The mob lives, is agitated, indignant, and thrills the public more than Antony's oration.[2]

In *Romeo and Juliet* Vera Komisarjevskaya wanted 'some idea of the balcony, and nothing else'. She got a great deal more.

It must be remembered that the German theatre was so organized, with a state supported playhouse in every city of moderate size, as to favour a respectable ensemble in default of individual genius. The stars were prepared to alter their courses when a visiting planet entered the radius of their galaxy. George Henry Lewes recalls how the great – in his opinion the only great – tragedian Seydelmann stood down from Hamlet when the young Emil Devrient came to Berlin. The result was an unforgettable Polonius. Ludwig Devrient (1784-1832), the father of Emil, played many of the great Shakespearian parts in Breslau; a strongly oriental Shylock and a successful Falstaff. It is remarkable that with his small presence and little volume or sonority of voice he should have been

[1] *Monthly Letters* (1929) p.92
[2] B. V. Varneke *History of the Russian Theatre* (1951) p.348
[3] L. Rellstat *Blumen und Ahrenlese* p.356
[4] Raoul Auenheimer
[5] William Winter *Shakespeare on the Stage* (1912) pp.442-3

Adolf von Sonnenthal as King Lear

Below: Josef Lange as Hamlet

among the outstanding Lears of the century. True. he emphasized the milder aspects of the character, and his mastery of make-up did much to conceal his physical deficiencies. A contemporary writes of

One of the noblest old man's heads I have ever seen. . . . Sometimes he would pass his hand, in weariness and despondency, over his bald forehead, as if he would brush away the crushing weight of sorrow from his brain. At the words: 'I would not be mad', spoken with this gesture, a cold shudder ran through the audience, as they saw, with him, the awful, inexorable spectre of madness glide forth from the gloomy background, and laying a hand upon his, mark him as its destined victim.[3]

There were times when Devrient fell down in an epileptic fit after the second act, or at the end of the play he would be carried out of the stage door in costume, disordered and pale, like a dead man from the battlefield. In later years he was obliged to give up the part altogether. In 1832, the year of his death, he was playing Shylock at the Burgtheater in Vienna, and those who saw him in his dressing-room could hardly believe that a body so enfeebled was capable of sustaining a performance.

It was at the Burgtheater – once compared to 'a planet whose orbit lies between opposite points of attraction, society and literature'[4] – that Adolf von Sonnenthal, the other famous Lear of the German stage made his name. An early recording of his voice may still be heard at the Theatermuseum in Münich. The deep groundswell, like waves breaking over rocks or the rumbling of a distant avalanche, indicate his emotional and vocal range. His failure as Hamlet is as easy to imagine as his success as Lear; and the vices of that production went far beyond the clichés of nineteenth-century convention.

The scenery ranged from the garish opulence of an Eighth Avenue barber-shop to the tawdry luxury of a railway-station lunch-room, with an occasional suggestion of a country church. The Ghost was a brightly caparisoned phantom that gleamed in the attendant limelight like a burnished warming-pan and told its doleful tale from the middle of a burning bush. . . . Queen Gertrude's apartment was provided with two full-length and very hideous portraits of her two spouses, and when the Ghost penetrated into that bower of nuptial bliss he abruptly took the place of his 'counterfeit presentment' and remained within the picture frame. . . . The corpse of Polonius, visible beneath the arras, becoming weary of the protracted proceedings, presently conveyed itself away in a manner more expeditious than impressive.[5]

William Winter is not always to be trusted on foreign actors, but when he describes Herr Barnay – a noble Mark Antony, but as Hamlet no more suitable than Sonnenthal – lowering the curtain after the Prince's first meeting with the Ghost and taking a call before proceeding to 'another part of the platform', one rubs one's eyes and takes him at his word. Barnay had played leading rôles with the Meininger, and was now enjoying a holiday from team work.

The Burgtheater had a canonical status similar to that of the Comédie Française. Less overpowered by its past, it was more open-minded. Josef Schreyvogel, who directed it from 1814 to 1832, wished to make it 'a world theatre, a forum for intellectual exchange covering American and European, as well as Austrian and German, theatre life'. Shakespeare had from the first an important place in its repertoire. There, in the long gallery today, are the portraits of Josef Lange as Hamlet in powdered wig; Zerline Gabillon as a very serious Beatrice; Stella Hohenfels-Berger as – one thinks – an Ophelia too

Charlotte Wolter as Margaret in
Richard III, Hofburgtheater 1874

Josef Kainz as Romeo and Anna von
Hohanberger as Juliet, Deutsches
Theater, Berlin, 1886

strong minded to go easily out of her wits; and Josef Kainz (1858-1909) as Richard II with the long hair and falling head-dress under the crown. The son of a station-master on the line from Vienna to the west, and the protégé of the mad King Ludwig of Bavaria, Kainz was himself the king of all those who have won their laurels at the Burg. Listen to his voice, as an old recording brings it to us,[1] climb the scales in the *legato maestoso* of '*Sein oder nicht sein*' and you will understand all that the *vox humana* can accomplish. You will receive an impression of delicacy as well as power. Kainz was a highly cultivated man, illustrating the old Viennese principle that taste and elegance are the expression of an inner nobility. 'A proper man' he wrote to Baron Berger 'is and must be a gentleman.'[2] His startling physical beauty made him a natural Romeo, Prince Hal, and Claudio in *Much Ado*. A certain feyness that can be read on his features evokes his Fool in *Lear*.

A contemporary describes him as Orlando when he was only ten years old: 'In word, gesture, and expression Kainz has not changed by a hair's breadth. As a boy and as a young lad in the gymnasium he was already a perfect and accomplished actor.' His immediate idol at the Burg was Fritz Kastel, with his black hair, superb stature, and eyes that blazed like live coals. Kastel was known as the 'Helden-tenor of tragedy'; he was not a thoughtful actor, and his characterization was weak. His elocution, like that of Charlotte Wolter, tended to turn a speech into an aria. This was a tradition at the Burg; they were said to handle words 'like a courtier's wand'. Although Kainz had his eyes and his ambition on the Burg, it was with the Meininger that he began to mature his extraordinary art. He joined them at the age of twenty when nature designed him for Lorenzo. His Jessica – Thérèse Grumert – described his opening to the last act as a 'little jewel of grace and fire'. The dialectical sharpness and contrapuntal composition of his speech showed him, already, as a successor to Josef Lewinsky, considered the greatest speaker of his time. He left the Meininger for the state theatre at München where he was an obvious Laertes and Malcolm, and was given his first great opportunity, being called upon to play Romeo after only three rehearsals. Here he laid the ground plan for a performance of the part which can rarely have been equalled in the history of the stage. The dreamy and physically inert patrician youth of the opening suddenly took fire as he enquired of the servant: 'What lady's that which doth enrich the hand of yonder knight?' The soliloquy at the opening of the balcony scene was 'a gentle outcry of the heart' where 'a boy's voice dissolved the words in music, and thought was lost in jubilation.'[3] The rich vowel sounds in German lend themselves to effective prolongation, and Kainz was quick to take advantage of this. 'Schule', as he spoke it, became 'Schu——le'. He was also a master of the pause and the abrupt transition. 'Tybalt, the love I bear thee...' is usually spoken in an even tone; but with Kainz 'Tybalt' was rapped out in the heat of temper – then came a pause as he controlled himself; and the remainder of the speech was quiet. The nuptial parting was no consolatory *au revoir*; Kainz thumped the stage with his clenched fist in a positive fury of heartbreak.

From a Romeo of this quality the step was easy to Richard II. Kainz was fortunate in playing both these parts with his Hamlet still before him. As Richard he showed the boyish tyrant, clinging with desperate fanaticism to the last discredited shreds of the Divine Right of Kings. The young man who had played with his own happiness, and the happiness of others, like a toy, indulging his wit and sarcasm at their expense, was reduced, in the abdication scene, to a man whose nerve would hold out no longer. Alternating between 'Yes' and 'No', he pressed the fingers of both hands to his forehead, and in his grating voice were the tears of an unspeakable misery. He held the mirror high above his head, and then his fingers opened as if they had lost all strength; as if happiness had slipped through them, and that he no longer had the will or could make the effort to retain it. The gesture was at once simple and symbolic. This Richard had foundered through his own exorbitance; the misuse of a talent which he had wasted through lack of self-control, and of an authority which he had sought to place above the law. As he waited for death in the dungeon at Pomfret, all his features suddenly brightened under the influence of music, and then, as he stopped his ears to it, they became like those of a sick child. Some thought, when he played the part in later years, that he drew a parallel between Richard's downfall, and the very different catastrophe which had overtaken the King who had been something more than his friend.

Kainz stayed for three years in München, playing many different parts. Then, in 1883, he joined the newly opened Deutsches Theater in Berlin. In 1891 he played his first Hamlet at the Ostendtheater, and between October 1897 and December 1909 gave twenty-six performances of the part. The interpretation changed and deepened with experience of life and intensive study of the text. Kainz was not afraid to better Schlegel's instruction when he thought fit to do so. Marked at first by a patrician grace and nobility, the performance gradually acquired a more cutting edge. Here was no languishing Werther; one felt the muscles tauten as anger, hatred, and irony were emphasized at the expense of melancholy. It was reflection, not fear, that prevented the marriage of the right act and the right intention. More tense in some respects, this later Hamlet was more relaxed in others, walking to and fro with his hands in his pockets, or sitting on the edge of a table, and coming that much closer to average humanity. But while he summed up the universal significance of the part, he seemed at the same time to be a consciously German Hamlet, and awoke for the sophisticated onlooker echoes of Nietzsche, Schopenhauer, and Kant's categorical imperative. His was the tragedy of a nature essentially noble, frustrated by the excess of ability, not by the lack of it.

Josef Kainz as Richard II

Josef Kainz as Hamlet

There was no heartbreak in the 'nunnery' scene as Kainz held Ophelia's head in his two hands, pushed it back, looked into her eyes, and reading the deception there, let her go. It was clear that he had renounced her for good and all, and that his experience of life was the richer for it. In the play scene his doubtful gallantries were the cloak for a gathering excitement as he moved closer and closer to the King, 'ready like a beast of prey to spring at his throat until he was bent over him with clenched fingers and blazing eyes, a very genius of revenge. Then, in a wild and orgiastic outburst of jubilation, the lines came shrill and piercing as he sprang and danced around.' With Gertrude he was a stern judge, though never forgetting the Ghost's injunction: 'Taint not thy mind, nor let thy soul contrive against thy mother aught.' The mingling of passion and fantasy was shown in the final scene when he kicked Claudius into eternity, after sealing his fate – and exhausting his own rage – with rapier, dagger and poison. Kainz had throughout reserved a deep tenderness for Horatio. 'Now he leaned upon him, and dragging himself along a few paces, either sank upon the steps of the throne' – as in Berlin, or – as in Vienna – 'allowed Horatio to help him to a couch'. He brought out 'The rest . . .' in a broken voice, and then with a movement of the hand to his mouth and a scarcely perceptible shake

[1] Also to be heard in the Theatermuseum, München
[2] Helene Richter: *Kainz* (1931) p.239
[3] For these and other details of Kainz's performances, see Helen Richter *Kainz* (1931)

of the head, 'is silence' signified the failure of speech, and was followed by a last sigh. 'A shiver went through the outstretched limbs; the eyes stayed open; and the head fell on to the breast. As Horatio closed the lids, the pale, unseeing features flickered into a beatific smile.'[1]

When Kainz played Richard II for the last time at the Burgtheater, the audience noticed an unaccustomed shrillness in his voice, and in his whole performance a special depth of feeling. It was observed that as he met the challenge of Bolingbroke tears were running down his cheeks. These were the signs of a fatal illness, and in a few months he was dead. A German critic wrote of him:

> As Kainz was a force of nature in his own right through the richness of his personality, his effect upon the spectator was that of an elemental force. Thereby he set himself against theatrical convention. He found the way to a romantic vision of nature, while masters in the other arts were still groping in the dark. . . . Kainz interpreted in his art the spiritual transition which occupied the last quarter of the nineteenth century. This is his abiding significance. He was the first and greatest of those who have brought impressionism to the stage. The entire cultural *ambiente* of our times could be read in his acting and that was the secret of his effect.[2]

3

Pavel Mochalov

When Peter the Great had the first public theatre built in the Red Square in Moscow, there is every reason to believe that the German actor Johann Kunst presented *Julius Caesar* on its stage. This was early in the eighteenth century, and for some time French notions of dramatic refinement dictated Russian taste. Alexander Sumarokov (1718-77), theatrical advisor to the Empresses Elizabeth and Catherine II, working on La Place's translation of *Hamlet*, turned Horatio into a 'confidant' and the theme of the play into a conflict between love and duty – the former represented by Ophelia. Sumarokov found cause for congratulation in the fact that his play 'bore hardly any resemblance to Shakespeare's tragedy'. What remained of Hamlet was played by Dmitrevski, an actor of considerable power and well acquainted with the French stage. The British Ambassador at St Petersburg admired 'the decency, order, and rich mise-en-scène' that Sumarokov had introduced. With Karamazine (1766-1826) the liberating breezes of romanticism began to blow across the Vistula. He regarded classical French tragedy as 'a formal garden where nature has been concealed by the gardener's art', and opposed to the sophistries of Voltaire 'the plenitude of Shakespeare's genius which embraces the whole world'.[3] Karamazine had great authority as a critic, but the Shakespeare he presented was seen through the eyes of Schiller. The romantic 'sublime' had replaced the classical 'sublimity'.

Meanwhile, under the shock of the French Revolution, both *Richard III* and *Julius Caesar* were forbidden by the censor, and it was not until the first decade of the nineteenth century that Shakespeare reappeared with any frequency on the Russian stage. Adaptations of Ducis' *Othello* and *King Lear* were given in 1806 and 1807. Iakovlev, trained in the classical school by Dmitrevskoi, was a romantic Moor; and Ivan Choucherine (1753-1813), having muted the violence of Lear under instruction from Prince Chakhovski, took the bit between his teeth in the storm scenes to great effect. The décor was a Gothic castle, with Gothic furniture upholstered in velvet. This was not Elizabethan, but it was more Shakespearian than Stonehenge. Chakhovski was at last prepared to sacrifice the classical properties, and in honour of his mistress, the actress Iéjova, he mounted a spectacular *Tempest* in the Grand Theatre at St Petersburg. He rearranged, but did not mutilate, the text into three acts, with a good many musical interludes and magical effects. The shipwreck was a masterpiece of scenic virtuosity. Later he amalgamated the two parts of *Henry IV* into a single play entitled *Falstaff*. Doll Tearsheet, who appears in only two scenes of the original, became a central character under the name of 'Mrs Tirshit'. The action all took place in an enclosed garden with a gate in the middle, a Gothic tavern to one side, and on the other a table and chairs for the customers. Roast beef and partridge were on the menu.

Ivan Panaiev (1812-62) compared his emotion on reading Ducis' *Othello* to his emotion on reading Hugo's *Notre-Dame de Paris*. Eulogy could go no further. He translated the play, which was advertised as a translation from the original, and indifferently performed. In the following year, 1837, two celebrated actors presented their Hamlets for comparison by the connoisseurs – Pavel Mochalov (1800-48) in Moscow, and Vasily Karatygin (1802-53) in St Petersburg. Both played it in Polévoi's translation, the first to be made in Russian from the English text. Critical opinion was ready for it, since Pushkin had already stated his conviction that 'the outworn forms of our theatre are due for renovation' and that 'the popular conventions of Shakespearian drama are better suited to our theatre than the courtly conventions of Racine'. Lermontov, too, had written that if Shakespeare was great, it was in *Hamlet*. Mochalov was an actor splendidly endowed both in temperament and physique. His voice that could charm a snake had already lent conviction to the wooing of Lady Anne in *Richard III*, and the transformation was described as 'terrible' when she had left the stage. But he had not served the apprenticeship which, in the theatre as elsewhere, is the essential basis of consistency. At his best he was so natural and yet so passionate that the audience were indulgent to his lapses of taste. His features were as beautiful as his voice, and when anger possessed him he was compared to 'an enraged tiger or a Nero seized with wrath'.

Vasily Karatygin as Hamlet

Even in Polévoi's sentimental translation he challenged Goethe's conception of the part, which was the law and the prophets to a generation reared on *Wilhelm Meister*. His irresolution came from no native weakness, but from a world that was 'out of joint'. He emphasized the energy, not the melancholy, of the rôle. This was evident – almost perversely, one thinks – in 'To be or not to be':

> He did not enter slowly, sunk in deep meditation, but came in almost running in a state of extreme nervous excitement, and then, stopping, cried: 'To be or not to be' – and after several minutes of contemplation threw himself into an armchair, and uttered despairingly – 'that is the question'. Then he recited the rest of the monologue, at times leaping from the armchair, or again throwing himself into it, with the same pathological nervousness.[4]

The important critic, Vissarion Belinski (1811-48), thought that, except for this soliloquy and one other scene, everything that Mochalov did was 'beyond any possible conception of perfection'. Here was 'a real, living, concrete Hamlet' – even though it was 'less Shakespearian than Mochalovian'. Mochalov comes down to us like a character out of Dostoievsky, masochistically aware of his own weakness. When the director of the theatre discovered him in the

[1] Helene Richter *Kainz* (1931) pp.288-92
[2] Egon Friedell *Die Schaubühne* (13 November 1910)
[3] *Revue d'Histoire du Théâtre* (October-December 1964)
[4] P. I. Weinberg, quoted by B. V. Varneke in *The History of the Russian Theatre* (1957) pp.257-8

Opposite: Ludwig Devrient as King Lear, Nationaltheater, Berlin, 1815

middle of a drinking bout with a deacon of the Orthodox Church, Mochalov exclaimed: 'You come to see Mochalov when he is drunk and dirty – not when he is a genius, but when he is no longer a human being. Shame on you! get out! get out quickly!' 'The great actor of Weltschmerz', as he was so often described, died after he had taken to the road where he could give full rein to the daimon that ruled him; and the monument over his grave bears this moving epitaph:

> So sleep, great Shakespeare's friend insane!
> Our Lord has vindicated you.

Mochalov and Karatygin were compared as follows – and the comparison was valid not only for Hamlet, but also for Othello and Coriolanus where they were again in competition:

> Karatygin is a gracefully laid out garden with clean walks, gorgeous flower-beds, and velvety lawns rather subordinated to the norms of art, cleanly washed, trimmed and neatly dressed. Mochalov is a thick forest: here are the enormous pine-trees, the weeping birch, and the giant oak tree growing alternately, with roots and twigs twisted together – in short, this is Mother Nature.[1]

Karatygin was a friend of the Emperor, and conformed to a general pattern of polished behaviour. Herzen cruelly described him as 'a Guards tragedian in whom everything was so memorized, studied, and ordered, that even passion arose in him in tempos; he had learnt the ceremonial march of despair, and having correctly slain somebody, he buried him in a masterly fashion'. Belinski bluntly described Karatygin's clientèle of officers, gentlemen and court officials as 'a menagerie of monkeys and ourangatans, a disgrace and insult to humanity'. Karatygin's Hamlet was the pensive and melancholy prince, graceful in movement and mellifluous in speech. A critic, evidently impartial, contrasted him with Mochalov:

> Karatygin controls himself in moments of high emotion; and this is a great art . . . Mochalov has the superior talent, but Karatygin is an incomparably finer actor. No amount of study can acquire what nature has refused, but art is always possible to acquire.[2]

The rivalry had political repercussions. The Liberals applauded Mochalov because a Hamlet so obviously capable of cleansing the Augean stables of Elsinore suggested other stables, nearer home, which could also do with a cleaning. The Conservatives favoured Karatygin for the opposite reason. In fact, to be 'anti-Shakespearian' became a mark of political respectability. Nevertheless Mochalov had set a pattern of simplicity that was to influence other Hamlets of the century – notably Maximov in 1854 with Jouleva as an Ophelia who enchanted the town. In the case of Polavtsev – like Karatygin, a magnificent Lear – Rybakov, and Lensky, the Schiller tradition of unsullied nobility withstood the trend towards naturalism. It is interesting to note that when Mounet-Sully came to Russia he had no popular success.

In 1903 the Moscow Art Theatre presented *Julius Caesar*. This had been seen in the Meininger production, but the ban on its performance by a Russian company had been lifted only in 1897. It was regarded as republican propaganda, although a closer look might have suggested the contrary. Stanislavsky played Brutus, and also assembled 150 supers to each of whom he assigned a separate identity. 'We shall play *Julius Caesar*', he told the actors, 'in the tones of

[1] Apollon Gregoryev *Revue d'Histoire du Théâtre* (October-December 1964)
[2] Serge Aksakov *Revue d'Histoire du Théâtre* (October-December 1964) pp.402-3

Hinweg erborgter Plunder!

DEVRIENT
als
König Lear,
in dem Trauerspiele: König Lear.

Verlag v. Gbr. Crepius i. Diorama.

L. Sachse & Cⁱᵉ

Chekov', and it was said that he and his designer 'glimpsed Brutus' garden through the flowering branches of a cherry orchard'. The Meininger lessons had been thoroughly – too thoroughly – digested; there was the same search for antiquarian detail at the expense of artistic truth.

> The theatre was transformed into a veritable scientific institute. A special commission, with Nemirovitch at its head, went to Rome to assemble the topographical and archaeological data. A special office was set up; one section dealt with textual prob‑ lems, stage tradition, cuts, information, and literary criticism; another with every‑ thing concerning the manners and customs of Caesar's time; a third with the décors, a sixth with the music, a seventh with the crowd scenes, and so on. It was not alone the theatre that went to work; the whole of Moscow was enthusiastic to lend a hand. Museum directors and librarians placed their knowledge and their treasures at its disposal.[1]

Nemirovich-Danchenko tells the story himself: there were

> more than 200 in the cast; actors, pupils, and university students, all working with great enthusiasm as idlers, senators, warriors, patriots, conspirators, priests, con‑ jurers, dancers, courtesans, vestals, matrons, and market women.

But fatigue and boredom set in. Stanislavsky's Brutus was not understood; he had conceived the character as

> the last Roman – something bright, burning, and revolutionary, while the public wanted to see in Brutus one of the 'gentle' wavering images of Shakespeare. No matter how he perfected his design from performance to performance, this gap between him and the public refused to be bridged.[2]

    Kachalov was a brilliant Caesar, anxious and complex, but in general the suggestive undertones and elusive rhythms suitable for Chekov were quite inappropriate for a play in which the *res publica* was the theme, whether your sympathies were republican or absolutist. Stanislavsky realized this. 'Apart from Kachalov' he admitted 'the acting was all wrong. We were inferior to our décors.'

    He never had much luck with Shakespeare. It was said that he had 'been to Venice and brought back a bit of a gondola'. He had played, and produced, *Othello* at the Solodovnikov Theatre in April 1896. In spite of much inventive detail the performance fell completely flat. The great realist was unsuited, both temperamentally and physically, for romantic and heroic parts. He had modelled his appearance on an Arab met in a Paris restaurant, as Salvini had modelled his on an Arab met in Gibraltar. But good Othellos do not depend on meeting live Arabs. The Iago, too, was miscast; nor, in spite of an effective voice, was he helped by being left to speak the first of his soliloquies in the midnight gloom of the Doge's palace. Here the messengers bringing news that the Turkish fleet was at sea were cleverly differentiated between an old sea dog, and a negro slave who put one of the Doge's feet on his head while he was delivering his speech. In the second act a Turkish coffee stall was placed at the corner of two narrow streets. Here the Venetians were carousing, and the Turks lounging around in groups, when a number of Cypriots were seen approaching. On Iago's line 'Cry – a mutiny', the scene developed into a brawl between Turks and Cypriots *versus* Venetians, with Venetian soldiers standing with their backs to the audience in the foreground. Othello, on his entrance, separated the fighting

V. Kachalov as Julius Caesar, Moscow Art Theatre 1903

Opposite: Design by Alexander Tischler for *A Midsummer Night's Dream c.* 1930

[1] Nina Gourfinkel *Théâtre Russe Contemporain* (1931)
[2] *My Life in the Russian Theatre*

Julius Caesar, Moscow Art Theatre
1903

parties with his sword. Fifty years later this treatment of the scene would have had a certain topicality. Another original idea was to insist on a heavily padded Roderigo; but there was something in Ernesto Rossi's comment that 'all these baubles become necessary only where there are no actors. What you want is art.' To which Stanislavsky enquired, a little naively for so considerable an artist, 'Where is one to learn it from?' 'Yourself' came the categoric reply. When he had retired from active work in the theatre Stanislavsky published a detailed 'score' for a new production of *Othello* which he never lived to direct. It bore the imprint of his magnificent mind, but a great deal that had happened in the interval had evidently passed him by.

Much Ado about Nothing and *Twelfth Night* followed in 1897. For the second the scenic artist of the Moscow Imperial Theatres had designed, in chocolate-box style, an open-air landscape in front of the painted back-cloth of a castle, and in such a way that the actors at the back were two or three times as big as the houses or trees beside them. The setting for *Much Ado* was inspired by a castle that Stanislavsky had seen near Turin. The delicacy of Shakespearian comedy is generally beyond the scope of a foreign actor, and this Benedick was needlessly coarse-grained.

In 1908 Stanislavsky invited Gordon Craig to direct *Hamlet* for the Moscow Art Theatre. This was asking for trouble, for the two men preached and practised a quite different aesthetic of the stage. Craig believed that the theatre must be theatrical, albeit in a new way. Stanislavsky wished to disabuse his audience of any notion that they were in a theatre at all. Craig saw the conflict in *Hamlet* as one between the mutually destructive forces of spirit and matter. He held that, contrary to Chekov, Shakespeare's plays contained no feelings to be read between the lines; against which Stanislavsky argued that the lines in Russian were not the same as the lines in English. Craig maintained that Hamlet regarded Rosencrantz and Guildenstern as his friends until they proved themselves to be otherwise; Stanislavsky disagreed. There was also debate over Ophelia whom Craig insisted was as stupid as Polonius and Laertes; he wanted their scene together (act I scene iii) to be played very fast and without movement. His idea for the Ghost hardly corresponded with 'my father in his habit as he lived' – a tall, rigid skeleton devoured by worms, with the flesh – mistaken for armour – whitening on its bones, and a torn shroud hanging about them. The production suffered from Stanislavsky's method of rehearsing a play in segments, so that the total effect was lost sight of; and when he pleaded that 'we have to do something to make the audience hear the words', Craig replied 'That's exactly why I propose to have such simple scenery, and why I'd like the movements to be so few and simple.'[1] In fact, Craig's screens were anything but simple; they had their own startling and memorable splendour, as well as their occasional collapses. A rich gold designated the luxury of the Court and the 'divinity' that 'hedged' the King. Among other pictures, Stanislavsky recalled the long, semi-circular corridor, its walls so high that their tops could not be seen,

> covered with gilt paper and lighted by the declining rays of projectors. In this long and narrow cage the black and suffering figure of Hamlet, silent and solitary, paced in melancholy, reflected in the golden mirror of the walls of the corridor. From beyond the corners he was watched by the golden King and his courtiers. Along the very same corridor the golden King passed with his golden Queen.[2]

Here and elsewhere the effect was simple as well as splendid, but the actors, divorced from the realism they had perfected, could not conceal their insecurity.

Konstantin Stanislavsky as Benedick in *Much Ado about Nothing* 1897

[1] For this and much of the foregoing see *Stanislavsky* David Hagarshack (1951)
[2] Stanislavsky *My Life in Art* (1924) p.515

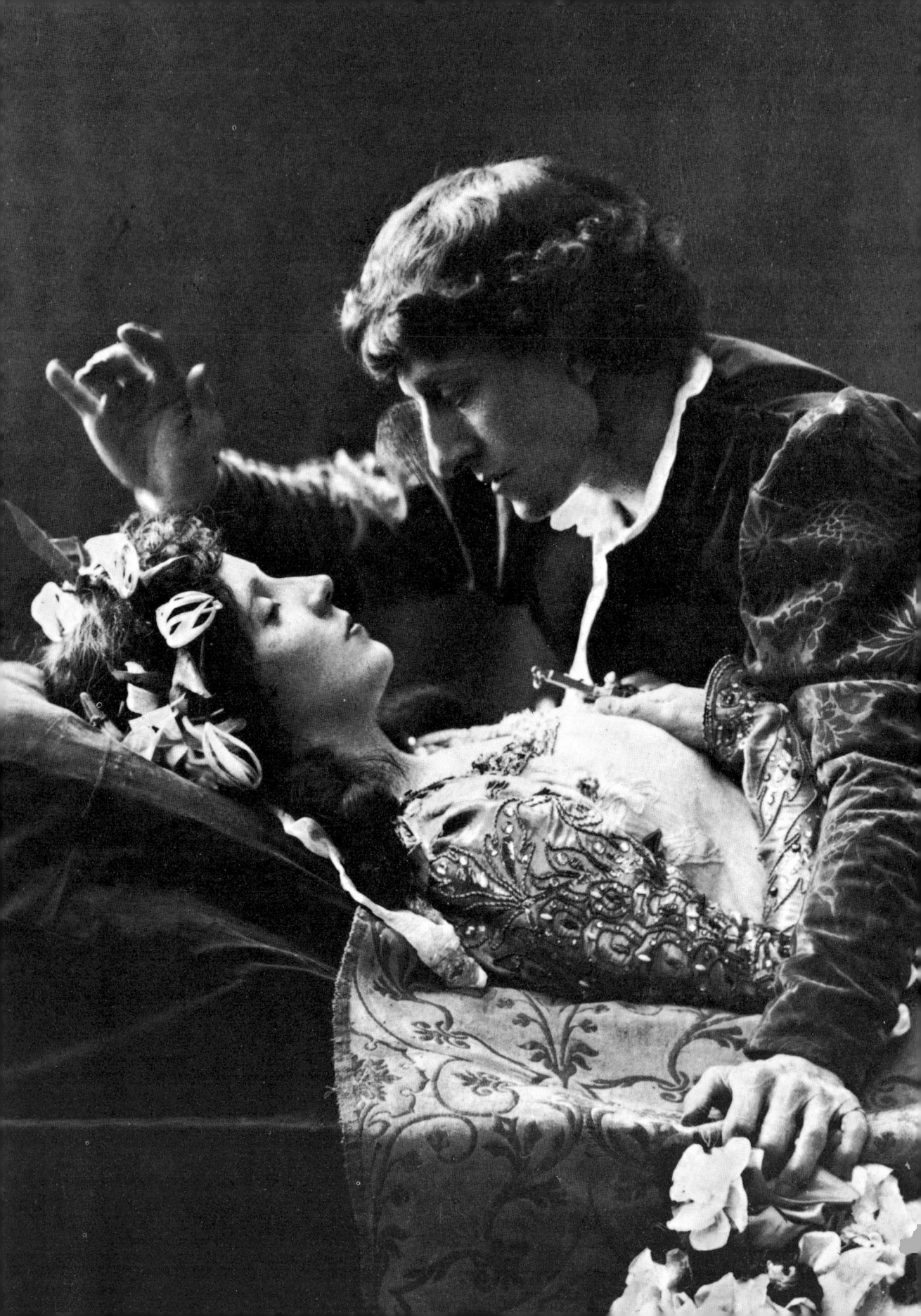

VII The Challengers

If Irving had disproved the managerial lament that 'Shakespeare spells ruin' – although he had come near to ruining himself in doing so – Augustin Daly (1839-99) was giving himself a long run for his money by giving Shakespeare a short run for his. He certainly spared no pains in making him presentable, and a good deal of plastic surgery went into the operation. In *The Two Gentlemen of Verona* Shakespeare makes it clear that Proteus lives with his father and Julia with hers. Daly had father, son, and putative daughter-in-law under the same roof. Again it is made clear that Valentine travels from Verona to Milan, followed by his faithful servant. But when the servant arrived in Milan it was equally evident that he was still in Verona. These discrepancies would not have mattered in a *décor simultané*, but the notion of a *décor simultané* had not yet occurred to commercial managements, although it had been taken for granted by the author of the play in question. Having thus confused the plot, Daly was ruthless in cutting the poetry, and Valentine was stripped of his lovely *aubade*.[1]

Johnston Forbes-Robertson as Romeo and Mrs Patrick Campbell as Juliet, Lyceum Theatre 1895

Nor did the scenery rival Lyceum standards. For 'a street in Verona', according to Bernard Shaw, the audience were served up with 'a Bath bun coloured operatic front cloth with about as much light in it as there is in a studio in Fitzjohn's Avenue in the middle of October'; and the elaborate set in which Julia first entered showed how far Mr Daly preferred 'the Marble Arch to the loggia of Orcagna'. Classical façades and pale green cypresses banished any suggestion of 'San Zeno and the tombs of the Scaligers'.[2] The iconoclast of the *Saturday Review* was left hankering for *Cavalleria Rusticana* at Covent Garden. Fond as he was of opera, his tastes normally lay elsewhere.

In *A Midsummer Night's Dream* the panoramic illusion of Theseus' barge on its way to Athens seemed to Shaw 'more absurd than anything that occurs in the tragedy of Pyramus and Thisbe'. Titania was shown, centre stage, in full limelight, where the rustics, gathered for their rehearsal, were supposed not to see her. Theseus was obliged to pick his way between the sleeping lovers, apparently unaware of their existence, although 'the four lions in Trafalgar Square' were 'not more conspicuous and unoverlookable'.[3] No wonder that others besides Bernard Shaw thought it time for Shakespeare production to submit to the laws of reason; which is as much to say that it was time it submitted to Shakespeare.

We have already noted the success of Johnston Forbes-Robertson (1853-1937) as Claudio in *Much Ado* and as Buckingham in *Henry VIII*. Of the latter Sir George Arthur, an inveterate and discriminating playgoer, was to write:

> For sheer beauty Forbes-Robertson's delivery of Buckingham's farewell speech remains something of a sacred memory. The impression, night after night, left on the audience whose eyes were riveted on the actor as they drank in the intonations of his matchless voice, was that one of the noble army of martyrs had already crossed the dark river and was speaking from an unseen world.[4]

In 1895, while Irving was away on an American tour, Forbes-Robertson took

[1] 'Who is Silvia . . .'
[2] *Our Theatres in the Nineties I* (1932) pp.172-3
[3] Ibid p.180
[4] Quoted in *The Tragic Actor* p.392

the Lyceum for a production of *Romeo and Juliet*. Here was the actor that Shaw was looking for, and as Romeo many other people were glad to have found him. He had youth of person, grace of movement, and a sovereign beauty of voice and feature. The voice was not only beautiful in itself, but it had been rigorously trained. Yet he never gave the impression of listening to it, because thought and feeling were always in command. He neither chanted – which had been the reproach levelled at Betterton, nor croaked – which was the reproach sometimes levelled at Irving. He had played Fenton with Phelps in *The Merry Wives*, and repaid the debt by painting him as Wolsey (*see* page 48). The core of Phelps's teaching was the perfect combination of melody and meaning in the spoken word. Limited, in a sense, as Forbes-Robertson's achievement proved to be, for want of the ambition to sustain it, his mastery of speech has become a legend of the English theatre.

It was undoubtedly a limitation that he was so conspicuously a gentleman. Irving could be just as gentlemanly – or as imperiously aristocratic – when he chose, but he realized that the behaviour of Shakespearian protagonists, whatever their pedigree, is not invariably gentlemanly. Shaw was no admirer of Irving's Romeo, but he missed in Forbes-Robertson the 'dim figure dragging a horrible burden down through the gloom "into the rotten jaws of death"'. In Forbes-Robertson's production they were far from rotten; the tomb of the Capulets was 'tidily kept, well lighted . . . quite like a new cathedral chapel'. Paris was laid out by Romeo 'as carefully as if he were folding up his best suit of clothes'. The hot blood was anything but stirring in the market-place, with the ladies of either party looking on as if the members of opposing football teams had forgotten the rules of the game, and Romeo challenging Tybalt with 'unconcealed repugnance'.[1] It was not thus that Forbes-Robertson, as Orlando in *As You Like It,* had wrestled with Charles.

The Juliet was Mrs Patrick Campbell (1865-1940). It seemed possible that the 'Second Mrs Tanqueray' might develop into a second Sarah Bernhardt. She would never have developed into a second Ellen Terry. As Juliet she had the southern temperament of which Forbes-Robertson had only the physical envelope. To dance 'like the daughter of Herodias' is hardly the right prelude to the almost liturgical duet with which Romeo and Juliet accompany those stately measures. Shaw wrote of this Juliet that 'there is not a touch of tragedy, not a throb of love or fear, temper instead of fear'.[2] One has the impression that Salome had wandered into the wrong play; obviously a woman who could be satisfied only by the head of John the Baptist knew nothing whatever about the serious business of love. Mrs Patrick Campbell was too sophisticated for Shakespeare, and, except for her Ophelia, always failed in it. But one sometimes dreams of what she might have done with Cleopatra.

So far, then, Forbes-Robertson's reputation and promise rested mainly on his Buckingham. But two years later Irving, with characteristic generosity, again put the Lyceum at his disposal, and on 11 September 1897 he appeared as Hamlet. Irving had also lent the scenery. Forbes-Robertson was forty-four, a little old for his début in the part, and the 'heyday in the blood' was tame. What he gave was

> The courtier's, soldier's, scholar's, eye, tongue, sword:
> The expectancy and rose of the fair state

illustrated by a natural method, shaped to classical proportions. Ears attuned to the slow motion then in vogue, complained that he spoke too quickly whereas he was in fact following Shaw's advice to Ellen Terry – on the word, and to the word, and with the word, but never between the words. What then did Shaw mean when he described Forbes-Robertson, as so many others described him, as a classical actor?

> He can present a dramatic hero as a man whose passions are those which have produced the philosophy, the poetry, the art and the stagecraft of the world, and not merely those which have produced its weddings, coroners' inquests, and executions. And that is just the kind of actor that Hamlet requires.[3]

Yet Shaw did not find Forbes-Robertson cold. The 'O what a rogue and slave' soliloquy, 'as passionate in its scorn of brute passion as the most bull-necked affirmation or sentimental dilution of it could be', was still given without violence – though one rather wonders how. Missing was 'the relentless parental tenacity and cunning with which Sir Henry nurses his own pet creations on Shakespearian food like a fox rearing its litter in the den of a lioness; but we get light, freedom, naturalness, credibility, and Shakespeare'.[4] Most surprisingly of all, they got Fortinbras, and even a fleeting glimpse of Reynaldo. It is worth noticing, however, that many of the qualities admired in Forbes-Robertson's Hamlet – the breeding, the thoughtfulness, the pictorial appeal – were also admired in Irving's. But with Irving the shadows were deeper, the lights more sudden, the passion more electric. Everything that Forbes-Robertson did well – the advice to the players, the conversation with the grave-diggers, the profession of friendship for Horatio – Irving had also done well. But the beauty of Forbes-Robertson's voice and diction, his total absence of mannerism, made the old part seem like a new thing. On the appearance of the Ghost he had a low, long-drawn intake of breath and faint, appalled whisper on 'Angels and ministers of grace defend us'; he murmured to himself the text of the *Murder of Gonzago*, except for Lucianus' crucial lines; showed considerable passion with Ophelia, and deep affection for Gertrude; and died upright on the throne with the crown upon his knees. The work of a classical actor, his Hamlet at once took its place among the classics of the English stage. Others have rivalled but not dislodged it. Sarah Bernhardt observed to James Agate that it was 'a jewel to be worn on the finger of the poet himself'.

The quality of his acting in *Hamlet*, and other classical parts, was described in a memorable passage by C. E. Montague:

> It is not in his art to trouble; rather to tranquillise; it soothes you like some Augustan architecture, with its just proportions, the ranged masses of its declamation, its expression of dependence on sound reason, lucidity, intellectual balance. Romantic acting, like other romantic art, is adventure, almost gambling; it comes off and it seems to have found new worlds, or lit on the floor of magic, or it fails and flops into grotesqueness. Classical acting like Forbes-Robertson's runs lesser risks; it may not take your breath away, or send a momentary wave of coldness across your face, or elicit whatever your special bodily signal may be of your mind's amazed and sudden surrender to some stroke of passionate genius. But there is one glory of the sun and another glory of the moon.[5]

Deduce Forbes-Robertson's Hamlet from that and you will not be far wrong; it differed from Irving's as the new cathedral of St Paul's differed from the old.

Forbes-Robertson was not, it seems, a passionless Othello, since there were

[1] *Our Theatres in the Nineties I* (1932) pp.200-2
[2] Ibid
[3] Ibid III p.201
[4] Ibid p.203
[5] *Dramatic Values* (1910)

Hamlet: the final scene, Lyceum Theatre 1897

moments when he terrified his own wife, Gertrude Elliott, who was playing Desdemona. William Winter thought it his best part, characterized as it was by a lofty chivalry, and maintained that not even Edwin Forrest had surpassed the anguish of 'By the world, I think my wife is honest and think she is not'. The performance, admired in the provinces, had become muted when it came to London, but this was a part in which the great Italians were rivalling each other, and Forbes-Robertson – with the voice that Shaw compared to the 'chalumeau register of the clarionet' – was no match for their emotional orchestrations. In *The Merchant of Venice*, his exit from the court seemed to imply that Shylock's death was imminent, and the lines in the fifth act suggesting that he lived on were omitted. Forbes-Robertson retired, only too willingly, from the stage at sixty-three. Even ten years later he would hardly have been too old to play Prospero with his daughter Jean as Ariel or Miranda. To have abdicated on the stage as well as from it – what an *abschied* that would have been! For although the 'magic' of Forbes-Robertson was anything but 'rough', it had worked its spell. James Agate quoted him as an example of 'the great actor's power to sweep away chairs and tables'; and Agate had heard the cheers at midnight when Irving came to Manchester.

2

Theatrically speaking, the twentieth century opened with Herbert Beerbohm Tree's production of *A Midsummer Night's Dream* at the newly-built His, or Her, Majesty's, according to the reign. Tree had moved from the Haymarket where extensive wicker-work had inadequately padded his lean figure and lush personality as Falstaff in *Henry IV, Part One*. Later, as Falstaff in *The Merry Wives,* he managed to get through the whole play before a Boston audience without raising a single laugh. He was forty-six years old and already an established actor-manager. His supper parties had emulated Irving's *convivia* in the Beef Steak room at the Lyceum, and his productions had emulated, not very tastefully, its scenic splendours. He never knew when to leave things out, even within a misguided convention, and the idea of leaving Shakespeare alone would not have entered his head. He represented, with prodigality and a certain perverse imagination, the heavy materialism of the time. He was an aesthete, not an intellectual. Where Irving was happy with Burne-Jones and the Pre-Raphaelites, Tree would have leaped upon Aubrey Beardsley if he thought he could risk *Salome* in his repertoire. One is only surprised that he funked it.

In *A Midsummer Night's Dream* live rabbits scampered across the stage, and a female Oberon (Julia Neilson) sang 'I know a bank whereon the wild thyme grows'. For *Twelfth Night* Hawes Craven copied Olivia's garden from a picture in *Country Life* – terraces, topiary, and all. There was a splendid flight of steps down which Malvolio – always followed by four miniature Malvolios, under-stewards so to speak – elected to fall, and upon which he proceeded to sit surveying the formal landscape. Shakespeare often had to wait a long time during these parentheses. Richard II was probably the best of Tree's parts, for here the vein of self-pity – the artist contemplating his own misfortunes – suited his self-consciousness. 'For God's sake let us sit upon the ground' was an open invitation to pathos; yet all Bernard Shaw could remember of the scene was a note passed to him in the stalls by a well known elocutionist. 'If you will rise and move a resolution, I will second it.' Tree was putting in a great deal that Shake-speare had left out, and omitting a great deal that he had put in. You will look in vain for a dog among the *dramatis personae* of the play; yet the dog assisted one of Tree's most effective *coups de théâtre* when he turned from Richard and licked the hand of Bolingbroke. Exit Richard with a sob. The introduction of horses on the stage is even more inconvenient, but Tree could not forego the great white horse that carried him through the jeering crowd, nor the look he gave them. 'No one since Chaliapine' wrote Shaw, had 'done so much by a single look and an appearance for an instant on horseback.' If Shakespeare described something, Tree did it.

In 1906, the jubilee year of Ellen Terry's first appearance on the stage as Mamillius in Charles Kean's production of *The Winter's Tale*, Tree presented her as Hermione in the same play. She traced the cycle of life, death, and resurrection with consummate art; Ellen Terry always made it easy to believe in the resurrection of the flesh. Bohemia was irrigated by a babbling brook, in which Autolycus bathed his hands to the accompaniment of 'When daffodils begin to peer', and – horses being out of place in these humbler surroundings –

Herbert Beerbohm Tree as Shylock,
His Majesty's Theatre 1908

the Clown brought on a donkey. *Antony and Cleopatra* followed in the same year. Opening with a dissolving Sphinx, it passed immediately to Rome and the fourth scene of the first act; then to Alexandria and the two lovers entering to 'If it be love indeed, tell me how much'. When they had gone out Enobarbus was handed the comment with which the play properly begins, 'Nay, but this dotage of our general's o'erflows the measure'. Tree, alert as ever to seize an opportunity which Shakespeare had missed, picked on a single reference to Cleopatra's appearance as the goddess Isis. This was elaborated into a *tableau vivant* of the 'serpent of old Nile', robed and crowned in silver, walking in procession through the streets of Alexandria among the screaming populace. The Sphinx returned in the middle of the play, looming out of the darkness 'while a thrumming, vibrating, aromatic kind of music fell on our ears to suggest the maddened luxury of the East, and the exasperating, enigmatic attraction of the queen'.[1] In *The Merchant of Venice* Tree was not content to follow Irving's business, and knock once, or twice, on the door of Shylock's house. He 'knocked again and again, thrust open the door – not locked after all – cried "Jessica", entered the house, raged round its rooms (visible through lattice-work and open windows), emerged, still crying hoarsely, saw a gondola pass on the horizon, flung himself to the ground in a paroxysm, rent his garments, and poured ashes upon his head'.[2] This was neither comical-tragical nor tragical-comical, but the hysteria of actor-managerial hubris.

Tree's virtuosity in make-up and his inventiveness in scenic accessory had almost unlimited scope in *The Tempest*. The ship foundered as surely as Charles Kean's, and when it set out, fully rigged, on its homeward voyage, Caliban, no longer chewing at his raw fish, watched it disappear over the horizon's rim. One transposition Tree could not resist. The play ended with an abridgement of 'Ye elves of hills', but when the curtain went up for the call, Caliban was seen alone on his rock. Not yet sueing to the gods for grace, his arms were stretched out, hopelessly, towards the vanishing ship. It had not occurred to Tree that the one person whose back he would have contemplated with relief was Prospero.

Macbeth opened with the Witches flying on wires – for which Tree had surer textual warrant than he probably suspected; Duncan was accompanied to his last night's sleep to the music of a harp; and before the play could be proceeded with, the Witches must suddenly reappear in the middle of the castle, cackling their overture to that 'night's business'. Strange, indeed, that such a conjuror of theatrical effect should not have seen the value, at that moment of all others, of silence and an empty stage. In the sleep-walking scene Lady Macbeth descended a steep staircase without benefit of hand-rail. Tree did, it is true, restore the murder of Lady Macduff; but probably the only one of his Shakespeare productions to which we should now give qualified approval was his *Henry VIII*. It was cut heavily, ending with the coronation of Anne Boleyn, and still ran for four hours. The play suited Tree's method, and the part of Wolsey his magnificence. Entering under a canopy, with a suite of choristers and the *cappa magna* trailing behind him, he was not only the prelate but the parvenu. The last scene with Cromwell was the downfall of a statesman, where Irving had hinted at a saint *manqué*. Violet Vanbrugh evidently came from beyond the Pyrenees, born to a throne – and tragedy. Arthur Bourchier, bluff and brutal, was Henry to the life. It was not until many years later that Donald Sinden indicated a different Henry, sensitive below the self-assertion, clutching the infant Elizabeth in his arms as he wondered why God had not yet given him a son.

As an actor Tree was an empiricist, like Irving, but he was also an improviser. He trusted to the most fallible of all theatrical guides – the inspiration of the moment. He had never been trained; he had not even trained himself; but in founding the Royal Academy of Dramatic Art he realized that training might be good for other people. Desmond McArthy put a finger on his qualities and his limitations:

Tree possessed the power of conceiving character in a very high degree. . . . But an actor must, of course, also possess the faculty of representing the characters he understands. . . . In the case of Herbert Tree his power of understanding character was far wider than his power of representing it; and his extraordinary skill in making up, in which he was unmatched, often tempted him to play characters which were outside his temperamental and physical range. He had not the animal vigour which is necessary to great excellence in violent tragedy or in robust comedy. He could make himself look like Falstaff; he understood and revelled in the character of Falstaff; but his performance lacked fundamental force. Hence the contradiction in his acting: his performance as a whole often fell short of high excellence, yet these same impersonations were lit by insight and masterly strokes of interpretation, which made the spectator feel that he was watching the most imaginative of living actors.[3]

Herbert Beerbohm Tree as Macbeth and Violet Vanbrugh as Lady Macbeth, His Majesty's Theatre 1911

[1] Desmond MacCarthy *Theatre* (1954) p.51
[2] J. C. Trewin *Shakespeare on the English Stage 1900-1964* p.41
[3] Max Beerbohm *Herbert Beerbohm Tree* (1920) pp.221-2

Herbert Beerbohm Tree's *Henry VIII*,
His Majesty's Theatre 1910

Tree's productions of Shakespeare never achieved the dignity of Irving's. They
were magnificent; they were munificent; but they were not Shakespeare.

  Others were also in the field. Only a month after Tree sent his rabbits across
the stage in *A Midsummer Night's Dream*, Frank Benson brought his troopers to
the Lyceum, where he had once appeared as Paris. Benson also was self-
trained, but he had the gift of training other people. Their names resound like
a saga of the best Shakespearian acting over the next forty years: Henry Ainley,
Oscar Asche, Matheson Lang, Baliol Holloway, and Dorothy Green were
notable among them. They trudged the provinces, and for a few weeks in
spring descended on Stratford where, for many years, Benson was the genius of
the Festival. J. C. Trewin has chronicled their happy vagabondage.[1] They
broke no new ground, although they mobilized many new audiences. For a
year the young William Poel was Benson's stage-manager and learnt a great
deal from his character and policy, though less from his productions.

> The Benson Worthies lived in the open air. The leader himself of this happy band of
> Arcadians was a typical Greek in nobility of thought, in seriousness of purpose, in
> physical fitness and energy, a worthy model for the chisel of a Phidias. At the age of
> twenty-three, as a young graduate fresh from college,[2] his costume consisted of a
> flannel shirt, a grey pea-jacket, cricketing trousers, no cap and a red necktie. That
> necktie proclaimed his political opinions. He was a disciple of William Morris. . . .
> It was in the early eighties that I first heard spoken by Benson those memorable
> words of Morris, 'Commercialism and competition have sown the wind recklessly,
> and must reap the whirlwind'.[3]

  Arthur Machen, who had trebled the rôles of Duncan, the Porter and the
Physician in *Macbeth*, describes how the mythical personage of 'Lord Essex'
represented several members of the nobility in the Historical plays. He goes on
to recall the ambience of that unique *camaraderie*.

[1] *Benson and the Bensonians* (1960)
[2] Oxford
[3] *William Poel and the Elizabethan Revival*
(1954) p.60
[4] *Theatre Arts Monthly* (September 1931)
[5] *Dramatic Values* (1910)

And some, thinking of those old days, hear again the old music sounding from the orchestra – King Lear's march, let us say, as Christopher Wilson, the Musical Director of those days, wrote it, and the hot dressing-room piled heavy with suits of armour, with barbaric costumes, returns; and the steps hurry in and out of those whose steps are still and silent now forever, and young men become old and old men young in a few minutes; and the strange distant rumour of the stage sounds as the door opens and shuts.[4]

It was consonant with a stained-glass quality in Benson's acting that he should have the church bells ringing for the Feast of Crispian, while exceedingly respectable *vivandières* dallied with the French on the eve of Agincourt. As Hamlet, for which he was physically the *beau idéal,* A. B. Walkley described him as '*aigre-doux*' – which is exactly what Hamlet should be. As Richard III he could frighten as well as fascinate, and of his Richard II – where he borrowed, metaphorically, Tree's faithless hound from His Majesty's – Montague has left an illuminating picture: 'In him every other feeling is mastered, except at a few passing moments, by a passion of interest in the exercise of his gift of exquisite responsiveness to the appeal made to his artistic sensibility by whatever life throws for the moment in his way'.[5] Benson, with no one to look after him while he was so usefully looking after other people, developed some curious vocal mannerisms, and his productions – tailored to repertory and to changing trains at Crewe on Sunday mornings – were too unspectacular for metropolitan

Herbert Beerbohm Tree's
Julius Caesar, His Majesty's Theatre
1898

Martin Harvey's *Hamlet*, Lyric Theatre 1905

tastes. But they were only provincial in the sense that they primarily served the provinces. He was not quite a great actor, but he was the master of a great school – or, as we might turn the compliment to please him, the Captain of a great Eleven.

Oscar Asche was the bull-necked, *basso profundo* of Benson's team, leaving it to skipper his own side with *As You Like It* in 1907 at His Majesty's, while Tree was away, and *The Merry Wives of Windsor* at the Garrick in 1911. In *As You Like It*, Mr Trewin records for us, the stage was strewn with 'a collection of moss-grown logs, two thousand pots of fern, large clumps of bamboo, and leaves by the cartload from the previous autumn'. In one of his big sets 'the cast walked through ferns, two feet high in places, that had to be renewed weekly'.[1] In *The Merry Wives* street and field were covered four inches deep in salt, for Asche had had the intelligence to see that this was a winter play, though the fires burned merrily in the hearths. 'Everyone wore mufflers and gloves or mittens; every nose was red with cold.'[2] The production did not have the stellar casting of Tree's, with Madge Kendal and Ellen Terry, but it may well have been closer to Shakespeare.

Tree, to his credit, had never been afraid to surround himself with the best actors available. Of these Lewis Waller, with his panache, was more than the matinée idol of the hour. His Henry V spoke for England with the confidence of 'Land of Hope and Glory' – striding down stage in the crescendo of the Crispin speech, and speaking the last lines with his back to the audience, and the more than 'two or three most ragged foils' facing him in a semi-circle. Heraldic in a rougher vein was his Hotspur, which he played with Louis

Calvert – the finest Falstaff of them all. Martin Harvey, a Lyceum graduate of long standing, struck out on his own and, like Benson, bestrode the provinces more successfully than the West End. Authority sat on his features, though not on his figure; inches are important for Petruchio, but they matter less for Richard III. He was a Maeterlinckian actor, suggesting Debussy or Ravel in the way that Waller suggested Elgar. The ineffable, with a hint of the infernal, gave distinction to his Hamlet, and his production owed a good deal to a talk with Reinhardt. Although in some respects he had taken over the *mystique* of the Lyceum, and the kind of theatre it stood for, he was more receptive than most actors of his standing to those who were already challenging the current orthodoxies of Shakespeare production. So, oddly enough, was Herbert Beerbohm Tree; he walked with his head in the air, but his ear pretty close to the ground.

H. B. and Laurence Irving (1870-1919, 1871-1914) were rather more than impressive shadows of a mighty substance. It was significant that friends addressed the father as 'Henry', and the son as 'Harry'. H. B. suffered, of course, from a close physical resemblance, with the daimon left out of the picture – very much as Millais left it out in his portrait of the greater Irving at the Garrick Club. H.B. played Hamlet first in 1895, then in London ten years later. A. B. Walkley found him too cerebral in 1905, 'a little didactic, almost donnish; . . . impressive rather than charming, perhaps almost harsh after the conspicuously charming Hamlet of Forbes-Robertson',[3] but he softened a good deal in subsequent revivals. Older playgoers compared him to Fechter. Two innovations may be noted; as a prelude to 'To be or not to be':

Frank Benson as Richard II, Lyceum Theatre 1900

> He entered from the back of the stage reading a book, which he carried in his hand, and was so wrapped in what he was doing that he walked into the table in the centre of the stage. He then seated himself sideways on the table, swinging his leg, and held his hand out over a brazier which contained a live coal, still absorbed in the book. After warming and withdrawing his hand two or three times, he became more absorbed in the book, and withdrew his hand very hurriedly from the brazier, having been brought to a sense of his surroundings evidently by burning his hand. He then sighed, and resting the book on his knee, began the soliloquy.[4]

Wishing in the closet scene to contrive appropriate darkness for the entrance of the Ghost, he banged his uncle's portrait on the table, thus extinguishing the light.

Laurence had the more original talent. He resembled his father very little, except that you felt the daimon stirring under those dark brows. He must have had much of Irving's flair for fantastic comedy, since his Justice Shallow became legend, a 'figure of greedy, timid, boastful, leering, crackling dotage . . . embroidered into a kind of brilliant and humorous exposition of the whole psychology of senility'; inferring 'a human quality or a deficiency from the rhythm of a sentence or the idle repetition of a word'; and piecing out 'that grotesque and awful image of a weak mind's and soul's decay from the broken fragments of drivelling reminiscence in the text'.[5] Laurence had his own unconventional idea of Hamlet as a 'very young man and very spoilt child',[6] and he also had the wit to put the play into Elizabethan dress. Afterwards he played Iago with Tree; 'no honest, burly ensign, but a limber devil, a word-player, a snapper-up of unconsidered trifles . . . the essence of cold, intellectualised malignity.'[7] Some criticized the interpretation, while admiring the

[1] Ibid pp.60-1
[2] Arthur Barker *The English Dramatic Critics* (1932)
[3] *Pastiche and Prejudice* (1921) p.169
[4] Austin Brereton 'H.B.' and Laurence Irving (1922) pp.123-4
[5] *The Manchester Guardian* (probably C. E. Montague), quoted by Brereton Ibid pp.177-8
[6] Ibid p.189
[7] *The Outlook* Ibid p.191

Laurence Irving as Iago, His Majesty's Theatre 1912

Opposite: Martin Harvey as Richard III 1910

performance. A tendency to turn the blank verse into prose was noted, and this suggests that Laurence Irving would have found his natural place where Shaw had wished to lure his father – in the realistic theatre of ideas which had yet to win its way to popularity. But all that promise went down into the Atlantic with the *Empress of Ireland*, early in the summer of 1914.

3

The challenge had been going on quietly for some time, although it resounded in the trumpet blasts of Bernard Shaw. We cannot do better than take it up from the day in 1899, when William Poel rang the bell of Harley Granville-Barker's flat in York Buildings. Poel was then in his forty-eighth year, still a lean and ardent figure possessed with a mission that he pursued until his death in 1934. It has been described as 'Elizabethan Methodism'. He believed that only by rediscovering and, as far as possible, reproducing the conditions of the Elizabethan stage, with its unlocalized platform and swift, musical speech, could Shakespeare and other classics be properly performed. Salvini was the example that Poel held out to everyone who worked with him. His approach to acting, like Shaw's was essentially musical, and he found Lyceum Shakespeare sadly out of tune. If you got the 'tunes' right, and observed certain principles of deportment, the rest would look after itself. It did not always do so.

With a sovereign contempt for the land of milk and honey where Beerbohm Tree pastured his horses, dogs, and rabbits, Poel was perfectly content to work in the wilderness. Indeed he was the nearest approach to John the Baptist that any theatre has either ignored, or followed with little idea of who was leading it or where it was being led. His prophetic intransigence matched, and occasionally belied, his Pre-Raphaelite appearance, for in these early days he seemed like a firebrand to the half-trained semi-amateurs whom he flayed into an imitation of his tunes. Since his demonstration of these was highly idiosyncratic, whatever good reason may have been behind it, imitations of them were even more peculiar. Poel was a rationalist on top and a mystic underneath, and it was not always easy to tell with which one was dealing.

He had begun in 1887 as instructor to the Shakespeare Reading Society gathering his disciples round him to read the plays in such places as University College, Gower Street, the London Institution, the Royal Academy of Music and St Mark's Vestry room in Battersea, the last of which could not be suspected of a proscenium, and all of which forbade the usual notion of entertainment Gradually his performers were allowed to put on costumes and at last, in 1892 to give a production of *The Two Gentlemen of Verona* in the open air. Already, in 1890, Bernard Shaw had attended a recital of *Much Ado about Nothing*, in which a gentleman called Samuel Johnson – one is delighted to learn – read the part of Dogberry. 'From these simple recitals' Shaw wrote in *The Star* 'without cuts, waits, or scenery, and therefore without those departures from the conditions contemplated by the poet which are inevitable in a modern theatre I learn a good deal about the plays which I could learn in no other way. What i more, I enjoy myself.' Out of these recitals grew the Elizabethan Stage Society which was Poel's chief title to fame.

In the autumn of 1893 Poel converted the interior of the Royalty Theatre into as close a likeness of the old Fortune Playhouse as was possible in a roofed building. The play was *Measure for Measure* in which he played Angelo

himself. He insisted that Isabella, not yet being professed in the religious life, should not be dressed as a nun, and argued convincingly that, if she had been, the Duke would never have sought her in marriage. He also argued that Angelo must not be presented as a reprobate, for, after all, he had won and retained the affection of Mariana. What he required was 'a charming Angelo, a boisterous Lucio, a passionate Isabel', insisting that the Duke was the centre of the play. 'A man of about forty, alert, full of resource and energy, adored by all for his easy-going and kindly ways; always helpful, never willing to hurt, and far too witty and wise for anyone to be dull in his company.' It was going a little far to suggest that 'Be absolute for death' should be given 'with ease and spirit, for the Duke here ironically proclaims the triumph of death over life, laughing to himself while he says the words, for he is not a religious man in the conventional sense'. Neither was William Poel, and for that reason he was able to keep the play within the bounds of tragi-comedy.

Although Poel stood before the world as an apostle of textual integrity, the reputation was not altogether deserved. He cut drastically, but to spare blushes or boredom, not to save time. His excisions from *Measure for Measure* were rather like depriving Marion Bloom[1] of her last soliloquy. If he had occasionally frequented a public house, and chosen the right one, he could have heard people talk like Lucio and Mistress Overdone any evening of his life. But the conversation at the Emerson Club ran on different lines.

The Elizabethan Stage Society was constituted in 1894, and in the following year two performances of *Twelfth Night* were given, the first in Burlington Hall, Savile Row, the second in St George's Hall. The play was performed with a single interval of ten minutes. Arnold Dolmetsch supervised the music, and all the members of Olivia's household were dressed in black. Shaw wrote that 'nobody can pretend that the Society had any advantage over Mr Daly or Sir Henry Irving in the histrionic talent at its disposal. But what it had went so much further under the Elizabethan conditions that everyone present took the acting to be much better than it really was'.[2] Nevertheless here Poel encountered the most formidable critic of his work. William Archer was no reactionary. The translator of Ibsen, though he admired Irving in certain parts, was anything but a Lyceum devotee. He understood, and in a measure approved, what Poel was getting at, but he maintained that Poel's perversity defeated his own aims. He described the *Twelfth Night*, advertised as 'Acted after the manner of the sixteenth century', as in fact 'staged (more or less) after the manner of the sixteenth century and acted after the manner of the Nineteenth Century Amateur'. He also reproached Poel with the omission of 250 lines, which were neither improper nor obscure.

In a subsequent production, two years later, most of them were restored; and the hall of the Middle Temple reproduced many of the features of an early Jacobean performance of *Twelfth Night* at the Blackfriars. Orsino's household were dressed in two shades of crimson, and Olivia, as before, in black. Halberdiers stood at the side of the stage throughout, as well as on the stage itself and in the corridors outside the Hall. The Dolmetsch ensemble again contributed the music on an Italian virginal of 1550, a treble and a bass viol, and a lute made in Venice about 1560. Poel orchestrated the voices of his cast as follows: Viola (Mezzo Soprano), Olivia (Contralto), Sebastian (Alto), Antonio (Basso Profundo), Sir Toby (Bass), Sir Andrew (Falsetto), Malvolio (Baritone), Maria (High Soprano), Orsino (Tenor), Clown (Tenor). He maintained that

Opposite: H. B. Irving as Hamlet

[1] James Joyce's *Ulysses*
[2] *Our Theatres in the Nineties* (1932) vol. I, pp.188-91

neither Olivia nor Orsino were more than seventeen, and that Viola and
Sebastian were no more than sixteen, years old. The Hall of Grays Inn was
equally suitable for *The Comedy of Errors*, which was given to celebrate the
tercentenary of an Elizabethan performance of the play in the same place. The
costume of the Dromios reproduced exactly the dress and equipment of an
Elizabethan serving-man; the Antipholi were costumed in the Dutch fashion of
the period; and the Halberdiers in attendance were played as servants of Gray's
Inn, wearing the Griffin on their sleeves. The play was given without an interval
and praised by Shaw as 'a delectable entertainment which defies all description
by the pen'.[1] Poel's visual sense was as strong as Irving's or Tree's, and far more
selective. The artist Byam Shaw expressed the wish 'that others would follow
your notable example and allow us to listen to Shakespeare instead of looking at
what Mr So-and-So thinks is like a sunset or a cherry-tree'.[2]

Nowhere did Poel challenge Irving more defiantly than in restoring Burbage's
red wig to Shylock. If Shakespeare had intended Shylock to be a tragic figure –
or so Poel argued – he would never have written his fifth act. Only if Shylock
left the trial scene in a rage, would the audience be interested in the comedy of
the rings. But Shakespeare makes it clear that Shylock does nothing of the sort.
'I pray you give me leave to go from hence; I am not well.' In avoiding Heine's
view that Antonio was unworthy to tie Shylock's shoelaces, Poel was blind to
Shakespeare's power of seeing all round a situation or a character, of writing on
more than one level, of giving to his comedies the qualities of chequered
sunshine. He could not see that *The Merchant of Venice*, in John Palmer's
valuable definition, is 'a comedy in which ridicule does not exclude compassion,
in which sympathy and detachment are reconciled in the irony which is
necessarily achieved by the comic spirit in a serene presentation of things as they
are'. Poel's Shylock was deficient alike in dignity and pathos; yet for such
experienced Shakespearians as George Wyndham and Edward Dowden 'this
was the Jew that Shakespeare drew'. Minor innovations were the introduction
of a priest and four acolytes while Portia's suitors were making their choice – the
religious character of Portia's obligation to respect her father's will being thus
emphasized – and of a hermit standing by. However, in a play so packed with
improbabilities, one hermit more or less in a country house was unlikely to have
troubled the spectators. This was the kind of liberty that Tree would have taken;
and there was more than a grain of truth in Archer's criticism that Poel was 'a
non-scenic Beerbohm Tree'.

So we are brought to that crucial morning in the autumn of 1899 when Poel
called on Granville-Barker at an hour which may well have found Barker less
wide awake than usual. Barker was twenty-two years old, and quite unknown.
Like Poel himself, he was that rather rare person – an intellectual in theatreland.
We do not know whether Poel had seen him act, but he had heard of him, and
thought that with his graceful physique, sensitive features, and light, flexible
voice he might do well as Richard II. Barker was to write to him many years
later:[3] 'Such light as has shone for me on W.S. dates from an earlier day on
which you came to see me and shook all my previous convictions by showing me
how you wanted the first lines of *Richard II* spoken.' He must also have
lamented the thirty-seven lines of priceless introspection at Pomfret, which were
senselessly cut out. Poel's genius shone in fitful flashes; Barker's brain threw an
equal, electric gleam. They were each to go their own way – wilful in the case of
Poel, steady but less persevering in the case of Barker, whose *Prefaces* are in fact

William Poel's *Comedy of Errors*, Grays Inn Hall 1895

lucid exposition of Poel's principles. Barker's mind was more balanced and flexible; his grasp on theory was not stiffened or distorted by fanaticism. Poel, essentially a Victorian, was really closer to Irving, his antagonist, than Barker, his disciple, was to him. Barker talked the language of the twentieth century, and his ideas were correspondingly more accessible to it. It was curious, and also characteristic, that Poel himself failed to appreciate the *Prefaces*. Where a production was afoot, there was steel in both these men. The rehearsals for *Richard II* took place in an empty house, and on one occasion Poel locked his actors in one of the rooms, declaring that he would keep them there all night until they had mastered his inflections. If Barker had written a *Preface* to *Richard II*, we might have had a clearer picture of what Poel's production was like. We know that the Duchess of Gloucester was dressed as a nun from Barking Abbey, as represented on her brass at Westminster; and in the third act Poel had historical warrant for the appearance of Richard as a friar.

Granville-Barker was not the man to content himself with an obscure platform, or even with a platform stage – a dream of Poel's that was still a long way from realization. He was determined to invade the theatre, as the theatre was commonly understood. In April 1904 he directed a production of *The Two Gentlemen of Verona* at the Court Theatre in Sloane Square, which left A. B. Walkley 'under so strong a charm that I almost told the cabman, "To Mantua –

[1] Ibid
[2] Letter to William Poel (8 June 1896)
[3] (14 January 1930)

by sea"'. Six years later Beerbohm Tree, who had an impresario's nose for novelty, invited Poel to present the same play during a Shakespeare Festival at His Majesty's. This was to ask the wolf to step into the sheepfold. For the first time an 'apron' was built out over the orchestra pit of a theatre which had always guarded the conventions, and front lighting was installed in the balconies. Both were retained for Tree's *Henry VIII* in 1912; it was the thin edge of the Elizabethan wedge, and no one has since dislodged it. Walkley described the production as 'an entertainment of absorbing interest. The literary quality of the play, the verve of its dialogue, the lyric beauty of many of its passages came out with unusual freshness and clear-cut relief'. He was reminded of some 'trifle of de Musset', some '*marivaudage* of Marivaux', or the 'fervour of Cyrano de Bergerac serenading his *précieuse*'.[1]

Yet here Poel had indulged one of his most disconcerting perversities – that of putting women in men's parts – and one for which he could claim no Elizabethan precedent. Bridges-Adams, his assistant stage manager, discovered him one morning wrapped in a grey muffler, nibbling at a biscuit and sipping a glass of milk. In front of him a lady shimmering with sequins, no longer in her first youth, was standing in an attitude of visible distress. Poel's voice was raised in querulous criticism. 'I am disappointed, very disappointed indeed. Of all Shakespeare's heroes Valentine is one of the most romantic, one of the most virile. I have chosen you out of all London for this part, but so far you have shown me no virility whatsoever.' When people dismissed Poel as a visionary crank, it was not always easy to gainsay them. Most of his productions had a lunatic fringe, and some of them a lunatic foreground.

In the following year (1909) he produced *Macbeth* for six performances at the Fulham Theatre. He had seen it, rightly, as an Elizabethan tragedy where the blood-guiltiness of Holyrood and Kirk o'Fields darkens the corridors of Dunsinane. For Lady Macbeth he took his cue from what Mrs Siddons had conceived and Ellen Terry tried to execute: 'fair, feminine, nay, perhaps even fragile'; the amoralism of the Renaissance contrasted with Macbeth's awareness of personal responsibility, which Poel held to be the gift of the Reformation. Lillah McArthy, one of the two actresses alternating in the part, described his tigerish energy at rehearsal, as his face grew taut with the intensity of the truth he was trying to convey, and then relaxed into the most disarming of smiles. He had imagined Lady Macbeth down to the smallest detail of her appearance and make-up; bright red hair and pink complexion; a clear and carmined mouth; white hands and neck tinted with a pale blue; moving with a slight swing, head erect, straightened back, and squared shoulders. She should suggest a woman of about thirty-five.

There were two notable innovations. At the opening of the sleep-walking scene Lady Macbeth was shown at her dressing-table, mechanically playing with her brushes and comb and going through the motions of doing her hair. Later she rose and began to walk about, moving gradually into the rhythm of somnambulism. In the banquet scene Poel argued that since the second apparition of Banquo's ghost is evidently more terrifying than the first – 'take any shape but *that*' – and since it is not described as '*re*-entering', it *might* not have been the ghost of Banquo at all. 'Can such *things* be?' – 'When now I think you can behold such *sights* . . .' – did the plural tense indicate that there had in fact been two separate apparitions? And was the second, and more frightening, the ghost of Duncan? Such reasoning was plausible, though not conclusive; but so produced, the effect was doubly telling. Poel took the Witches from Reginald Scot's *Discoveries of Witchcraft*, which had certainly been Shakespeare's source, bringing on Hecate slap on the top of Macbeth's 'We are yet but young in deed', and surrounding her in the cauldron scene with three attendants, all four being dressed in masque costumes. The effect of retaining Lady Macduff was illustrated by a letter from Bernard Shaw: 'I never before had realized with absolute certainty that Macbeth was a doomed man if he ever let Macduff catch him.'[2]

Poel's last wrestle with Shakespeare before the outbreak of war in 1914 was *Troilus and Cressida* in December 1912. This again he pulled back from the period of its subject to the century of its birth. The Greeks were dressed as Elizabethan soldiers smoking the tobacco which Raleigh had brought back from Virginia, the long pipes rising and falling with the argument at Agamemnon's GHQ. The Trojans wore masque costumes of the period, thus emphasizing the sophistication of a society which thought Helen worth a war. This was further underlined by a Cressida in her late twenties – a plausible 'daughter of the game'. For subsequent performances in the Memorial Theatre at Stratford-upon-Avon, Thersites, conceived as the camp jester and speaking with a Scots accent, was unaccountably played by a woman – but so convincingly that when Israel Zangwill remarked to his neighbour in the stalls: 'How good that man is who is playing Thersites!' he got the reply that the man in question was his neighbour's wife.

Troilus and Cressida is a long play, and can bear cutting. But Poel's surgery was breath-bereaving. The five lines of Cressida beginning 'When water drops have worn the stones of Troy' were left out, and Ulysses' great speech to Achilles was ruthlessly truncated and senselessly transposed. Troilus' adieu to Cressida was similarly mutilated. 'He fumbles up into a loose adieu' is of the deep Shakespearian essence, a line that very few other poets could have written. But Poel's 'Elizabethan Methodism' did not give him an ear for the melodic line of a speech. Moreover he excised completely Troilus' frenzied challenge to the Greeks, which expresses all the Trojan despair at the death of Hector. No doubt this jarred against Poel's inveterate pacifism. But in the name of what principle did he censure Irving for cutting Shakespeare when he himself took such liberties with the text, stripping one of the least poetical of the plays of such little poetry as it contained?

The production will always be remembered for its Cressida. On the fly-leaf of Poel's prompt book a name now famous was scribbled in hardly legible pencil: 'Miss Edith Evans'. She was then a milliner – but Poel had a nose for the right amateur. After the performance the young Bridges-Adams wrote to him: 'I wish I knew how you contrived to teach an amateur to give such a perfect and such a classic performance: it seemed to create Cressida once and for all for this generation.'[3] We owe this to William Poel, if nothing else, that the greatest English comédienne of the twentieth century finally gave up her hats.

4

A third challenger had entered the lists. In 1903 Ellen Terry, having now left the Lyceum, took the Imperial Theatre where her son, Gordon Craig, directed a production of *Much Ado about Nothing*. In spite of Ellen Terry's Beatrice, it was too audacious in its simplifications to compete successfully with the scenic

[1] *The Times* (21 April 1910)
[2] Letter to William Poel
[3] R. Speaight *William Poel and the Elizabethan Revival* (1954) p.199. See also for much else in the foregoing.

Design by Edward Gordon Craig for
Hamlet 1907

clutter at His Majesty's. The church was indicated by a broadening light
throwing its beams on a huge, multi-coloured cross, and the other scenes by
curtains with pillars painted on their long folds, and by elaborate wickerwork
for Leonato's garden. Successful or not, it is melancholy to record that this was
the only production of Shakespeare that Gordon Craig ever directed in his
native country. The theatre, like politics, is the 'art of the possible', and Craig's
visual imagination soared far above its practicalities. He prepared for Beerbohm
Tree a series of designs for *Macbeth* which met the objection by Joseph Harker
that 'if the scenery were made to the scale of the models, it would have risen
through the roof of His Majesty's and overtopped the Carlton Hotel'. Craig

[1] Introduction to acting edition of
A Midsummer Night's Dream (1914)

brought an action against Tree for the destruction of the models – which was settled out of court – and wrote off the affair as 'a solemn farce'. Yet the loss of Gordon Craig to the English theatre is a solemn thought rather than a solemn farce. The designs he has left us make the eyes water with regret for what he might have done. The monolithic battlements for the opening of *Hamlet*, with the narrow canyon running between them; the huge central pillar for *Macbeth*, with the great sweep of steps curving round it – these were far removed from Poel's 'Elizabethan Methodism', or Barker's brilliant derivation from it. They were a declaration of visual independence to which even Shakespeare was expected to subscribe; as boldly as Beerbohm Tree, they claimed a priority for the producer's theatre; and, all in all, it was fortunate for Shakespeare that Harley Granville-Barker was not only a producer, but also an actor and a dramatist. He maintained that the dramatist must have the last word, if only for the reason that he had written it.

Barker was now married to Lillah McArthy, whose embryonic Lady Macbeth Shaw had admired and Poel brought to maturity. She was as anxious to play in Shakespeare as Barker was to produce him. In September 1912 a gift of £5,000 from a friend who sold his pig farm enabled Barker to take the Savoy Theatre for a production of *The Winter's Tale*. This was in the heart of theatreland, and the challenge to His Majesty's correspondingly keener. Barker had taken what he needed from Poel, and this was, primarily, an Elizabethan flexibility of speech.

> In the teeth of ridicule he [Poel] insisted that for an actor to make himself like unto a human megaphone was to miss, for one thing, the whole merit of Elizabethan verse with its consonantal swiftness, its gradations sudden or slow, into vowelled liquidity, its comic rushes and stops, with, above all, the peculiar beauty of its rhymes. . .
>
> We shall not save our souls by being Elizabethan. It is an easy way out, and strictly followed, an honourable one. But there's the difference. To be Elizabethan one must be strictly, logically, or quite ineffectively so. And even then, it is asking much of an audience to come to the theatre so historically sensed as that.[1]

Here was the problem succinctly stated – how to be faithful to Shakespeare and the stage for which he wrote, without falling either into pedantry or pastiche; how to be essentially Elizabethan and dynamically modern at the same time. The solutions will vary from one generation to another; but Barker's productions at the Savoy from 1912 to 1914 looked ahead in a pretty straight line to Peter Brook's *A Midsummer Night's Dream* at Stratford more than fifty years later. They stimulated, even where they did not completely satisfy. From Poel's demonstrations of what the theatre once had been, and Craig's dreams of what it might become, they were a long step forward towards the distillation of an authentic Shakespearian magic, and the creation of a new Shakespearian audience. Barker declared that Craig had opened his eyes to the possibilities of real beauty and dignity in stage decoration, and that Poel had taught him 'how swift and passionate a thing, how beautiful in its variety, Elizabethan blank verse might be when tongues were trained to speak and ears acute to hear it'.

Lillah McArthy as Hermione in Harley Granville-Barker's *Winter's Tale*, Savoy Theatre 1912

The Savoy productions were also a triumph of vote-catching by a candidate who did not bother to canvass. Barker came to the Strand from Sloane Square with the prestige of his partnership with J. E. Vedrenne behind him. That is another story. Enough to say that the Fabians, the feminists, the vegetarians, the teetotallers, the suffragettes, the reverend agnostics, and many others besides, who had flocked to the Court would willingly flock to the Savoy. They were a receptive audience, although they were not in the least Elizabethan. Barker may well have chosen *The Winter's Tale* to open with because Shaw admired the play so much; because it would test his method to the utmost; and because Hermione was an excellent part for his wife. Declaring that all the historical and sartorial problems of the play were settled for him by the mention of Giulio Romano, he demanded a '*décolleté* stage' – neither completely bare, nor cluttered with conventional scenery. It was divided into three acting areas:

> a fairly small one at the back within a false proscenium that reduced the depth and width of the stage; a second one, four steps lower, that was spanned by the proscenium arch and covered the front of the stage proper; and a third, slightly lower again, an apron twelve feet deep in the centre, eleven feet deep at the sides, that spread out over the orchestra pit.[1]

These areas were divided by green-gold traverse curtains painted with flat Japanese landscapes to represent exteriors, and with a leaf pattern design for interiors. The palace furniture consisted of gold settees. The hard white lighting – sweeping shadows from the stage, 'as if they harboured germs', according to Bridges-Adams – came exclusively from projectors fixed on the front of the dress circle; two box lights in the centre, three cylinders on either side, a light in each stage box, and four white arc lamps above and across the centre of the main stage. There were no footlights. To soften the impression of actors stepping out of a picture frame on to the forestage, Norman Wilkinson designed a décor of white pilasters for Leontes' palace; these were removed for the pastoral scene, where the shepherd's cottage with its green door stretched right across the stage. The costumes by Albert Rutherston were of no definable period, and executed in strong variations of emerald, scarlet, lemon, and magenta. Henry Ainley as Leontes, a great performance with another man's brain behind it, paced like an enraged tiger to and fro around a brazier in the middle of the stage. Only six lines of a difficult play were cut, and the scene of the four gentlemen – essential to an understanding of the plot – was restored, much enlivened by Nigel Playfair, playing for his usual salary but with a good deal less than his usual scope.

Barker made his actors read the play, fixed their moves, and then sent them away for two or three weeks. Later, he would rehearse till three or four in the morning, and no one complained. He was patient and persistent until Lillah McArthy begged him to let them run a scene without interruption. Presently a curious noise was heard from the dress circle. It was Barker with his back to the stage, kicking the seats in exasperation. His insistence on speed disconcerted a number of critics; but he argued that it was of little importance that every word should be understood. The meaning was in the sound as well as in the sense. The production detonated like a bombshell, but the public support was hesitant and it ran for only six weeks.

Twelfth Night followed to unanimous acclaim. It has often been regretted that Barker wrote no Prefaces to the plays he actually produced. This is not quite true, since he did in fact write short introductions to his acting editions of all three. He had looked without enthusiasm at *Much Ado about Nothing* and *As You Like It*, and with a liberal's distaste at the jingoism of *Henry V*. Shakespeare's finest comedy, he maintained, was in the Falstaff scenes of *Henry IV*; and since comedy was what he was now after, he preferred to find it shot with

[1] *Shakespeare on the English Stage 1900–1964* (1964) p.52

romance in *Twelfth Night* rather than weighted with history in *Henry IV*. Wilkinson designed the costumes, and the black and silver setting with a formal garden and staircases right and left. Ainley's Malvolio was a Puritan prig, flashing out at Feste on his final exit. Arthur Whitby's Toby might have drowsed away the afternoon in the bow window of White's, but his 'I'll have a drop of that malapert blood from you' to Viola recalled an outraged Colonel in an officers' mess at Aldershot. This Toby was always a gentleman, with the beaming roundness of a full moon. Leon Quartermaine's Aguecheek had a vapid elegance, and the scenes between them, stripped of much traditional business, never degenerated into farce. Barker wrote that one might come upon a score of Aguecheeks 'in greater or less perfection, any day after a west-end London lunch, doing what I believe is called a slope down Bond [Street]'. He caught the whiff of the stable in Fabian; and Antonio reminded him of 'Sir Richard Grenville chewing a wine-glass in his rage'. Orsino, he argued, would have regarded Antonio very much as a Spanish grandee would have regarded Sir Francis Drake. And what was the point of Maria's diminutive stature?

Lillah McArthy as Viola in Harley Granville-Barker's *Twelfth Night*, Savoy Theatre 1912

Surely because the part was written for a very small boy. Barker set the play in the 'half-Italianised court of Elizabeth . . . . Its serious mood is passionate, its verse is lyrical, the speaking of it needs swiftness and fine tone; not rush, but rhythm, constant and compelling.' John Masefield wrote that the production was

much the most beautiful thing I have ever seen done on the stage. . . . The speaking of the verse was beautiful: Lillah often got the most exquisite effects with a sort of clear uplifting that carried us away, and I believe the women scenes were never allowed to drop to the dreamy and emotional; they were always high, clear, and ringing, coming out of a passionate mood.[1]

Barker's third Shakespearian revival was *A Midsummer Night's Dream*, which opened on 6 February 1914. This would always be remembered for its 'ormolu fairies, looking as if they had been detached from some fantastic, bristling old clock'.[2] Barker admitted that the fairies were the 'producer's test', and that it was partly in the hope of passing that test that he had decided to produce the play at all. They could not sound too beautiful, but 'how should they look? . . . They must not be too startling. But one wishes people were not so easily startled. I won't have them dowdy. They mustn't warp your imagination – stepping too boldly between Shakespeare's spirit and yours. It is a difficult problem.' It certainly was, and not even Barker himself was sure that he had solved it. Theseus' palace was again in black and silver, its definition contrasting sharply with the diaphanous wood, where a green velvet mound, spangled with white flowers, was set below a terracotta wreath. Fireflies and glow-worms flickered in the gauze canopy suspended from it, and 'in the background were curtains lighted in various changing tones of green, blue, violet, and purple with a backcloth of green rising to a star-spangled purplish-blue'.[3] There was all of Robin Goodfellow in Donald Calthrop's Puck, a creature of medieval folk-lore brewing his mischief from the vantage point of some Gothic cathedral, and none the less closely bound to the earth for his ability to survey it. Mendelssohn was discarded in favour of Cecil Sharp, and the rustics, with Nigel Playfair in command as Bottom, had to rely upon Shakespeare for their laughs. The production aroused furious controversy. To some it was too metallic to the eye and insufficiently melodious to the ear. One or two people suspected that those gilded sprites were the creations of a man who did not believe in fairies; and wondered if, when it came to *Macbeth*, Barker's witches might not prove to be the creation of a man who did not believe in witches.

It never came to *Macbeth*; the Great War came instead. Barker retired from all public work in the theatre except, on two occasions, to direct his own plays. He gave us his *Prefaces to Shakespeare* instead of his Shakespearian productions, and against these any director will break his teeth in vain. Yet the productions at the Savoy have become a part of theatrical legend, influencing all who saw them, and many who did not. They were a crucial break-through in the evolution of Shakespeare on the stage. Perhaps, as Bridges-Adams has suggested,[4] the challenge to tradition was too strident. The visual effects literally hit you in the eye, so that you remembered Hermione's gold umbrella more vividly than Hermione, and so caught your breath at the sight of Malvolio's cloak when he turned upstage that you momentarily forgot the letter he was about to pick up. There was a conspicuous absence of boot and saddle,

[1] C. B. Purdom *Harley Granville-Barker* (1955) p.142
[2] Desmond MacCarthy *Theatre* (1954) p.53
[3] *Shakespeare on the English Stage 1900-1964* (1964) p.58
[4] 'The Lost Leader' from *A Bridges-Adams Letter Book* (1972)

Far left: Donald Calthrop as Puck and (left) a fairy 'with gilded face and golden dress', *A Midsummer Night's Dream*, Savoy Theatre 1914

which did not matter in any of the plays that Barker had chosen to produce, but would have mattered a great deal in *Macbeth*. His was the urban, sophisticated and rational revaluation of a poet who had his roots in the Warwickshire earth; everything was very spick and span and wonderfully lucid beneath those implacable projectors. John Palmer described the *Dream* as 'the child of Mr Granville-Barker's perfect sanity – that perfect sanity whose pitiless iron seems finally to have entered Mr Granville-Barker's soul'. What would Barker have done with Shallow's orchard, or the Boar's Head? These questions are vain, though tantalizing. But the Barker of the Savoy was only thirty-five years old; he was growing all the time; and he grew into the *Prefaces*. He had thrown down the gauntlet – a gesture that must be made defiantly, if it is to be made at all. It was a declaration of war; and by the time the other war was over, there were few that ventured to take it up.

VIII Actors and Institutions

The story of Shakespeare on the stage in Britain and the United States had, up to the outbreak of war in 1914, been a record of individual achievement. The institutions, in so far as they could have been said to exist, counted for much less. Irving's Lyceum and Tree's His Majesty's were both institutions in their way; but when Irving died, or Tree, nobody cried 'The King is dead, long live the King'. The kings had departed, and the captains were soon to follow them. From now on the actor will gain from the institution as well as give to it, and the institution will survive his departure. It also follows that the director will count increasingly. Where we have thought hitherto of what Booth did with Hamlet or Salvini with Othello, we shall now speak of Ayliff's *Hamlet* in modern dress or Guthrie's *A Midsummer Night's Dream*. Neither of these would have been possible without the institution that supported them.

In 1833 Charles Kingsley wrote of the Royal Victoria Hall in the Waterloo Road as 'a licensed pit of darkness'. The darkness remained unrelieved until, in 1880, Miss Emma Cons took over the lease and baptized the drinks that were served at the bar and the songs that were sung on the stage. After the death of Miss Cons in 1912, her niece Lilian Baylis assumed the direction of the theatre, and also the governorship of the Governors. Hers was, and always remained, the last word. She was ruthless, dedicated, and sentimental, with a sure instinct for good acting; and she was adored by everyone who worked for her, however little she paid them. Her primary interest was opera, but in April 1914 the first Shakespeare play, *Romeo and Juliet*, was staged at what became known as the Old Vic. Two seasoned Bensonians, Matheson Lang and Hutin Britton, produced *The Merchant of Venice, Hamlet,* and *The Taming of the Shrew*, with shreds and patches of their own scenery and costumes. Sybil Thorndike joined them and played a variety of leading parts all through the war. In 1918 Philip Ben Greet (1857-1936), who had been touring his own company for years, took over the direction of the plays, with George Foss to assist him. It was now possible to see *Hamlet* performed in its entiréty – an annual ritual at the Vic for many years to come. Maurice Baring, that most sophisticated of playgoers, wrote that

> Shakespeare's play was face to face with the best of all publics; the public which wanted to see the play, and were ready to sit listening to it from one to six p.m. – on hard seats and on a stuffy afternoon. The public enjoyed it; they listened with absolute attention, and they applauded enthusiastically at the right moments throughout, and deliriously at the end. I think if Shakespeare's ghost was there he must have been pleased. Anyone seeing that performance could tell what the author was about, and could follow the story he had to tell without difficulty.

Russell Thorndike was the Hamlet, with that rasp in the voice that gave a memorable edge to his repartee, and a macabre tinge to his melancholy. Baring went on to say that, with the exception of Sarah Bernhardt, he was the only Hamlet in his experience who had 'carried on the excitement of the play scene into the following scene with Rosencrantz and Guildenstern'. There was a touch of which Tree would have approved. 'A jester gambolled about in the court scene [act 1] and stood looking ghastly with his painted clown's cheeks while Hamlet fought with Laertes.'[1]

Two years later Robert Atkins took over from Ben Greet. Here was a ripe character indeed. He had played with Greet, and imbibed as much of Poel's gospel as was good for him. A natural Elizabethan, he had a sixth sense about Shakespeare which served him better than the scholarship to which he never pretended, or the sophistication which no one would have suspected in him. He was the reverse of Barker in every way – a man about the taverns, you might say, rather than a man about the town. Unlike the more stellar directors of our own time who are rarely actors, he was able to demonstrate to a novice what he wanted him to do and how he wanted him to speak. The demonstration could be as rough as it was always ready; and when James Agate observed that there was a little too much of the *petit caporal* about Atkins's Richard III, he was putting a sure finger on the Napoleonic side of his character.

Between 1920 and 1925 Atkins directed every play in the First Folio, with the exception of *Cymbeline*, and *Pericles* was thrown in for good measure. The Old Vic auditorium was an orthodox Victorian horseshoe, with the *stimmung* that so often attaches to such theatres. As John Gielgud was to write:

> It is warm, alive; and it has a tattered magnificence about it. It smells and feels like a theatre, and it is able to transform a collection of human beings into that curious, vibrant instrument for the actor, an audience.[2]

Although it resisted a radical Elizabethan methodism, Atkins built out a fore-stage which brought the actors nearer to the audience and eased their speaking. The productions were swift and vigorous with simple elements of décor and traverse curtains; and the old grooves had been removed from the floor of the stage. Sensitive lighting always satisfied the spectator's eye, and did its duty by the actors' faces. 'Nothing left undone', Atkins ponderously observed after a performance of *Titus Andronicus*. But there was nothing crude about that production of Shakespeare's crudest tragedy. Instilling red blood into his actors, if he thought they did not possess enough of it already, Atkins never allowed them to outstep the modesty of nature. He had a sure ear for inflection, and the right instinct for pace.

He was fortunate in much of his material. The beautiful Florence Saunders, whose Ophelia Baring remembered as 'really mad and not just pretty', and whose early death robbed the English stage of an actress where authority, stature, personal warmth, and physical appeal were combined as they had hardly been since Ellen Terry; John Laurie, taut in speech and tense in feeling; Hay Petrie who made one feel that Dick Tarleton and Robert Arnim must have had a drop or two of Scottish blood; Ion Swinley, heraldic as Henry V and heroic as Troilus, speaking verse better than any one else on the English stage; George Hayes as Richard II, only semi-sincere in his sincerity; and Ernest Milton whose Hamlet many have considered the finest of his generation. This was an exotic plant in Elsinore, until you remembered that Shakespeare's Elsinore is high Renaissance; a graduate of Bologna rather than of Wittenberg; lonely, prehensile, and mysterious; de Musset's Lorenzaccio filled out to an Elizabethan scale; a performance of international 'class'. Atkins himself played when there was a part to suit him. 'Mr Atkins has taught me Caliban'

Ernest Milton as Hamlet, Old Vic 1925

[1] *Punch and Judy* (1924) pp.333-7
[2] *Theatre Arts Monthly*

wrote Herbert Farjeon, and here there was a certain correspondence between the part and the personality. Whatever Atkins put upon the stage had guts and more glamour than people now remember, but these sprang, you felt, from soil where the compost had been laid upon the earth to make it richer. It was not until ten years later (1935-6) that he seized his true Elizabethan opportunity in the Ring – normally a boxing stadium – at Blackfriars. Here, under a hard white light, with the audience on three sides of them, actors played *Henry V, Much Ado about Nothing,* and *The Merry Wives of Windsor* on a platform normally reserved for pugilists, backed by an inner stage and balcony.

Atkins was followed at the Vic by Andrew Leigh, and in 1925 Edith Evans, fresh from her triumph as Millamant in *The Way of the World*, turned her back on the North Bank for the New Cut. She had set an example that many were to follow. She was Dryden's Cleopatra rather than Shakespeare's, but the wit of Millamant went back to nature in her Rosalind. Baliol Holloway, most versatile of old Bensonians, came to partner her. In 1928 Jean Forbes-Robertson joined the company. All her father's steadiness and strength, the clear-cut profile and gravity of mien, the unswerving gaze, were there in her Juliet and especially in her Cordelia. But the next important break in the fortunes of the Vic came in 1929 when Harcourt Williams took over from Andrew Leigh and persuaded John Gielgud, then only twenty-five, to come as his leading man. The choice of Williams reflected great credit on Lilian Baylis's judgment. He had played with Benson without becoming too Bensonian; his idol was Barker, whose *Prefaces to Shakespeare* he put into practice as far as his cast and his circumstances permitted. As a man – teetotal, pacifist, and vegetarian – he stood at the opposite pole to Atkins, but he carried what Atkins had tried to do a stage further, so that one could see the influence of Poel and the influence of Barker harmonized in what one recognized as the Vic style of acting and production.

Where speech was concerned he went faster, at first, than his company or his audience were trained to follow him. Resolved, like Barker with whom he was in regular correspondence, that *A Midsummer Night's Dream* should be an English, not a German, fairy tale, he threw Mendelssohn overboard, and substituted folk tunes arranged by Cecil Sharp. There were other musical options less reminiscent of the Morris dancers at Much Wenlock. Those who did not believe in English fairies – Lilian Baylis herself among them – missed the muslin and gauze. Leslie French's lyrical and athletic Puck was as definitive as Gielgud's Oberon. Gielgud had matured his Romeo since he had played it, some years before, with Gwen Ffangcon-Davies, but it was with Richard II that a classical actor of the first rank announced his arrival on the English stage. Inheritor of the Terry charm – which has been defined as 'a delight in pleasing and in rapid cerebration combined with bodily grace' – Williams leaned upon him a good deal during the two seasons that he had him at his side. The brittle elegance of Richard, and then the long, elegiac descent into self-pity were conveyed with a beauty of diction matched at that time only by Ion Swinley. But Gielgud had the consistency of purpose and sophistication of approach necessary to hold the position he had won. After an imaginative Macbeth – where only the martial toughness was missing – he was ready for a Hamlet which became a *locus classicus* for the generation that applauded it. To begin with, no Hamlet within living memory had been so young. If it lacked the strangeness of Ernest Milton, and something of Milton's rich colouring and tragic depth,

Opposite: Costume design by Roger Furse for Tyrone Guthrie's *Hamlet* (Alec Guinness as Hamlet), Old Vic 1938-9

it was spontaneous and unmannered; striking successfully every note in the character; meditative but not mooning; lucid but not explanatory; active with a feverish, misdirected energy; swift and subtle without making complexity more complicated; discovering its effect in the lines and not in the business; new without striving after novelty; and likely, had he been put on, to have proved most royally. He was to play the part many times over the next ten years, and wisely refused to play it any longer. Some people thought his first Hamlet, in that unpretentious production, was his best; this is often the case with first thoughts in the theatre, as it is in literature and painting. Certainly no Hamlet since Forbes-Robertson has made so many of the judicious glad.

In the middle of his second season, the new Sadlers Wells, designed to do for the north of London what the Vic had done for the south, was opened by Forbes-Robertson who recalled his early memories of Phelps. No theatre could have been more misconceived for its purpose, and it was later handed over to opera and ballet. Ralph Richardson and Dorothy Green had now joined the company and Richardson's Enobarbus wonderfully deflated Gielgud's Antony, inevitably on the lighter side both in years and physique. Dorothy Green's Cleopatra after Veronese – Williams again having taken his cue from Barker – was exemplary in speech and feeling, but the 'serpent of old Nile' does not easily slither on the banks of the Thames or the Avon. Gielgud's Prospero was an embittered sage, not a testy schoolmaster, and Leslie French's Ariel – his Puck converted to the higher realms of mischief – was turned into stone by Eric Gill and may now be seen over the entrance to Broadcasting House. John Gielgud's Lear, which closed the season and crowned his achievement at the Vic, held all the promise of his later performance in the part; with sweeping brow and short grizzled beard, he was every inch a King whose instinct for authority was as strong as his capacity to exercise it was weak.

The last two seasons of Harcourt Williams's direction of the plays suffered from Gielgud's departure to bigger salaries and lesser parts. For the first of them Richardson remained as a pillar of strength; a resonant *arriviste* speaking for England as Falconbridge; a Bottom who had spent a night in Mahomet's paradise and would not forget it; a Toby Belch who might have stepped out of a painting by Franz Hals; and a Petruchio whose madcap mastery of Kate seemed no more than the ebullience of a heart of gold. This was Petruchio as Bridges-Adams imagined it – D'Artagnan crossed with Bluntschli. His panache blew several holes through a rather niminy-piminy, 'Commedia del'Arte' production of the play, at which Christopher Sly would have slept more soundly than he did already, and which that fellowship of strolling players would most improbably have included in their repertoire. One noticed a fascinating difference in the elocution of Richardson and Gielgud. Richardson shaped his words like a draughtsman; with Gielgud they flowed like a sonata.

Edith Evans strengthened the season at its close with an Emilia 'vulgar and lackadaisical' who 'seemed to fill out the whole background of her life with Iago',[1] and a Viola who swept into her own with the 'ring' soliloquy. Elsewhere the vulnerability was missing. In Williams's final season Gielgud returned to direct *The Merchant of Venice* in Motley's single set 'with fluted columns, curtains, and rope balcony, all executed in unpainted hessian that could be lit to a rich gold'.[2] Décor at the Vic was moving with the times. For *As You Like It* Williams used 'a blue net curtain that hung in a half circle, with a glade of great tree trunks just visible beyond',[3] and a movable geometrical

[1] J. C. Trewin *Shakespeare on the English Stage 1900-1964* (1964) p.140
[2] Ibid p.141
[3] Ibid p.140

Hamlet   Claudius

King Lear   Regan -
Last costume - widow

Miss Fay Compton -

Same black moirée
skirt as in second cost.
black moirée bodice with
jet trimmings and black
ring velvet sleeves bor.
with gold braid & decora
with pearls

black velvet surcoat
with black satin rev.
as before -

soft veiling zengette
going up under roll
hat of black ring ve

hillock in the centre of the stage. Peggy Ashcroft, then in the April of her prime, tempted Walter Sickert to sketch her Rosalind, and many others to wonder what she would do with Juliet in the years ahead.

Some had already seen it in the year behind, when Gielgud produced *Romeo and Juliet* for the Oxford University Dramatic Society. Charles Morgan wrote of this in *The Times*:

Miss Ashcroft's Juliet is the youngest and freshest that we remember. What faults it has springs from a too plaintive overstraining of the voice in the passages of tragic despair. . . . But her balcony scene shines with all its magic. 'Well, do not swear . . .', the superb farewell that follows it can never have been spoken with a lovelier gravity; and the scene in which Juliet is impatient for her nurse's news . . . is brilliant in its zest and inventiveness, proving that in comedy Miss Ashcroft can go where she pleases. And above all, this Juliet is in love – not rehearsing phrases, but passionately in love. The high music of that love's despair sometimes tests her too far, but its melancholy is a rapture and its delights are delight itself.

Beside this Juliet Edith Evans as the Nurse was

busy with a contributory masterpiece. She has the walk of an old woman, the hands of a sly one; and all the nurse's experience of ribaldry and affection are in the curious tortoise-like movements of her head. Never a strain, never an affectation; laughter proceeding naturally from character and all controlled; in movement, in speech, in the light of the eye, above all in restraint masterly.[1]

Like two flowers – the one of spring, the other of autumn – these two performances would bloom for a few years yet upon the stage, and they would never wither in the memory.

Harcourt Williams appropriately bade farewell to the Vic in the rôle of Prospero. He was succeeded by Tyrone Guthrie who remained for only a single year. In spite of its window dressing – the most brilliant young director of the day, and six fashionable players from the West End, including Charles Laughton, Athene Seyler, and Flora Robson – the season was only a qualified success. Shy both of poetry and pathos, Guthrie was not – or not yet – a dedicated Shakespearian. Long associated with good acting, there still clung about the Vic the odour of good works. People began talking about 'starved' Shakespeare; and William Archer never forgot how, in earlier days, a rat had gnawed at his hobnailed boot as he was sitting in the stalls. Guthrie had no reverence for good works. On the other hand, where production was concerned, he was already moving towards his later advocacy of the open stage. For the moment all he could do was to build a permanent set which he found difficult to light, and which the actors found hard to negotiate. Laughton missed the good humour in Henry VIII, and everything essential in Macbeth. The one part, Caliban, where his husky voice would have done no harm, he declined in favour of Prospero where it did no good. Only as Angelo, a flabby sensualist with the thin blood boiling in his veins, did he triumph over his inability to speak Shakespearian verse. Realizing, perhaps, that he had missed the wave-length both of his author and his audience, Guthrie left – but only for the time being.

The interim, under Henry Cass, was remarkable for the emergence of Maurice Evans. His story really belongs to the American stage, but his triumph in New York was grounded in the Richard II which he gave at the Old Vic.

Peggy Ashcroft as Miranda and Harcourt Williams as Prospero in *The Tempest*, Old Vic 1933

Opposite: Costume design by Roger Furse for Harley Granville-Barker's *King Lear* (Fay Compton as Regan), Old Vic 1940

[1] (February 1932)

Laurence Olivier as Romeo,
Edith Evans as the Nurse and
John Gielgud as Mercutio in
Romeo and Juliet, Old Vic production
at the New Theatre 1935

Completely master of voice and movement – an indefectible technician – his
'We are amazed' was described as 'the last flare before the sun of the
Plantagenets fell beneath the horizon'.[1] It was also the last flare of Maurice
Evans before a British audience. In the meanwhile Tyrone Guthrie, and a
good many other people as well, had discovered Laurence Olivier. Only the
year before, Gielgud and Olivier had alternated the parts of Romeo and
Mercutio in Gielgud's production of *Romeo and Juliet* at the New Theatre,
and again with Peggy Ashcroft and Edith Evans. Olivier had challenged a
generally hostile press with a realistic Romeo, deliberately, even defiantly,
unpoetical. But the poetry was there in his acting, if it was absent from his
speech. This was apparent to Guthrie who wrote to him admiringly of 'terrific
vitality, speed and intelligence and *muscularity*, a lyric quality pictorially, if
not muscially'. And whatever may have been the limitations, and occasional
perversities, of Guthrie's handling of Shakespeare, he had the eye of an Old
Master. Olivier's Mercutio, advised by his friend Richardson not to hurry the
'Queen Mab', was 'all dash and swagger, a Mercutio well pleased with himself,
a Mercutio who had perhaps walked too much in the heat of the sun and was a
little mad'.[2]

   Guthrie had been wrong; it was not Shakespeare who was starved at the
Old Vic; it was the Old Vic that was starved of John Gielgud. Here, then,
maybe, was an actor to fill the gap; and one, moreover, so different, it seemed,
as to run no risk of challenging improperly the idol of the New Cut who was
now the idol of the West End. Looking back shortly before he died on these two

en who have divided the Shakespearian stage between them, Guthrie arrived
t an interesting comparison – although he and they had matured considerably
nce Olivier was first lured across the Thames.

Gielgud, although the range of his acting is smaller than Olivier's, is the more sophisticated rhetorician. When he is suited by the material, he speaks with a matchless
musicality. . . . Olivier, also extremely musical (I don't think it's possible to be an
important actor without a strong musical talent), has developed, as he expresses it
himself, the brass of his orchestra but never mastered the strings. That is to say, he
commands marvellous tones for violent, exciting vocal crises and challenges, but the
soft, tender, luscious tones are considerably less marvellous; or, to put it technically,
nasal resonance has been cultivated at the expense of the deeper, softer, resonances
of chest and throat.[3]

nother observer put the contrast more succinctly: 'John is claret; Larry is
urgundy' – to which it may be added that when either is at its best there is
othing to choose between them.

   Guthrie, on his return to the Vic, persuaded Miss Baylis to important
hanges of policy; a small permanent cast, recruited as required; each play to
un for as long as there was an audience to see it; and Sadlers Wells to be
eserved for opera and ballet. Guthrie had already produced a sparkling
ove's Labour Lost – albeit heavily cut – at the Westminster. Now, with its
wo pavilions and wrought-iron gates, and Ernest Milton's fantastic *hispanidad*
s Don Armado, the play proved once again an unpopularity which sub-
equent productions have belied. But Edith Evans's Rosalind, with Michael
edgrave as Orlando, triumphed in an Arden where Millamant might have
at down to a *fête champêtre*. Then, early in the New Year of 1937, Olivier's
Iamlet streaked, meteoric, across a stage where the echoes of Gielgud's
eductive *legato* still lingered. The audience remembered them to Olivier's
isadvantage; nor did the Oedipan emphasis, which Guthrie had bought lock,
tock and barrel from Dr Ernest Jones, make the expected impact in spite of
Gertrude's kiss wiped in revulsion from Hamlet's face. Nevertheless Olivier
onquered the Gielgud loyalists with his portrait of a man whose weakness
was to do too much rather than too little, and with too many minds to make
ather than one which he could not make up at all. 'I do not know why yet I
ve to say this thing's to do' was the outcry of one caught in the vice of an
ntolerable dilemma, whose hand was itching for his sword. Indeed Ivor
Brown observed that there was 'more of thistle and sword-grass than of sensi-
ive plant in his composition', and Agate thought that he had given 'the best
erformance of Hotspur the present generation had seen'.

Laurence Olivier as Hamlet and
Esme Church as Gertrude, Old Vic
1937

   Guthrie had devised an architectural set ascending to the left of the spectator
y a broad flight of steps leading to an upper platform, where the levels were
gain broken, leading on one side into the wings and on the other forming a
eeper platform at the head of the first flight. This was used with great effect
n the play scene. The visiting actors brought with them their own stage – a
ow circular platform with properties and hangings. Claudius and Gertrude
ere seated on the topmost platform, their faces well lit, while the play pro-
eeded below and Hamlet moved up and down the steps. At the climax the
King rushed down them into the lowest stairway below the stage, and by the
ime the lights he had called for were brought, there was nothing above but the
lare of torches and Hamlet jubilant beside Horatio.

[1] J. C. Trewin *Shakespeare on the English
Stage 1900–1964* (1964) p.162
[2] Felix Barker *The Oliviers* (1953) pp.67–70
[3] *On Acting* (1971)

Olivier went on to play a sharp-nosed Sir Toby, indulging all his virtuosity in make-up, and a Henry V given, at first, against the grain. There is precious little humour in the part, but what there is reminded him of a scoutmaster. He overcame his dislike, however, when Charles Laughton reminded him that he was 'England'. In Westminster Abbey they were getting ready for the Coronation, and it was in the spirit of the time that all the trumpets should be sounding on the other side of the river, and the banners waving over that precarious *entente*. At the end of the season the company played *Hamlet* in the courtyard of Kronborg Castle at Elsinore. Not since 1585 had an English company performed there. On the first evening rain compelled them to move the production at short notice to the ballroom of the Marienlyst Hotel. Ivor Brown made an instructive comparison between this performance and the one he saw the following night.

Hamlet, Kronberg Castle, Elsinore

> Next evening we saw the same players on a huge platform built up in many levels at one end of the huge open courtyard of Kronberg. The scene of natural stone was imposing and the grey ghost of Hamlet's Father seemed to have stepped straight out of the grey wall behind. But naturalism died at nine-thirty. When day waned and the artificial light was turned on, the castle itself became artificial. . . . So it happened that *Hamlet* 'on the very spot' became, except for the coldness of the night air, which, true to the text, bit shrewdly, very like *Hamlet* in a modern theatre, whereas *Hamlet* in a ball-room had been strange and different and perhaps more truly Elizabethan.[1]

Olivier returned in the autumn of 1937 to play a Macbeth considerably madder than his Hamlet – the powerful sketch for a later portrait – and Judith Anderson as his Lady was more forceful than fascinating. The production was

[1] *Theatre Arts Monthly* (November 1937)
[2] Barker p.133
[3] Ivor Brown *Theatre Arts Monthly*
[4] Quoted in Marvin Rosenberg *The Masks of Othello* (1961)

dogged by the misfortune which so often attends the play. Michel St Denis, who directed, with music by Darius Milhaud, though happily at home in the English theatre, was never at home with Shakespeare. His approach was perhaps too theoretical. The lighting was too dim; the costumes too mannered; Motley's barbaric masks helped neither the Witches nor Banquo's ghost, and Olivier's make-up with false gums, slanted eyes, raised cheek-bones, and yellow complexion did not assist his humanity. Vivien Leigh's comment was to the point: 'Well, you hear Macbeth's first line, then Larry's make-up comes on, then Banquo comes on, then Larry comes on.'[2] To make matters worse, Olivier was suffering from a bad cold, and an accident to St Denis forced the production to be postponed. Lilian Baylis's beloved dog was killed; and on the day before the play was due to open, Lilian herself suddenly died in her sixty-fourth year. The 'odd little Empressario, with her fire of faith, her queer face, her spluttering speeches, and her vanities of cap and gown'[3] had gone to the reward she so fervently believed in. The Old Vic survived her passing, as she intended it should, but *Macbeth* did not.

The burden fell upon Guthrie. At Christmas (1937) he retorted to Granville-Barker with a fully-fairied *Midsummer Night's Dream*, Mendelssohn restored to the throne, Robert Helpmann's Oberon and Vivien Leigh's Titania making what Guthrie described as a 'nice noise' and an exquisite pattern of shimmering movement – a flagrantly Victorian fantasy in what had once been the Royal Victoria Hall. *Othello* followed with a fresh collaboration between Guthrie and Dr Ernest Jones. Guthrie rallied to Jones's suggestion of an unconscious homosexual motive for Iago's jealousy. Richardson, who had returned to play Othello, was kept in the dark about this. It was thought, no doubt, that being a far more sensible person in such matters than Dr Jones, he would not have understood it. The audience did not understand it either. Olivier acted under instruction, but he later rejected a theory which remains among the more ludicrous aberrations of psychoanalysis.[4]

The season ended with *Coriolanus*, directed by Lewis Casson, and Olivier's first incontestably great performance. This was partly due to a fruitful clash and fortunate accommodation between Olivier's realism and Casson's essentially musical approach to a Shakespeare text. The play was given in a unit set, with the customary togas discarded for neo-classical costumes. Sybil Thorndike's Volumnia was eloquent alike in her pleading and her pride. Olivier was very much the 'boy' of Aufidius' final taunt, his arrogance excused by youth as well as by patrician birth and martial achievement. Sarcasm, invective, and an occasional impish humour flashed alternately in voice and gesture. In 1938 Guthrie, a late convert to the growing fashion, put *Hamlet*, with Alec Guinness, discreetly into modern dress. This was an Elsinore where the Rassendyls would have sat comfortably on the throne; the poison was distilled beneath the protocol; and Guinness's performance was sensitive and *intimiste*, shunning spectacular effects. The umbrellas for Ophelia's funeral were an appropriate suggestion of a rainy day.

Vivien Leigh as Titania in
A Midsummer Night's Dream, Old Vic
1937

Sybil Thorndike as Volumnia and
Laurence Olivier as Coriolanus,
Old Vic 1937-8

2

The Stratford story can be more simply told. In 1919 the control of the Festival passed under the joint management of London's 'Shakespeare Memorial National Committee'. They appointed Bridges-Adams to assume a responsi-

John Gielgud as Richard and Peggy
Ashcroft as the Queen in *Richard II*,
Queen's Theatre 1937

bility which had been Benson's for as long as anyone could remember. He
eased the transition by engaging a number of Bensonians – Murray Carrington,
notable as Richard II, among them. Stanley Lathbury – his Cloten in *Cymbeline*
'straight out of Cruikshank', as Bridges-Adams described it – had a wry twist of
the lower lip which lent a striking acidity to the character and comedy parts.
Bridges-Adams had learnt a good deal from Barker and Poel, but he was more
romantic than either, with a hankering after boot and saddle and a reverence
for the Lyceum which he had never known. The intimate Victorian horseshoe
of the Memorial Theatre was ill-suited for drastic experiment, and the exiguous
budget forbade expensive actors or elaborate scenery. The company were
expected to rehearse six plays in five weeks, an impossible task if they had not
so often rehearsed them before.

Bridges-Adams designed the sets himself, building a false proscenium of
movable pillars to be adjusted as required. The plays were given virtually uncut
– which earned him the soubriquet of 'Mr Unabridges-Adams' – but he conceived a chronic aversion to Christopher Sly and had him away altogether when
he felt secure enough to do so. He also felt, with his instinct for dramatic
momentum, that the scene between the Old Man and Ross in *Macbeth* delayed
the move to Forres and 'that haunted throne'.[1] Less excusably, he cut the
prison scene from *Twelfth Night*. He was not afraid of reasonable innovation.
Richard II wore black armour, supposedly inherited from the Black Prince;
the Clown in *All's Well that Ends Well* made better sense if he were treated as
Countess' gardener; the apparitions in *Macbeth* represented the Stuart Kings,

leading up to Mary, Queen of Scots herself; Macbeth actually took hold of
Banquo's ghost and turned him round in his chair; and it re-entered not as
Banquo but as Duncan. The settings were simple and illustrative; Antonio's
counting house for the opening scene of *The Merchant of Venice*, the mound of
Agincourt, and – in later years – a shipwreck in *The Tempest* based on arcane,
but no doubt accurate, nautical calculations. The company was strengthened
when Baliol Holloway and Dorothy Green came as further legacies from Benson.
Holloway played Falstaff as only a lean man with a rich temperament can play
him; and his Richard III – the furrowed face twisting itself into sardonic
smiles, the voice curling itself round the words with a rough masculine caress,
power and presence and agility – was unapproachable until Olivier put the
part beyond immediate competition. In general, however, the performances
lacked metropolitan 'class'. W. A. Darlington wrote of 'a certain lack of finish
and precision', and many would have agreed with his summing up. 'The production and settings at Stratford are certainly better than anything the Waterloo
Road house can show, but for team-work and acting ability the Old Vic has it
nine times out of ten.'[2] But this was an early verdict before either company
had really got into its stride.

On 12 March 1926 the Memorial Theatre was mysteriously burned down.
Bernard Shaw had already suggested that this was the ideal solution for a
theatre so unsuited to the production of Shakespeare. Bridges-Adams was
promptly on the spot, tracing in the mud with his umbrella the design for an
enlarged stage. Within an hour it was announced that the Festival would
proceed as planned, and it took the citizens of Stratford only half as long to
raise the money required to adapt the local cinema. Models for seven productions were sent out to the contractors; costumes were lent from America
by E. H. Sothern and Julia Marlow; and the curtain went up on time. As
St John Ervine wrote, looking back at the opportune conflagration, 'If there
were any sponges about that day, none of them were thrown up.'

Controversy was soon raging as to where the new theatre should be built;
what sort of theatre it should be; and whether it should be built in Stratford
at all. The Elizabethan Methodists would be content with nothing less (or
more) than the Globe reconstructed on the banks of the Avon. Once the
architect – Elizabeth Scott – had been chosen, and the money was coming in
from America, Bridges-Adams, who had both the talent and the temperament
of an architect, made his views unmistakably clear:

> the true need is for absolute flexibility – a box of tricks out of which the child-like
> mind of the producer may create whatever shape it pleases. It should be able to offer
> Mr Poel an Elizabethan stage after his heart's desire. It should be no less adequate
> to the requirements of Professor Reinhardt[3] . . . To reproduce at Stratford, and to
> the detriment of the new theatre as a normal modern playhouse, a stage construction
> which, in pursuit of this alleged intimacy, condemned Hamlet to speak 'To be or
> not to be' with his back to one third of the audience would be little short of insanity.
> . . . The Stratford theatre has to serve us for at least the next 100 years. That its basic
> design should be normal should be self-evident. But so far as is humanly possible,
> that design should also provide for future developments in stagecraft. It should not
> bar the door to any producer of genius because it cannot afford him the means to his
> effects.[4]

Until quite recently the Stratford stage – for his writ did not run beyond

Baliol Holloway as Falstaff in the
Merry Wives of Windsor, Royal
Shakespeare Theatre,
Stratford-upon-Avon, 1923

[1] Letter to the author (19 June 1955)
[2] *The Daily Telegraph* (28 April 1921)
[3] *The Observer* (8 January 1928)
[4] *The Daily Telegraph* (14 January 1928)

Fabia Drake as Rosalind in
W. Bridges-Adams's *As You Like It*,
Royal Shakespeare Theatre,
Stratford-upon-Avon, 1933

Randle Ayrton as Lear in
Theodore Komisarjevsky's *King Lear*,
Royal Shakespeare Theatre,
Stratford-upon-Avon, 1936

the proscenium – was the stage that Bridges-Adams designed, with the exception of the revolve which he regarded as a needless temptation; and it was quite as important as any production he put upon it. In the meanwhile the company – strengthened by Randle Ayrton, a magnificent Lear, and Fabia Drake, whose Portia, Beatrice and Rosalind were each a perfect distillation of Shakespearian comedy – performed for six years in the cinema, and gathered prestige on three American tours. It was the first America had seen of what may be described as the English Shakespearian style in the conditions of repertory. The new theatre was opened by the Prince of Wales on 23 April 1932. The company were perhaps too travel-tired to be at their best for the occasion, and it still contained a certain amount of dead wood; but Bridges-Adams had reason to complain that he was not given the means to bring the best actors to the 'British Bayreuth', which Stratford had now become. Perversely, he hankered a little after the small rural festival it had been when he took it over. But then, as now, it was threatened by the parochialism of those who held its purse-strings.

Nevertheless he was able, for the first time, to invite directors and designers from outside. He flattered Barker and flirted with Reinhardt – to no avail. But Aubrey Hammond centred *Love's Labour Lost* round an immemorial oak, with a tree-crowned slope in the background, and provided beetling cliffs for *The Tempest*. Norman Wilkinson's olive-green façade for *Romeo and Juliet* had four openings, two of which could disclose a musicians' gallery, or Juliet's balcony, or the Friar's cell, or the Prince of Verona's judgment stand. Behind there were glimpses of a garden, or a street, or Capulet's ballroom. Rachel Kempson's Juliet had 'the April in her eyes' and sparkling water in her speech. Most beautiful of all were Wilkinson's designs for *A Midsummer Night's Dream*. Stratford has seen nothing lovelier than that sextet in white trooping up the staircase to their nuptials while Geoffrey Wilkinson's Puck – with something of the vinegar he had so memorably poured into the wounds of *Lear* – brought the epithalamium to a close. The effect of this production was of 'a nocturne in blue and silver . . . Elizabethan figures in alabaster slipping

Setting for Theodore Komisarjevsky's
Macbeth, Royal Shakespeare Theatre,
Stratford-upon-Avon, 1933

through some fold of time across the centuries from a golden age when love
and all the world were young.'[1]

At last the moment came when Bridges-Adams invited Theodore
Komisarjevsky to dinner in a Soho restaurant. With pencil or pen they
sketched out a production of *The Merchant of Venice* on the check tablecloth.
If, as one critic suggested, the Stratford stage was 'a machine for acting on' –
which is what a stage should be – the great Russian director was being used as
a *machine de guerre*. The result was an excitingly topsy-turvy *Merchant*,
balanced with music by Bach, followed by *The Comedy of Errors* – a play which
blushes at no experiment – and a *Macbeth* which, in the opinion of many, did.
The supernatural element was removed; the Witches were squalid fortune-
tellers; and the cauldron scene was enacted in Macbeth's own nightmare-
ridden brain, much of the dialogue being spoken by the sleeper himself. The
play was removed from time and place, with its aluminium screens and
circular stairway. It opened on a scarred battlefield with a howitzer, and a
skeleton round which the 'weird sisters' crouched. The soldiers wore modern
steel helmets and great-coats, and Banquo's ghost appeared as Macbeth's
own shadow. Here was a brilliantly conceived phantasmagoria of neurosis,
but hardly the *Walpurgisnacht* of Shakespeare's imagination. Komisarjevsky
did not pretend to be at home with his verse; fortunately George Hayes and
Fabia Drake were on hand to fight a rearguard action on its behalf. 'Stratford'
Mr Trewin reminds us 'spoke of Komisarjevsky's *Macbeth*, not of Shakespeare's'.[2]
But Komisarjevsky had proved, if nothing else, that the new Memorial Theatre
had become a place, as Bridges-Adams intended it to be, where the greatest
directors and designers could create a masterpiece or make a mistake. *Macbeth*
was his own favourite play, but what he remembered from its fortunes or misfortunes on the Stratford stage was Edmund Willard's voice of bronze in 'Arm,
arm, and out!' ringing out over the gardens which adjoin the theatre.

Bridges-Adams now, in 1934, felt that it was time for him to go. He maintained that six or seven consecutive openings were as oppressive to everyone
working behind the curtain as they were inimical to what they achieved there.
He wanted a closer link with other bodies engaged in similar enterprises, giving
him larger resources in personnel, even at the cost of some independence. He
wanted an international status for the theatre, and more guest-directors of

[1] *Birmingham Post* (20 April 1932)
[2] J. C. Trewin *Shakespeare on the English
Stage 1900-1964* (1964) p.167

international repute. When he saw no evidence that these policies would be endorsed, he resigned. Of all those applying themselves to the production of Shakespeare in England between the two wars Bridges-Adams probably had the best mind; it was not his fault that he was not always given the best means.[1]

B. Iden Payne succeeded him. A scholarly 'Elizabethan', nurtured on the pure milk of Poel, he was rather too academic for a theatre clamouring for imaginative size both in acting and production. It received the second from Komisarjevsky's *Lear*, mounted on the same metaphysical pyramid of rostrums that the Oxford University Dramatic Society had seen in 1927:

> These were set at different angles and led in different directions to achieve a sense of altering locality . . . nowhere was the studied congregation of characters used so meaningly as in the closing moments of the play when the light died out slowly in the sky, and darkness descended step by step down the stage. Line by line the motionless soldiers and courtiers faded from view: the light lingered for a moment on the dead Lear and Cordelia before they too dissolved into the dark. Rolling drums died away, and the curtain crept slowly down to cover the darkened stage.[2]

Size in performance came from Donald Wolfit, not too young at thirty-five to challenge Gielgud (and *Wilhelm Meister*) with a Hamlet deficient in physical grace and charm, but unerring in vocal stress. The latter he had learned from Poel, and Iden Payne was at hand to underwrite the lesson. It was a bourgeois Hamlet, but what it lacked in grace it made up in guts. Agate admired the 'complete grasp of character mapped as a general maps out a battlefield, enormous virtuosity of expression, and depth of genuine, as opposed to manufactured, passion'.[3] There was no doubt that a significant individual had come to maturity on the Shakespearian stage; but as time went on he would have some trouble with the institutions.

3

Of these the Birmingham Repertory Theatre, under Barry Jackson, broke new ground with its modern dress *Hamlet* in 1925. This production by H. K. Ayliff, at the Kingsway Theatre, stated its case with ingenuity and intelligence, but did not prove it. Some characters survived the treatment better than others. Claudius, superbly played by Frank Vosper, was all the more real for losing his trappings, and the gilded youth of Elsinore presented no difficulty to a public which had recently been applauding *The Vortex* – a play, incidentally, in which the closet scene had already been rehearsed. But it was not easy to imagine either Noel Coward or John Gielgud in plus-fours, and Colin Keith-Johnston – under no circumstances a natural Hamlet, whose 'rough and furious actuality' gave one 'the prose side of the medallion'[4] – was further handicapped by being obliged to wear them. This *Hamlet* at least induced a number of people to come to the play who would normally have run a mile from it. Ayliff's *Macbeth*, wrongly cast and wrongly chosen, rebuffed a similar handling; but he was safe with *The Taming of the Shrew*, with the electric heater in Petruchio's house, the tailor as an obsequious Jew from Whitechapel, Petruchio and Katharina in a broken-down car, and photographers with flashlights for the wedding.

The most interesting of these experiments was Michael Macowan's production of *Troilus and Cressida* at the Westminster Theatre in September 1938.

[1] For a more detailed study of Bridges-Adams, see *A Bridges-Adams Letter Book*, edited with a memoir by Robert Speaight: *Society for Theatre Research* (1972)
[2] T. C. Kemp *The Stratford Festival* (1953)
[3] Ronald Harwood *Sir Donald Wolfit* (1971) p.127
[4] Ivor Brown

Colin Keith-Johnston as Hamlet in
H. K. Ayliff's modern dress production,
Kingsway Theatre 1925

The play – very modern in its disillusionment with love and war – came near to the bone at a moment when war seemed round the corner. The Trojans were seen as products of the best British Public Schools, the Greeks rather more Gallic, and Thersites as a seedy journalist. Robert Harris was a deeply moving Troilus; and Ruth Lodge, with Max Adrian as Pandarus, generated the heated eroticism of life behind the Trojan lines. One had the impression that the play had been *written* in modern dress.

At the other end of the spectrum Nugent Monck – again a faithful disciple of Poel – had in 1921 acquired a disused baking-powder factory in the Maddermarket at Norwich. He built a gallery round three sides of the hall, connected with the balcony over the stage which occupied half of the original floor space. A modified apron projected in front of it. The background was composed of figured tapestries of plain, painted sackcloth, closed or opened in full view of the audience as the action required. For *A Midsummer Night's Dream* formal flights of blue steps zigzagged up to the balcony, with pillars festooned for the Court scenes, or conventionally disguised as trees. For *Hamlet* steps connected the balcony with the stage. By 1933 Monck's production of all three parts of *Henry VI* completed the Shakespearian cycle. Thoroughly professional himself, he worked exclusively with local amateurs.

It was not alone the Maddermarket that drew the connoisseurs to East Anglia. At the Festival Theatre in Cambridge, Terence Gray, inspired by Continental experiment, did what he chose with Shakespeare when he troubled to produce him at all. In a galvanized steel set he presented *The Famous History of Henry VIII* as a 'masque in the modern manner with the text attributed to Shakespeare and others'. The costumes and make-up were designed to look like playing cards, and the smaller parts were represented by cardboard models, their lines being spoken from the side of the stage. The Court entrances were danced, and the scenes in the palace yard were played in the auditorium where the rabble rushed and the messengers brought their news. The tempo was slow for the Court, excited for the mob, and characterization was sketched by appropriate mime. The play was stylized from start to finish, with the result that the *dramatis personae* naturally disappeared with their personalities. In *The Merchant of Venice* Portia pleaded for mercy from a swing, and Shylock and Tubal were shown fishing for lobsters in the Grand Canal. If fish were to be so literally baited, they might have picked upon the right ones. Frank Birch, however, did scholarly, as well as theatrical, justice to *Troilus and Cressida*. In Doris Paston's imaginative setting the heads of mythical beasts glared at each other in a diagonal pattern from either side of the stage.

Robert Atkins had produced a *Twelfth Night* in black and white at the New Theatre (1932), with Jean Forbes-Robertson. While Viola was asking the sea-captain: 'When did you last see my brother?', many in the audience were asking Viola: 'When did you last see your father?' – so startling was the likeness. Ivor Brown wrote that 'the directness of the performance, its lack of fuss, is as enchanting as the physical beauty of the small, dark figure in its courier's uniform of white'; and St John Ervine, more succinctly, 'she can do no wrong'.[1] In 1935 Atkins also presented George Robey as Falstaff in *Henry IV, Part One*, at His Majesty's. It was some time before the great comedian had to admit that Shakespeare's 'gags' were so good that he wondered why he had spent a lifetime inventing so many of his own. Atkins had now moved over to pastoral Shakespeare, where a natural setting was to hand in Regent's Park. *Twelfth Night*, *As You Like It*, and *A Midsummer Night's Dream* were obvious favourites. The *Dream* especially, wrote Ivor Brown, was

Robert Atkins as Sir Toby Belch in his *Twelfth Night*, Open Air Theatre, Regents Park, 1953

> admirably suited by spaciousness of grass; all the hide-and-seek business in the play, which is so tiresome on a small stage, comes to boisterous life amid the trees. Nature at night is itself enchanted, and with the play of the flood-lights after half time, there is real bewitchment of the eye even for those who find the silvery speeches inevitably impaired by mechanical amplification.

An unexpected visitor to the Park was Meyerhold from Moscow. He noted that the dresses were 'more theatre dresses than open-air dresses' and that they 'stood out from the pastoral background instead of melting into it'. He recommended Burne-Jones's *Green Summer* in the Tate Gallery as an 'example of dresses that make pastoral harmony'. Others complained that these were reminiscent of Shakespeare's heroines as they appeared in exhibits of the Royal Academy.

Shakespeare made occasional appearances in the West End of London, but few of these call for detailed mention. Gielgud matured his Hamlet and Richard II in seasons of his own at the Queens (1935). Charles Morgan wrote of the *Hamlet*: 'If I see a better performance of the play than this before I die, it will be a miracle.'[2] Ellen Terry made her last appearance as the Nurse in *Romeo and Juliet* (1919). Her memory now almost gone, she sat by a curtain behind which the prompter was ready. She lacked the earthiness of Edith Evans, but the gentle sunshine of her seventies warmed a generally cold production to which, among the others, Leon Quartermaine's Mercutio alone lent a lyric fire. Doris Keane's 'brave, lovely motion across the stage'[3] had not saved her Juliet, and Basil Sydney's Romeo never took wing. Lewis Casson had less than merited luck with *Macbeth* (1926), and *Henry VIII* (1925). Katharine and Lady Macbeth were natural parts for Sybil Thorndike. For the second she had waited until Henry Ainley was ready to partner her. He gave an electrifying performance at the dress rehearsal, and never gave it again. Charles Ricketts had designed a tapestry indicating the slaying of the Holy Innocents for the scene in England; and for *Henry VIII* another where the angels were identical with those in Katharine's vision. The production had much beauty, with Anne Boleyn in white and green for her Coronation, and the crowd suggested by a white and green barrier stretched across the front of the stage. Sybil Thorndike captured all the pathos of outraged dignity – a queen by right of virtue as well as blood – but Lyall Swete, whose Warwick in *Saint Joan* had seemed to mark him out for Wolsey, was a damaging disappointment.

In a brilliantly designed set by McKnight Kauffer, Ernest Milton, moving bravely into management, tried his luck with a lithe and Levantine *Othello* (1932). Here the lightning flashed, but the thunder was not at his command. *The Merchant of Venice* followed, with the secretive and implacable Shylock that the Old Vic had applauded some years before. Neither production had much success. Milton's Timon of Athens at the Westminster, three years later, in Nugent Monck's production, was the very genius of misanthropy – the last authoritative Shakespearian creation of an actor who had something of Irving's hypnotic presence, and power to make you forget his mannerisms.

The days of the actor-manager were numbered. One of them, however, had kept the flag of costume melodrama successfully flying in London and elsewhere. Matheson Lang, a romantic juvenile with Benson, a Hotspur whom Tree had taught to stammer, and a memorable Shylock, had won immense popularity in *The Wandering Jew* and *Mr Wu*. If an actor wanted big receipts at the cost of little effort, he was safe to play a Chinaman – a maxim that Oscar Asche had triumphantly tested in *Chu Chin Chow*. Lang was a powerful, impressive, but not particularly energetic actor. *Carnival*, in which he played an actor who murders his wife during a performance of *Othello*, did not tax him unduly. He thought, nevertheless, that he might risk the real *Othello* for matinées (1926), with Arthur Bourchier as Iago. The result – according to the few who saw it – was one of the greatest Shakespearian performances of the century.

Lang was disappointed by the trivial response of the daily press, and certain members of the audience. Middleton Murry remembered Lucien Guitry smoking a cigarette in the interval, impatient to call on his son's mistress; but when the Sunday papers came out, the size of Lang's achievement was apparent. One critic was 'so carried away by its beauty' that he 'found it difficult to write of it in cold blood'; for another 'the final scene surpassed everything which the writer . . . could recall after a quarter of a century's experience'. The performance was not repeated, for lack of the institution to support it, and it has been so largely forgotten that the tribute of J. T. Grein, a man with an intimate knowledge of the European stage, deserves quotation. Lang, he tells us, was an Othello 'black as night', all restraint at the opening, deferent before the Doge, protective and even paternal to Desdemona, slow to suspicion, and when doubt became certainty, there was 'still dignity, but his wrath tears his soul, strains his muscles, fells him to earth like a pole-axed animal'. Grein was reminded of 'the wounded bulls at St Sebastian in their awful agony', and in the killing of Desdemona of an auto-da-fé. 'In that scene Matheson Lang is so real, there is such an absence of theatrical effect, that, although we shudder in awe, we do not avert our faces . . . Victor Hugo was right when he said: "*Le laid, c'est le beau*".'[4] Here, at last, was an English Othello worthy to be set beside Salvini.

George Robey as Falstaff in *Henry IV, Part One*, His Majesty's Theatre 1935

[1] *Theatre Arts Monthly*
[2] *The Times*
[3] Stark Young
[4] Quoted in Matheson Lang *Mr Wu Looks Back* (1940)

In many respects the years between the two world wars were a golden age on Broadway. It was aptly said that the Theatre Guild had 'brought the American theatre into the twentieth century'.[1] But Shakespeare's part in this activity was a relatively small one; there were no institutions to support individual endeavour. The actor-managerial tradition lingered on with Walter Hampden's Hamlet, Shylock, and Othello. Hampden – it used rather snobbishly to be said – was popular with middle-class audiences, and John Mason Brown wrote of his 'forbidding coldness and deadening nobility'.[2] Thornton Wilder described his Othello as 'a thoughtful and hesitant educator',[3] outclassed by Baliol Holloway's Iago. By 1930 Hampden was apparently infected by the prevailing heresy that if you treated Shakespeare's poetry as prose, you would make his characters come alive. According to Stark Young, the finest critic of his day:

> He broke up into thoughtful phrases and detailed readings speeches that should come to us as a great swell of sound. . . . Eloquence disappears with analytical pause and any patent intricacy of thought. Mr Hampden's sin was that he made people apologise for Shakespeare as artificial, bombastic, and worthy.

John Barrymore as Richard III, New York 1925

Other voices[4], however, as well qualified to judge, have given Hampden higher marks than this. Mason Brown found his Hamlet 'excellent and touching before [he] had become so scholarly that he substituted a Phi Beta Kappa key for a rapier'.[5] In 1916, on the morrow of Barker's visit to New York, he was playing Prospero on an Elizabethan stage at the Century Theatre. With Louis Calvert as Caliban, the performance cannot have lacked vitality. Of the older generation of impresarios David Belasco was still in the field. His *Merchant of Venice* was bulkily scenic with David Warfield's Shylock playing for pathos, and four intermissions. James K. Hackett had played Macbeth with Mrs Patrick Campbell in London. Not for the first time Mrs Pat was overpowered by Shakespeare; her only memorable moment came at the end of the banquet scene when she drew down Macbeth's head upon her breast, removing the crown as she did so. They had both had enough of crowns. In 1924 Hackett played the part in New York with Clare Eames, tense, neurotic, and staking out a claim that, in other parts, London was quick to accord her. The play was ruthlessly cut, with seventeen intermissions, and neither Banquo nor Lady Macduff were allowed their murders. Hackett, in defiance of the text, lay down to die on an empty stage, while three singing voices accompanied the downfall of the curtain. The ghost of Shakespeare, if it stalked on Broadway, must have stood beside that of Banquo, less in sorrow than in anger.

One would like to think that it looked back to its own tercentenary, in 1916, when a group of coloured actors were performing – or were they only reading? – *Othello* in Harlem. George Jean Nathan wrote that he had 'heard Othello from many tongues in many lands, but never . . . ·have I heard a reading now more liquid and silver, now more full-throated and golden, than this reading of the Moor's fable by these ambitious darkies'. It would be interesting to know

[1] S. R. Behrman
[2] *Theatre Arts Monthly* (December 1925)
[3] *Theatre Arts Monthly* (May 1930)
[4] A. C. Sprague to the author
[5] *Dramatis Personae* (1963)

Top: Design by Robert Edmund Jones
for John Barrymore's *Hamlet*:
the madness of Ophelia, New York
1925

John Barrymore as Hamlet, Haymarket
Theatre 1925

Opposite: Walter Hampden as Hamlet

whether the young Paul Robeson heard it too. His own Othello had to wait until 1943 until it was thought safe to present it on Broadway; London had already seen it in a pretentious and ill-judged production into which Peggy Ashcroft and Sybil Thorndike knocked a little Shakespearian sense. Meanwhile, in 1915, a tiny but vital link had been established, quite fortuitously, between fresh minds on either side of the Atlantic. Granville-Barker produced Anatole France's *The Man who Married a Dumb Wife* as a curtain-raiser at Wallack's Theatre, and the set for this was designed by Robert Edmund Jones (1887-1954).

It was his first, and unlikely to have shown much evidence of what he was presently to accomplish. The revelation came with John Barrymore's Hamlet in 1925. Here the permanent setting of architectural forms and play of steps, delineating significant space – 'princely, austere, and monumental'[1] – only failed of its purpose in the graveyard scene, which can always do with a touch of tangible and visible earthiness. But Stark Young had reason to describe Jones's set as 'one of the glories of our theatre'.[2] Agate maintained that it was 'the most beautiful thing I have ever seen on the stage'; and Ivor Brown declared that it was 'the best setting of the play in my experience'. Barrymore proved not unworthy of these superlatives. Arthur Hopkins, who directed, described his voice as 'furry', and Barrymore, realizing his shortness of vocal range and complete lack of breath control, had studied with a retired opera singer, Margaret Carrington. He came to her, as she recalled, 'tremulous, modest, and extremely shy', and she literally 'built' his voice in six weeks. The performance wanted something of tenderness and mystery, but it had subtlety, complexity, and tremendous power. Careless and indeed ignorant of tradition, Barrymore acted the part as if he had never even read the play before. Every thought came fresh-minted – if a little slowly – from the pressure of mind and heart. Ivor Brown spoke of his 'deliberate painstaking virtuosity'. The voice was hoarse with grief on 'I'll rant as well as thou'; and in the 'O what a rogue' soliloquy it rose to a sustained scream on the call for 'Vengeance'. In the closet scene the Oedipan emphasis was strongly marked, and as Hamlet moved towards the Ghost, he fell back in his mother's arms. The naturalism and the bravura did not always go easily together; you were excited by Barrymore's Hamlet, but you were less often moved by it. For George Jean Nathan it was 'critically so precise that it is at times histrionically defective . . . . His Hamlet, like a diamond, is glittering, vari-coloured, brilliant – but cold, intensely cold. We get from it the reflected rays of intelligence, but never – or at best rarely – the rays of heat.'[3] Arthur Hopkin's production matched the nobility of the décor. The graveyard scene was played at night; one remembered the *cortège* of mourners with their torches trooping through the lighted arch, and the Ghost who was a mere wraith of light. Barrymore remained on surprisingly easy terms with him.

Margaret Carrington performed the same useful service for his Richard III (1920). The part suited his mordant, rapier-like mentality, and unpredictable temperament. Yet no pains were too great for him. He ordered real plate armour – copper and black – from an armourer in Newark; made forty trips for fittings; and injured himself whenever he fell in it. He supervised his robes of state after correspondence with the British Museum. These fell in long folds over the dais to the throne, or trailed behind him as he glided across the stage like an unearthly spider with his swift limp. Asked how he contrived this, he replied: 'I merely turned my right foot inward, pointing it towards the instep

[1] Stark Young *Immortal Shadows* (1948) p.13
[2] Ibid p.14
[3] *Theatre Arts Monthly* (February 1942)

of my left foot. I let it stay in that position and then forgot all about it. I did not try to walk badly. I walked as *well* as I could.' He was remembering the exaggerations of Mansfield and Robert Mantell. Grace and deformity, beauty and wickedness were all combined in this performance, where the sinister chuckles, hoarse whispering and occasional screams never pushed the melodrama so far that it could not be pulled back to tragedy. Robert Edmund Jones again designed the setting for Arthur Hopkins's production. The Tower of London loomed, threatening, behind every scene, with variations in front; the lower part hidden by tapestry for King Edward's palace, the arras replaced by a throne for the coronation, an iron cage in the centre for Clarence's prison cell, and a grim gibbet in black silhouette for Bosworth field. These were the only Shakespearian rôles to which Barrymore brought his superb physique and magnetic personality. He was as variable on the stage as off it. Fundamentally, he lacked ambition – 'a smouldering coal from an ancient altar'.[1] Yet he had demonstrated as few other American actors of his day that 'acting is an art'; and had made of it 'an art of truths instead of a trade of mendacities'.[2]

That art was badly missed when his brother Lionel played Macbeth for Jones and Hopkins in 1921. Here the Gothic abstractions; the gold frames or sharp gold lines against black velvet; the vast daggers of light that fell upon the Witches from the suspended silver masks; Lady Macbeth moving from right to left behind pointed white screens, cross-barred and transparent, in the sleep-walking; her red robe for the banquet, and the candlesticks askew on the table; the tall white pillar in the cauldron scene; the brilliant illumination against dark shadows; and the distorted suggestions of wall and doorway and throne – filled the eye and excited the imagination. But *Macbeth* cannot live by décor alone. It is better to have an actor without a frame than a frame without an actor; and here such acting as there was bore no relation to the frame in which it was set.

Opposite: Maurice Evans as Hamlet

Jones's purpose was deliberately anti-decorative. However elaborate, his décor was conceived in terms of dramatic function and executed in terms of light as well as shape and substance. 'The beam of light' he wrote 'strikes with the precision of a *mot juste*. It bites like an etcher's needle or cuts deep like a surgeon's scalpel.' He was inspired by certain prints of Hiroshige – 'the light that never was on sea or land' – and certain paintings by Odilon Redon and Utrillo, by the etchings of Gordon Craig and Appia's drawings of the Elysian Fields for Gluck's *Orphéus*. But there was no imitation. He was to tell us later what was in his mind's eye for the sleep-walking scene in *Macbeth*:

Animula, vagula, blandula, little flame, little breath, little soul, moving before us for the last time. . . . And the shadow on the wall behind that 'broken lady' becomes an omen, a portent, a presage of her 'sad and solemn slumbers', a dark companion following her, silent and implacable, as she passes from this to that other world. . . . When we think of this scene we remember, not only the dreadful words and the distraught figure, all in white like a shroud; we see vast spaces and enveloping darkness and a tiny trembling light and a great malevolent shadow.[3]

If Clare Eames had been there to hold that light, and John Barrymore to occupy those spaces, what an historic production this would have been! In 1937 Jones both directed and designed an *Othello*, with Walter Huston, at the New Amsterdam Theatre; but this was deliberately pitched in too low a key and had little success. For *Much Ado about Nothing* he rehearsed a production which never saw the chiaroscuro he had designed for it, nor the background against

[1] Walter Pritchard Eaton *Theatre Arts Monthly* (February 1937)
[2] Percy Hammond
[3] *Theatre Arts Monthly* (February 1941)

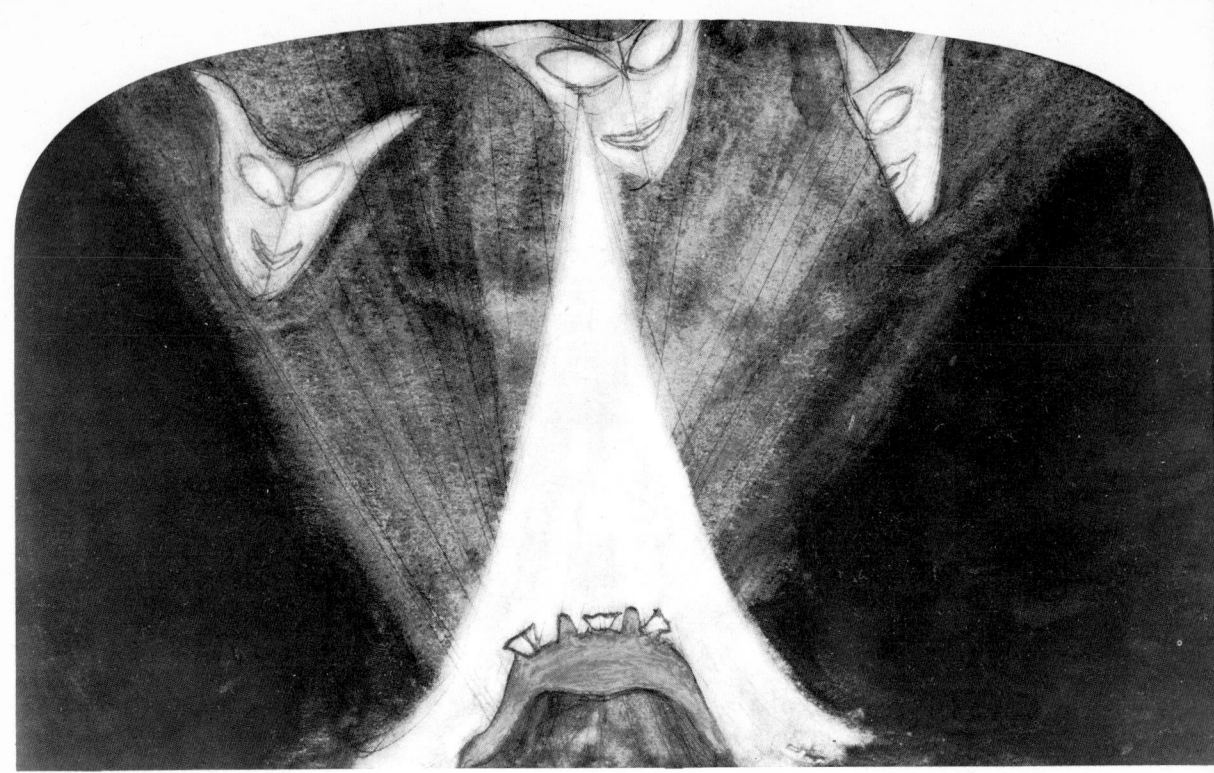

which the actors in their scarlet and gold costumes were to stand out. Jones was way ahead of his time when he planned for the company to appear in a kind of actors' uniform, and to put on their clothes for the play in view of the audience. He had left representation far behind; presentation was now the watchword. His dream stage was 'a structure of great beauty, existing in dignity, a Precinct set apart. It will be distinguished, austere, sparing in detail, rich in suggestion . . . its mood will be continually varied by changes of light'. He realized, and avoided, the danger of repeating himself: 'Above all else I seek to avoid doing a Jones setting.' His aim was constant: 'to carry the audience into that other region where the ideal play takes place' and 'to find the simplest, broadest, grandest way to take the audience there, and to keep them there'.[1] He had been more successful than Craig in giving substance to his dreams; but only in *Hamlet* had he found an actor to give them humanity. It was not his fault that, more often than not, they remained an unpeopled planet.

With few exceptions, Shakespeare on Broadway at this time comes to us in pictures rather than performances. In 1928 Douglas Ross directed *Macbeth* at the Knickerbocker Theatre. Gordon Craig sent his designs, but did not come over himself to supervise their use. The Wagnerian costumes were by another hand. By this time, as Stark Young observed, Craig had become 'a source rather than a sensation . . . some have fed their talents with his substance, some have turned it into paying enterprise'. The result was 'as if El Greco supplied somebody with a sketch and colour card to paint one of his pictures'.[2] Yet the designs – as they stood on paper – were an inspiration to the eye; the furled banners, deep blue, orange, and green, on either side of Duncan, as he stood above the steps of the throne room for 'Is execution done on Cawdor?'; the castle's 'pleasant seat' seen through the arched span of a bridge; the jutting

Design by Robert Edmund Jones for Arthur Hopkins's *Macbeth*: the three Witches, 1921 angles of large block screens throwing their weird shadows for the scene following the murder; the 'leafy screens' of gauze forming a hanging veil of purple, orange and green for Birnam wood; the great canopy covering the whole length of the banqueting table; the heavy gates and broken bits of wreckage strewing the rostrum, with its double flight of curving stairs, for the final scene.

Norman Bel Geddes designed an impressive *Hamlet* for Raymond Massey in 1932 – a 'vision of theatre-wise beauty betrayed at the heart of its secret by a negative performance'.[3] He also directed the production, and his rehearsal book was as minutely detailed as a musical score. The setting was so devised that the play could be acted with only two intermissions, and that the background should suggest only the mood and facilitate the action of the particular scene. Here, again, was the anti-decorative approach. Every movement, vocal variation, light cue, and sound effect was worked out in advance on a cork model into which pins could be stuck, indicating the position of the actors. The basic platform with its steps could become, in turn, the dais of a throne, Ophelia's grave, or a stage for *The Murder of Gonzago*. The opening between two blocks was now a corridor, and now an abyss separating Hamlet from the Purgatory of which the Ghost was speaking to him – 'between two worlds become much like each other'.[4] There were twelve entrances to the set, although none were visible. A jutting, triangular apron gave intimacy with the audience where required. The setting was permanent, but never, from one scene to the next, looked the same. Geddes did not, like Craig, work from drawings. His approach was plastic, not pictorial; pragmatic not theoretical.

More traditional was Jo Mielziner's treatment of *Romeo and Juliet* for Katharine Cornell (1934). He went back to the earlier Italian Primitives, since they offered lightness of key and purity of colour, and freed the designer from the stricter rules of perspective. By using his full set for only a few scenes, he was able to place the others on the apron, between the proscenium, or further back. In this way Juliet could step out of a Gothic window on to her balcony, or

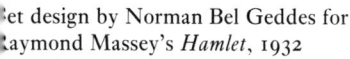
Set design by Norman Bel Geddes for Raymond Massey's *Hamlet*, 1932

Ibid
Immortal Shadows (1948) p.97
John Hutchins *Theatre Arts Monthly* (June 1932)
T. S. Eliot *Little Gidding*

Lilian Gish as Ophelia (above right);
John Gielgud as Hamlet and Judith
Anderson as Gertrude in
Guthrie McClintic's *Hamlet*,
Empire Theatre 1936

drink the potion under the high canopy of her bed, Romeo summon the Apothecary with the arcading of Mantua behind him, Friar Lawrence greet the morning
from the door of his cell, without interrupting the movement of the play. The
intention throughout was frankly pictorial, but then *Romeo and Juliet* is a play
which frowns on austerity. Paul Nordoff's music was used as preludes to several
of the scenes, as well as for the ballroom and, most inappropriately, the wedding.
Clandestine marriages at crack of dawn can dispense with musical accompaniments. Katharine Cornell had come to Juliet a little late; like Julia Marlow
before her, she was the woman that Juliet might have become if she had had the
sense to follow Romeo to Mantua. But she was supreme in movement, 'literally
running' – as Richard Lockridge remembered her – 'with her arms outstretched
to love'.

There was a greater unity in Mielziner's designs for *Hamlet* when John Gielgud, in Guthrie McClintic's production, repeated his London success on Broadway – with perhaps just this shade of difference that New York had not forgotten Barrymore. The last scene with Claudius and Gertrude on the open rostrum between two cliffs of crenellated walls, was deeply impressive. For the other court scenes the gap was closed. There was no dearth of Hamlets on Broadway. Maurice Evans had come over to play Romeo with Katharine Cornell, and then – on the spur of the moment, so to speak – had taken the town by storm with his Richard II (1937). Here was a new actor and, virtually, a new play; for no professional performance had been recorded in New York since 1878. Margaret Webster's production had a splendid sweep of movement and colour within an economy of means to which her experience at the Old Vic had well accustomed her. The settings by David Ffolkes played effective variations on arches, hangings, and portcullises, and gave at one point – 'Dear

Maurice Evans as Richard II, 1937

earth I do salute thee with my hand' – a glimpse of ships at anchor, as Richard
landed at Bristol from the Irish wars. When his murdered body was placed at
the foot of the throne, with Bolingbroke looking down at him and the courtiers
standing silently around, memories of a more recent abdication by another
King were naturally aroused. In 1938 Evans played Hamlet in its entirety, also
at the St James Theatre, and Margaret Webster was again in command. Here
there was less unanimity of approval. Stark Young admired the vigour and
clarity of speech, but also noted a lack of princely form and little evidence of
inward struggle. The transitions were blurred, and it seemed as if the actor were
approaching the words 'as if he had planned every one of them and intended to
put it into action'.[1] Maurice Evans had always been a master strategist. For
Mason Brown the extrovert interpretation was justified by the unabridged text;
here was a 'healthy young intellectual', only paralysed by the ultimate doubt.
Evans's Richard II, when it was recorded, reminded some listeners of Alexander
Moissi; the work, it seemed, of a cantor rather than an actor; and Richard, the
most lyrical of Shakespeare's tragic protagonists, was particularly suited to his
style. A comparison was made with Gielgud, whose performance in the part – no
less lyrical to English ears – New York was not to see. Gielgud's renunciation,
as one heard it, seemed more psychological than Evans's 'song of sorrow'; the
degradation more painful; 'down, down, I come' more realistic. Evans's 'like
glistening Phaeton', beside this, had 'the wildness of the sun-chariot out of
control and flying down the sky'.[2]

Certain other performances stand out from those years, when so many
British actors thought of Broadway as a place they would like to go to when they
died, even if they did not get there while they were alive. Otis Skinner's Falstaff –
described as a 'rotund old devil of the taverns'[3] – in a mediocre production by the
Players Club; a link with Booth, whose portrait presided there, and the great
old days when the special theatrical trains spanned the continent, and the
railroads still condescended to passengers. Basil Sydney's Hamlet in modern
dress (1925) – 'expertly read' – taking a quick cue from Barry Jackson, but not

Basil Sydney as Hamlet and
Percy Warren as Horatio, 1925

Eva le Gallienne as Juliet and
Richard Waring as Romeo, 1930

yet starting a fashion. Ethel Barrymore's Portia delivering the 'quality of mercy'
as a tête-à-tête little sermon, not as an aria, in a voice sometimes very dramatic,
often moving, and in its use very little varied in any speech anywhere.'[4] Jane
Cowl as Viola in a *Twelfth Night* (1930), directed by Andrew Leigh, where
Raymond Sovoy's décor opened like the pages of a huge book, set upstage; and
as Juliet in Frank Reicher's production (1923), where the general intention of
speed did not prevent fifteen intermissions. Stark Young thought she only
lacked a kind of 'impalpable distinction'[5]–a quality that others missed in Evans's
Hamlet. And there was Eva le Gallienne's Juliet, with the stage divided in half
for the tomb scene.

The king and queen of Broadway were Alfred Lunt and Lynn Fontanne. One
did not look to them for Shakespeare, but they could not resist *The Taming of
the Shrew* (1935) – and the public could not resist it as they gave it to them;
Katharina in her wedding dress being led away on horseback by Petruchio in
his *apache's* cloak and sombrero, or mounted gaily on his shoulders; the pair of
them riding off into the clouds in a chariot at the end of the performance, and
leaving behind them a roistering mêlée of music, dancing and acrobatics. Brooks
Atkinson compared the production to a 'game of ninepins ... stuffed with all the
horseplay their barn-loft holds' with its 'band, a troupe of tumblers, a cluster of
midgets, a pair of comic horses, and some fine songs set to good beer-garden

[1] *Immortal Shadows* (1948)
[2] *Theatre Arts Monthly* (June 1940)
[3] John Mason Brown *Dramatis Personae* (1963)
[4] Stark Young *Theatre Arts Monthly* (October 1926)
[5] *Immortal Shadows* (1948) p.28

Alfred Lunt and Lynn Fontanne in
The Taming of the Shrew, Theatre
Guild 1935

music by Frank Tours'¹ – and the whole directed with 'the versatility and dispatch
of a ringmaster'. The *Shrew* is so tough a play that you can take pretty well any
liberty you like with it; the Lunts had hilariously justified theirs.

2

Broadway is notoriously short of elbow-room, and it was soon apparent that
Shakespeare needed a new stage and a new public. In the summer of 1935 Joseph
Papp inaugurated his open air theatre on the shore of a tiny lake in Central Park
with what has now become known as the New York Shakespeare Festival.
Admission was free for 2,236 people, and the actors wore body microphones.
The weather could be inconvenient; on one occasion when the wind blew over a
standing torch, Romeo rose from the dead to blow it out. The plays were given
on a permanent platform, with an upper level, and the audience on three sides.
Papp acknowledged a responsibility to an audience 'composed of persons who
insist that we serve them a style of Shakespeare they can relate to their contemporary experience . . . and will settle only for characters with whom they can
identify.' This was to open the door both to experiment and eccentricity.

There was no lack of either in the work of Michael Chekov, who came over as
director of the Second Moscow Art Theatre in 1923, and gave productions of
Hamlet, Lear, Twelfth Night, and *The Taming of the Shrew.* He left Russia for
good in 1928, and established his studio in New York. Another arrival from
overseas made a more spectacular mark on the history of Shakespeare production. Orson Welles, then a young man in his middle twenties, was familiar to
audiences at the Dublin Gate Theatre at a time when he was quite unknown to
America. He was quick to remedy an ignorance which, in retrospect, seems   ¹ Works Progress Administration

astonishing. In conjunction with John Houseman and the WPA[1] Federal Theatre, he took the Lafayette Theatre in Harlem and presented *Macbeth* with a negro cast. The play was set in Haiti in the early nineteenth century, with settings and designs by Nat Karson. Rank and tropical greenery formed a background to the castle, and to the uniforms of pale blue, scarlet and gold. Macbeth was in canary yellow, emerald green, and shining top-boots; Macduff wore epaulettes a foot wide of heavy red cord, and satin-striped red and white breeches. The guests at the banquet danced to nineteenth-century waltzes, and the ghost of Banquo was represented by a luminous death-mask seen high up on the battlements. It was from the same battlements that the 'cream-faced loon' was shot dead, and kicked eighteen feet into the courtyard below. Malcolm and Donalbain fled, not to England, but to the 'coast'. Jack Carter, who played Macbeth, was the light-skinned son of a famous beauty from the Floradora Sextet; he had been born in a French château and was for long unaware of his negro blood. He stood six feet four inches in his boots, and was the original Crown in *Porgy*. Edna Thomas had both the power and the presence for Lady Macbeth; there was all the temperament for the spirits to 'unsex', and the nerves that broke under their response.

This production became known as the 'Voodoo' *Macbeth* – with its naked witch doctor and primitive negro masks. Five black goats were sacrificed in the theatre and skinned for the drums which reiterated the black magic of the play. These were under the command of Absadata Dafora Horton, later to be Minister of Culture in the Republic of Sierra Leone, and they accompanied the chants which Virgil Thompson thought a little lacking in evil spell. The drummers replied that they had gone to the limits of wickedness, but afterwards admitted that the music was intended to warn off the evil spirits, not to conjure them. Had they given the real thing, it might have worked – disastrously. In fact, it appeared to have done so. An unfavourable review by Percy Hammond in the *Herald-Tribune* was considered 'the work of an enemy', and on the night after it appeared the basement of the theatre echoed to a sinister cacophony. At the same time Hammond was taken seriously ill and died a few days afterwards –

Orson Welles's 'Voodoo' *Macbeth*: costume design by Nat Karson (above) and Macbeth's castle (below), Lafayette Theatre 1936

officially of pneumonia. Generally speaking, however, the press was warm in approbation. The *Brooklyn Eagle* wrote that 'with all their gusto they play Shakespeare as though they were apt children who have just discovered and adore the old man'.[1] Brooks Atkinson spoke of 'fury and phantom splendour', and saw in this Macbeth and his Lady 'an alliance in crime between a middle-aged wife-mother and a passionate husband-son'.[2] Carter disappeared later in the middle of a performance and was replaced by the principal stage-manager, who had been walking on as one of Macduff's barefoot soldiers. The production was taken on tour bringing to 100,000 people throughout the country 'a tragedy of black ambition in a Green Jungle shot with such lights from both Heaven and Hell as no other stage has seen'.[3] To one spectator it seemed like 'the Emperor Jones gone beautifully mad';[4] and a particularly vivid impression was recorded by Ernst Stern:

> When Macbeth and Lady Macbeth planned the murder, their plottings were accompanied by the background throbbing of the drums. It merged naturally into the knocking on the door: 'Wake Duncan with thy knocking! I would thou could'st.' Sometimes the throbbing was subdued, like the insistent throbbing of a guilty conscience, like a steady pulse-beat; sometimes louder and more insistent, according to whether it conveyed the memory of past horrors or the suggestion of new horrible deeds to come.[5]

Orson Welles's *Julius Caesar*,
Mercury Theatre 1937

The following year (1937), and again with Houseman and the WPA, Welles produced his *Julius Caesar* in modern dress at the Mercury. The bare brick walls of the stage were stained blood-red from floor to gridiron, with the lighting equipment, superbly handled by Jean Rosenthal, fully visible, and a wide low platform set squarely in the middle of the stage. When the production was transferred to the Empire, Sam Jeve designed a number of large, subtly graded platforms covering the whole floor of the stage. These led in a gentle rake to shallow steps and a plateau eight feet in width, and from there to a crest six and a half feet above the stage level. There were several trapdoors, and no padding on the platforms. The steps were deliberately uneven – in one case twenty inches in height. The background was simply the back wall of the theatre painted a blood red. The patricians wore military uniforms with black belts, and Brutus a double-breasted, black, pin-striped suit. Casca's snap-brim black felt hat and raglan coat were cleverly in character. Daggers were used for the killing of Caesar, and short bayonets for the suicides. Certain lines for the citizens were borrowed from *Coriolanus*. The crowd, recruited from students at Bennington, Yale, and Carnegie Tec, was kept in continual movement during Antony's oration, and the lynching of Cinna was omitted until the final dress rehearsal, when it became a high point of the production. Welles himself played Brutus as 'the bewildered liberal . . . the man of character and principle in a world threatened by fascist destruction'.[6]

This was the general motif, underlined by the use of spotlights and flagpoles, of a production which had, as John Mason Brown was quick to acknowledge, 'the touch of genius upon it'. His tribute deserves quotation:

> Something deathless and dangerous in the world sweeps past you down the darkened aisles at the Mercury and takes possession of the proud, gaunt stage. . . . In its stream-lined simplicity this set achieves the glorious unimpeded freedom of an Elizabethan stage. Mr Welles . . . keeps drumming the meaning of his play into our minds by the scuffling of his mobs when they prowl in the shadows, or by the herd-like thunder of

their feet when they run as one threatening body. . . . Like the setting in which it is used, it is pure theatre – vibrant, unashamed, and enormously effective.[7]

The Mercury *Julius Caesar* was exciting, but incomplete. Where Shakespeare holds the scales even between petrified order and dissolvent anarchy, between devious diplomacy and high-minded regicide, the focusing of interest on Brutus left Antony victorious in the Forum but virtually absent from the battlefield – since there were no battles to be fought. The play's grip was consequently relaxed for want of contrast, and there were times when the very deliberate speaking – though it made the meaning clear – slowed down the momentum where it should have been gathering speed and urgency. Nevertheless as a result of the extensive cuts, the play ran for only one hour and forty-nine minutes, without an intermission. What was lost in the labouring or mutilation of the text was recovered, partially at least, by concentration and continuity.

It would be ungenerous to labour unduly the failure of *Five Kings* (1939) where Welles's native exorbitance over-reached itself. He had conceived the idea of welding the two parts of *Henry IV*, and *Henry V* into a single evening's entertainment, with the selected fragments linked together by quotations from Holinshed and some of the choruses from *Henry V* – spoken from the well of the orchestra which would have been better occupied by an apron. This must always be ruinous; you can no more easily or sensibly abridge the *Ring der Nibelungen*. You can perform the parts, but you cannot pretend that pieces of the parts are the whole. It was realized, too late, that even *Five Kings* would have kept the audience in their seats well into the small hours of the morning, and further desperate curtailment was necessary at the last moment before the production could open in Boston. It travelled, very laboriously, to Washington, and grounded to a halt in Philadelphia.

Welles had designed his permanent setting in three parts to cover the three segments of a revolve. These represented a castle with huge circular walls, a tavern, and a ramped street with an open court at one end and a narrow alleyway at the other. The actors moved with the revolve, in full view of the audience, from the Boars Head to the palace, or from the palace to the battlefield. Various dispositions of ramps and platforms were signposts for Shrewsbury, Agincourt, or Harfleur. The revolve could move more quickly when a battle was in progress, but never fast enough for the actors who marched or fought upon it. On occasion it disconcertingly jumped into reverse. The décor was built of burlap and wood, double-faced with thin veneer cut into narrow slats and stained a light blue-grey without any paint or shadowing. It was beautiful to look at, and took easily the lighting that Jean Rosenthal devised for it. A better frame for *Henry IV, Part One*, could hardly be imagined – but alas! there was *Henry IV, Part Two*, and *Henry V*, and long before one had reached the field of Agincourt the iron tongue of midnight was threatening to give its unheeded cue to the curtain. Welles's Falstaff appeared in massive contrast to Maurice Evans, who had been playing the part in Margaret Webster's more orthodox production of *Henry IV, Part One*. Evans had the cutting wit, Welles the 'bulk and thews and big assemblance' that belonged to him by right of nature. A little more geniality, and a little less distraction from the unmanageable child that his invention had brought forth, would have placed this Falstaff in the highest class. One further question remained to puzzle the audience – where were the *five* Kings? Only two of them were visible to the naked eye.

Orson Welles as Falstaff and Burgess Meredith as Prince Hal in Welles's *Five Kings*, Mercury Theatre 1939

[1] Quoted by John Houseman in *Run-Through* (1973) see also for much of the foregoing
[2] Ibid
[3] *Theatre Arts Monthly*
[4] Ibid
[5] *My Life, My Stage* (1951)
[6] Archibald Macleish
[7] *New York Post*, quoted in *Run-Through* p.314

X The Animateurs

Like so many French words, *animateur* is not easy to translate, at least in a theatrical context. It implies a man with a formulated aesthetic approach to the theatre, and at the same time one who works in it. In France Lugné-Poe, Antoine, Copeau, Dullin, Baty, Jouvet, Pitoeff, Vilar, Planchon, and Jean-Louis Barrault all qualify for the title. Dullin defined their common ideal. 'Nothing, it seems to me, is forgotten so quickly as that which clings to the problems of the passing hour. Once it deserts the poetic imagination, the theatre becomes boring and strictly *sterile*.' After turning his back on realism, Antoine produced nearly every one of Shakespeare's plays in Paris, including *Titus Andronicus*. Working in the first decade of the century, he was anxious to rescue Shakespeare from the 'English cant, the severe censure which Protestant rigour has imposed on all dramatic production, and which has for centuries since dried up the sap of the great Shakespearian tree.' An Elizabethan realist in method, he was equally Elizabethan in mind.

Not until 5 December, 1904, at the Théâtre Antoine, had Paris seen a play by Shakespeare produced in its entirety. That production of *King Lear*, in a translation by Pierre Loti, ran for a hundred nights; Jean Vilar described it as 'the first theatrical revolution since *Le Cid*'. Antoine had conceived a sequence of décors, quickly and silently changed behind a forestage embellished with draperies. For the first time the public could watch a Shakespearian play unfold in tune with its natural rhythm, and no interruption but a single interval of ten minutes. Antoine had proved what Firmin Gémier was to preach. 'The greater a work, and the closer it brings us to the sublime, the less need it has of décor and pictorial production. The words carry the décor in themselves.' – although with Gémier they did not always do so. The same scenic formula was employed for Antoine's production at the Odéon, varied for *Julius Caesar* by certain structural elements suggested by the play. In *Romeo and Juliet* the Montagues had their dwelling on one side of the stage, the Capulets on the other, and the double doors of a central pavilion could open to indicate other localities. Rigid in principle, Antoine was reasonably eclectic in practice. Léon Daudet compared him to a 'fox terrier who ran after all the pebbles one threw at him, and sometimes brought back a diamond, and sometimes a rough stone, but who couldn't help running'. His production of *Coriolanus* was simplified into an archway for the Volscians, a suggestion of Rome, and a wall between them. The attraction exercised by the opposing cities was thus symbolically represented and effectively conveyed. An absolute obedience to the text, and the transformations within a permanent décor, enabled Antoine to reduce the most complex material to simplicity.

Similar ideas were fermenting elsewhere. Lugné-Poe, a former associate of Antoine at the Théâtre Libre, had seen William Poel's production of *The Two Gentlemen of Verona* in the Merchant Taylors' Hall, with music by the Dolmetsch ensemble. Inspired by this example, he took the Cirque d'Eté in 1898 for a production of *Measure for Measure*. Here was a mingling of actors and

Lugné-Poe's *Measure for Measure*, Cirque d'Eté 1898

Firmin Gémier's *The Merchant of Venice*, Théâtre Antoine 1917

audience, revolutionary – not to say disconcerting – for its time. But Lugné-Poe did not share Antoine's respect for the Shakespearian scriptures, and the translation by Louis Ménard respected them even less. It was all very well to proclaim that the word created the décor; but it did nothing of the kind when it was the word of an insensitive intermediary.

It was at the Théâtre Antoine that Firmin Gémier produced *The Merchant of Venice* in six scenes, and an adaptation by Lucien Nepoty. This inaugurated the Shakespeare Society which Gémier had founded. Many speeches were transposed; Morocco and Aragon appeared simultaneously; and Shylock returned in the last act. The text was less Elizabethan than the *mise-en-scène*. Gémier suppressed the footlights, and built a staircase from the stage to the auditorium. In all this the influence of Reinhardt was apparent. Gémier subsequently appeared with Ida Rubinstein in *Antony and Cleopatra* at the Comédie Française (1918). Three orchestras were disposed about the auditorium, more than enough to drown such poetry as the translation had managed to preserve. The gratuitous orgy which concluded the second act would have brought a blush to the boards of His Majesty's. Colette described it, not without admiration.

A unanimous exclamation went up from the house when the curtain revealed that carpet of women on the steps, palpitating and motionless, like beautiful reptiles. At a signal from the orchestra they all got up and hurled themselves into a mêlée, at once brutal and harmonious, and obedient to the rhythm of the dance. The audience was stirred by a healthy pleasure, like the trickling of grapes during the vintage, or like the stacks of wheat at harvest time – like the pleasure that you always get from looking at the riches of the earth.[1]

Another spectator, Jacques-Emile Blanche, reminding Gémier that a father had felt obliged to escort his son out of the theatre during the scene, pleaded that realism of this kind ran clean contrary to the Shakespearian aesthetic. If Matisse had designed the costumes it might have been a different matter; and

Firmin Gémier's and Lugné-Poe's
Hamlet, Théâtre Antoine 1913

Blanche could not help but admire 'the macabre and lubricious effect of voluptuous frenzy suddenly assuaged'. But all the audience would take away from Shakespeare's *Antony and Cleopatra* were the 'beautiful naked thighs kicking in the air under the embrace of rough boxers'.[2]

These embellishments or deformations did less harm to the comedies. Nobody complained of an operetta based on *The Merry Wives of Windsor*, or even of music from Offenbach's *La Belle Hélène* introduced into *Troilus and Cressida*. And whatever one did with *The Taming of the Shrew*, it would still be left standing. Robert Brasillach remembered Gémier as Petruchio at the Odéon. 'He was 60 years old with his grimacing features under a blonde wig and his pitiless articulation, and bearing no resemblance whatever to the Petruchio of the play. All the same he was the only Petruchio who has ever convinced me.'[3] Here the actors were caricatures of Renaissance strolling players, and performed against simple flats and draperies. In *Hamlet* (1925) an equally simple variation of curtains and arches showed that Gémier had learnt something from Antoine. The scenes of ensemble or hysterical emotion were acted on the stage proper; but whenever Hamlet was engaged in soliloquy or intimate dialogue he played on the steps of a low apron which brought him close to the audience. Where Antoine and Lugné-Poe had appealed to an *avant-garde*, Gémier, in his own revolutionary way, was eager to capture the *grand public*. He was an impressive and popular actor, and a snapper up of other men's considered trifles. But he deserves a place among the *animateurs*.

Of these by far the most important was Jacques Copeau (1879-1949). A literary critic of distinction, he had been closely associated with André Gide and Jacques Rivière in the founding of the *Nouvelle Revue Française*, but he already had his eyes on the theatre as it was, and as he would have liked to make it. Even when he had converted a corner of it into his own likeness, it was still too much for him. He then retired to a hillside in Burgundy with a few disciples, and found a willing audience among the *vignerons* of the Côtes d'Or. All that is another story. What concerns us here is primarily Copeau's production of

[1] *Etudes Anglaises* XIII, no. 2 (1960) p.271
[2] Ibid
[3] *Animateurs du Théâtre* (1954)

Opposite: Set design by
Lucien Coutaud for Jacques Copeau's
As You Like It, Boboli gardens,
Florence, 1938

Set design by Pierre Sonrel for
Charles Dullin's *King Lear*

Twelfth Night at the Vieux Colombier Theatre on the 15 May 1914. It is significant of Copeau's appeal to an intellectual and artistic *élite* that Debussy should have been there in the tenth row, and observed afterwards that he expected Shakespeare himself to take a curtain. The audience, as Jules Romains observed, was then largely composed of people 'who have a library, buy the new books, and gladly say "I would rather read a good novel by the side of the fire"'.[1] Others described it as a 'public des Ballets Russes'. Copeau (Malvolio) and Jouvet (Aguecheek) had worked all through the previous night, and the company were in a state of collapse. Duncan Grant, who had designed the costumes, was still painting them when they were already on the actors' backs. There was Suzanne Bing as Viola in white doublet with thin black stripes, and black tights; Blanche Albane (later Mme Georges Duhamel) as Olivia; Copeau in his long Puritan gown, and Jouvet in his sky-blue top hat; Feste in pink and blue, and a red cap shaped like the claws of a lobster. The play was presented in curtains, with Malvolio's prison under the trap door, stylized trees, and simple cubes for seating. Behind the central opening a scenic element was in place, and against this simple background the mere grouping of the actors formed a succession of enchanting tableaux, as they wove a pattern of beauty and fun.

Copeau's famous prayer 'Donnez-moi un plateau nu' had been granted, but the nakedness was lit up by the bulbs in octagonal lanterns, revolving on an axis and presenting different sides. These were hung in the auditorium, were movable to throw the light as required, and came to be known as '*les jouvets*' after the great technician who had invented them. The production was revived in 1920 with a décor on two planes, designed by Jouvet, and sixty changes of lighting. He was still playing Aguecheek, and a critic wrote of his 'bloodless face, his girlish look, his drawling voice, his limp, exhausted movements, . . . a comic figure, at once bleak and impressive'. (In his dressing-room the picture was very different, as he missed his cue sipping a glass of Sauternes!) It was Jouvet who said of Copeau: 'Everyone owes him something; I owe him everything.' Copeau's *Twelfth Night* entered into theatrical legend as surely as Barker's production of the same play. Indeed there was something in common between the two men, except that with Copeau the Messianic tendency was rather more pronounced. Both deserted a theatre that would not receive their gospel, and there was a shade of truth in the complaint that Copeau was a Jansenist in a milieu where Jansenism is rightly rejected as heretical, and a Cartesian who trimmed the Elizabethans into a geometrical pattern alien to their genre. His principles were the same as Antoine's. 'Any originality in our interpretation' he wrote in 1913 'will come only from a deepened knowledge of the text.' He began by reading the play aloud to the company. This gave them the 'linear direction' of the work, and its 'essential shape'. He then rehearsed it in no particular order, sometimes calmly and sometimes with a feverish energy. For Copeau, as for Barker, the text had the sanctity of a musical score; neither the archaism nor the license of Poel would have met his demand for a theatre that was aesthetically alive without being impudently modernist. Great teacher as Copeau unquestionably was, all taint of exposition had faded from that production of *Twelfth Night*, when Barker saw it in 1921 and gave his views to *The Observer*[2] in three columns of close print.

He made the 'appalling discovery' that French actors spoke Shakespeare better in French than English actors spoke him in English. They had the 'precision, variety, clarity, and above all passion', which he had tried to instil

[1] *Vieux Colombier*
[2] (1 January 1922)

into his own actors at the Savoy. He noted with approval the apron, set a step lower than the stage proper, but thought that it had not been used to its full advantage as an indication of time and place, or to relate the Court of Orsino to Olivia's mansion. He was severe on the costumes of Duncan Grant, which had already been criticized in New York as 'bright and garish in a Greenwich village way'. The artist should have realized that Olivia and her household were in mourning. Barker reminded Copeau that Sir Andrew Aguecheek was not a village idiot; that Malvolio, now played by an actor short of inches and authority, should not be turned into a 'mechanically outrageous figure of fun that even the wildest horse-play could not animate'; and that Maria was not a kitchen maid, but a lady-in-waiting. These were all mistakes that a closer acquaintance with English manners and society would have avoided. But he had nothing but praise for Jean le Goff's exquisitely spoken Orsino, slightly reminiscent in costume and make-up of Charles II, or even the Roi Soleil; for the excellent, if slightly sentimental, Antonio; the first-rate Fabian in what was by no means a third-rate part; and the 'richly coloured, totally unexaggerated, and really amusing Sir Toby' of Romain Rouquet, where an American critic had already caught a 'hint of Rabelais'.

Barker devoted the bulk of his essay to the Viola of Suzanne Bing; this was not only an extraordinary tribute to the actress, but a classic of dramatic criticism. After noting an emphasis on the 'background of tragedy in the girl's life at the expense of the youthful high spirits' – with the result that certain important passages, notably the 'ring' soliloquy, slipped into a minor key and endangered the 'contrasting effects around them' – Barker admitted that this reading brought its compensation in the duel scene where the usual clowning was avoided, and the romantic interest of the story sustained. He continued:

> You may know her in just one minute for a supreme actress, not only by her perfect physical repose, but by the lack of all anxiety to impress the part – far less herself – upon you. . . . Madame Bing spoke very beautifully; she moved with grace. But the movements did not exist apart from their meaning, and every sentence came out conceived as a whole, as a thought and a feeling, not as a variously valued collection of words. . . . And certainly one learnt as much more about Orsino by following the lights and shades of this Viola's love for him as Orsino himself declared. And as much more about Olivia; though here Shakespeare has been verbally downright, and Viola's attitude to Olivia is one of the obvious tests of the part's playing. Madame Bing was almost impeccable in this . . . her Viola is fine, I think, chiefly because it is fine all through. There are no purple passages, no doubtful ones. She has visualised a Viola, and with certain art, by complete self-abnegation, she makes her vision ours.

By the time Barker saw the production Copeau had attracted a much wider audience; not only the *beau monde* and the intellectual *avant-garde*, but workers and students, and a sprinkling of foreigners like himself. They left the theatre 'exhilarated, not exhausted, not as having seen a show, but as having helped, they too, even actively, in the consummation of a worthy work of art'.

Two vignettes, even more strikingly than Barker's analysis, convey the magic of the production. Copeau himself described the opening:

> While the Duke, followed by his gentlemen, slipped into the shadows on the left, Viola emerged from the other side in a different light, veiled in pink and holding a palm leaf in her hand. So, right from the beginning, the comedy discovered its rhythm and began to trace its winding pattern. Hardly had the grave and slightly

Opposite: Set design by René Allio for Roger Planchon's *Henry IV*, Théâtre de la Cité à Villeurbanne 1957

melancholy voice finished speaking . . . than a woman's voice – Suzanne's – clear and bell-like, transported us elsewhere without the slightest jolt. 'What country, friends, is this?' 'This is Illyria, lady'.

In New York Jouvet's architectural décor lent itself to the drinking scene – not played, as long custom had dictated, in a kitchen.

In the blue shadows pink columns rose like phantom shapes. Gilded trellis-work enclosed the back of the stage. On either side staircases led from the mansion of the beautiful Olivia. A shadow lay on the upper balcony, so that one could hardly make out the slender vases with their strange blossoms. Only a ray of moonlight fell straight on to the big semi-circular seat in the middle of the stage. The revellers were there, lit by round, multi-coloured lanterns. They were singing. The whole of a summer night, misty and blue, was called up before us, and the invisible garden rocked and accompanied the clown's melancholy song with the murmur of a 'cello.[1]

François Mauriac was enchanted 'by this unique poetry where the bells on the cap of foolery tinkle more lightly than the sighs of love. So many sighs were never mingled with so much laughter to delight the heart.'[2]

The same décor served, not always happily, for *The Winter's Tale* produced in February 1920, again at the Vieux Colombier. Copeau had translated the play himself with Suzanne Bing. Fauconnet gave symbolic colouring to the costumes, Hermione in pale mauve, Leontes in red, and a bowler hat for Jouvet's Autolycus. The Vieux Colombier closed in 1924 – certain hostile critics had already rechristened it 'Les Folies-Calvin' – but Copeau's flight to Burgundy was not quite definitive. In 1934 he returned to Paris for a production of *As You Like It*[3] at Dullin's Atelier. It was most unfortunate that the excellent translation of Jules Supervielle was not available to him, since this was then being used in a rival, and over-elaborate, production by Victor Barnowsky at the Théâtre des Champs Elysées, where live sheep were pastured on the stage. He had to rely

Jacques Copeau's *Twelfth Night*, Vieux Colombier 1914

instead on the adaptation – altogether too free – of Jules Delacre. Supervielle was content to entitle his version *Comme il vous plaira*; with Delacre it became *Rosalinde*. This was a typical infidelity. Copeau, who played Jaques himself, had a fair acquaintance with English and brought the text into a closer conformity with the original when he judged it proper to do so. Nevertheless there remained a disconcerting difference between the faithful translation of *Twelfth Night* by Théodore Lascaris, and the liberties Delacre felt justified in taking. Copeau, with his profound culture, knew better than to abstract Shakespeare from his Elizabethan moment of time, simply because his sense of humour is not always ours, and his play of words not always readily understood.

It was ten years since a production by Copeau had been seen in Paris; and those who imagined that his self-imposed exile had only deepened his austerity quickly had their fears relieved. Dullin, in his own productions at the Atelier, had given an important place to music and mime, and Copeau was not afraid to follow him. There was not quite the same subordination of the production to the play, which had resulted in the miracle of *Twelfth Night*; but he was still careful to relate the one to the other.

All my efforts have been concentrated on that wonder of wonders – on Rosalind. A gigantic rôle beneath its fragile envelope. To discover the right note – throughout two acts – for this boy who is really a boy and this girl who is pretending to be one is certainly one of the most difficult problems that any director can set himself today.

This was obviously beginning at the right end. Copeau thought in terms of character before he thought in terms of costume or make-up. His exiled Duke was fifty years old with young features and silvery hair, wearing the same frayed costume throughout until, in the final scene, Rosalind and Celia adorned it with flowers. The usurping Duke was in red, with curly hair; Oliver was a hard-faced country gentleman, but sufficiently good-looking and softened by adversity for Celia to fall in love with him.

Robert Brasillach remembered 'the charming fête that preceded the wrestling bout, with the glow of Venetian lanterns to caress it, like the carnival in a painting by Guardi . . . and the green landscape where, for a fleeting second, a furtive roebuck came dancing by.'[4] The music, which included twenty-seven numbers, was composed by Georges Auric – a rather hazardous choice, since one did not look to 'Les Six' for romanticism. Apart from the prescribed songs, Copeau had asked that Touchstone (Jean-Louis Barrault) should be humming a tune underneath the window while Rosalind and Celia were preparing for their journey – and that elsewhere he should be chasing butterflies; atmospheric music for the beginning of Act II to evoke the forest at daybreak, with a suggestion of sheep-bells, birdsong, and murmuring streams; a dance of shepherds for Act III; and a wedding dance for the end of the play, interrupted twice by the departure of Jaques and the arrival of Jacques de Boys. In default of the more open stage at the Vieux Colombier, Copeau built a false proscenium and included the stage boxes in the area of play. Two curtains, appropriately painted, indicated the dwellings of Duke Frederick and Oliver. These were raised for the wrestling match and, later, for the forest where the décor was varied from scene to scene. An ingenious device was to open an immense sunshade, behind which the exiled Duke's picnic was prepared, while Adam and Orlando were playing their scene in front of it. When they had left, it was removed to disclose the Duke and his courtiers at table. The revolve, decorated

[1] Pierre Seize *Etudes Anglaises* XIII, no. 2 (1960) p.187
[2] Ibid p.185
[3] For a detailed account of Copeau's productions of *As You Like It* see Jean Jacquot in *Revue d'Histoire du Théâtre* (January-March 1965) pp.119-137
[4] Ibid

with a half-circle of greenery, was used only once to allow Corin to go in search of Rosalind and Celia; when it had completed its round Silvius and Phoebe were discovered with the others peeping through the branches. The costumes were designed by Marie-Hélène Dasté, blue predominating for the suite of the exiled Duke and red for the usurper. A touch of tartan for the former might have carried a reminiscence of Rob Roy to a reader of the Waverley novels.

The list of properties for the use of Touchstone in the first act alone suggests an almost exaggerated preoccupation with detail. He was furnished with a pint of ale, bread and cheese, a clown's bauble, an ambassador's three-cornered hat, a sporting cap, field-glasses, a small trumpet, a fan, and a wooden horse! But this load of accessories was not, it seems, too heavy for the impression of lightness which the production was intended to convey. Copeau's management of the wrestling match was a good example of his capacity to keep the stage alive. Charles was allowed to demonstrate his prowess before a group of enthusiasts, whom the referee had some difficulty in separating from the contestants once the bout had started. Oliver made himself scarce when he had confirmed the defeat of Charles, while Touchstone waved his fan in the face of the humiliated champion. The young men about the Court gathered around Rosalind were sharply called to heel by the Duke when he found himself alone. Returning to a stage, empty but for the two girls, he began to threaten in a low voice and it was Rosalind who raised the emotional temper of the scene. After he had gone out one heard his footsteps echoing in the wings. At the end of the play it was Duke Frederick himself who placed the crown on the head of his brother, and wrapped the ducal cloak round his shoulders.

In the summer of 1938 Copeau presented *As You Like It* in the Boboli gardens at Florence. This gave him the possibility of placing the action of the play in different parts of the same décor – in this case necessarily permanent. Facing the audience, a little to its left, was a circular pavilion of two storeys, with a small revolving stage inside it. The upper storey was occupied by musicians whom a curtain could discover or conceal. Adjacent to this, on its left, was an artificial hill with several flat levels, and paths leading up and down, into which the actual trees of the site were cleverly integrated. On the extreme left of the audience was a pond, with an island in the middle of it, fringed with greenery; and on its extreme right a foot-bridge crossed the natural path of the gardens, with circular steps descending from it on the further side. The Boboli gardens themselves, and the wall enclosing them at the back, composed a frame in which the pavilion, the pond, and the artificial hill were conveniently set. Reinhardt had used the same site for *A Midsummer Night's Dream*; it suited *As You Like It* just as well.

Copeau made effective play with his lighting – or with its absence when darkness fell. After Duke Frederick, followed by his dwarf and his dog, had left the scene of the wrestling bout, the shadows closed in; Orlando went towards the gardens; Rosalind appeared on the steps of the pavilion; and the Duke re-entered over the bridge. Later, as the pavilion was lit up inside, one saw the shadows of the two girls as they made ready for their journey, before disappearing in the direction of the hill. One did not see them again until the first pink light of dawn had touched its summit. Copeau – who was himself a man of deep religious conviction – thought it necessary to introduce the hermit – an impressive figure in his Franciscan habit – who had been the instrument of Duke Frederick's conversion, and was followed by a lion, a tiger, and a bear. He ppeared something of an uninvited guest at that highly mythological wedding, but it was not complete without his benediction – from which the lion, the tiger, and the bear were not excluded.

All this suggests a certain competition with Reinhardt, but Copeau had not forgotten Rosalind. From the moment she discovered Orlando with his arm in a sling, she ceased to play the boy. Copeau's direction was clear:

> She goes towards him and, from behind, puts her hand on his shoulder. These are vows that they are about to exchange, strangely formulated: 'Why then tomorrow I cannot serve your turn for Rosalind?' 'I can live no longer by thinking.' He has bowed his head and shaken it. She is behind him; tender and mysterious.

In its general outline and conception, and despite additional embellishment, this production differed little from the one applauded at the Atelier. They had both moved a good way from the *plateau nu* of the Vieux Colombier. Copeau was now seeing theatre in terms of celebration, almost of liturgy; and towards the creation of this *fiesta* he was prepared to use all the arts of music, mime, and ballet. But the music of humanity, still or sparkling, sad or merry, could always be heard above the orchestra.

Among Copeau's intimate collaborators Louis Jouvet was a total man of the theatre. He looked back, not necessarily to the *plateau nu* of the Vieux Colombier which he had himself done much to clothe, but to the Elizabethan stage – for never had 'there been an arrangement so favourable to liberty of movement, to the dignity of theatre conventions, to the participation of the public in the action'. It was due to the radically different tool forged by the Italian Renaissance that the actor had 'ceased to develop any genuine depth, presenting to the audience an action diminished in scope, with refinements induced by the exigencies of perspective to the detriment of dramatic illusion and with its most precious qualities lost'. Jouvet dreamt of rediscovering the dramatic function of Shakespeare 'from that vanished creation that was the Globe Playhouse', for when he re-read the Elizabethan drama it was with the feeling of warming himself 'at a great fire now almost entirely reduced to embers'.[1] Jacques Copeau had done much to rekindle them.

2

In 1933 Charles Dullin produced *Richard III* in an adaptation by André Obey. Marie-Hélène Dasté designed the costumes, and Georges Vakalo the décors, inspired by medieval miniatures. The Atelier was a small theatre, and for this production Dullin used the stage boxes. With his small, squat, humped-back physique and drooping lower lip, he could exert fascination and inspire fear – especially the fascination of evil. This served him wonderfully in Richard. It was said of Dullin that he had only to crook his forefinger and any woman was at his feet. Lady Anne, for all the suppressed violence of Marie-Hélène Dasté's playing of the part, had no difficulty in falling there. Brasillach recalled the moment when 'the hideous hunch-back in his crown and cloth of gold, drunk with murder and ambition, whirled round on the stage, abandoning himself to the four winds'; and the battle of Bosworth 'mimed by a dozen supernumaries – a warlike ballet danced by anonymous actors – while the royal hunch-back, bent under the weight of his huge lance, rose up like one of Hokusai's warriors, and the battlefield resounded with the drums'.[2] Dullin's aim was to create a western

[1] *Theatre Arts Monthly*
[2] *Animateurs du Théâtre* (1954)

aesthetic of the theatre, as indigenous and as unmistakable as the theatre of China or Japan, and as far removed from naturalism.

Richard III enjoyed a tremendous popular success, and was followed in 1937 by *Julius Caesar*, for which Bakst designed the costumes and Darius Milhaud composed the music. Dullin played Cassius 'stunted with hate and poisoned with rancour, and not particularly Roman' – as one observer described him. This, it seems, was hardly his intention. More to the point was his comment on a man who had committed suicide after the German invasion in 1940. 'He finished like Cassius, without any fine phrases, and as nobly as he had lived.'

The little stage of the Atelier was very skilfully used so that neither the Forum nor the Senate seemed absurdly reduced in scale. Semi-circular fragments of steps indicated a corner of the street or the Senate house, and a rostrum rose up when required, virtually in view of the audience. The crowd scrambled and vociferated on the apron. In Brutus' garden a single olive tree gleamed in the moonlight, like a painting by di Chirico. Jean Marchat was a brilliant Mark Antony, and the name of Jean Vilar appeared on the programme in a tiny part. Habib Benglia, a well-known coloured actor, made a deep impression as the Soothsayer.

The rediscovery of Shakespeare by these gifted *animateurs* coincided with the rediscovery – as Gaston Baty put it – of that 'wooden O where Shakespeare recreates the world'. Baty's conception of the theatre was just as basically religious as Copeau's eventually became. Where Shakespeare was concerned he saw the Elizabethan schism as a purely political affair in no way altering the popular sensibility, and the Elizabethan theatre as the late and logical flowering of the medieval stage. But he did not share Copeau's respect for the written word.

The poet dreams up a play, and puts down on paper whatever can be reduced to words. But words can only express part of his dream. What is left over does not exist in written form. The business of the director is to restore to the work of the poet whatever was lost on the way from the dream to the manuscript.

Marguerite Jamois as Hamlet,
Théâtre Montparnasse 1928

ma fièvre ? Tu es là, pourtant. Tu parais aussi palpable que celui-ci que je tire de sa gaine.② Tu me montres le chemin que j'allais prendre, l'instrument que j'allais employer. Sont-ce mes yeux qui me trompent ou mes autres sens ? Je te vois toujours, et sur ta lame, et sur ton manche, des gouttes de sang qui n'y étaient pas tout à l'heure...Mais non,④ tout cela n'est pas. Seulement ma pensée qui prend forme. A cette heure, sur la moitié de ce monde la nature semble morte et les mauvais rêves se glissent sous les rideaux pour violer le sommeil. La sorcellerie offre ses sacrifices à la pâle Hécate, et le meurtre livide, éveillé en sursaut par le loup, sa sentinelle,⑤ d'un pas furtif marche à son but... Toi, terre solide et ferme, n'écoute point mes pas, de peur que tes pierres mêmes ne crient où je vais, et ne brisent l'horrible silence qu'il faut à cette minute.⑦

　　　　(La cloche sonne)　　Entre lady Macbeth)
　　　　　　　　　　　MACBETH
J'y vais, j'y vais.⑧ La cloche m'appelle.⑨ Ne l'entends pas Duncan : c'est ton glas qu'elle sonne, pour le ciel ou l'enfer.
　　　　(Il sort.

　　　　　　　　　　LADY MACBETH
Ce qui les a enivrés m'a enhardie ; ce qui les a éteints m'a enflammée.⑩ Chut !...Non. C'est le hibou, fatal veilleur qui saluait la sinistre nuit.- Il est au travail. Les portes sont ouvertes. Les valets ronflent. J'ai si bien drogué leur boisson que la mort et la vie doivent disputer à qui les aura.

　　　　　　　　　　UNE VOIX ensommeillée

age from Gaston Baty's *mise-en-scène*
r *Macbeth*

This was a large presumption, for who could tell what had been lost of Shakespeare's 'dream', or if indeed anything had been lost at all? Nevertheless it was with these ideas that Baty presented the First Quarto *Hamlet* at the Théâtre Montparnasse in 1928, Marguerite Jamois walking intrepid in the wake of Sarah Bernhardt – an essay in transvestism, which was certainly not Elizabethan. Baty believed that the Folio version had been padded out in the interest of literature rather than stage effect. Such argument was easily refuted; but he adopted a suggestion of Dover Wilson that Hamlet overhears the conversation between Claudius, Gertrude and Polonius at the beginning of Act II, thus explaining the pointed dialogue with Polonius that follows it. In the single décor for the play symbolism and realism were ingeniously combined. All the action took place in the courtyard of the castle, with the door to Polonius' house,

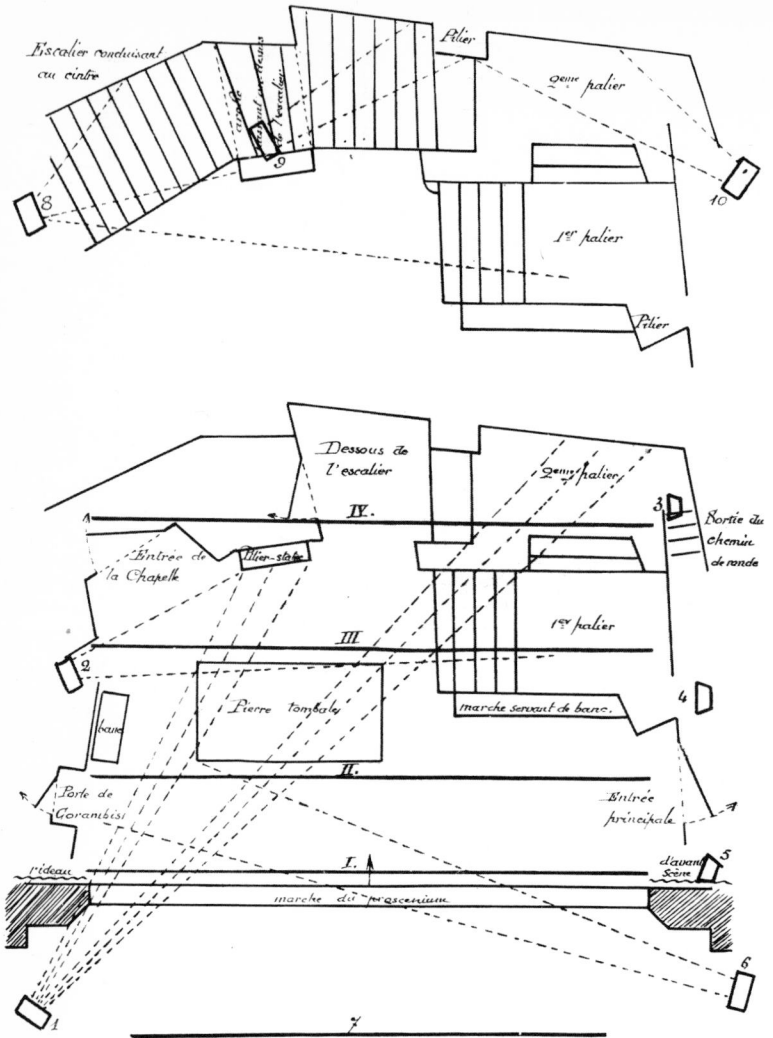

the entrance to the chapel, and a gravestone before a pillar clearly marked. A sculptured effigy on the pillar, representing Hamlet's father, turned conveniently into the Ghost. Draperies were lowered for the closet scene, and for ceremonial occasions. The text of the play had been reduced to shreds and patches, but the costumes were sumptuous. Nobody ever accused Baty of Jansenism, and whatever he did with his stage it was never a *plateau nu*.

At the outbreak of war in 1939 he had ready the designs for a *Romeo and Juliet*.[1] These were never to be carried out, although it would be worth the pains of another director to appropriate them. No play is a greater challenge to Elizabethan simultaneity, for the audience are invited to believe themselves in a market place, a ballroom, a garden beneath a balcony, a friar's cell, and a funeral vault – not to mention a passing glimpse of Mantua. Without any recourse to traverse curtains, Baty solved the problem by a semi-circular arch, with steps on either side, and a playing space above and below. Either space could be lit or blacked out as required, and scenic elements of décor concealed

Left: Stage plan for Gaston Baty's *Hamlet*, Théâtre Montparnasse 1928

Set design for Georges Pitoeff's *Hamlet*, Théâtre des Arts 1926

the steps when these were not in use, or illustrated the background. Juliet's balcony was set high up and dead centre – which might have made things difficult for Romeo; and in the final scene he was able to enter, and fight with Paris, above before descending into the vault. It would not be surprising to learn that Baty had seen Goethe's sketch for *A Midsummer Night's Dream*; conscious or otherwise, there is a straight line of derivation between the two.

Louis Jouvet said of Georges Pitoeff: 'Four times out of five he is mistaken; but it is he who has the genius.' Pitoeff's mistake was to attempt, heroically, parts for which he had not the physical means, and productions for which the means were lacking also. Nevertheless, a profound understanding of Shakespeare transpired through his imperfections. His first productions were given in Geneva with a company of amateurs who became professional when they moved to Paris. Here, in 1926, he presented *Hamlet*, in Marcel Schwob's translation. The 24 décors in black and grey were reduced to a single permanent setting for the subsequent production at the Théâtre des Mathurins. Pitoeff was afraid lest the pleasure of seeing so many changes should distract the audience from the play. He relied on the barest auxiliaries; one or two pieces of furniture, a carpet, and an opening well lit, relieved by black or blue curtains. Fortinbras and his soldiers were in white – an indication (contestable perhaps) that political virginity had returned to Denmark.

Pitoeff spoke 'To be or not to be' standing quite alone in the middle of the stage, and evidently saw the 'let be' to Horatio in the last act as the resigned answer to it. Brasillach wrote of his 'blank voice, his suffering and questioning look, his large ungainly figure' – the perfect incarnation of contemporary man at war with his instincts, 'burning to live with a greater intensity, and dreaming of the absolute'. Colette described how he

> showed his teeth when he laughed; the incurable crack in the voice; a kind of deep-seated negligence; the agility and ease of a man who walks about with bare feet . . . the way he looked above the head of the person he was talking to; the poetry and the instability and the need to go off the deep end – cruelly, if need be – and then the insolent come-back if he were checked.

However cracked the voice and unpleasing the accent, Georges Pitoeff's Hamlet spoke for his generation very much as he might have spoken for the generation of another *après-guerre*. Brasillach writes again:

> No other Hamlet was so perfectly identified with the Hamlet I have lived with since I was a boy, and before I saw any Hamlet on the stage. This was a young dreamer of the sixteenth century, living outside theatrical invention; and his anxiety, travelling across time and space, gradually became ours. One had the undeniable certainty that Hamlet really existed, and also that the whole of mankind shared his anguish; that he was, as I had been that evening, its immortal and insignificant legatee. . . . He turns the most ordinary fear into metaphysical anguish, and in this, no doubt, he is rather Russian. But he also translates into noble language the sum total of our discontents.[2]

Pitoeff was sensitive to the connection, as well as to the contrast, between *Hamlet* and *Macbeth*.

> The same three elements compose the basis of these two tragedies – the divine element, the thought, and the action. In *Hamlet* the divine element intervenes from the beginning. Hamlet, dreamy and thoughtful by nature, does nothing of his own accord, but

[1] Denis Gontard *Revue d'Histoire du Théâtre* (January-March 1965) pp. 137-40
[2] Ibid

divinity, in the shape of the ghost, *gives* him an order that he is obliged to obey. Macbeth, on the other hand, is at the very heart of the action, and it is divinity that provokes him to thought.

Pitoeff had not attempted to reproduce in his décors an historical setting for the play; his aim was to translate its inner conflict. As H. R. Lenormand, a gifted dramatist of the *entre deux guerres,* described it:

> Nothing could be more ethereal than the upper platforms of the huge ogive in which the action of the play was framed; nothing more embedded in matter, more irremediably lost in the mud of animality, than the dark well from which the couple came up, and in which they were finally engulfed. A series of steps and landings allowed the characters to circulate from the lowest to the highest levels; and this circulation was at once real and symbolic, giving life and breath to the drama.[1]

The music was composed by Henri Breitenstein who had composed two principal motifs – one for Macbeth and the other for his victims.

> By means of successive transformations Macbeth's theme becomes also that of Lady Macbeth . . . and afterwards, in a freer rhythm, the theme of Ambition; and finally, losing its sadness and austerity, it lights up in the last act, almost unrecognisably, to symbolise the Liberation. It then becomes a gay, striding, march like the quick pace of soldiers who will rush to the assault. The *initial phrase*, sombre and funereal, only recurs at the last moment when the hero dies.[2]

Ludmilla Pitoeff as Ophelia, Théâtre des Arts 1926

Pitoeff himself, according to Lenormand, gave no more than a sketch of Macbeth. In the violent passages his hoarse voice and excessive tension were tiring to the audience. 'It was only in thought that he belonged to the character. His appearance and diction let him down. Like a painter who leaves a portrait unfinished he disdained theatrical effects. He knew the actor's business too well.' This was acting of 'suggestions, allusive and nuancé'. In *Macbeth*, as in his other rôles, Pitoeff's characterizations were embryonic, overwhelming for the artist or psychologist who could see what he was getting at, but disconcerting for the general public.

His last Shakespeare production was *Romeo and Juliet,* in the superb translation by Pierre-Jean Jouve. He had conceived it as his theatrical testament to which everything he had done hitherto was leading up. His disappointment at its failure was correspondingly acute. The ingenious simultaneous décor – which lacked the simplicity of Baty's – was designed for the large stage of the Théâtre des Champs Elysées, and it seemed uncomfortably cramped at the Mathurins. Despite the innovation of placing Juliet's tomb under a trap–door – whence she must presumably have been lifted – the *mise-en-scène* left the audience confused. Pitoeff had misconceived Romeo as Hamlet's brother, and the misconception was emphasized by the dark hangings which enclosed the stage. His mistake was not, as Lenormand pointed out,

> to play Romeo when he was over fifty, but to play a part in which he would have been no better at twenty. On the stage, and in Romeo's costume, he was Romeo. Internally, he was not; internally he was Hamlet. In his 'real' life, as they call it – his life outside the theatre – Georges was Romeo to Ludmilla. That is why he found it natural to infuse the character with the lyrical and carnal exaltation which possessed him from his youth until the day he died. With any other Juliet but Ludmilla, he could not have played Romeo, nor would he have wished to.

[1] *Les Pitoeff* (1943)
[2] Henri Breitenstein
[3] Ibid

At the end of the preview, the fatigue of a heavy evening had thickened his diction. His voice was the voice of his bad first nights, and the sense he had of the public's polite hostility lowered it still further. We suffered for him to hear the tomb scene through a mist, where the words left his lips as if they were exhausted by the necessity of crossing a barrage.[3]

It was a sad conclusion to a gallant and imaginative enterprise. Nothing the Pitoeffs did was quite perfect; but their failures were excused because they were so loved, and because they so loved one another.

3

No play lends itself more easily to a political *parti-pris* than *Coriolanus*. Militarism, patriotism, and oligarchy are at odds with the revolt of the masses, who invoke the constitution in their support. The production at the Comédie Française in December 1932 was a calculated risk, since the socialist city council of Geneva had already refused to harbour it, in spite of the fact that a Swiss, R. L. Piachaud, had made the translation. This was approved by Copeau: 'Not the least of the writer's merits is to have introduced, with an admirable tact and discretion, a sonority closer to the language of today.' It was in fact a good deal too close for the comfort of the house of Molière. The anti-democratic sentiments received a standing ovation; cries of 'Vive Boulanger' came from all parts of the auditorium; the curtain had to be lowered twenty times during the performance; several enraged deputies left before the end; and the *Action Française* declared, not surprisingly, that the Comédie Française had 'never chosen a better play, nor mounted a more magnificent production'.

This was later simplified into a more structural décor of curtains and steps. For some spectators, however, the performance – so far from being inflam-

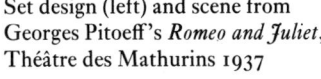

Set design (left) and scene from Georges Pitoeff's *Romeo and Juliet*, Théâtre des Mathurins 1937

matory – was too academic. Both Colette, and Brassillach who would have sympathized with the anti-democratic manifestations, confessed themselves bored. Copeau wrote:

> Shakespeare's plays can only be given their proper style and movement – the *poetry* of representation can only serve the *poetry* of the text – if we place ourselves back in conditions analogous to those with which these plays were originally satisfied, and to which they submitted. It's not a question of erudition, or still less of reconstruction; we must re-invent in the spirit of a tradition. M. Boll has brought this method to perfection for *Hamlet* and *Coriolanus*. He employs a basic structure, modified by curtains and light flats.

But the actors were less capable than the designer in capturing the Shakespearian style.

The play was directed by Emile Fabre, using his upper and lower levels to indicate the rise and fall of Caius Marcius. Bridges-Adams came over from Stratford and invited him to produce *Othello* or *Richard III* at the Memorial Theatre. With 231 supernumaries it was small wonder that the assistant, rehearsing them all through the night, lost his voice. But political passions were now running high. Victor Hugo's *Ruy Blas* was forbidden the boards between November 1933 and August of the following year; the speech beginning '*O ministres intègres*' was too much for a public infuriated by parliamentary incompetence and corruption. On 20 December 1933 the Commission des Finances – which held the purse strings of the Comédie Française – declared war on the 'adaptation by the foreign fascist Piachaud'. In January 1934 the play was interrupted by an outbreak of applause and hisses; and in the following month it was temporarily suspended at the request of President Doumergue. This invited the obvious headline: '*Coriolan en exil*'. In March the run of the play was resumed. The house was sold out, and the anti-democratic tirades of Jean Hervé, who was playing Coriolanus, were received once again with wild applause.

Shortly afterwards *Coriolanus* was produced at the Maly Theatre in Moscow as a 'drama of individualism' to show 'a superman who had detached himself from the people and betrayed them'.

It has been said that Gordon Craig and Adolphe Appia forced the plastic upon the stage; and experiments in the Cirque Medrano in Paris looked forward to the arena productions of the future. Appia's designs for *Hamlet* were an inspired dialogue between structure and space. The long, straight rostrum for the battlements, its line only broken by a short slope at one end and an upright mass closing it at the other. The single octagonal pillar giving Hamlet strength and focus for 'To be or not to be'. All light on a central dais for the play scene. The passage of Fortinbras down an inclined ramp, bordered by what looked like milestones, from which the Captain was to jump down for his few words with Hamlet. For 'the rest is silence' Appia conceived a suggestion of infinity, with an idealized light tinged with gold creating the limitless freedom of the open air. On 'Why does the drum come hither?' pages were partially to open the curtains at the back, discovering Fortinbras at the top of four steps and a sweep of sky beyond. Hamlet's body would be carried on a long shield to the platform, and left lying in profile to the audience. Four torches would rise above the level of the platform, as the ordnance was fired.

The same reduction to essentials, and an equal satisfaction to the eye and mind, was evident in Appia's conception of *King Lear*. He built his scenes with light as well as with matter, using shadows to give significance to form, to translate emotion, and to define by delicate suggestion. His influence was visible in Jones's *Richard III*, Bel Geddes's *Hamlet* and, in Germany, on Jessner's *Othello*. He claimed for the *régisseur* the authority of a *chef d'orchestre*. 'I am happy' he said shortly before his death in 1932 – and they were among his last words – 'to have been able to show the way to a few people.' He is showing it to them still.

Set design by Adolphe Appia for *King Lear* 1926

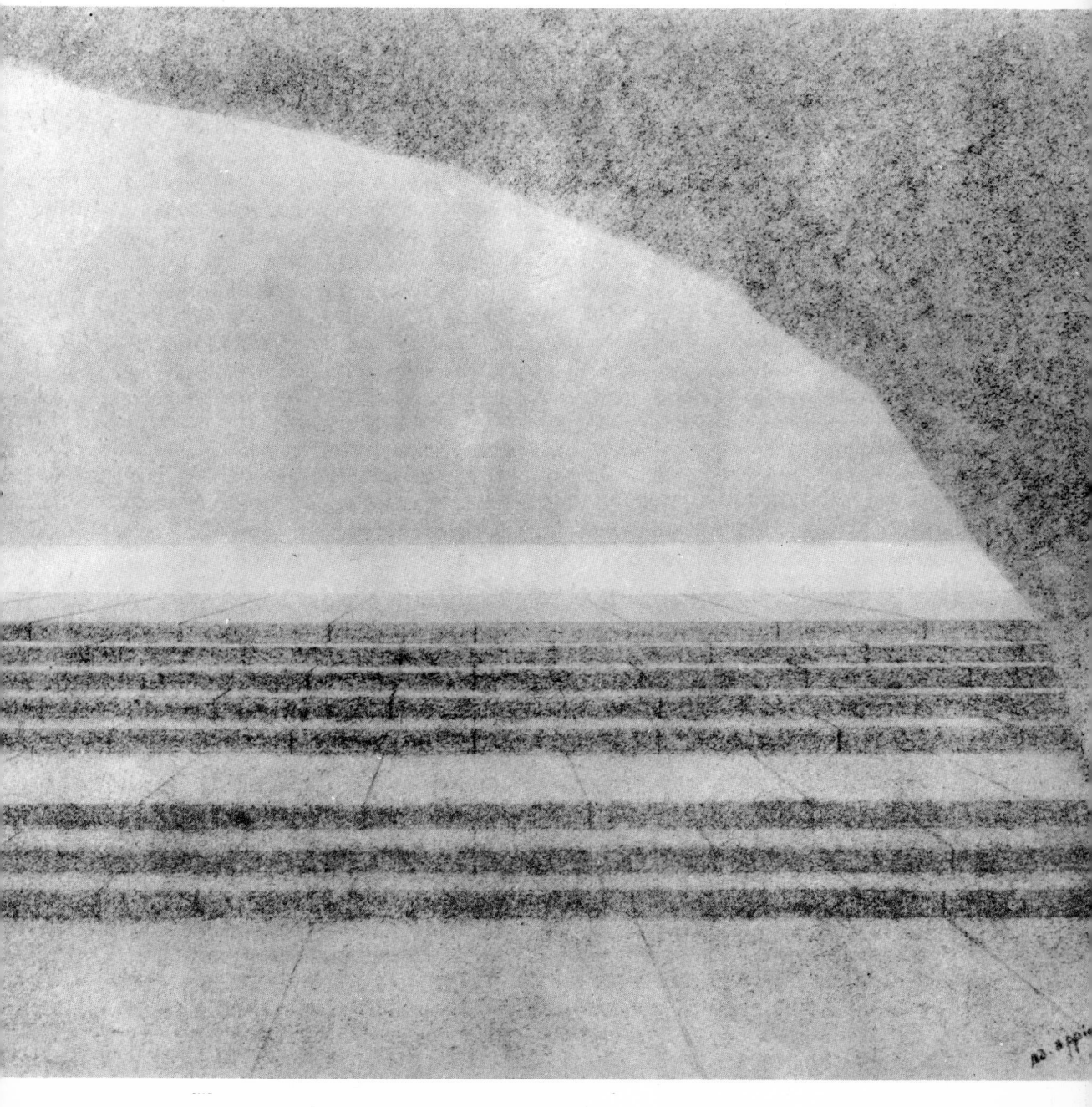

The international scale and success of his operations give Max Reinhardt (1873-1943) a place apart in the history of the Shakespearian theatre. Where Copeau and Pitoeff had registered their tactical victories or defeats with depleted battalions, Reinhardt deployed his grand strategy with several divisions, and was difficult to approach except through his Chief-of-Staff. He was unlikely to engage in battle unless he were assured of success beforehand, and his control, though it was remote, extended to the smallest detail. A Napoleon of the stage, he did not waste his breath in theory; and if he had an aesthetic he kept it to himself. 'The art of lighting' he declared tersely 'consists in putting light where you want it and taking it away where you don't want it.' That, he might have added – echoing Lady Bracknell – was all there was to say about lighting. Excellent, as far as it went; and it went a long way.

Reinhardt had the Jewish power of rapid assimilation, allied to a genius for showmanship. As an actor under Otto Brahm (1856-1912) at the Freien Bühne in Berlin, he had learned a good deal about ensemble, the workings of repertory, and psychological interpretation. He had been impressed by the Meininger, and jumped like a child at the possibilities of real wind and real rain. When he produced his own *Julius Caesar* at Drury Lane, he showed what he – and they – could do with a crowd, letting the voices start at one point and then be picked up at another. (Louis Calvert, let it not be forgotten, had already done this for Tree at His Majesty's.) There were other influences at work; Wagner, where music, song, dance, speech, and décor contributed to a unitary effect; the Berlin and Münich Secessionists; and, at the other end of the scale, Savit's Elizabethan simplicities at Münich.

Reinhardt took over the direction of the Kleines Theater in 1902, the Neues Theater in 1903, and the Deutsches Theater in 1905. Here he produced *The Winter's Tale,* with Emil Orlik's décor, and implied acknowledgements to Gordon Craig. It was a child's vision of the play – much criticized – where the bright green velvet grass of Bohemia, the conventional flowers and fruit trees, the toy cottage, and the masts and pennons in the background, opened up like the illustrations from a child's picture book. When Hermione entered for her trial, word went round from mouth to mouth, cries of love and rage, and then a sudden shriek. Reinhardt, taking another cue from Dumont and Lindemann at Dusseldorf, was a pioneer of symbolic staging. At the Deutsches Theater the actors' silhouettes stood out against a whitewashed wall, and all lines converged upon the centre. Later he introduced a circular cyclorama – a light structure of iron, covered with plaster, supported on columns to allow the passage of scenery, and hidden when required by curtains of the same colour. He used no footlights except for interior scenes, where they counteracted the effect of the upper lighting. But Reinhardt was more than an inspired technician. Brahm had taught him to look for actors who could think as well as feel – Gertrud Eysoldt was one of them – though he found in Alexander Moissi, who could feel more easily than think, the Romeo and Hamlet of his dreams. Moissi's Hamlet,

Alexander Moissi as Hamlet in Max Reinhardt's production, Künstlertheater, Munich, and Deutsches Theater, Berlin, 1919

where the traces of an Italian accent softened still further the 'cello resonance of the voice, seemed a little tired and disembodied by the time Maurice Browne brought it to London in 1932; but it had long enraptured continental ears. He first played the part for Reinhardt at the Deutsches Theater in 1910. Here the orchestra was covered and three rows of stalls removed to provide an enlarged apron; and the painted pine trees stretching up into the proscenium for the outdoor scenes, with the tapestried interiors, showed the influence of Tree's production which had been seen in Berlin. In the closet scene two large portraits of Hamlet's father and Claudius occupied the back wall.

Reinhardt was in fairly close touch with the English theatre. He so admired Arthur Bourchier as Henry VIII that he invited him – without success – to learn German and play the part in Berlin. He also envied the elegance of English playgoing – white ties in the dress circle and stalls – and thought a good digestion after a good dinner made an audience less critical. A genial epicure himself, Reinhardt looked down his nose at the beer and sandwiches of a German buffet. He did not particularly want his audience to think; he wanted them to laugh or to cry. Even when he failed to tap the springs of tears, or tapped too grossly the springs of laughter, his practice never belied his conviction that the purpose of the theatre was to entertain. Shakespeare might well have agreed with him.

Reinhardt exerted a direct influence on the English stage when Martin Harvey, with Poel at his elbow, produced *The Taming of the Shrew* at the Prince of Wales (1913). He suggested the placing of Christopher Sly on a carved stone seat over the well of the orchestra to which he was conducted by the Lord's major-domo. The stage, steps and cloth masking the proscenium arch were all in grey. Behind were three false prosceniums; the first framed with huge green laurels, tied with bows of gilt ribbon, and the arch of black wood patterned in gold. The effect was that of a hall opening on to a broad landscape and a road disappearing in the distance. From a terrace and black stone balustrade three steps led down to it. Two bay trees festooned with gold marked the opening at the back. For the Induction tapestried curtains described an Italian landscape, and the Lord's 'wanton pictures' were painted on white Roman satin. The stage was fully disclosed for the entrance of the players, their scarlet and yellow waggon in tune with their costumes. The following scenes were played against curtains or screens eight feet high, run into position by a servant. A large canopied seat, with a table in front, hoisted into the 'flies' for the outdoor scenes, indicated Petruchio's house.

Reinhardt produced his own *Taming of the Shrew* as a rumbustious farce, played entirely for the benefit of Sly – for this alone, he thought, would excuse Petruchio's intolerable behaviour. The actors appeared in the costumes of the clowns, harlequins, columbines, and pantaloons of the Commedia dell'Arte, inspired by the engravings of Callot. They wheeled their cart into the hall of the great house, used its staircase as it suited their convenience, and made packing-cases serve as furniture. Reinhardt had installed a revolving stage at the Deutsches Theater, which enabled him to produce *Much Ado about Nothing* in fourteen scenes, vividly coloured by Ernst Stern. A double row of old-gold walls seen in perspective ran out to a thin streak of blue sky. As with *The Winter's Tale*, it was a festal, child-like, vision of the play, all the bushes and hedges on the stage seeming to resound with music. But Reinhardt's first great success with Shakespeare in Berlin was *A Midsummer Night's Dream* (1905), designed by the Danish artist, Max Rée. Here a northern wood of plastic trees

Victor Arnold in Max Reinhardt's
The Taming of the Shrew,
Deutsches Theater, Berlin, 1909

Gertrud Eysoldt as Puck in
Max Reinhardt's *A Midsummer Night's
Dream*, Neues Theater, Berlin, 1905

and tall grass revolved to show the fairies in green tights and green wigs, and
Gertrud Eysoldt as a shaggy Puck in yellow-brown tights and a leopard-skin
round her bosom. Reinhardt later changed his conception of the part, and
allowed a larger freedom to his comedians – which, in the way of German actors,
they did not scruple to abuse. Then, in 1925 he produced a baroque *Dream* in
Vienna at the Theater an der Josefstadt, where the light from flaring candelabra
fell on the thick, corkscrew pillars. This was also seen at the Salzburg Schauspielhaus. Oskar Strad designed the settings, and Ernest de Weerth the costumes;
Tilly Lösch danced; and the Hippolyta was Rosamund Pinchot, who had played
the nun in the New York production of *The Miracle*. Ernst Stern waged a
successful campaign against Reinhardt's unnecessary use of tights, but he
recognized his sense of colour; Iago in green, 'glistening like a reptile', Tybalt
flaming like a fighting cock, Mercutio matching the glitter of his speeches,
Rosencrantz and Guildenstern as sportsmen because – a sure intuition here –
they were really Englishmen.

Reinhardt handled *The Comedy of Errors* 'like a puppet-master', employing

Set designs by Ernst Stern for
Max Reinhardt's *Merchant of Venice*,
Deutsches Theater, Berlin, 1913

Design by Ernst Stern for
Max Reinhardt's *The Tempest*,
Volksbühne, Berlin, 1915

Right: Max Reinhardt's
Merchant of Venice, Campo San
Trovaso 1934

music to set the rhythm of the entire play. A bridge spanned the width of the
stage, with a view of houses above, and below of ships at anchor. The actors
performed either on the bridge or the apron. His *Macbeth* (1915) was conventionally costumed in kilt and tartan. Stern's décor of movable towers, with
walls, buttresses, steps, and archways, did not prevent the creation of space.
Lightning flashed, clouds scudded, and wind whistled or howled over a
background of treeless heather; and the deep groundswell of an organ mingled
with the night owl's shriek to sound an accompaniment to crime. Bagpipes were
commanded for the banquet scene, but a Scottish prisoner of war refused to
play them 'for a bloody lot of Boches'.

In the summer of 1916 Stern was staying with Reinhardt on Hildensee off the
Baltic coast. 'I see this Hildensee as Bermuda' observed the *régisseur*, as they
watched the cattle driven over at low tide to feed, 'the right scene for Caliban,
Ariel and Prospero'.[1] The result was a *Tempest*, with Rudolph Schildkraut as a
notable Caliban, where the revolving stage could be raised or lowered at will.
For the opening scene the ship rolled and lurched over the cavity and disappeared beneath on Gonzalo's 'I would fain die a dry death.' Then the island
rose in its place, strewn with brown and yellow rocks, and reddish cactus-like
vegetation. Reinhardt afterwards produced *The Tempest* in the natural stone
theatre at Hellbrunn. He had the artist's – and the impresario's – eye for a site,
seeing the Summer Riding School at Salzburg, with its three tiers of boxes hewn
out of the rock of the Monschsberg and the greensward below, as an appropriate
setting for *As You Like It*.

He was particularly at home with the comedies. In *Twelfth Night* Humper-
dinck accompanied the love scenes, and in *The Merchant of Venice* – with Albert
Bassermann as Shylock – the singing and humming city, with violins in the
distance, effervescent with the *joie de vivre*, was a popular reply to the Meininger
production and its gliding gondolas, princely retainers on horseback, and
carnival processions. This Venice was hot and quick of tongue, its tempo slowed
down to a lyrical *andante* in the park at Belmont. The stage pictures were
inspired by Carpaccio, Giovanni Bellini, and Veronese; and 'when the play
was over' wrote George Brandes 'you had been in the fantastic Venice of the
Middle Ages'. You were in it even more immediately when Reinhardt produced

[1] Ernst Stern *My Life, my Stage* (1951)

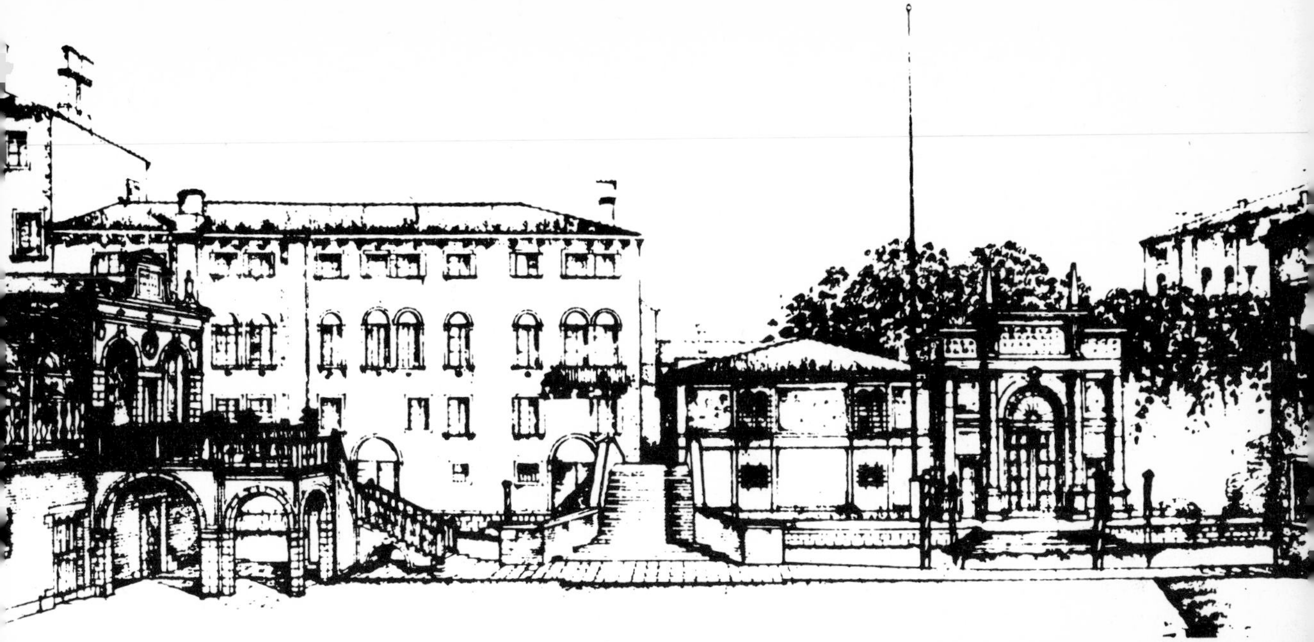

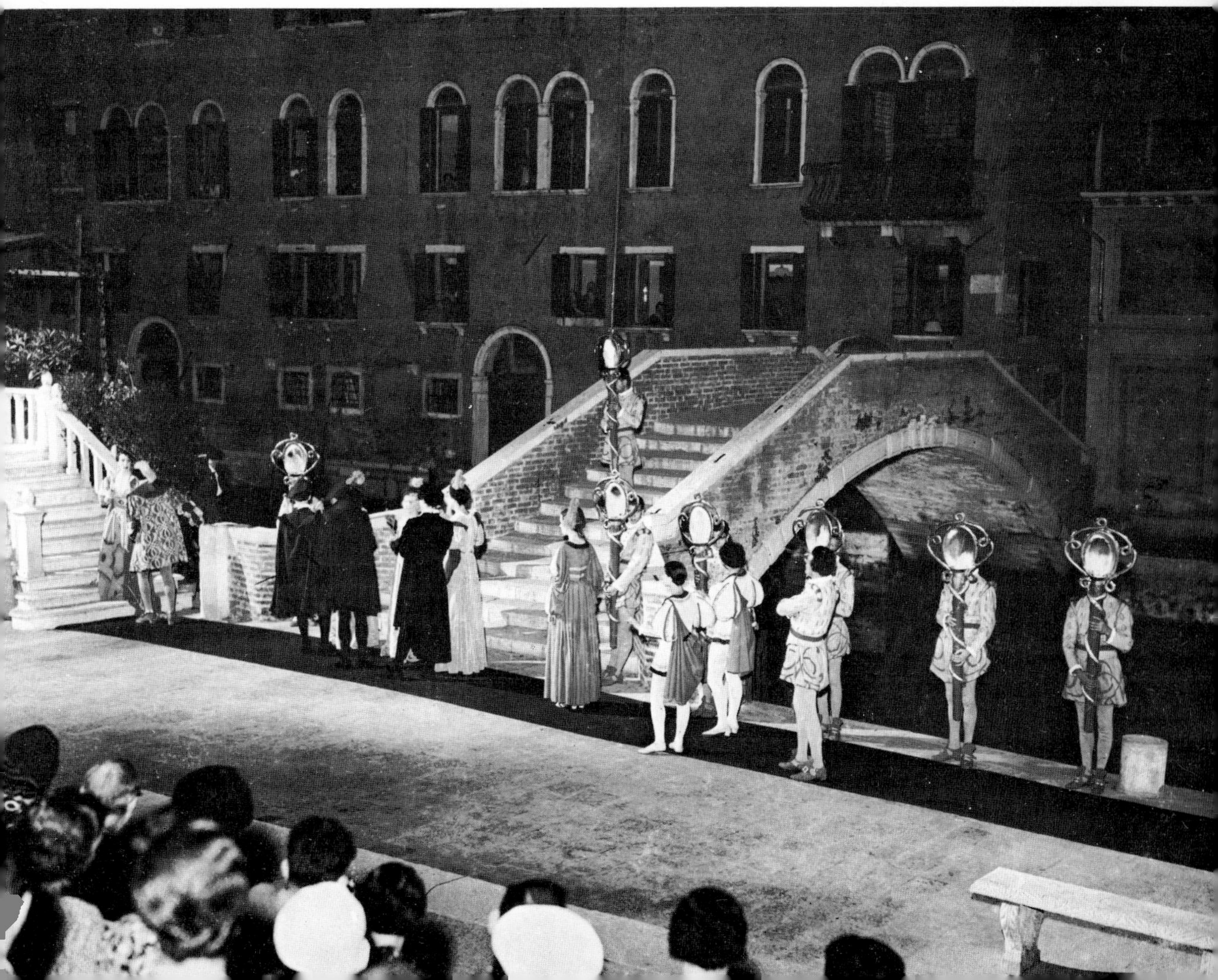

the play, with Memo Benassi as Shylock and Marta Abba as Portia, on the Campo San Trovaso. Nine tenths of the piazza was occupied by spectators, facing the bridge that crossed the Rio d'Ognissanti. On their right was the *casino* of the noble Venetians, designed by Duilio Torres, and on their left – also designed by Torres – stood Portia's *castello*, a little close for plausibility, but with an appropriate suggestion of Palladio. Shylock's house was on the left, at the end of a short lane. Here there was no artificial construction. Reinhardt played ravishing variations with light and water. The characters met and conversed on the bank of the canal, and arrived and departed by gondola, the Doge descending from his gilded barge for the trial scene in the piazza. In the last act a garden was improvised on the steps of the bridge, so that it seemed as if all the characters, as they stepped out of their gondolas, were disembarking at Belmont from the Brenta. The balconies of Portia's mansion, the windows of Shylock's house, and the rim of a well which formed part of the natural site, were all used effectively. Titina Rota's costumes showed with particular brilliance in the retinue of the Prince of Aragon, and Victor de Sabata's music did its best to supply what was missing in the Tuscan adaptation of the text.

In 1919 Reinhardt had opened the Grosse Schauspielhaus in Berlin – the old circus Schumann – with a production of *Hamlet* in semi-modern dress. Moissi and the other characters wore fur caps and trimmings, high gaiters, loose coats, and voluminous capes. The Ghost and the soldiers appeared in the steel helmets of the German army. *Julius Caesar* followed; but in 1920 Reinhardt left Berlin for Vienna and became in due course the uncrowned King of Salzburg. After the *anschluss* he lost his throne, but continued to deploy his grand strategy in the United States. The more fastidious would not dissent from the earlier judgment of Stark Young that Reinhardt was a director

of great energy and a vast power to assimilate the ideas encountered; of a remarkable fighting force; of an extraordinary sense of the theatrical, of the spring and life necessary to real theatre, of a vast talent for management and a prodigious achievement in reducing to order the welter and abundant variety and wide range of theatrical elements, theories, forms, movements, dramas, not only of our day but of former

Design by Ernst Stern for
Max Reinhardt's *Julius Caesar*,
Grosse Schauspielhaus, Berlin, 1920

times as well. In a more strictly artistic sense Reinhardt's achievement seems never of the first-rank.[1]

Set design by Emil Pirchan for Leopold Jessner's *Richard III*, Staatliches Schauspielhaus, Berlin, 1920

Nevertheless it was considerable. Shakespeare had served him well; how well he served Shakespeare depended on one's priorities. Arthur Hopkins, for one, thought that he had got them right.

> He has swallowed Craig, but he has digested him. . . . To my mind Reinhardt does more to assist and less to impede the author than any living producer. If he wants a great scenic effect, he is careful to play it in such a way that it is not going to kill the lines. He makes his effects belong. They are not dragged in. They are not glaringly apparent. A little of Craig goes a long way, and Reinhardt knows how to use him.[2]

2

Leopold Jessner (1878-1945)[3] was a disciple of the Reinhardt school who denied the teachings of his master. Where the temperament of Reinhardt was emotional and romantic, and his vision impressionistic, Jessner was essentially an architect, gripped at first by the dead hand of expressionism. Although he believed with Appia that 'all stage settings should be a point of departure for the actor', he was less concerned that they should be a point of delight for the audience. There was plenty of space in the décors that Emil Pirchan designed for him at the Staatliches Schauspielhaus in Berlin, but not very much room for humanity. He became known for his 'Jessnertreppen', so constantly did he depend on steps and levels. His *Richard III* powerfully anticipated Jan Kott's vision of Shakespeare's

[1] *Theatre Arts Monthly* (May 1924)
[2] *Max Reinhardt and his Theatre* (1924) p.339
[3] See Denis Bablet in *Revue d'Histoire du Théâtre* (January-March 1965) pp.58-69

Design by Saladin Schmitt for Johannes Schröder's *Henry V*, Stadttheater, Bochum, 1927

Below: Gustav Singer's simultaneous set for Shakespearian productions, showing the Expressionist influence

historical plays as the 'mechanism' of power up which the protagonist ascends, and from which he is precipitated. Richard was crowned in a red cloak at the head of a huge red staircase, while eight retainers, also in red silk, sank down below him. It was from here that he called 'my kingdom for a horse' after the curses of those he had murdered had come to him from the wings, his sleeping body beating a tattoo to their imprecations; and on the same steps that his army, dressed in red, fought symbolically with Richmond's who were in white. The end had moved a century away from Kean's desperation – 'drunk with wounds' – for Jessner did not believe in Shakespearian battles. Richard, naked to the waist, mounted his sword, hopped down the steps, and fell. The staircase, when it was required, concealed the two levels on which the rest of the play was acted; an upper terrace from which Richard and Buckingham bamboozled the Lord Mayor and citizens of London, and the stage proper with an opening into Clarence's cell. A symbolic representation of the Tower composed the background, except for the final scene. The production eschewed realism at every point, giving the shape and essence, rather than the historical substance and detail, of the play. The murderers of Clarence squatted on the prompter's box, and a mere plunge of the dagger in his direction was enough to indicate the *coup de grâce*. Fritz Kortner's Richard reminded people of a humped toad, a grinning Japanese mask, or Rodin's Balzac; but the grotesquerie was without grandeur, and the frightfulness held no fascination. His voice alternated between a studied and semi-whispered staccato, and a scream or snarl. Jessner's over-simplified symbolism often defeated its own ends, even in a play that invited simplification. Light and shadow were given the best parts, and it was said of this production that it was 'an explanation in black and white, which occasionally ventures to whisper in white and red'.

In *Othello* the yellow light played on the canvas cyclorama, a pale, neutral

[1] Charles Maurras

wall of faintly salmon pink, and on the double podium which occupied the centre of the stage. Desdemona's bed, with its white curtains, occupied – very impressively – the upper level of this. Elsewhere a corner of Brabantio's house, two pillars and some seats for the Senate, and the large trunk of a tree for the garden in Cyprus, were a sufficient indication of locality. Jessner's aim was to dramatize an event, not to interpret a character. Motivation did not interest him in the least; the audience was invited to watch, with the minimum of emotional involvement or decorative distraction, *what* was happening, and not *why*. This objectivity was a long way from Reinhardt, who in his production of the same play had hunted for motives with the keen nose of a foxhound. Kortner's Othello had a bovine strength, but the leonine beauty of the part was beyond him.

Between 1922 and 1926 Jessner produced nothing by Shakespeare. Expressionism was going sour on him, but he was looking for something other than the romanticism of Reinhardt, the intellectualism of Barker, the archaism of Poel, or the aestheticism of Gordon Craig. He found it in politics. A social democrat of advanced views, he was not satisfied to see what a play had meant to Shakespeare; he had to decide what it could mean for him, and for those who thought – or could be made to think – as he did. With communism to the east and fascism to the south, and a stricken Germany secreting the seeds of its desperate recovery, it was a case of '*politique d'abord*' – little as he would have relished the quotation.[1]

'Any art' Jessner wrote 'which is not of its own time is without roots . . . and at the best can offer us only a superficial pleasure.' His aim, therefore, was to create a theatre which should be political, but should not be the theatre of a political party. He would preserve his cherished objectivity to 'express a spiritual content, set in motion the facts of which it was composed, and show what he had seen, brutally, without mask or make-up'. *Hamlet* was an obvious

Leopold Jessner's *Hamlet*, Schauspielhaus, Berlin, 1926

Opposite: Set design by Ernst Stern
for Max Reinhardt's *A Midsummer
Night's Dream*, Deutsches Theater,
Berlin, 1913

Set design by Rochus Gliese for
Jürgen Fehling's *Love's Labour's Lost*,
Staatliches Schauspielhaus, Berlin,
1930

Overleaf: Set design by Emil Pirchan
for Leopold Jessner's *Othello*,
Staatliches Schauspielhaus, Berlin,
1921

choice. Prussian militarism was scarcely concealed in the uniforms of the Court, and Claudius bore a certain resemblance to William II. *The Murder of Gonzago* was played in a baroque theatre, with the king and queen in the Royal Box. Hamlet smoked a pipe as he chatted with the gravediggers. But these adjuncts were incidental. The character of Hamlet interested Jessner not at all; he was only concerned to illustrate the 'something' that was 'rotten in the state of Denmark' – and this was principally the espionage of which Hamlet was the victim. Denmark was visibly a 'prison', and it was by no means certain that Fortinbras had opened its doors. Here was no image of political virginity in a white uniform, as Craig and Pitoeff had conceived it, but a Prussian officer mounting with firm steps the 'great mechanism' of power.

Jessner's production scandalized many of the critics, and a large section of the public. They saw that beneath the gold braid and epaulettes he had dressed the play in what 'all good Prussians take to be the red dress of socialism'. The National Party introduced a motion in the Landtag inviting the authorities, in the name of culture, art, and morality, to suppress it. In 1930 Jessner resigned from the Staatliches Schauspielhaus, and in 1933 left Germany altogether. In 1945 he died in Los Angeles, virtually forgotten. He was a hard, honest, humourless, intractable character, and as dictatorial as the dictator who had forced him into exile. He had not a tithe of Reinhardt's talent, but he belongs to the Shakespearian theatre of today in a way that Reinhardt does not. White ties (or black) in the stalls and dress circle would have caused him no pang of envy.

3

There were other stages. Jürgen Fehling, who directed the Schiller Theatre in Berlin, and succeeded Jessner at the Staatliches, made less of an international noise than Reinhardt or Jessner, for he was neither a showman like the first, nor a doctrinaire like the second. Basing his productions on a deep feeling for the text, it was not until he presented Werner Krauss as Richard III on an open stage that he allowed political overtones to become audible in his work. Here, exceptionally, the influence of Brecht was apparent. Fehling was at once a visionary and a superb technician. Käte Gold and Lucie Mannheim were among the actresses he inspired, and he directed Krauss as a memorable Shylock. A tragic figure – for he died insane shortly after the war – he is still spoken of in Germany as the greatest director of his time, although in later years his eccentricity got the better of his judgment.

In Münich Richard Kellerhals' Grumio – with 'his odd wizened little face, inordinately simple, just a bit loony; his acrobatic legs, quick and comic' – pretty well stole the *Shrew* from a bull-necked Petruchio. At the Schlosspark Community Theatre in Berlin *Timon of Athens* was played within the walls of the annexe to the old Schloss at Steglitz (1921). A play in which 'language was packed with content to the point of disruption' was compared by the same critic to 'flagons of steel into which superabundant quantities of gas have been forced', and was thought, as such, to satisfy the prevalent taste for expressionism. The Volksbühne productions in Berlin were all designed for a revolving stage with an interior and exterior set, and on either side a flat which moved on a swivel. These were tilted downstage for exterior scenes, and the gaps left open formed entrances from the ends of streets. For interior scenes they were swung upstage to join the main set. It was a convenient formula. After Jessner had

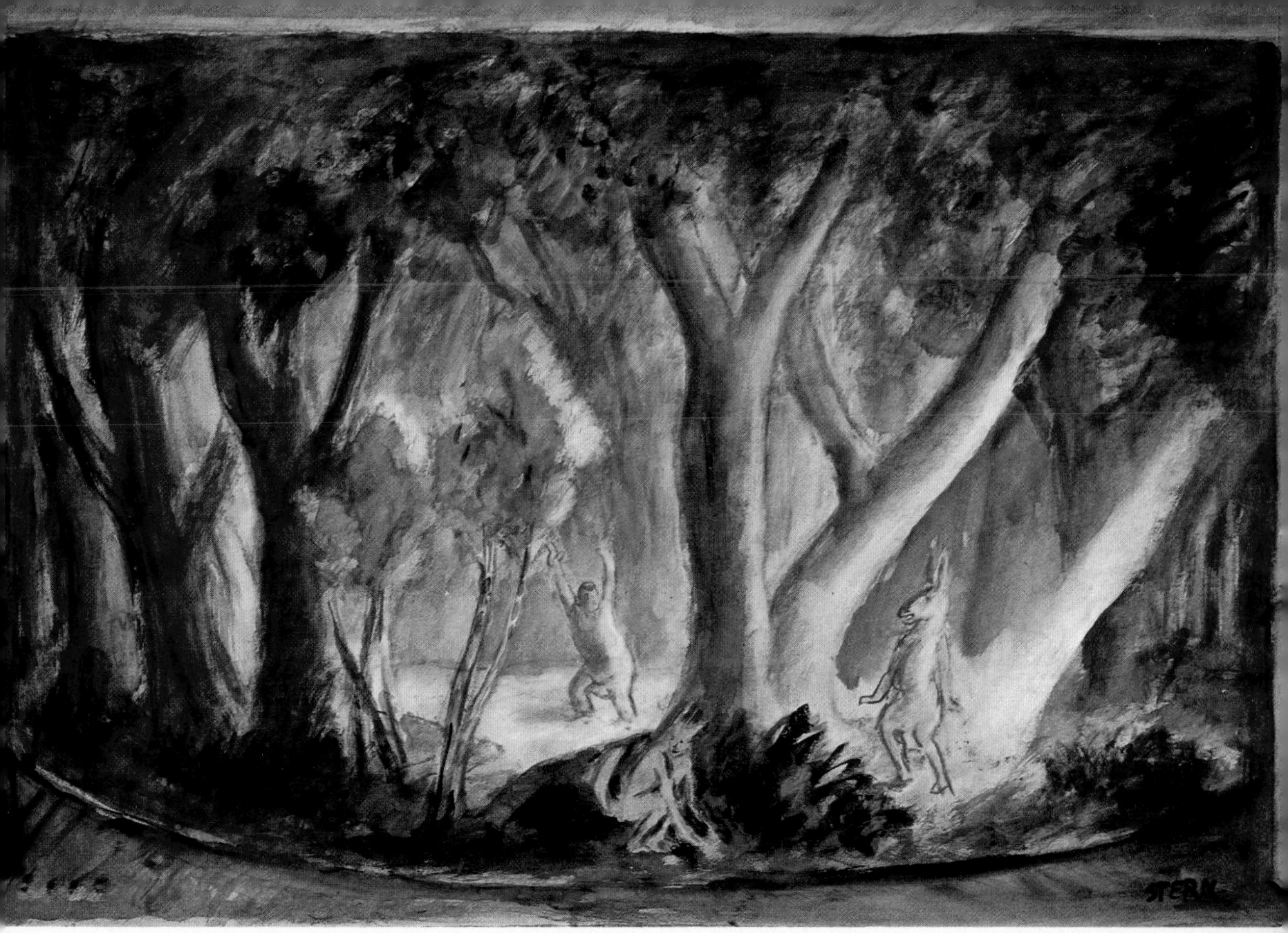
STERN

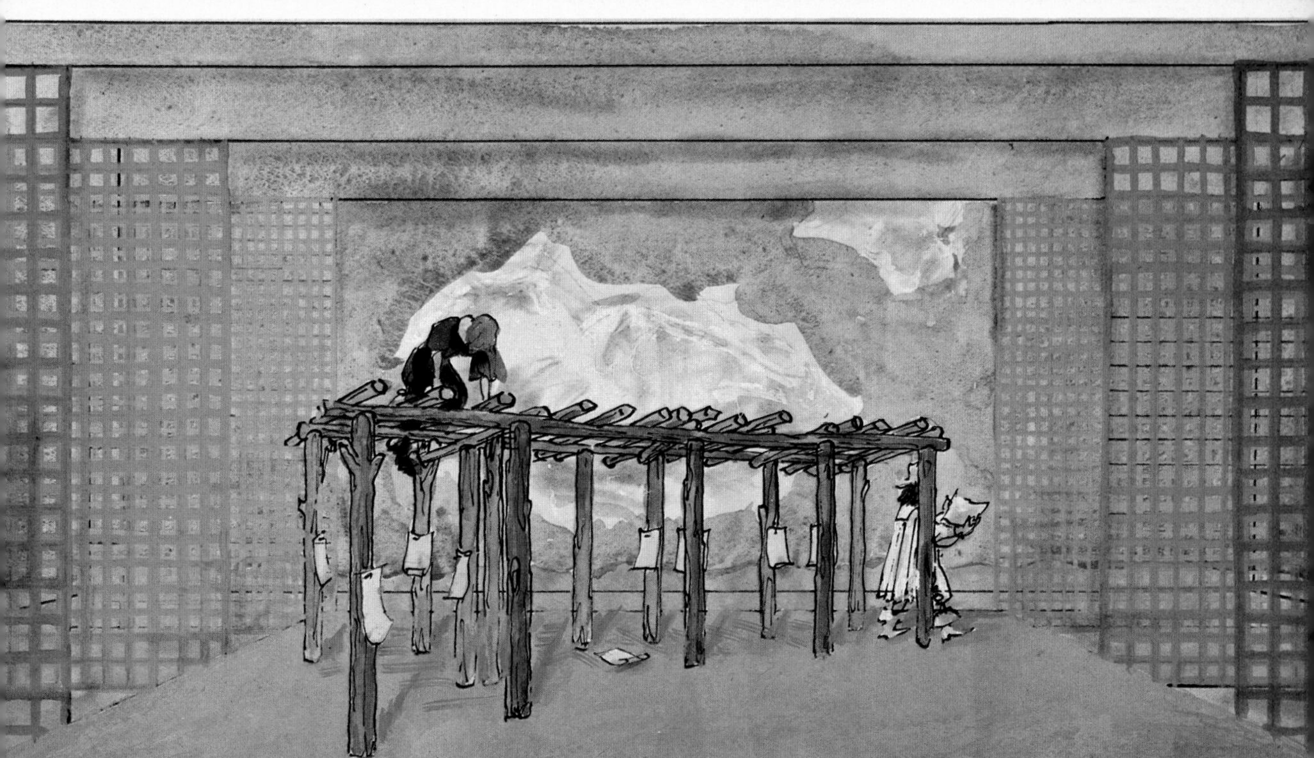

WINTERMÄRCHEN : AVTOLICVS

gone into exile the Staatliches Schauspielhaus, put a *Twelfth Night*, freely
adapted by Hans Rothe, into modern dress. Orsino lounged in white ducks on a
round pouf, with his attendants in shirts and tennis flannels. Bodeslaw Batlog,
also in Berlin, had previously given *Twelfth Night* in a middle-eastern setting;
Rothe's version, though it might have suggested the Dalmatian coast, was still
a long way from Shakespeare's Illyria.

Much more successful was the same adapter's version of *The Comedy of
Errors*, first seen in Breslau and subsequently in Berlin. Ashley Dukes, better
acquainted than any other English critic with the German stage, wrote of this as
follows:

> The *mise-en-scène* devised for this Berlin production was witty in itself and wholly
> satisfying from a dramatic standpoint. Structurally its basis was an abruptly sloping
> stage, rising from the footlights to a height of six or seven feet in the background –
> the slope of one in four or five on which players can still move in comfort and produce
> the illusion of movement on level ground. The wings of this receding platform were
> formed in the opening scene by box pictures of the Ephesian harbour, and in the
> later scenes by architectural wings, with the house of Antipholus, seen alternately
> from the front and from the inner courtyard, forming the background. By an original
> twist of presentation this background came gradually forward as the play advanced,
> so that the house deep-set at first on the summit of the sloping stage was finally
> brought almost to the proscenium, where the tangle of mistaken identity could be
> cleared up with the characters in closest proximity to the audience . . .[1]

Hans Rothe similarly adapted *The Two Gentlemen of Verona*, which was also
produced at the Staatliches Schauspielhaus.

In Vienna the Burg maintained its solid, and sometimes inspired, traditions.
Lotte Medelsky was probably the finest Cleopatra of the century on any
European stage, but Raoul Aslan's Antony was too neurotic for a part that should
be played on anything but the nerves (1923). In the same year the theatre gave a
nobly acted *Coriolanus* in sepia, with etched lines, mottled skies, and trees too
weakly coloured for its heavy frame; and in 1935 it presented *As You Like It*
for the first time in its history, and *Julius Caesar* with Werner Krauss in the
title rôle. Krauss' Lear stood in legitimate descent from Devrient and Sonnenthal. The Redoutensaal was skilfully adapted for productions of *Romeo and
Juliet* and *Twelfth Night* by Irving Pichel, Rudolf Schaeffer and Norman
Edwards. In Prague the productions were considerably more adventurous.
Krapel's *Winter's Tale* discovered a luxurious garden exotic with monstrous
plants. All the early scenes were played here, or in front of black curtains.
Hermione's prison was entered through a low round arch. For her trial the
stage had the colour of slate with an unlit cyclorama at the back. She stood in a
yellow light, and on the message of the oracle – 'Hermione is chaste' – there was
an acclamation from the crowd, a roll of thunder, and Leontes' crown crashed
to the ground. The décor of the pastoral scene in Bohemia was not unnaturally
conceived as a fantasy on Czech folk-lore. The last act was played behind a
gauze, with the snow falling, and Paulina's house – a kind of richly decorated
pagoda with a tree on either side – stood against the open sky.

Hilar's production of *Hamlet* at the National Theatre opened with a semi-
circular platform, four steps high, framed by black curtains, and the Court
scene that followed was equally severe. The arras behind which Polonius is
stabbed in the Queen's closet was suggested by a curtain hung over a detached

Werner Krauss as Falstaff in
Heinz Hilpert's *Merry Wives of Windsor*
in modern dress, Deutsches Theater,
Berlin, 1929

Opposite: Rudolph Schildkraut as
Autolycus in *The Winter's Tale*

[1] *Theatre Arts Monthly* (September 1934)

Romeo and Juliet, Moscow Chamber
Theatre 1921

frame; and the portraits of the two kings were fitted into the panels of three
screens diminishing in height as they extended towards the back of the stage,
each partially hidden by the one in front of it. The graveyard scene was played
before a church – very mittel-European in the modern style – with three oval
windows, and a semi-circular arch through which Hamlet and Horatio made
their entrance. *The Taming of the Shrew* was placed fairly and squarely in the
twentieth century; and Karel Dostel's *Merchant of Venice* at the Stavoske
Theatre employed a unit set which achieved the maximum of fussiness with the
minimum of means. Pictures by Botticelli were thrown on to the cyclorama,
and the Prince of Morocco was played by a negro from a city dance hall. The
heresy dies hard that when Shakespeare described someone as a Moor he did
not know what he was talking about. A Hamlet in 1926 was described as 'not a
Dane but a half-mad and completely lost post-war youth' – a refrain that was to
have its encore. Post-wars are very useful for actors and directors who want to
get away from *Wilhelm Meister*. In this case, we are told, he 'mused about human
vanity on a stage sparsely decorated with a throne, a curtain, and a few dejected
arches'. There was no reason, in that corrupted court, why the arches also
should have hung their heads. More to the point was Georges Freika's *Julius
Caesar* at the National Theatre, where a few broken columns and a low wooden
platform, imaginatively lit, revived the grandeur that was Rome.

In Hungary[1] Shakespeare had enjoyed his first real chance with the trans-

[1] See Lazlo Bati in *Revue d'Histoire du
Théâtre* (January–March 1965) pp.50–58

lations, excellent for their time, of Ferenc Kazinczy who saw in Hamlet's indecision the hesitant revolt of his countrymen against the Hapsburg domination. Shakespeare in Hungarian was also a declaration of war against the German theatre, and the authorities were quick to regard it as such. The Othello of Ira Aldridge, partly no doubt because he too belonged to an oppressed minority, made a deep impression. The Meininger influence, with its realistically encumbered *mise-en-scène*, was also felt until it was displaced by the theories of Appia and Craig. Of these Sandor Hevesi, who carried on a long correspondence with Craig, was the ardent exponent. For thirty years he worked at the National Theatre and directed it from 1922 to 1932. An early production of *The Tempest* (1902) tried to recreate Elizabethan conditions on a stage reluctant to accommodate them, but the later influence of Reinhardt and the German theatre of the twenties tended to diminish the popularity of Shakespeare. In the season of 1937-8 only one of his plays was performed.

In 1923 both *Lear* and *Othello* were given at the Polizama Nationale in Florence – a circular, barn-like arena with seating for 2,000. A semi-circular, olive-green drapery was hung across the stage in three folds, one section of which was drawn aside to reveal the scene required, although the whole stage was used if necessary. Lear's map was the rug at the foot of his throne. The plays, in full and faithful versions, were generally overacted with an eye to the groundlings, and the *Othello* presented in the courtyard of the Palazzo San Marco in Venice (1935) was at once more sensational and more sophisticated. Here the turrets, galleries, and balconies of the building were inventively harmonized with a wooden stage on several levels which suggested on one side the hump of a small Venetian bridge, and on the other the open space of a *campo*. The artificial lighting was contrived by projectors and flood lamps suspended from one gallery to another, and by concealed flood-lamps on the ground. All Venice appeared to swarm from a dozen entrances and openings as Brabantio was summoned to hear the news of his daughter's elopement; the entrance of the Doge was preceded by the insignia of the Senate; and when these had divided, the Senators were shown in formal session, Brabantio's chair alone being vacant. For Cyprus there was a gay coming and going of citizens until, when the clash of swords suddenly rang out, a shocked stillness as suddenly descended on the piazza, and the heads peered down from every balcony until Othello called the combatants to order The later scenes lost nothing of their tension and poignancy, except that the intoxication of the starlit night tempted the players to overact.

Costume design by Alexander Ekster for *Romeo and Juliet*, 1921

Sofronov as the Clown in *Twelfth Night*, Bolshoi Drama Theatre, Leningrad, 1921

4

'Shakespeare belongs to us,' Turgeniev had written, 'he is part and parcel of our flesh and blood.' The early years of the Revolution did not give Turgeniev the lie. Maria Andreéva, an accomplished actress from the Moscow Art Theatre, with the support of Gorki, Alexander Blok, and Chaliapin, created the Theatre of Tragedy in 1918. Productions were given in the Ciniselli circus – a setting which assisted the massed movements, and interchange between stage and auditorium, proper to a revolutionary theatre. For *Macbeth* the director, Douboujinsky, built two turreted castles in hard granite on either side of the arena, flanked by staircases with platforms, to represent the fortresses of Duncan and Macbeth. When the Theatre of Tragedy developed into the Grand

Set design by Alexander Tischler for
Richard III, State Theatre, Leningrad

Dramatic Theatre, the production was transferred there, with only such changes as a former music hall made necessary. *Othello, Lear, The Merchant of Venice, Twelfth Night* and *Julius Caesar* followed; but by the end of 1921 Blok was dead, Gorki had gone for a second time into exile, and for some years Shakespeare disappeared from the Soviet repertoire. The hour of socialist realism had sounded; a 'fatal bellman', indeed, who sounded a stern good-night to 'Shakespeare under a canopy of ostrich feathers' – as one critic described the productions mentioned above.

When he returned it was under the restless genius of Meyerhold, with whom the actor became a bio-mechanical acrobat on the rigging of a constructivist décor. Only Michael Chekov, before he emigrated to New York, preached and practised in the second Moscow Art Theatre what had always been the gospel of the first – that nothing mattered in the theatre but psychological truth– and offered his own Hamlet as an example of it. Tairov, at the Kamerny, at least clung to aesthetic standards, although they were not those of yesterday. Capulet gave his ball in a vorticist décor; and an amalgamation of *Antony and Cleopatra*, Shaw's *Caesar and Cleopatra*, and Pushkin's observations on the same subject, summed up under the title of *The Egyptian Nights* was too much for a public which still had a little of Shakespeare in its 'flesh and blood'. At the State Theatre in Leningrad (1923) an authentic *Antony and Cleopatra* was given in Schillingowsky's handsome, if conventional, décor of steps and pillars. Beerbohm Tree would have been at home in it. Alexander Tischler's design for *Richard III* in the same theatre was a good deal more imaginative. A narrow defile of stairs, broadening at the base, led up between the walls of two curving and crenellated bastions which occupied the whole width of the stage. The rough stone and architectural detail illustrated a world where power was wrested by violence, and the same tones were reflected in the costumes. Tischler's later *King Lear* (1935) saw the play in a manor-house setting, with twelve gigantic wooden sculptures set against red brick walls to suggest a family which had been ruling for generations. The Jacobeans would have understood what he was driving at.

Elsewhere socialist realism imposed its inflexible decrees. Romeo and Juliet,

at the Theatre of the Revolution, were seen as heralding the unitary, centralized state, and the family brawls as the dying gasp of feudalism. Helena in *All's Well that Ends Well* appeared as the proto-feminist, so admired by Bernard Shaw; and casuistry went to its limits in claiming Katharina in *The Taming of the Shrew* as a champion of Women's Lib! The popularity of the play was such that it could not be forbidden, but the public could still be told what it really meant. Desdemona was enlisted in the same gallant company, and *Othello* treated as a play in which wicked imperialists employed a Moorish general to assert their naval supremacy. By the time the Maly presented *Coriolanus* (1934) in reply to the Comédie Française, the 'fascist beasts' were ready for the slaughter.

Hamlet at the Vakhtangov Theatre (1932) was the climax of frivolous perversity. Four and a half hours of elaborate settings, gorgeous costumes, and exciting music were more than enough to put the original out of sight and mind. A stocky and jovial Hamlet dressed up as his father's ghost, while Horatio's voice came from the cellarage – the purpose of this charade being to impose a belief in the apparition on a court supposedly ready to unseat the usurper. The philosophizing over Yorick's skull took place in the first act instead of the fifth; the graveyard scene was cut altogether; and only the first line of 'To be or not to be' was spoken – as a necessary reassurance that *Hamlet* was in fact being performed. Rosencrantz and Guildenstern were received by Claudius in an artist's studio, where the King was sitting for his portrait; and Hamlet pretended to go mad in the market-place, dressed in a nightgown, a carrot in his hand, and a saucepan on his head. The play scene was performed twice – first on stage as a rehearsal, and then overheard in the wings, after which the King and Queen were seen scurrying in panic down a vast flight of steps, and Ophelia, in a crisis of unsatisfied nymphomania, took to drink, was carried out on the shoulders of her competing admirers, and drowned herself while still in her cups. Several characters in the outdoor scenes entered on papier-mâché horses, and a stag hunt was not thought irrelevant to a play that does not sin by brevity. A Marxist interpretation of *Hamlet* is a perfectly reasonable option, as Kozintsev was to show in the finest Shakespearian film ever made; but the fatuities of this production were too glaring, even for a public conditioned to accept pretty well anything in the name of proletarian solidarity; and with it all, according to one critic, there was 'not a single performance of power'.

Left: Set design and (far left) costume design by V. Shchuko for *Antony and Cleopatra*, State Theatre, Leningrad, 1923

Hamlet, Vakhtangov Theatre 1932

For this we must turn to Salomon Mikhoels, who helped in 1925 to create the Jewish State Theatre in Moscow. It was not, however, until ten years later that he gave a performance of Lear, which is still talked about as one of the classics of the Russian stage. (The talk has only recently been open, since Mikhoels was assassinated on Stalin's orders in 1948.) The rôle had obsessed him for years, and he saw it in terms of Biblical imagery; not as a descent from majesty to madness, but from wisdom of one kind to wisdom of another; from the wisdom of the world to the wisdom of fools. This conception strained the text not a little, and Mikhoels had difficulty in finding a director ready to accept it. To give his features freer play, he insisted on appearing without a beard; and he traced the itinerary of the part, 'not from old age to death, but from a static and limited ideology towards a stormy renovation and a second youth. Lear's tragedy is to have become young and fresh in thought and vigour only on the brink of the grave.' And so, after the preliminary fanfares and processions, all one saw was a little old man of eighty, who took his seat upon the throne with no affectation of authority. Mikhoels was aware of his unimpressive physique, and he argued that, if he had entered in all the habiliments of royalty, the audience would have found it hard to see him as a king, and impossible to accept him as a sage. All that mattered were the thoughts passing through his mind. When Kozintsev produced *King Lear* in 1941, with music by Shostakovitch, he summed up the play in a formula with which nobody need disagree: 'A king dies and a man is born.' This was the conception that Mikhoels had embodied in what Gordon Craig described as 'one of the finest performances I have seen at any time in any country'.

A close correspondence with Craig was the secret of Léon Schiller's productions of Shakespeare in Poland. He described him – and with reason – as 'my Prospero'. Schiller had radical political ideas in a country which viewed them with suspicion, and for this reason he was rarely given the authority to realize his Shakespearian projects. The opportunity came to him on his appointment as director of the Boguslawski Theatre in Warsaw, and he seized it to present *The Winter's Tale*. The contrast was striking between the dark background, veiled lighting, and solemn declamation of the first three acts, and the white draperies which framed the bucolic caperings in Bohemia. In the last act an amber light illustrated the expiation of Leontes. Some critics accused the production of 'expressionism' when they should have addressed their complaints to Gordon Craig. The play ran for eighty-five performances in a single season.

Schiller's greatest triumph was his *Julius Caesar* at the Polski in 1927. Here the crowd acted and reacted collectively, although they were separately grouped; in contrast to the Meininger tradition, it was not conceived as a sum of individuals. For those who saw the play as an intimate drama, and Brutus as prefiguring Hamlet, the production was too monumental – although 'geometrical' would seem a better description of the irregular décor stretching on either side of a low semi-circular arch with entrances, again irregular in height and width, opening to right and left, and steps leading down to the stage level. But *Julius Caesar* is a play about public matters, and Schiller had reason on his side. When he came to produce *Coriolanus* eight years later, at the Grand Theatre in Leopol, he was searching for a new aesthetic and also for a new technique – 'We must learn everything, right from the beginning; we must go to school to nature, and give up our stylisation.' The result still had the monumental stamp of Schiller's previous work, but the emotion flowed more easily despite an indifferent performance. In *A Midsummer Night's Dream* at the Polski (1934) his intention was to break with an operatic tradition, but this was not helped by adding other songs of Mendelssohn to the existing score, not to mention a number by Hugo Wolf to be sung by Bottom. Nor was it easy to justify the substitution of a 'Homage to Shakespeare' for the epithalamium which closes, and resumes, the play. It would seem that Schiller's exceptional musical sensibility had tempted him too far, in default of a poetry necessarily impoverished by translation. *The Dream* was an intelligible option; and it led naturally to *The Tempest*. Already, in 1938, he had sketched out a production of this for the Jewish theatre at Lodz; but not knowing Yiddish he reserved his definitive treatment till a later time. In the interval his country would have been crucified between two thieves – and by them.

Salomon Mikhoels as King Lear and (right) with Zuskin as the Fool, Jewish State Theatre 1935

XII The War Years

At the outbreak of the first world war, and in the years that followed, Shakespeare was often thought to spell risk for the actor and ruin for the management. By September 1939 the case had been substantially altered. After the initial flurry of gas-masks and evacuation, Britain settled down to the expectant inactivity of the phoney war. Actors not previously enlisted in territorial regiments found themselves as yet unwanted in the Services, and there seemed no reason, in the absence of aerial bombardment, why the bored and embarassed population should be starved of entertainment. A company was therefore assembled at the Old Vic, early in 1940, under the leadership of John Gielgud and Lewis Casson to mount a production of *King Lear*. It was by all odds the finest team that had ever battled with the play. Supporting Gielgud, now ripe to mature his previous performance, there were Cathleen Nesbitt as Goneril, Fay Compton as Regan, Jessica Tandy as Cordelia, Robert Harris as Edgar, Nicholas Hannen as Gloucester, Casson as Kent, Jack Hawkins as Edmund, and Stephen Haggard as the Fool. The production, designed by Roger Furse, would have been safe enough in the hands of Casson, but he and Gielgud spied a possibility that was not too good to be true.

Harley Granville-Barker was then director of the British Institute in Paris (an annexe of the Sorbonne) and living, most comfortably, in the Place des Etats-Unis. To many of his admirers it seemed that he had long deserted the higher life for the higher living. Nevertheless he was now persuaded to come over to London for ten days and superintend the rehearsals of *Lear*. What Barker thought about *Lear*, and the way it should be presented, is plain to read in his published Preface to the play. But whereas he there rejected Elizabethan dress, he now favoured it. The option is always difficult. Oswald, Edmund, and the Fool all belong to the world that Shakespeare knew; even Goneril and Regan are conceivable in farthingales. But Lear himself? Ashley Dukes felt that he harmonized well enough with his costume 'as long as he was a monarch in power, a sort of Holbein sovereign . . . his curses were good Tudor stuff, his tempers might have been those of King Hal.'[1] But as the tragedy thickened, and the elements took a hand in it, and the pagan ambience became more pronounced, the attachment of the play to a period recognizable and not too remote seemed more open to question. It would be interesting to know whether Barker himself felt that his first or second thoughts on the matter were the more appropriate.

What is not in doubt were the value of his insights, and his extraordinary attention to detail. When Cordelia was crying in the first scene he said to her: 'You are crying not because your father has been cruel, but because France has been kind.' When Lear, in the last act, announces that he has killed 'the slave' that was hanging Cordelia, the Captain remarks tersely: ''Tis true, my lord – he did.' The line, spoken by an actor of humble status and modest attainment, commonly goes for nothing. But this was not good enough for Barker. 'Do you realise what you are saying?' he exclaimed, 'you have just seen a *miracle*. Here was this old man, "four-score years and upward", and tottering on the brink of

Opposite: Laurence Olivier as Richard III, 1944

[1] *Theatre Arts Monthly* (1940)

the grave, who has actually *killed* a tough campaigner in the act of murdering his daughter. What you must express is utter, bewildered amazement. "'Tis *true*, my lord – he *DID*!"[1] The searchlight of Barker's mind played on every word that was spoken in a production which remains among the glories of the Shakespearian stage.

The combination of so many talents and the alliance between Barker's method and Gielgud's receptiveness, with his physical and imaginative powers now at their height, had an overwhelming impact. 'Lear is an oak; you are an ash' he told Gielgud – and the acorn was surely planted. Long absence from the theatre had not dulled his brilliance. He was neither conventionally old-fashioned, nor fashionably *avant-garde*. Where ringing declamation or noble gestures, the ceremonial entrance or the distraught exit, were required he was ready for them; but all these had to serve the truth of character and pulse of dramatic rhythm. Clear about what he wanted, and in absolute control of every detail, he nevertheless encouraged his actors to experiment, driving them, as he drove himself, to the limit of fatigue. Day by day he sat on the stage 'with his back to the footlights, a copy of the play in his hand, tortoise-shell spectacles well forward on his nose, dressed in a black business suit, his bushy red eyebrows jutting forward, quiet-voiced, seldom moving, coldly humorous, shrewdly observant, infinitely patient and persevering'.[2]

Lear was followed by *The Tempest*, designed by Oliver Messel, where Gielgud's Prospero – with something of Bacon, and much of Shakespeare's 'beating mind' – stood embittered, mystical, and ultimately forgiving, on the summit of a theatre itself in process of transformation. Marius Goring, as a slim and ageless Ariel, brought the breath and the slight hostility of a magic that survived his master's renunciation of it. The Old Vic was very much itself again at a moment when the same was presently to be said of Britain.

In 1942 Gielgud produced *Macbeth* at the Piccadilly. Michael Ayrton designed pale colours of greenish-blue, yellow, and pink for the scenery, and stronger tones of steel-blue and dark red for many of the cloaks and draperies. The Witches were in shades of lemon-yellow, white and pale-blue; wore antlers on their heads; and their monstrous arms and legs were veined like figures out of Hieronymus Bosch. William Walton composed the music; storm effects with strings, an unearthly march for the 'show of Kings', and a weird strain for the appearance of Banquo's ghost. Here again was a rich combination of talents. Gielgud played for imaginative intensity, using his voice with tremendous power, and for deep psychological insight; a solitary and sombre figure within the imprisoning fantasy of his ambition. Only the warrior's muscle was missing. This would have mattered less with a stronger Lady Macbeth, but there was no hint either of steel or seduction behind Gwen Ffrangcon-Davies's willowy movements and wavering voice. Vitality was wanting just where it was most required.

Another *Macbeth*, in a careful production at the Lyric, Hammersmith, gave Ernest Milton a chance to show how far the magic of personality could compensate for inadequate physique in a part that obviously demands it. James Agate declared that he had 'never known the verse to be spoken so beautifully, not in this passage or that, but everywhere. Here at last was that tapestry, at once splendid and sombre, which Shakespeare hung on the walls of Glamis.' He also noted the 'touches of Irvingesque humour', and 'the hushed, almost hypnotic delivery of the "Tarquin's ravishing strides" speech'.

Top: Jessica Tandy as Cordelia and John Gielgud as King Lear, Old Vic 1940

John Gielgud as Macbeth and Gwen Frangcon-Davies as Lady Macbeth, Piccadilly Theatre 1942

Opposite: Maurice Evans as Macbeth and Judith Anderson as Lady Macbeth in Margaret Webster's production, 1941

[1] Recorded by Cathleen Nesbitt in a broadcast talk
[2] John Gielgud *Stage Directions* (1963) pp.51-5, 121-9

For Gielgud's two productions at the Haymarket – *A Midsummer Night's Dream* and *Hamlet* – he called upon two scholars, Nevill Coghill and George Rylands, both of whom had worked with undergraduates – as Gielgud himself had done – respectively at Oxford and Cambridge. Rylands was here the more successful. His *Hamlet* was a classic of lucidity, letting the daylight in upon the mystery; too explanatory, maybe, for those who see the play in chiaroscuro; but telling the audience, without condescension, what it was about. Where Motley had gone to Cranach and Mielziner to Van Dyck, Rylands turned to Dürer and the court of Henry VII for costumes that suggested the watershed between the Middle Ages and the Renaissance. Gielgud's performance had acquired a sharper edge – here, more emphatically than before, was the '*scholar's* eye, tongue, sword' – but nothing of the feeling or the fluency had been lost. His Oberon, still matchless in speech, had become a little more larded with Warwickshire earth in the masque which Coghill had devised for the *Dream*. But – inevitably in the circumstances of the time – the sap of youth was running low in the company; and when Coghill told them that this was a play about love, they seemed surprised.

It was running pretty high, five years later, when he deployed his undergraduates in *The Tempest* beside the lake in the gardens of Worcester College, Oxford. Caliban rose from a submerged tank, and at the end of the play Prospero's boat was rowed round from the side by a crew of stalwart undergraduates. Still holding his book – an ancient tome provided for each performance by Blackwell's bookshop – he embarked upon the waiting galleon, and standing on the prow plunged it into the water. A duckboard had been fixed to run from the shore to where the galleon had anchored. Along this, when he had been given his *congé*, Ariel sped to freedom – so that he seemed to be literally skimming the water – and a few minutes later he was picked out by the lights, apparently poised on the top of a clump of bushes. Caliban, left alone to work out his salvation, relapsed into his tank. This was the acme of scenic Shakespeare in a production that had no need of scenery.

One of Coghill's most memorable effects was fortuitous.

I had based the production on the idea that Prospero was an Adam figure, flung out of his Paradise (Milan) for the neglect of his duties and allowed to return when he had shown forgiveness – the New Adam taking over (so to speak) thanks to Ariel (the spirit) from the Old Adam. So I made Prospero up to look like the Adam in Van Eyck's *Adoration of the Lamb*, the most beautiful man's face I know, which is the same face as that of the traditional Christ – combining the two Adams, Old and New, by adding a silver streak to the hair that rippled to his shoulders, and with a touch of silver in the beard. When he stood up in his magic robes he was my idea of a true Prospero; well and good. But mark the miracle! Ariel returned, put on his doublet, rapier, and short cloak and, last of all, put on his plain Elizabethan hat. I *gasped*! It was William Shakespeare standing before us. I had never before realised his Christ-face.[1]

Théophile Gautier once wrote that his ideal performance was a Shakespeare play acted by amateur ladies and gentlemen. He would have enjoyed this one.

German bombs had robbed the Old Vic of its stage, but Tyrone Guthrie mustered a company with Ernest Milton, Lewis Casson, and Sybil Thorndike, and its headquarters – most improbably – at Bury in Lancashire. Milton clothed the neurosis of King John with a baleful beauty, and Dame Sybil as Constance, with her gift for democratizing tragedy without forfeit of dignity,

[1] Letter to the author (14 September 1972)
[2] See Ronald Harwood *Sir Donald Wolfit* (1971) pp.157-67

called a plague on compromise in accents which should have echoed at Yalta. The company descended on London from time to time. In the autumn of 1942 Frederick Valk joined it for an Othello which was already famous in Prague. In terms of sheer power and pathos the performance was overwhelming – a fight, not quite successful, against overwhelming odds, for the symphonic movement of the verse was beyond the capacity of an actor who normally played in Czech. Indeed, there is a certain *beauty* in Othello, which Valk might not have compassed even in his own language. This was a bull – albeit a prize bull – skilfully baited by Bernard Miles's Iago, but hardly the monarch of the jungle. As Shylock Valk was positively helped by his foreign accent; his adamantine purpose left little room for pathos when it was frustrated.

Meanwhile a definitive *King Lear* was hibernating in the provinces. Donald Wolfit had formed his own company – not a very good one – and in 1942 he presented the play in Cardiff, though not as yet to his satisfaction. Ernst Stern, now a refugee from Nazi Germany, remembered what Reinhardt had done with a hundred knights; he also remembered what he had done with six – and it was much better. This suited Wolfit's slender resources; and an appropriate variation on Stonehenge was devised for touring purposes. Nugent Monck was engaged as associate director. The production was shown in London at the St James's Theatre during the winter of 1943, and excited no more than polite comment. Not until the spring of the following year was Wolfit's performance ready for the accolade of critical approbation. One or two of the pundits were hesitant at first, and it was left to James Agate to blow their hesitations to the wind. He set out the qualities that an audience demands of Lear.

First, majesty. Second, the quality Blake would have recognized as moral grandeur. Third, mind. Fourth, he must be a man, and what is more, a king, in ruins. There must be enough voice to dominate the thunder, and yet it must be a spent voice. Lear must have all of Prospero's 'beating mind', but a mind enfeebled like his pulse. . . . Mr Wolfit had and was all the things we demand, and created the impression Lear calls for. I say deliberately that his performance on Wednesday was the greatest piece of Shakespearian acting I have seen since I have been privileged to write for the *Sunday Times*.

Agate also said that it was the greatest tragic performance he had seen on the British stage since the death of Irving. Charles Morgan, who had left his column on *The Times*, wrote to the actor that when his son was 'an old man in a chimney-corner, he would tell people not yet born how, when he was twenty, he saw Wolfit play Lear'. Edith Sitwell wrote that 'all imaginable fires of agony and all the light of redemption' were in a performance which became famous – and even, unlike the actor himself, fashionable – for the brief moment that it cast its spell. But the kind of theatre in which Wolfit would have been at home was gone beyond recall; it was nervous of giants; and the theatre that lay ahead offered him only a restricted hospitality. His personality was too emphatic, and his method too large, for him to accept or to decline it gracefully. The accolade he received from his admirers was confirmed by his Sovereign; it was less willingly bestowed by the members of his own profession.[2]

Laurence Olivier, caught in America by the outbreak of war, put everything he had into a *Romeo and Juliet* with Vivien Leigh. For the only time in his career he lost the wager; returned to England; enlisted in the Fleet Air Arm; but was later released, with Ralph Richardson, to pursue the business of the Old Vic at the New Theatre. 13 September 1944 was an historic date. Olivier, limping

Top: Donald Wolfit as King Lear

Frederick Valk as Othello and Bernard Miles as Iago, Old Vic production at the New Theatre 1942

Top: Laurence Olivier as
Justice Shallow in *Henry IV, Part Two*,
Old Vic 1945

Ralph Richardson as Falstaff in
Henry IV, Old Vic 1945

with a slight stoop, sidled on before the front traverse to open his Richard II
with 'Now is the winter of our discontent . . .', incorporating some necessary
lines from *Henry VI* into the soliloquy. He had modelled his make-up on two
sketches – one full-face, the other in profile – and his voice on the thin resonance
of Irving, as tradition reported it. This was indeed the 'limping panther'
described by J. C. Trewin, 'the true double Gloucester, thinker and doer, mind
and mask', racing through the part with 'diction mill-race swift'. Or, as Agate
was to put it, 'his high shimmering tenor has not the oak-cleaving quality; it is a
wind that gets between your ribs'. Olivier died slowly, after fighting punch-
drunk with wounds, and glimpsing – perhaps in some spasm of remorse – the
cross-hilt of his sword. A little later he was presented with another sword. Irving
and Kean had both fought with it in their day, and it was given him by John
Gielgud. The gesture had a characteristic generosity. For fifteen years Gielgud
had reigned, virtually unchallenged, over the classical theatre in Britain; now
he had a competitor who was none the less a friend.

A dazzling Hotspur followed in 1945. Having decided to play the part in a
red wig, Olivier spent three hours in making up to it – a good example of genius
taking an infinity of pains. It was not the first time that Hotspur had stammered
but Olivier's actor's instinct hit upon the infallible letter in the alphabet. 'Food
for w... w... w——' earned a rich dividend of pathos. And again the death was
spectacular, as he stood motionless for a second and plunged down two steps,
headlong, on to his face. In the second part of *Henry IV* – where Richardson's
Falstaff was again sharp with an etcher's blade, the mind never muffled by the
padding – Olivier again dazzled with his Justice Shallow. Here was Montague's
portrait of Laurence Irving come back to life. Lear, in 1946, was a more difficult
challenge, if only because Gielgud's majestic performance was recent in
memory. It would not perhaps be unfair to suggest that if Olivier succeeded
more completely in doing what he set out to do, what Gielgud had attempted
was better worth doing.

Olivier was not helped by Roger Furse's opening set, such as a child might
have built with a box of bricks. If you insist that *Lear* is a fairy-tale, you rob it of
its rock-bottom reality; and you diminish the height from which majesty must
stoop to folly. In many passages, particularly towards the end, crowned with
flowers or beseeching the onlookers to 'howl' over Cordelia's body, Olivier was
wonderfully moving. His 'terrors of the earth' was torn out of his bodily and
spiritual entrails. Elsewhere one missed 'the surge and thunder of the Odyssey'[1]
which is never far below the surface of this Homeric play. If he looked and even,
as Alan Dent observed, '*sounded* like a Blake', it was still a Blake in a minor key.
There was something in Agate's suggestion that Olivier is 'a comedian by
instinct, and a tragedian by art', and the tragedian's art can gain much from the
comedian's instinct. This it is that gives Olivier his quicksilver rapidity, daring
changes of tempo, and kaleidoscopic shiftings of mood. They were all of service
to his Lear, except where the part called for a more massive structure, a more
symphonic groundswell of emotion. The performance, with all its flashes of
lightning, had not quite Gielgud's firm intellectual grasp – but then Barker was
not at Olivier's elbow, rehearsing him *tête-à-tête* for one and a half hours a day.
If he had been, the mind harbours the suspicion (perhaps unworthy) that
Olivier might have wished he were somewhere else. The sadistic relish of
Margaret Leighton's Regan, and the mixture of vinegar and holy water in
Alec Guinness's Fool, notably enriched the production.

[1] Andrew Lang

2

It was not until the autumn of 1943 that Paul Robeson's Othello came to Broadway. The production had the authority of Margaret Webster as director, and of Robert Edmund Jones to design the scenery and costumes. Walled-in streets and a sequence of palatial interiors were contrived to create an intimacy where the workings of conspiracy or emotion were plain to read. The sober magnificence of Robeson's dress when he appeared before the Senate; the tiger-striped burnous that he wore in Cyprus; and the scarlet cloak that he flung over Desdemona's murdered body – all this showed a great designer's eye for colour as well as for form. (Jones was now having further thoughts about *Richard III*, but no theatre ever saw that huge white rose on the bare brick wall, and Richard playing with his shadow in the circle of light below.) Robeson's performance illustrated the disadvantages, no less than the assets, of casting a negro for the part. The voice was a glorious instrument which the actor was not trained to use for Shakespearian verse. The *négritude* had textual warrant but quarrelled, at times, with what should have been a native habit of command. The tenderness, simplicity, and trust were deeply moving, but one did not quite believe in the volcano which their betrayal would stir into eruption. Othello is an exotic stranger in Veronese's Venice; he is not a second-class citizen. José Ferrer as Iago set down lightly 'the stops that should untune this music', and Miss Webster drove Emilia, and the play itself, with the momentum they both require.

In 1941 she had directed Maurice Evans and Judith Anderson in *Macbeth*. Dame Judith was an ambitious matron rather than the siren of Glamis, and Evans's Macbeth had his usual vigour and consistency, speaking the verse as no other actor on Broadway was then capable of speaking it, and only lacking a certain dimension of epic grandeur. The cauldron scene was presented as a projection of Macbeth's fevered imagination, although this made little sense of 'I will to the weird sisters, and betimes I will.' Miss Webster, inheriting the best traditions of English speech, had never found it easy to secure a reasonable homogeneity with actors not bred in that tradition. Some refused the parts offered them for fear of not being able to speak Shakespeare properly, or afraid that if they did so their future engagement as gangsters would be imperilled. Miss Webster steered a successful middle course between the refinements of Oxbridge and the vernacular of Brooklyn and the Bowery. Provincial audiences, who might never have seen an actor in the flesh before, not to mention a play by Shakespeare, had to be coaxed into sympathetic attention. When children in the Middle-West realized that Polonius was meant to be laughed at, they were cowed into silence by the police. Webster/Evans Shakespeare, whatever its concessions and shortcomings, was opening up the country in one way, as the 'covered waggon' had opened it up in another. Evans himself was shortly to be playing his abridged *Hamlet* to the GIs.

Top: Alec Guinness as the Fool in *King Lear*, Old Vic 1946

Paul Robeson as Othello

In the same year (1941) Margaret Webster directed Helen Hayes and Maurice Evans in a Theatre Guild production of *Twelfth Night*. The intention behind this was 'baroque' – a convenient label for pretty well anything between the accession of James I and the accession of Queen Victoria. The link established was between Elizabethan and Restoration comedy – uneasy allies. Stewart Chaney added a black hat and gloves, black buttons and trimmings, to Viola's white costume; and Evans's Malvolio wore a black bow tie, and wide, winged, upstanding wide collar. His genteel cockney accent brought the part closer to

Pinero or Wilde than to Olivia's household. The décor was inspired by the private or Court theatres of the Restoration with their ornate prosceniums, painted perspectives, and pendent chandeliers. Viola and Sebastian recognized each other at the foot of a double staircase; Olivia was followed by a little blackamoor carrying a pink parasol – but why pink in that house of mourning? – and the scenes were bridged by a snatch of song by Feste, a passing lamp-lighter, or Viola, with Orsino's gentlemen in attendance, striding, with mingled resolution and reluctance, on her distasteful errand. The sum effect was of merry and picturesque invention, and much individual accomplishment; but the lyrical pulse of the play beat rather faintly, and its underlying melancholy was smothered by the sophistication to which Broadway lends a ready ear.

The Tempest had not been seen on Broadway since a neo-Elizabethan production in 1916, and for some time Margaret Webster, with Eva le Gallienne, had been working on designs for décor and costumes which were executed by Motley. The principal scenic element was mounted on a revolve, and changes of location were indicated by light and colour and surface texture; a soft grey for Prospero's cave, smooth edges for the cliffs under which Caliban, Stephano, and Trinculo weave their abortive conspiracy. For the latter two Czech comedians of considerable resource – George Voskovec and Jan Werich – had been engaged. Ariel was exquisitely danced, but inadequately spoken and sung, by the Norwegian ballerina, Vera Zorina. Arnold Moss was a passionate, energetic Prospero – not too old – and he was still playing the part twenty years later. The medley of accents matched the intricacy of rocks, stairways, arches, angles and planes. For the shipwreck Motley had taken the print of a caravel with bellying sails from Burnacini and painted this on a curtain. Through a scrim in the centre of it the passengers and crew could be seen huddled aboard. Miss Webster saw *The Tempest* not as a masque about magic, but as a play about 'the search for freedom, and about power, and the abuse of power'; as a transformation act of the inner man. With Dover Wilson's authority behind her, she dropped the curtain after 'Our revels now are ended'.

The low comedy of *Twelfth Night* – but is it ever really low? – was seriously overstressed by Michael Chekov. Here Malvolio was pushed into a barrel, and the scene changing in view of the audience became ultimately tedious. More ambitious, though undercast and unsuccessful in performance, was Erwin Piscator's *King Lear* on the lecture platform at the New School for Social Research. This was transformed by Antonin Heytum into a spectacular stage with a revolve, backed by a grey fish-net cyclorama. The action was framed in huge semi-circular arches with the minimum of scenic accessories. Piscator was the legitimate heir of Jessner and Meyerhold; but there was no Moissi or Werner Krauss, Kortner or Bassermann, to give flesh and blood to his fantasies.

3

In France the catastrophe of 1940 had liberated the energies of the theatre, if it had liberated nothing else. In 1942 Dullin revived his *Richard III* at the Théâtre Sarah Bernhardt, a much larger theatre than the Atelier which invited, and received, a more lavish production. The revolve was used to display the ebb and flow of battle. But the stylization and concentrated dynamics imposed by a smaller stage were missing. After the Liberation, in the spring of 1945, Dullin presented a controversial *King Lear* in an adaptation by Simone Jollivet. Jumping on the existentialist band-waggon, she saw in the play a tragedy of the absurd. Twenty years later Peter Brook had the same idea, and made better sense of it. An attempt was made to recreate the atmosphere of a barbarous antiquity, but what resulted was a never-never-land of contradictions where characters from the *Très Riches Heures du duc de Berri* jostled cheek by jowl with Tibetan lamas, African sorcerers, and knights out of a Japanese *Nō*. Dullin's own performance had its moments, but it was now clear that his achievement at the Atelier owed as much to economic stringency as aesthetic principle. That, however, had not diminished its importance.

In the same year (1942) Baty presented a *Macbeth*, on which he had been at work for three years. He had seen in the play

> the most Aeschylean of Shakespeare's tragedies, which comes close to the *Oresteia* in its sacred horror. Written at the height of the Renaissance, the most inspired by the medieval vision; and the most Catholic, though written at the height of the Reformation.

This vision was translated, wherever possible, in the *mise-en-scène*. Duncan was almost liturgically apparelled and the figures of saints, incorporated in the décor, uttered their mute rebuke to the Witches. For a 'drama of mystery and horror which seems to be re-enacted outside of time by ghosts in the ruins of a haunted castle', Baty had devised a single décor, placed over the trap-doors. When Macbeth was finally defeated it appeared to be swallowed underground; only its rough superstructure remained above to form a semblance of rocks on the barren heath. Marguerite Jamois lent a sovereign presence and intensity to Lady Macbeth, and Baty was rather more respectful of the text than hitherto. Certain liberties, however, he still felt justified in taking.

> If we could believe that these texts at our disposal are Shakespeare's work throughout, pious revision would still be necessary. They were conceived for a noisy public, standing on its feet, highly imaginative and eager for strong emotions. We have to impose them on a public, seated and more or less silent, with more intelligence than sensibility, and its imagination atrophied for lack of exercise.

This begged a good many questions. It was a long way from Copeau and Antoine, and also from Jean Vilar whose opportunity was close at hand.

Jean-Louis Barrault had wedded himself – supposedly for life – to the Comédie Française, and here undertook his first Shakespeare production – *Antony and Cleopatra* in a translation by André Gide. He had conceived the play as a 'symphony' – and indeed it is more symphonic than structural – but Marie Bell was not an ideal Cleopatra; and twenty-three changes of scene, even with Jean Hugo's ravishing décors, instead of painting a decipherable map of the Mediterranean world, left it in unrelated fragments.

> Then, world, thou hast a pair of chaps, no more;
> And throw between them all the food thou hast,
> They'll grind the one the other.

The attentive listener, hearing these lines, would have jumped to the parallel with the two super-powers that were then dividing Europe between them. A great French writer, Georges Bernanos, had written that 'every high drama of history is Shakespearian'. For this reason, perhaps, Shakespeare had been able to hold his own at a time when all the world was indeed a stage, and all the men and women were either members of the audience, or performers in the play.

Alec Guinness as the King and
Irene Worth as Helena in Tyrone
Guthrie's *All's Well that Ends Well*,
Stratford, Ontario, 1953

Five days after Pearl Harbour, Maxwell Anderson declared at Princeton: 'I look for a rebirth of tragedy after this war.' Shakespeare was at hand to supply it, and much else besides. Tyrone Guthrie's restless temperament and inventive mind had not been satisfied with steering the Old Vic towards its eventual reconstruction, and later transformation into the home of the National Theatre. In the meanwhile he was looking for a stage, and stages, elsewhere. The Edinburgh Festival gave him his opportunity. Under the disapproving statue of John Knox himself, he produced in the General Assembly Hall of the Church of Scotland Sir David Lyndsay's satire, *The Three Estates*. This suited his genius for spectacle, and also for irreverence. A long, rectangular platform was built out into that rather inhospitable auditorium, with the public seated, not very comfortably, on three sides of it. The actors entered down the gangways; were kept in movement so that they should never have their backs for too long to any one section of the house; and, grouped effectively, supplied the décor for which there was no place. Having at last escaped from the proscenium, Guthrie had no wish to return to it.

The Three Estates set the pattern for Stratford, Ontario. Tom Patterson, nursing his dream of a Canadian Stratford on a Canadian Avon, called upon Guthrie to realize it. The response was quick, not to say Quixotic. The largest tent in the United States was hired from Chicago; four poles, each weighing one and a half tons, and sixty feet high, with ten miles of rope and cable. Inside it Tanya Moisewitch had devised her adaptation of an Elizabethan stage. This projected thirty-four feet, with a primary playing area eighteen by fourteen feet in width, with a trapdoor, and an inner playing area, fifteen feet wide. Outer staircases led to a balcony, with landings and doorways at their halfway point; and an inner stairway led down to the enclosed space between the nine small columns on which the balcony rested for support. The acoustics inside the tent were normal, although extraneous noises were troublesome. Guthrie opened the first Stratford Festival in the summer of 1953 with *Richard III* and *All's Well that Ends Well*. Alec Guinness played Richard with a spastic walk and one eye dropping lower than the other, and the King in *All's Well*; Irene Worth was the Margaret and Helena. The rest of the cast were Canadian. Seeing Helena as the proto-feminist, up to any dodge to capture her man, Guthrie put *All's Well* into Edwardian dress – an experiment that another Stratford was presently to applaud. Always particular about his footwear, he engaged Czech and Jewish craftsmen from Toronto to make the shoes for *Richard III* and the boots for *All's Well*. The auditorium may have been improvised; the productions certainly were not.

The Festival was twice extended from the four weeks originally planned, and drew 70,000 spectators, many of them from the United States. It became gradually clear that the stage, excellent for comedy or spectacle, was less suited to tragedy. *The Taming of the Shrew* in the following year was given a North American setting, with the Lord returning from a shooting party, and a certain

suggestion of California in the white coats of the servants. Five actors piled into Vincentio's red limousine; and Petruchio's Spanish hat and cape carried a reminiscence of Alfred Lunt and the silken smoothness of his 'I am rough and woo not like a babe.' As Robertson Davies wrote: 'There was a whole soldier's biography in this line and the soft laugh which accompanied it.' Hortensio in disguise looked like 'a back-street Paganini in a seedy woollen jumper', and Bruno Gerussi was a 'tough, back-alley Grumio'.[1] For all this, however, the production lacked a certain dimension of humanity and depth of humour. There is heart as well as heartiness in *The Taming of the Shrew,* and it should be heard beating, albeit fitfully, beneath the rough and tumble of the harlequinade. *Measure for Measure* was conceived in black, grey and silver, with the double-headed eagle of the Hapsburgs visible from first to last. This emblem of 'a little brief authority' did not obscure the mittel-European 'stews'. If the audience

William Needles as Petruchio in *The Taming of the Shrew,* Stratford, Ontario, 1954

winced at the heave of Pompey's codpiece on 'The valiant heart's not whipt out of his trade', Pompey himself recoiled before the stench of the prison cell coming up to him from below the trap.

In 1955 Guthrie handed over *Julius Caesar* to Michael Langham. At the end of the Forum scene Cinna's corpse was discovered, not only lynched but dismembered. This was too much for tender nerves, and the effect was modified later. In Guthrie's *Merchant of Venice* Frederick Valk repeated his powerful Shylock, and Antonio's affection for Bassanio was given a gratuitously homosexual motivation. Great tension was secured in the trial scene. Frances Hyland's fragile Portia moved in a Belmont of gauzy pink and white, and onlookers from the balconies watched Bassanio's choice of the right casket.

In 1956 Langham succeeded Guthrie as director of the Festival. For *Henry V* French-speaking actors from Montreal were engaged for the French parts. With such actors as Gratien Gélinas, Jean Coutu, and Guy Hoffmann, this worked admirably, and Christopher Plummer as the patriot king proved his great technical accomplishment. Within a very short time of its opening Stratford Ontario had produced its own star. If Stratford was in some sense the child of the Edinburgh Assembly Hall, it acknowledged the paternity when, in the same year, *Henry V* was presented there. In 1957 the present auditorium replaced Skip Manley's Homeric tent, with accommodation for 2,176 spectators, none of them more than sixty feet from the stage. Three plays by Shakespeare were given in 1961, *Love's Labour's Lost*, *Henry VIII*, and *Coriolanus*. The first was, by all accounts, among the prize productions of the Festival. Paul Scofield as Don Armado was described by one critic as 'a loon among swans';[2] and another recorded how 'his elegant feet can barely keep him touching the earth – his eye sees a world beyond'.[3] Langham gave a late September treatment to the play, dressing the gentlemen of Navarre as cavaliers, and the ladies in very pale satins. Boyet was in pink and white; and Mervyn Blake played Dull – Shakespeare already feeling his way towards Dogberry – 'with the drooping eyes of a basset hound'.[4]

Henry VIII was remembered for the blazing gold and yellow of its final scene, and for Douglas Campbell's blustering king. He had already blustered to great effect as Pistol – never more in his element than when he was storming about the stage like a baby elephant'[5] – but this tendency was properly muted for Menenius. Langham, hitching his waggon – unconsciously no doubt – to an idea once propounded by William Poel, had set *Coriolanus* in Napoleonic times. Both Harold Taubman in the *New York Times* and Walter Kerr in the *Herald-Tribune* were agreed that this did nothing to help the play; but the latter admitted that Langham had met its relative unpopularity 'by slyly, sternly, and most felicitously insisting upon every last ounce of ice that was in it'. The storming of Corioli was unhappily reduced to a 'folk-dance with rifle butts'[6] – the kind of nemesis that awaits a director when he takes an historical play out of history. If a battle cannot be fought convincingly, it is much better not to fight it at all.

In 1962 Tanya Moisewitch redesigned her stage, changing its sex–as Langham enigmatically asserted – from masculine to feminine. The balcony was raised eight inches, and the pillars supporting it reduced to five, larger than the previous ones. The side entrances were moved further towards the outer flanks of the stage wall, with larger platforms and overhanging canopies. The staircases were rearranged, the upper window balconies suppressed, and the main panels

1 *Renown at Stratford* (1954)
2 *The Guardian*
3 Herbert Whitaker
4 *The Guardian*
5 Ibid
6 Ibid

on the back wall hinged to provide additional entrances. A trapdoor was built into the floor of the central balcony. How all this amounted to a change of sex was not clear, but it has continued to serve the Festival, and to set a pattern for similar stages elsewhere. At a single stroke Guthrie had established the 'thrust', or open, stage as an orthodoxy for classical, and even for modern, productions on the American continent. The theatre which bears his name in Minneapolis is an outstanding example of it. Unencumbered by theatrical tradition, Canada had pointed a new way by returning to old principles.

The case so brilliantly stated was not, however, proved conclusively. A writer in the *Queen's (University) Quarterly*[1] – Nathan Cohen – looked back on fifteen years' achievement. He noted a number of exemplary performances: Leo Ciceri's Bolingbroke and Henry IV, Tony van Bridge's Falstaff, William Hutt's Justice Shallow, Plummer's Hamlet and Benedick. Others he might have added to them: Frances Hyland's Perdita, and John Colicos's Timon, in modern dress, afterwards seen at Chichester. He recognized the social and economic value of the theatre, which was also a gift to the *régisseur*. But he found the actors and the dramatist playing second fiddle to Gordon Craig's *Übermensch*. He noted what no apologia could disguise, that only a third of the audience could at any one time see and hear the actors. The enlarged perspective in which they stood to one another was annulled for the spectator. Moreover the public were embarrassed by the players hurtling down the gangways; a proximity and a kind of quasi-participation, helpful in some cases to comedy, were inimical to tragedy. For the two prerequisites for the performance of tragedy are perspective and repose – and the open stage denies them both. Neither Guthrie nor Langham were bothered by this. They kept their actors continually on the move in the interests of 'vitality'; and in thus securing that they should be visible to alternate sections of the audience, ensured that they would be imperfectly heard – if indeed they were heard at all. For when an actor speaks and moves at the same time, the significance of what he is saying is inevitably blunted. In comedy this may not matter; in Shakespearian tragedy, where the words are all important, it matters a great deal.

The Stratford stage and auditorium are very satisfying in themselves. The former escapes the least taint of archaism, and has lent itself, in the hands of several directors and designers, to a variety of beautiful effects. It has given to Shakespeare a new-found popularity in America, and to Canada a legitimate occasion for pride. Imagination and a reasonable level of accomplishment have rarely failed it. But when the hypothetical question is put – is this how Shakespeare would have liked to see his plays performed if he were alive today? – one can return only a qualified affirmative. The experiment was abundantly worth making, but it raises as many problems as it solves. It should not be regarded as the last word on a subject upon which the last word can never be spoken. Nevertheless it conveyed a warning which Christopher Plummer passed on to Laurence Olivier: 'You can't lie.' 'My God,' replied Olivier, 'what are we going to do?'

The clash of armies had not impaired the popularity of Joseph Papp's productions in Central Park, New York. Of their social value, at least, there could be no doubt, since they induced thousands of people to quit the relative safety of Fifth Avenue without fear of rape, robbery, or assassination. If Shakespeare himself was an occasional casualty, that did not trouble the police. An entirely new set was devised for each production within the same neo-Elizabethan

Opposite: Paul Scofield as Don Armado and Murray Scott as Moth in *Love's Labour's Lost*, Stratford, Ontario, 1961

[1] (Spring 1968)

framework. It did not make theatrical sense to pretend that Cleopatra was not in love with Antony; but there was some reason for the crowd to pelt Claudio (in *Measure for Measure*) with rotten apples, while beggars scrambled to pick them up. And if supernumaries with the stylized branches of trees impersonated a forest in *Titus Andronicus*, that did no great harm to a play which it was courageous to mount at all, although, in those surroundings, they were in uneven competition with the real thing.

But when, in 1967, Mr Papp took over the two 300-seat theatres in the Astor Library, in downtown Manhattan, his zest for the contemporary passed all reasonable bounds. The audience was surprised, but hardly enlightened, when Hamlet replied to Polonius' query 'What do you read my lord?' with 'The New York Times'; or when Ophelia sang her snatches through a hand-microphone; or when a game of Russian roulette supplanted the duel with Laertes. Simple and sophisticated alike must have had recourse to their science dictionaries when Mr Papp claimed that 'this production aims radioactive ididium 192 at the 19th century *Hamlet* statue and by gamma ray shadowgraphing seeks to discover the veins of the living original under accumulated layers of reverential varnish.' Hardly less provocative was the Actor's Workshop production of *A Midsummer Night's Dream* in San Francisco, inspired – disastrously – by Jan Kott, for whom that particular dream is an erotic nightmare. The set and costumes were designed by the pop artist, Jim Dine. Music by Mendelssohn and Mahler came from a jukebox; Hippolyta appeared in a cage; a light bulb flashed on and off in Demetrius' codpiece; and Helena was played by a man six feet four inches tall. Shakespeare had certainly moved a tidy distance from Broadway, and not always for the better. Beside these aberrations, an *As You Like It* set in the period of the American Civil War, at the Guthrie Theatre in Minneapolis, rang the changes with an almost timid peal.

It was almost inevitable that the success of Stratford, Ontario, should have gone to the head of Stratford, Connecticut. A medium-sized residential town within commuting distance of New York, with educational centres sprinkled along the length and breadth of New England, presented an ideal Festival opportunity. Here in 1955, Laurence Langner built a theatre on the banks of the Housatonic. Externally it bore a vague resemblance to the Globe, but there the likeness ended. *Julius Caesar* and *The Tempest* were given in heavy pictorial settings behind a proscenium beyond which the action was never permitted to stray. In 1956 John Houseman and Jack Landau took over the direction. They extended the forestage and presented *King John* and *Measure for Measure*; but this audience, too, had to be coaxed by novelties. In 1957 *Much Ado* was transferred from Messina to Texas, and *Troilus and Cressida* rather successfully recreated in terms of the American Civil War. The Confederacy was equated with the Trojans, boasting the better men and the worser cause. In 1960 *Twelfth Night* was set in an English seaside town during the nineteenth century, Orsino and his suite appearing in naval uniform inescapably reminiscent of HMS Pinafore. A little surprisingly Katharine Hepburn seemed miscast as Viola. The word began to go round that Stratford, Connecticut, was 'Shakespeare for people who hated Shakespeare'.

In 1959 Houseman resigned. A grant from the Ford Foundation was made available for training classes, and a more solid policy was inaugurated under Allen Fletcher and Douglas Seale. Fletcher's *Lear* in 1963 was memorable for Morris Carnovsky's performance, where pathos and majesty, senility and strength, were balanced in exactly the right proportions. Long experience with the Group Theatre and indoctrination with Stanislavsky's 'Method' had done nothing to impair his authority and power of theatrical projection. His deep and resonant voice met all the demands that were made upon it. This was probably the finest Shakespearian performance to be seen on the American side of the Atlantic after the second world war. The production, too, was rich in insight. Goneril and Regan were played from their own point of view, not Lear's, Regan working up the more slowly to her wickedness. Gloucester was a silly and adipose voluptuary, and Douglas Watson's Edmund was quick to get on terms with the audience. His Richard III, in 1964, played for a zestful charm, lost his wager against the more orthodox reading. Fletcher missed the melodrama in *Much Ado*, but little escaped him, a year later, in a balanced *Coriolanus* – although what exactly was intended, or conveyed, by a 'Freudian Volumnia' is difficult to assess from a distance. Other directors were brought in from time to time. Frank Hauser added bits of *Henry IV Part One* to *Henry IV Part Two* to justify a play entitled *Falstaff*; and in the same year, 1966, Margaret Webster sent the lictors to patrol the streets before the murder of Julius Caesar. Houseman returned in 1967 for a *Macbeth*, where Carrie Nye was allowed the exercise of a sinuous sex appeal; and once again, in *The Merchant of Venice*, Antonio's friendship for Bassanio was seen to be discreetly ambivalent. This was becoming a tiresome cliché on the part of directors who cannot distinguish between the ardours of friendship and the velleities of appetite. In *A Midsummer Night's Dream* Cyril Ritchard doubled the parts of Oberon and Bottom – an exercise that must have given him a great deal to do in his dressing-room. Whatever he may have done with his eyebrows, the audience would have lifted theirs.

In New York the 'reverential varnish' of traditional Shakespeare production could still gleam agreeably when the brush was in the right hands. It looked a little dull when Iden Payne – who had retired from Stratford-upon-Avon in 1942 – produced *The Winter's Tale* for the Theatre Guild, designed by Stewart Chaney. His flair was never quite equal to his fidelity, and he returned to the academic theatre in Texas where his profound theatrical scholarship was appreciated at its true worth. In February 1946 Maurice Evans, having drastically abridged his *Hamlet* for the armed forces, dressed it in Winterhalter costumes, still shorn of the graveyard scene. And in *Henry VIII* – always a play for veterans – Eva Le Gallienne and Walter Hampden gave one the taste of a vintage that had not been too long in bottle, although an older generation of playgoers might think it high time it were brought up from the cellar. As Buckingham walked to 'the long divorce of steel' down a long staircase with crenellated walls, one was not surprised that Margaret Webster was in command.

In 1947 Katharine Cornell appeared as Cleopatra, in a production by Guthrie McClintic which evoked Egypt and Rome 'without losing its way in a museum', and the battle of Actium by selective lighting that picked out the opposing flags and combatants on the various levels of Leo Kirz's décor. Antony's forces were in red, Pompey's in green, and Caesar's in blue. Godfrey Tearle's Antony flickered with a greatness going suicidally to seed; and Miss Cornell, walking 'with a panther's grace' was 'wanton and witty, lustful and regal, mischievous and sublime'.[1] There was no Cleopatra within sight on the British stage in whom the paradox of the character could have been stated so triumphantly. Three years later, in a Theatre Guild production of *As You Like It* by Michael Benthall Katharine Hepburn again puzzled her admirers, seeming in the eyes

[1] John Mason Brown *Dramatis Personae* (1963)

Opposite: Tony van Bridge as Falstaff, Mary Savidge as Mistress Quickly and Frances Hyland as Doll Tearsheet in *Henry IV, Part Two*, Stratford, Ontario, 1965

of one critic[1], to have mistaken the Forest of Arden for the campus of Bryn Mawr. An 'essentially deadpan' approach to comedy deprived Rosalind's high spirits of their conscious flourish.

2

Nobody in time of war would have claimed that their journey to Stratford-upon-Avon was 'really necessary'; even in time of peace they had sometimes doubted its necessity. With Iden Payne's retirement, and Komisarjevsky's emigration to New York, the Memorial Theatre settled down to the doldrums under Milton Rosmer, and was only intermittently stirred to life by Robert Atkins, who was unhappy with its stage. When the war ended the Governors were forced to look beyond the end of their own noses – or, at best, the confines of the Midland circuit. Bridges-Adams's dream of a 'British Bayreuth' was hardly likely to appeal to those who recalled the musical tastes of Adolf Hitler, but the triumphs of the Old Vic were a challenge that asked to be met. If Stratford were not to sink back to its original status of a rural festival, a new policy must be formulated – and paid for.

The Stratford story will now divide itself into three distinct, but overlapping, phases. From 1946 to 1949 Sir Barry Jackson, though not himself directing, was in charge. From 1950 to 1959 Anthony Quayle and Glen Byam Shaw, separately or in partnership, directed policy and productions. In 1960 Peter Hall succeeded them. Jackson immediately improved the working conditions, and imported eight directors for eight plays. Salaries were increased to meet the reasonable demands of London actors, Robert Harris and Valerie Taylor prominent among them. With so many minds at work, success was variable and consistency of style was not to be expected. Nugent Monck came from Norwich to direct *Cymbeline*. When asked by Jackson how he found the actors, he replied 'Not so bad; only *nine* of them *lisp*.' They ordered things differently at the Maddermarket. Michael Macowan had the courage to stage, at last, a Jacobean *Macbeth*, for one had got rather tired of the subtle reasoning and sophisticated imagery sitting on heads that might have worn the antlers of Hengist and Horsa. Macowan had imagined Stirling Castle at a time when Bothwell might have swaggered down the passages, or Holyrood when Rizzio lay murdered in a pool of blood, or Kirk o' Fields when Darnley staggered out to die. If the result fell short of the intention, the fault lay with a double staircase which served it awkwardly.

Barry Jackson had a genius for the discovery of talent. From the Birmingham Repertory Theatre he had imported the young Paul Scofield and the younger Peter Brook, who had only just come of age. Brook's *Love's Labour Lost* was the more than nine days wonder of the Festival. He had recently seen the first production of the play to be given in Paris for thirty years, in a translation where echoes of Marivaux and Musset, and even an epigram from Voltaire on the lips of Moth, seemed in no way out of place. This gave him his cue for a *fête champêtre* that Watteau might have painted. There were oddities as well as enchantments – Costard's water-pistol, and Dull with his policeman's uniform and string of sausages – and already several touches of the master's hand – notably the prolonged, stricken pause when Mercade brought his message of mortality. Scofield's Don Armado was compared by one critic to 'an overbred and beautiful old borzoi'.[2] Brook's method had at first been ultra-methodical, as

[1] Ibid
[2] Philip Hope-Wallace

JESSICA

Gold
stars
on
veil

T.M.
1955

he worked out the production with cardboard players and model sets. When he found the equation did not come out right, he scrapped it and worked with live actors instead. Henceforward he was to work to nothing but the brief in his own mind.

The wonder boy of 1946 was the whipping boy of 1947. Brook's *Romeo and Juliet* – all romantic abracadabra severely banished – was reduced to a tawny arena enclosed by low crenellated walls. Fascinated by the possibilities of the 'empty space', as Copeau had been obsessed by the *plateau nu*, Brook – with Rolf Gérard as his designer – filled it with the minimum of scenic accessories. Taking his cue from 'the mad blood stirring', he listened less attentively to the imperative rhythms of the verse. *Romeo and Juliet* passed for a moving and delightful play; Brook was concerned to make it dangerous. The peril recoiled upon his own head. Why preserve the musicians' chatter with Juliet cold upon her couch, and omit the Friar's instructions about the phial which had laid her there? Why cut the reconciliation between Montagues and Capulets which alone gives meaning to what is otherwise a tragedy of circumstance? Yet there were compensations, grudgingly recognized: a Juliet, Daphne Slater, still in her teens, and Paul Scofield's Mercutio spinning the fantasies of the 'Queen Mab', stretched on the ground with the flare of torches around him, and that crack in the voice that had not opened so wide that it let the poetry escape from it. In the same season Nugent Monck reduced the playing time of *Pericles* to an hour and a half, cutting the first act altogether on the grounds that the Shakespeare Memorial Theatre owed no hospitality to what Shakespeare evidently had not written.

1948 threw out a hint of changes to come. Anthony Quayle, whose ability to direct as well as to act was not widely suspected, joined the company with Godfrey Tearle and Diana Wynyard. With a single exception, he and Michael Benthall divided the productions between them. Tearle's Othello had nobility of voice and mien; was movingly subdued to the melting mood; and lacked only the extra depth of temperament and ounce of energy which might have converted it into a great performance. Quayle's Iago – a *rusé* sergeant-major, or adjutant risen from the ranks – found him an easy prey. Tearle may not have helped his own performance by directing the play himself. Scofield and Robert Helpmann alternated their Hamlets, a long-standing precedent from the Old Vic – Scofield's balance of strength and delicacy, and Helpmann's keen didactic edge of sophistication, contrasting with each other. Scofield then appeared the most *natural* Hamlet on the English stage, and it remains surprising that he did not make the part more definitively his own. A deliberate avoidance of theatrical, or even emotional, effect may have been responsible. Polonius would have said of him that by 'indirection' he found 'direction' out; and the audience, waiting for the explosive moment, too often missed the sign-post. Realizing that Hamlet, however magnetically, is *manqué*, Scofield was too honest to fill in the gaps. Here, as Kenneth Tynan pointed out in a brilliant page of criticism,[1] was C. S. Lewis's 'pale man in black clothes . . . with his stockings coming down, a dishevelled man whose words make us at once think of loneliness and doubt and dread, of waste and dust and emptiness, and from whose hands, as from our own, we feel the richness of heaven and earth and the comfort of human affection slipping away.' The black clothes were, in fact, the mourning weeds of a Victorian Ruritania in which Benthall had effectively set the play. In a very real sense Scofield's Hamlet was an *invitation au château*; he did not force you

Anthony Quayle as Iago and Godfrey Tearle as Othello in Quayle's production, Royal Shakespeare Theatre, Stratford-upon-Avon, 1948

Opposite: Costume design by Tanya Moisewitch for *The Merchant of Venice*, Royal Shakespeare Theatre, Stratford-upon-Avon, 1956

[1] *He that plays the King* (1950) pp.108-13

John Gielgud as King Lear and
Alan Badel as the Fool, Royal
Shakespeare Theatre,
Stratford-upon-Avon, 1950

inside. But the greater Shakespearian performances are generally importunate; and the laws of the château are not those of the stage.

At the end of the season Barry Jackson's three-year contract was not renewed, a disavowal which hurt him deeply. If he had done no more than bring Brook and Scofield to Stratford, he would have rendered a signal service to the theatre. But he had done much more than this. He had laid the indispensable foundations on which the future was to be built.

Anthony Quayle succeeded him, the first actor-captain of the team since Benson, with youth on his side – for he was only thirty-four. Two productions were outstanding – Gielgud's *Much Ado* and Guthrie's *Henry VIII*. The former, wittily served by Quayle and Diana Wynyard, held the promise of its future perfections. In *Henry VIII* 'Master Tony' – not for the first time – was at odds with 'Dr Guthrie'[1] – although the doctorate had yet to be bestowed. Prelates shambled on to the stage with copes and mitres askew, and Cranmer's sermon was interrupted by an irreverent sneeze. But Tanya Moisewitch's permanent set, with its broad sweeping staircase, under the 'steady truth of uncoloured lighting',[2] was an ample platform for the deployment of Tudor nobility. The play is a pageant of regalism, and Guthrie was a pageant master *sans pareil*. Tearle – who had disappointed as Macbeth – filled the eye and ear as Wolsey, and Quayle's Henry was as good as one had seen since Bourchier – the jolly features not yet frozen into the Holbein mask, but already suggesting them. The play was revived in the following season with Andrew Cruikshank as Wolsey and Gwen Ffrangcon-Davies as a Katharine too fragile for the strength of her long resistance, though not for the pathos of her fall. The panic desertion of Wolsey by those who had 'spaniell'd him at heels' was strikingly managed. One thought of 'rat week', as King Edward VIII prepared to abdicate.

On any count the next two years must rank as five star Stratford seasons. Gielgud revived his *Much Ado*, playing Benedick himself. Neither his temperament, nor his physique, suggested any great length of military service, but the glancing gaiety of his performance matched the warmth and wit of Peggy Ashcroft's Beatrice. The switch from comedy of manners to melodrama was deftly accomplished because the manners had never been bad. Scofield built a real person out of Don Pedro, and of all these players it could be said that, theatrically speaking, they had been well brought up. Peter Brook, sobered by a precocious maturity, returned for a *Measure for Measure* which is still definitive; the procession of prisoners that one expected at any moment to break into 'Freiheit, Freiheit'; and again the seemingly endless pause before Barbara Jefford's Isabella could bring herself to sue for Angelo. Seen as allegory, the fifth act carried a conviction far beyond a dramatist's contrivance. Gielgud's deep-seated pride was barely concealed beneath the plastic armoury of self-righteousness. Yet this Angelo, like any erring mortal, deserved that difficult forgiveness. A different crease in the soul was revealed by his biting Cassius, which the film of *Julius Caesar* was to bring to wider notice, matched at Stratford by the Brutus of Harry Andrews, playing as always the straightest bat in the eleven. Quayle, who was assisted in the production by Michael Langham, gave one the Olympic runner in Antony as well as the devious diplomat and the devoted friend.

But the season was above all memorable for Gielgud's *Lear*, produced 'with acknowledgements to the late Granville-Barker'. Barker had died in 1946, but Gielgud had not forgotten. Something went wrong on the first night, but

[1] T. C. Worsley
[2] J. C. Trewin

Cuthbert Worsley – the sharply perceptive critic of the *New Statesman* – sensing this, stayed over for the matinée on the following afternoon, and chronicled Gielgud's performance on the strength of it. He noted his

ability to exhibit the particular kind of simplicity that lies at the heart of passion in highly conscious, complicated personalities. . . . It is the weight Mr Gielgud gives to the ironies, the irresolutions, the subtleties, that gives the still moments when they come their extra turn. The razed vacant ruin that his Lear holds up to us at the height of his madness is only quite deserted for a few terrible seconds. Mostly it is thronged and peopled with the shuttled echoes and images from a whole long complex human history.

Particularly impressive was the short scene before Lear moves on from Goneril to Regan. Here Gielgud's look of unbridled self-indulgent authority had given place to

an amazed and frightened half-realisation of how far he has exposed himself. A projected self-pity makes him gentle with his fool as with a dog. But in between these indulgent caresses the follies of the last few days flash up one after the other, and are held there, each in a half-broken sentence; the last a premonition of the future.
'O let me not be mad, not mad, sweet heaven.'

Peggy Ashcroft again wrung the heart-strings with her Cordelia; and a young actor, Alan Badel, interpreted the Fool like an autistic adolescent, speaking the home-truths he would hardly have dared to speak if he had been a

John Gielgud as Benedick, Dorothy Tutin as Hero and Diana Wynyard as Beatrice in *Much Ado about Nothing*, Phoenix Theatre 1952

normal person, and yet of all the characters in the play the only one who knew the meaning of fear – and presumably died of it. Every word spoken by Badel as Octavius in *Julius Caesar* seemed to be incised on stone, and you might have met his Lucio, in *Measure for Measure,* any day of the week, peering at Books and Magazines in Soho.

The Festival of Britain in 1951 spurred Stratford to one of its finest efforts. If the youth of England was not exactly on fire, it was reacting with a healthy romanticism to the privations of austerity, prepared to look with unjaundiced eyes at the epic of its own history. Quayle was exactly the man to lead his company through the tetralogy of *Richard II, Henry IV, Parts One and Two,* and *Henry V.* Tanya Moisewitch provided them with a permanent, quasi-Elizabethan setting, which was a triumph of ingenuity and good sense. It served, with rapid and skilful adaptation, for court and countryside, tent and tavern – an oaken architecture against which her costumes swept and glowed. Seen thus in their historical sequences, the plays not only followed one another – they added up and multiplied. Bolingbroke, splendidly played by Harry Andrews with a sick mind and a physique that only weakened towards the end, became a major protagonist. Falstaff's comic stature was in no way reduced, but he was seen for what he is, a gigantic excrescence on the surface of the plays, the symbol of a genial but finally intolerable anarchy. We understood why it was time for him to go. Redgrave's reliance on precise characterization had sent him to Northumbria for the rough side of Hotspur's tongue. The casting of Richard Burton – a secret purpose plain to read in his steady gaze – took much of the callousness out of Hal and much of the chauvinism out of Harry. If the compulsion of the tetralogy slackened in the last of its four parts, this was less because Burton fought shy of heroics than because *Henry V* is an inferior play. Yet even here his vow to build 'two chantries' for the repose of Richard's soul was the more impressive because Michael Redgrave, not overstressing the effeminacy of Richard at the beginning, had muted nothing of his agony at the end. His imagination, kindled by misfortune, had an athletic quality which struggled with the tragedy it embroidered. It was well said that this was one of the rare Richards who might conceivably have met and overcome Wat Tyler's rebellion.[1] Alan Badel's Dauphin in *Henry V* was the *preux chevalier* from a medieval manuscript leaping from illumination into life; and his Justice Shallow the fussy and impotent husk of a man who had once known 'where the bona robas were', and paid his fiver to Jane Nightwork.

In 1953, while Anthony Quayle and Diana Wynyard were taking a company to Australia, Glen Byam Shaw moved in to direct the Stratford season. No other director has looked Shakespeare more straight in the mind, asking himself what a play had meant to the author and quite content if he could translate the meaning to us. This is really the height of ambition, although Byam Shaw's modesty concealed it. In partnership with Quayle until 1955, and then alone, he not only directed the theatre – he fathered it. Only when he found that the child had become a tyrant, did he take his talents elsewhere. His policy was consistent – to attract the leading actors and directors of the day to Stratford, and magnanimously to give them their heads. They did not often lose them.

Redgrave's lavish Shylock owed a good deal to the ghettos of Amsterdam, which he had been at pains to visit, and George Devine was invited to direct him in *King Lear.* The challenge, with Gielgud/Barker recent in memory, was nobly met. On either side of the forestage Robert Colquhoun had designed a

[1] J. Dover Wilson and T. C. Worsley *Shakespeare's Histories at Stratford: 1951* (1952) p.60

Peggy Ashcroft as Cleopatra,
Royal Shakespeare Theatre,
Stratford-upon-Avon, 1953

pair of gigantic doors which led into the castles of Gloucester and Albany. Behind, a curiously wrought construction in stone served, successively, for Lear's throne and hovel. It was a fine stroke of ironic imagination to make it do service for both; and when it was not in active use it led the mind back to the mystery of prehistoric man and the primal shapes of antiquity. Beside it, to right and left, were jutting rocks, and behind it formal backcloths; the one a cubist abstraction, fixing us on the universals of the play, the other outlining the contours of Dover cliffs. The effect was restful in a way that romantic scenery so rarely is. Lear is the tragedy of 'unaccommodated man', and the production, like the setting, was unconfused by anecdote. A classical spirit, serene but not unfeeling, seemed to preside over the whole performance.

The derivation of the play from pagan antiquity justified Devine in keeping it there, but the sophistication of wickedness, which Lear smells out with the antennae of his deranged reason, was communicated by the sickly colouring of the costumes. Redgrave presented an Ancient of Days, stooping and frail but immense in stature, wearing all the weight of his four score years. His voice rumbled, spurted, and subsided with the ebb and swell of passion, whimpered or thundered with alternating rage and grief. The case was made out for a Lear in some sense abstracted from quotidian reality – a remoteness that age can bestow and feebleness enforce – without which his folly is not dramatically acceptable. One remembered a Lazarus quality in the scene of reconciliation with Cordelia; the interplay with Gloucester and the Fool, beautifully conceived by Marius Goring, so that when Lear and the Fool were together they seemed like the two sides of a single personality; and the muted heartbreak of the close where Lear borrowed a wisp of his own hair for 'see – this feather stirs'. If the British theatre has proved nothing else in the present century, it has proved the actability of *Lear*; no other of the greater plays, or parts, has inspired so many fine performances.

Byam Shaw had already directed a production of *Antony and Cleopatra*[1] – an even greater challenge – with Godfrey Tearle and Edith Evans, and Anthony Quayle as a notably deflating Enobarbus. But Dryden's Cleopatra had trespassed upon Shakespeare's, and there remained very little of 'Nilus' slime' for Dame Edith to transmute into fire and air. Now, at Stratford, there was Peggy Ashcroft to remind us that where Dryden had written the part for a woman, Shakespeare had written it for a boy. The sexual nausea of *Lear* has evaporated in *Antony and Cleopatra*, and although Redgrave and Dame Peggy were never less than their sinful, senseless selves, lost to everything but each other, they never allowed the play to become bogged down in a cloying sensuality. A faithful submission to the verse had seen to that. There was something shaggy and lost about this Antony, like a great cricketer out for a duck in a Test Match. No art could give Dame Peggy the ineradicable essence of Cleopatra, but she went as far as character acting could take her; and from the tremendous outcry over Antony's corpse to the ineffable 'Peace, peace, dost thou not see my baby at my breast' – spoken as the staunchest lover of this play must have dreamt to hear it spoken – she conducted the fifth act to its transcendent close. The production was free and vivid. A furled sail on a suspended mast gave us Pompey's galley; a hot yellow light on the cyclorama recalled us from Rome to Egypt; and the imperial eagle was always there, in one form or another, to bring us from Cleopatra's palace to Caesar's tent. Not for seventeen years was *Antony and Cleopatra* again to be produced at Stratford. Expeditions to Mount Everest are not to be undertaken lightly.

The magnet of the Memorial Theatre drew Laurence Olivier and Vivien Leigh to perform, and Gielgud and Peter Brook once again to direct, there in 1955. In Gielgud's *Twelfth Night* Vivien Leigh had in Viola a part suited to her scale which, though exquisite, was not large. Olivier's Malvolio, with its vowels coaxed into gentility, had moved a long way up the servant's ladder, and was not deterred from further escalation. Byam Shaw was wrongly criticized for the wood fires burning in *The Merry Wives*, and the icicles hanging by the wall, for this is a play whose rough and tumble humanity takes the edge off a winter chill. As Macbeth, Olivier – as Kenneth Tynan put it – 'shook hands with greatness',[2] though they had met before. Far more restrained than formerly, he showed from the first a brooding acquaintance with crime, and in proportion as the character decreases in interest, the performance grew, reaching a climax of despair on 'I gin to be aweary of the sun.' Here was 'the anguish of the *de facto* ruler who dares not admit that he lacks the essential qualities of kingship . . . the valiant

[1] At the Piccadilly in 1946
[2] *Curtains* (1961) p.99
[3] *Life Magazine* (1 May 1964)

Vivien Leigh as Viola and
Laurence Olivier as Malvolio in
John Gielgud's *Twelfth Night*,
Royal Shakespeare Theatre,
Stratford-upon-Avon, 1955

usurper who can never comprehend what Ibsen calls "the great kingly thought".
He will always be a monarch *manqué*.'[2] He was also, in Olivier's own shrewd
definition, 'the kind of man whose arm you would never take as he crossed the
street'.[3] Byam Shaw's production, in settings by Roger Furse, sent the Witches
literally flying through 'the fog and filthy air'; and Maxine Audley's scream as
Lady Macduff has echoed down the years for anyone who heard it.

The sensation of the year, however, was Peter Brook's *Titus Andronicus* – all
in all, perhaps, the greatest Shakespearian production of our time, as Olivier's
Titus was arguably his greatest performance – the most intense exhibition of
sheer suffering that even this actor has given us, the individuation of character
reconciled with the impersonality of tragic art, lifting the play at times to
altitudes not yet within Shakespeare's reach. Who will forget that shambling,
hardly recognizable entrance, with the face furrowed by the endurances of a
dozen campaigns; and the all-encompassing desolation of – 'I *am* the sea?'
Brook had designed the setting and composed the *musique concrète*. It was an
extraordinary achievement to have rendered the atrocity of the play without

staining the stage, or the performers, with one drop of blood; and such perilous reefs as 'Why, there they are both, baked in that pie' were prudently circumnavigated. One remembers, too, the menace and magnificence of Anthony Quayle's Aaron, and the white hands of Maxine Audley's passionate Tamora clambering up his burnished thighs.

It may well have been Quayle's success as Aaron that prompted him to resign from the dual directorate and pursue a successful career elsewhere. Byam Shaw – realizing that the theatre, like the Church, relies upon an Apostolic Succession – now invited Peter Hall to produce a *Love's Labour Lost* which came and went without making any particular mark. He returned, however, in 1957 for a *Cymbeline* that did much to confirm his candidature. This realized exactly the mood of romantic melodrama which Barker saw as proper to the play. The set was framed by two gigantic oak-trees, ivy-entwined, and between them stood a miniature Norman tower and some flamboyant Gothic which might have come straight out of Monet's *Rouen Cathedral*. The morning dew lay fresh on Peggy Ashcroft's Imogen, and Richard Johnson's Posthumus was excused by the vanity of good looks. Clive Revill's Cloten was a cretinous Infante out of Velasquez, and Joan Miller as his mother, in arguably the worst part that Shakespeare ever wrote, reminded one of Mozart's Queen of the Night, having taken heavily to drugs. In Byam Shaw's *Julius Caesar* Alec Clunes's Brutus was never too good to be true, racked as it was by all the demons of the divided mind. The lynched body of Cinna hanging over the side of Antony's pulpit; the statue of Caesar casting its oppressive shadow across the opening scene; and the huge coloured map before which the Triumvirate planned their strategy – illustrated a clear statement of the play. Douglas Seale had taken out a director's patent for the Histories, but his *King John* was flawed by a lack of generosity in its Falconbridge. Robert Harris's refusal to turn the King into a gibbering neurotic had given to Alec Clunes an opportunity which he inexplicably declined. Here was a competent, foxy monarch yielding to a single overwhelming temptation. Seale had fought the static tendencies of the play, and here and there the warmer humanities of *Henry IV* began to make themselves felt beyond the feudal parley.

Peter Brook now came to grips with *The Tempest*. He understood what the play was about:

> When we realise that it takes place on an island and not an island, during a day and not during a day, with a tempest that sets off a series of events that are still within a tempest even when the storm is done, that the charming pastoral naturally encompasses rape, murder, conspiracy and violence; when we begin to unearth the themes that Shakespeare has so carefully buried, we see that it is his complete final statement, and that it deals with the whole condition of man.[1]

The difficulty was brutally put by a very young student to the present writer. 'Prospero said that every third thought would be his grave. What were the other two?' That is what the director has to find out, and Peter Brook was still searching. He might have added that although *The Tempest* is a play about magic, it is much more essentially a play about men and women, about a pure spirit, and about a monster who is on his way to being a man; that the magic of sounds and sweet airs, and miraculous transformations, is subordinate to the magic which operates in the minds and hearts of the characters. It is a play about emotion recollected, not in tranquillity but in storm and stress – yet recollected, for all that; and it is the director's business to bring it out into

[1] *The Empty Space* (1971) p.102

whatever light the theatre can afford. Brook's production at Stratford, and later at Drury Lane, was defeated by its own virtuosities; the *musique concrète* that came from what he called 'a mescalin world of sound', the dissolving gauzes and opening and shutting of trapdoors. Even with Gielgud's towering Prospero, absolute in conception and performance, this was not enough – or rather, it was too much. Ariel and Caliban – the spirit and the flesh – were both inadequate. Yet one detail, significant in its economy, remained to haunt the spectator – the ship's lantern swinging in the darkness at an angle of ninety degrees until the sea engulfed it. Peter Brook does not like to repeat himself; but suppose he were to have radical thoughts about *The Tempest* similar to the thoughts he had about the *Dream*?

In 1958 Michael Redgrave gave his last performance of Hamlet. Too old at fifty to carry all his previous conviction, he still acted so well that, as Bridges-Adams wrote, you never wanted him to stop. He seemed to be coming to the part for the first time, suffering from none of those second thoughts which Dr Madariaga had put into the head of Alec Guinness. All the colloquial passages were alive with irony and humour, and one had never heard the advice to the players better given. This Hamlet was an heroic failure, not a character out of an analyst's case-book. Athletic as well as imaginative, he was the man to defeat Laertes in a duel, and send Rosencrantz and Guildenstern to their doom; but winning all his battles, he lost his campaign. Life itself – the adversary with the invincible question-mark – got the better of him in the end. Byam Shaw's production had his usual virtues of simplicity and space, clarity and speed. The stage, its darkness stabbed with waving torches, was effectively used for the macabre hide-and-seek which followed the killing of Polonius; and the elaborate coats-of-arms hung between the pillars reminded one that *Hamlet* is a political melodrama as well as a private tragedy. Hamlet detected Claudius' hidden presence in the 'nunnery' scene from a sudden cry of Ophelia's, not from the usual fluttering of the arras; and the two pictures which he showed to Gertrude were respectively a miniature worn round his neck, and the back of a coin taken from his pocket. It was right that Laertes should return to Elsinore in mourning, and reasonable, at least, that Fortinbras – a cue taken here from Georges Pitoeff – should claim his sovereignty in white. Dorothy Tutin's Ophelia allowed one to guess, for a single moment in the mad scene, that she *might* have been Hamlet's mistress. Subsequent performances of the part have turned the doubt into a certainty. Byam Shaw's only affectation was a silver cross rising from the forestage, and making things very awkward for Claudius who must kneel behind it with his face to the audience, while Hamlet was rationalizing his scruples or refining his revenge.

John Gielgud as Prospero and Ian Holm as Ariel in Peter Brook's *The Tempest*, Royal Shakespeare Theatre, Stratford-upon-Avon, 1957

Tony Richardson, invited to direct *Pericles*, took the play's inconsequence and improbabilities in a richly imaginative stride, turning it into the kind of seafarer's tale which might have relieved the boredom of a dead calm on an Elizabethan galley. One was never long out of sight of the rigging, or out of smell of the salt sea spray. The play is a story of shipwreck, and here it was told, or sung, by a coloured West Indian actor, Edric O'Connor, as Gower. *Pericles* has both the absurdities and solemnities of opera, and music came naturally to its aid. So did London Sainthill's lovely and lavish settings, and a bunch of good performances. Richard Johnson's Pericles held the last great scene firm in face of the director's virtuosity; no other music drowned 'the music of the spheres'. Angela Baddeley's bawd had stepped straight out of Rowlandson. One was eager for Richardson to try his hand at one of the greater plays; when he did, one wished he had left it alone.

If Richardson had treated *Pericles* as one kind of libretto – a theme for Britten, with Peter Pears to narrate it? – Douglas Seale's *Much Ado* translated us to the world of Donizetti. The Bourbons reigned over Naples and the Two Sicilies, and Don Pedro obviously spoke for them. This was carnival time with the painted carts in procession, and the *elisir d'amore* was not slow to quicken in the veins of Benedick and Beatrice. Redgrave threw out what hints he could of mildly incredible campaigns, and Googie Withers – generosity of mind and heart aglow beneath the persiflage and the parasol – matched, if indeed she did not surpass, any performance of the part in recent memory. This production of *Much Ado* stood beside Gielgud's; no other has since come within a mile of it. Peter Hall's *Twelfth Night* – his favourite comedy – was an exploratory embrace; its consummation will be discussed later.

For his final season (1959) Byam Shaw mustered Peter Hall and Tyrone Guthrie to direct, Edith Evans, Paul Robeson, Charles Laughton, and Laurence Olivier to perform. There were times when the stars shot a little uncertainly from their spheres. The haunting voice of Robeson's Othello could still not quite compensate for the halting verse; and Richardson's production seemed intent on bringing it to a stop altogether. In *All's Well that Ends Well* there was really nothing to stop either 'Master Tony' or 'Dr Guthrie' on their way to town. Stratford, Ontario, had already seen this Edwardian fantasia. Robert Hardy's ailing King was *cousin germain* both to George V and Tsar Nicholas II; even the twitch of his fingers was patrician. Dame Edith as the Countess of Rousillon recalled a great châtelaine in the autumn of her days, and the ease of human relationships in a world of protocol where the seasons passed and yet time seemed always to be standing still. Cyril Luckham as Parolles was a loud-checked, latter-day bounder to the life; and the Stratford eleven made up a *posse* of officers from the Brigade of Guards, all of whom one could imagine playing cribbage at Pratts. When the Frenchmen were on active service the unities of time were rudely disturbed as the Duke of Florence, in a scene of gloriously gratuitous pantomime, addressed them through a microphone. The mind held a multitude of details within a coherent pattern – Zoe Caldwell's moving Helena getting her man by the scruff of his neck; a gloomy priest in a biretta blessing their union as if he were conducting their funeral; and all those immaculate supernumeraries fielding in the deep.

Byam Shaw's *Lear* suffered from a displacement of gravity due to Laughton's domestication of the opening scenes, and a deprivation of poetry due to his inability to speak Shakespearian verse. Words and meaning were huskily hammered out, but melody was missing. He was at his best in the scene with Gloucester, and in the arms of Cordelia, all passion spent, secure upon the summit of a second innocence. His mistake was to have arrived there too soon. Albert Finney distinguished very cannily between Edgar and Poor Tom and the unnamed rustic who sets Gloucester on his way to Dover; and Angela Baddeley showed a Regan who had taken to drink. By contriving an upper chamber above the entrance to Gloucester's castle, Byam Shaw enabled Lear and his companions to *return* to a hiding place in, or about, it after their wandering in the storm. The Elizabethan balcony would have served the same purpose, providing a strong visual parallel between the madness of Lear above and the maiming of Gloucester below.

Peter Hall's *A Midsummer Night's Dream*, rightly conceived as an epithalamium, accompanied by woodnotes wild that might have celebrated a wedding at Knole or Compton Wynyates, suffered from an obstinate double staircase which shattered the delicacy of Lila de Nobili's décor. We were never completely in the wood or out of it. The delicacy of the play itself was shattered by Laughton's overbearing Bottom, for once the innocent *hubris* of the character seems to have become part of the actor's own make-up, the innocence is lost, and our sympathies go with it. In the course of time and experiment Peter Hall was to get rid of that awkward staircase, and with a Bottom less coarse in fibre his *Dream* was an enchantment. His *Coriolanus* stood by Olivier's superb performance. It was more than twenty years since he had played the part, and now he was not better but different. The pride whose boyishness drew Aufidius' taunt was deep ingrained; the man's essential immaturity was fixed into a martial mould. After the 'common cry of curs', consummately delivered, one marvelled that the actor had so much up his sleeve, for thereafter he wore the look of a man doomed by his own conscience, his face frozen into a mask of fatality. Dame Edith's Volumnia lacked the edge of granite to show that mother and son were hewn out of the same block, and the production was not helped by a cumbersome and complicated décor. This gave Olivier a precipice for his cliff-hanging death fall, but its proportions were painful to the eye. From Heir Presumptive Peter Hall had become Heir Apparent; Stratford waited with confidence and curiosity for the new reign.

Judi Dench as Titania and Paul Hardwick as Bottom in Peter Hall's *A Midsummer Night's Dream*, Aldwych Theatre 1963

XIV Foreigners, and a Five-year Plan

A talented British director, John Blatchley, has written of his experiences in directing Shakespeare in France.[1] The article is a *locus classicus* of good sense, and it emphasizes among other things the difficulty of judging a Shakespeare production apart from the audience assisting at it. The familiarity of an English public with the plays tempts the director to novelty, if not to extravagance. People who have been seeing *Twelfth Night* all their lives naturally expect a new look. People who have never seen it before, and probably never read it, are content with a straightforward presentation. They are curious to know what happens, and it matters little to them whether Feste is a young or an aged clown, whether Sir Andrew is a walking scarecrow or simply a foolish knight. Never having set eyes on an English gentleman, they are incapable of asking themselves which club Sir Toby belonged to; and being quite ignorant of the social hierarchies, they cannot be expected to realize that Malvolio, though he may disdainfully decant the port, will be unlikely to set it in circulation. The predominantly middle-class audience, not necessarily well educated, that supports any of the Stratfords, expects to be titillated. The artisans who applauded Roger Planchon's *Henry IV* at Villeurbanne, or the rural public that crammed into a tent to see Blatchley's *Twelfth Night*, were very like an Elizabethan audience attending these plays for the first time. They might be bored, but they were not blasé.

Methods proper to a particular national tradition have often surprised the foreigner. When the Old Vic came to Paris after the war with *Lear* and *Richard III*, the French were stunned by Olivier's performances, but they found the productions old-fashioned. Those who remembered Mounet-Sully made their comparisons; there were no comparisons to be made with Copeau and Antoine. Again, when the same company went to New York, those who expected an ensemble to compare with the Moscow Art Theatre were disappointed. And whenever an English company has visited Russia, they have been astonished to find Shakespeare hamstrung by realistic productions which, in Britain, had been buried with Beerbohm Tree. Prepared for socialist realism, they found capitalist realism instead.

A defect of much French playing in Shakespeare is the avoidance of any *via media* between a shout and an incantation. Jouvet's haunting monotone would have wearied one in a tragic rôle, and there were times when even Vilar's impressive Richard II declined into sing-song. Certain exceptions, however, stand out: Debucourt's Jaques in *As You Like It* at the Comédie Française, entering the stage, as he so often did, like a man who had just been reading Montaigne in a well-stocked library; and Jean Dessailly's exquisite Henry VI at the Marigny. Another fault, as Blatchley pointed out, is a total misunderstanding of what Shakespeare meant by a 'clown'. The 'clown' in French comedy is a type; in Shakespeare he is a character. There is all the difference in the world between Lance in *The Two Gentlemen of Verona* and Lancelot Gobbo in *The Merchant of Venice*. Apart from anything else, you sigh whenever Lance

Jean-Louis Barrault as Hamlet, Théâtre Marigny 1946

Etudes Anglaises XIII, no. 2 (1966)

leaves the stage and whenever Lancelot Gobbo comes on to it. The same criticism applies to a good deal of German acting; self-indulgent lyricism on the one hand, crude buffoonery on the other.

Gaston Baty's last production of Shakespeare was *The Taming of the Shrew* in April 1941, and Copeau revived his *Twelfth Night* at the Comédie Française in 1940, not without a sigh of regret for the Vieux Colombier. The future belonged to Barrault and Vilar, and to Planchon a little later on. In 1942, at the Comédie Française, Barrault played his first Hamlet in a translation by Guy de Pourtalès. Jean Cocteau was quick to observe that Barrault was an *animateur* before he was an actor; that he needed to direct the play himself if his own performance were to move comfortably inside it. After his resignation from the Comédie Française he produced *Hamlet* at the Marigny in a new translation by André Gide, and décor by André Masson. It is natural for Hamlet to be surprised when he sees the Ghost, but Masson's conception of it caused the most seasoned playgoer to

Jean Vilar as Macbeth and
Maria Casarès as Lady Macbeth in
Vilar's production, Théâtre National
Populaire

catch his breath. Barrault had revised a romantic interpretation of the part to which his personality and physique easily lent themselves, presenting instead 'a hero of superior hesitation', drawn by his own lucidity to question the value of action and even of existence in a corrupted world, and offering himself in sacrifice, so that a new world may be born where faith will become possible once more'.[1] Apart from his quite exceptional intelligence and sensibility, Barrault's genius was for mime, and his movement as Hamlet not only helped the words but at times made them otiose. Wisely, he modified his plasticity when he brought the production to Edinburgh.

Honneger's music was partly live and partly recorded. Pierre Boulez was among the instrumentalists who followed the action of the play from the orchestra pit, while the trumpets came through the loudspeakers – never more significantly than on Fortinbras' final entrance. Barrault had seen him in his white and green cloak as the Angel of the Last Judgment – the messenger of life redeemed. 'Every year,' he was to write, 'towards the end of January, in midwinter, you have one or two days of false spring. The air is pale and green, and the sun is all white, like a mirage of the first leaf. When I hear this brief explosion in the air and in nature, I now say, "There are the trumpets of Fortinbras."'[2] Barrault left Oedipan speculations to the psychoanalysts; he found the notion of Hamlet's chastity, defined as sublimated sensuality, far more to the point. The ambiguity of the play was discovered in its situation between life and death, like the estuary of a great river belonging wholly neither to the sea nor to the land. After the death of Rosencrantz and Guildenstern Hamlet has set his face finally seaward, and the first thing he meets is the skull of Yorick.

A shrewd judge of his own work, Barrault has always placed his version of *Henry VI*, stitched together and adapted from François-Victor Hugo's translation, above his other Shakespeare productions. His intention was to show the transition between the decline of the Middle Ages and the first stirrings of the Renaissance. In the light of Buchenwald and Hiroshima, the young Henry's lamentation on the battlefield evoked a particularly sympathetic response. The Barraults – for Madeleine Renaud was closely associated with her husband's work – created an *avant-garde* which lost nothing of its enterprise in becoming, willy-nilly, an establishment. It was among the deeper ironies of the time that an ensemble which had brought Beckett and Kafka to Paris should have seen their theatre gutted, and their décors and costumes destroyed by the incendiaries of the Sorbonne – 'hogs' as Milton wrote 'that bawl for freedom in their senseless mood'. Rarely had so many teeth bitten the hands that fed them.

Where Barrault had confined himself to Paris and foreign tours, Vilar was in search of a different public. Conceiving the theatre as a popular 'celebration', he naturally profited from the post-war fashion for festivals. The courtyard of the Palais des Papes at Avignon gave him his opportunity. Here, in September 1947, he mounted *Richard II* before 3,000 spectators on a vast open stage, and in costumes by Gischia which 'stood out against the nocturnal brown of the walls or faded into isolated silhouettes, evocative of tyranny, under the pointed arches'.[3] Just as the play itself seemed to be liberated by this arena, the players felt themselves liberated with it. The performance was not improved when Gérard Philippe succeeded Vilar in the title rôle; and the case was altered, too, when Alain Cuny, with his hoarse, ear-splitting elocution, took over Macbeth. Where Vilar had seemed abstracted in his criminal fantasies, Cuny was 'more carnal and more combative',[4] and for that reason a closer partner to the Lady

[1] Ibid
[2] *Souvenirs pour demain* (1972) p.194
[3] *Spectateur* (September 1947)
[4] Madame Dussane *Etudes Anglaises* XIII, no. 2 (1960) p.225

Macbeth of Maria Casarès. *A Midsummer Night's Dream* (1960) presented a different challenge. Vilar had arranged his stage in three areas, one – in the centre – completely neutral, and one on either side of it to represent a clearing in the forest or Theseus' court. He emphasized the serious undertones of the play – discord in heaven disturbing a cosmic harmony – and only the excessive clowning of the artisans struck a note at odds with the general intention of the *mise-en-scène*. When the production was given at the Palais de Chaillot it seemed more appropriately housed. The eye which, at Avignon, had encountered a stone wall, however historic, could here plunge into infinite distance without any concession, except for the formal trees, to scenic realism.

Others were quick to follow Vilar's example, sometimes in places themselves associated with the play, or strongly suggestive of it; *Love's Labour Lost* in Languedoc, Jean Marchat's *King John* at Angers, *Julius Caesar* and *Coriolanus* in the Roman amphitheatres at Arles and Nîmes. Marchat also presented *Julius Caesar* in the ruins of Jupiter's temple at Baalbeck. Elsewhere the results were not uniformly successful; the quest for anecdote could be misleading. For *Hamlet* in the courtyard of the château at Annecy Gabriel Monnet constructed a stage which isolated the actors from their architectural setting but still left them sensitive to its atmosphere. What mattered, he maintained, was the 'instrumental value' of the site as a sounding board for the human voice.

Vilar and the Théâtre National Populaire had achieved their democratic aim of discovering a new, and younger, audience for Shakespeare, not only at Avignon but in the Parisian *banlieue*. The various dramatic centres in the provinces, now subsidized by the state, had also proved a congruity between the Elizabethan drama and contemporary taste: Maurice Jacquemont's *Cymbeline* at Quimper and Sarlat, Anouilh's translation of *Twelfth Night* at Arras, Dasté's *Tempest* at St Etienne, with décors by Bazaine, Guignoux's *Merchant of Venice* and Michael St Denis' *Romeo and Juliet* at Strasbourg – 'it was on the French bank of the Rhine' wrote one critic 'that for the first time I heard the lark of Verona sing a truly moving song'. In almost every case a straight look had been taken at the play, and a straightforward presentation given of it. But Roger Planchon at Villeurbanne, a suburb of Lyons, looked at Shakespeare through the spectacles of Berthold Brecht, choosing the two parts of *Henry IV* to inaugurate his Théâtre de la Cité. He had his own ideas of democracy, and they were not those of western democrats.

Planchon recognized in Shakespeare 'a dynamic theatre of men in the light of society, opposed to a static theatre of men in the light of eternity'. The first half of the equation was more valid than the second. He recognized, too, the sublimity of Shakespeare's verse, but acknowledged that 'the difficulty for us who are in search of a critical realism is to abstract this poetical "aura" which magnifies the stature of the characters, but runs the risk of masking them. We must exhibit, but not sublimate, them – diminish the poetry, but not extinguish it.' There was little doubt of the diminution; Henry's determination to join the Crusade, albeit abridged, was not easy to articulate while at the same time he was eating his dinner. Again, Prince Hal is not among Shakespeare's more attractive characters; call him an unhappy hypocrite, and you have said the worst of him. When Planchon allowed Hotspur to be stabbed in the back while the Prince was engaging him in front, he was falsifying both the character and the scene.

The plays were first performed in the open air for the Nuits de Bourgoyne. A

Maria Casarès as Lady Macbeth: the sleep-walking scene

Opposite above: Set design by Teo Otto for Leopold Lindtberg's *Henry V*, Burgtheater, Vienna, 1961

Set design by Lila de Nobili for Peter Hall's *Twelfth Night*, Royal Shakespeare Theatre, Stratford-upon-Avon, 1958

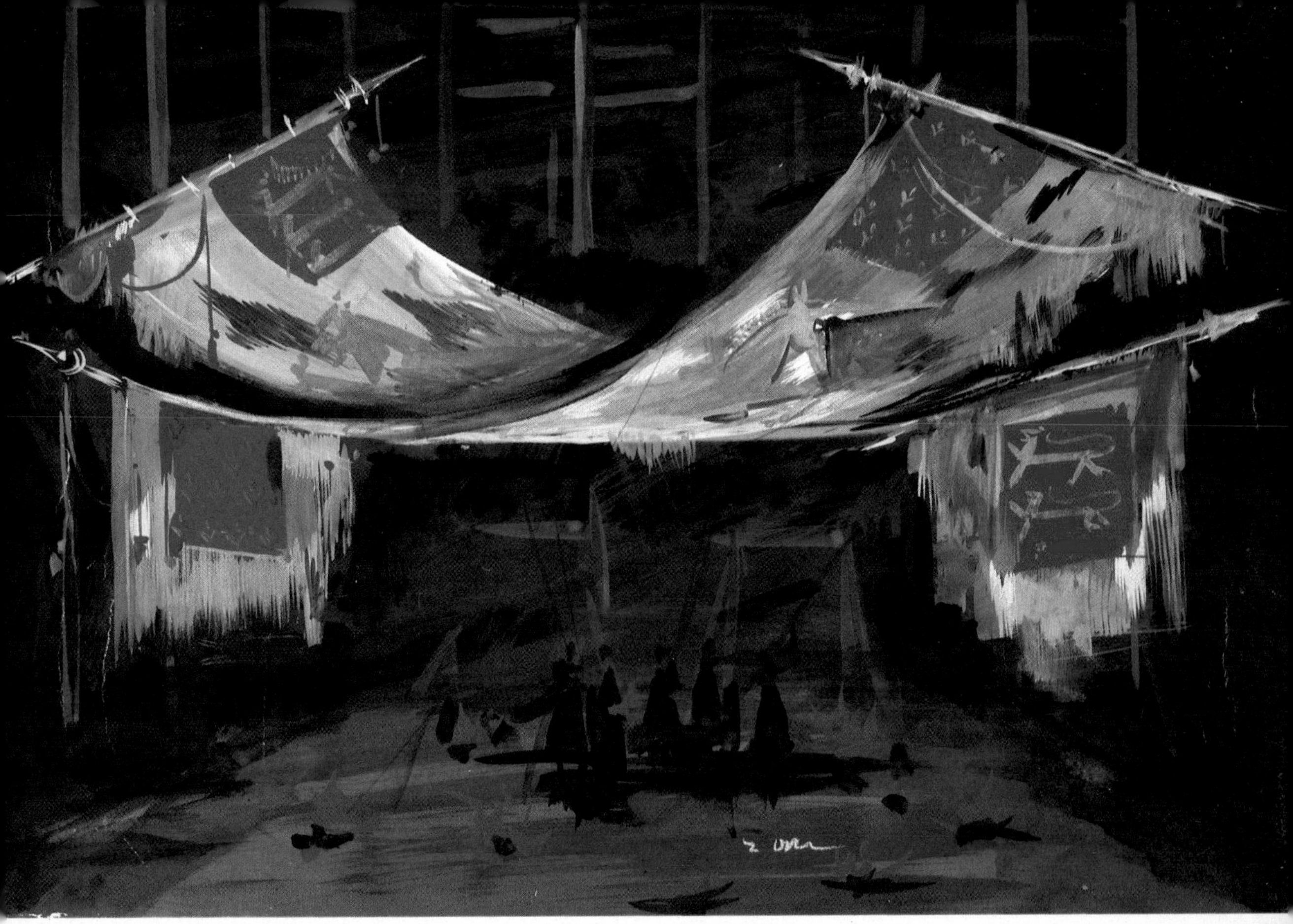

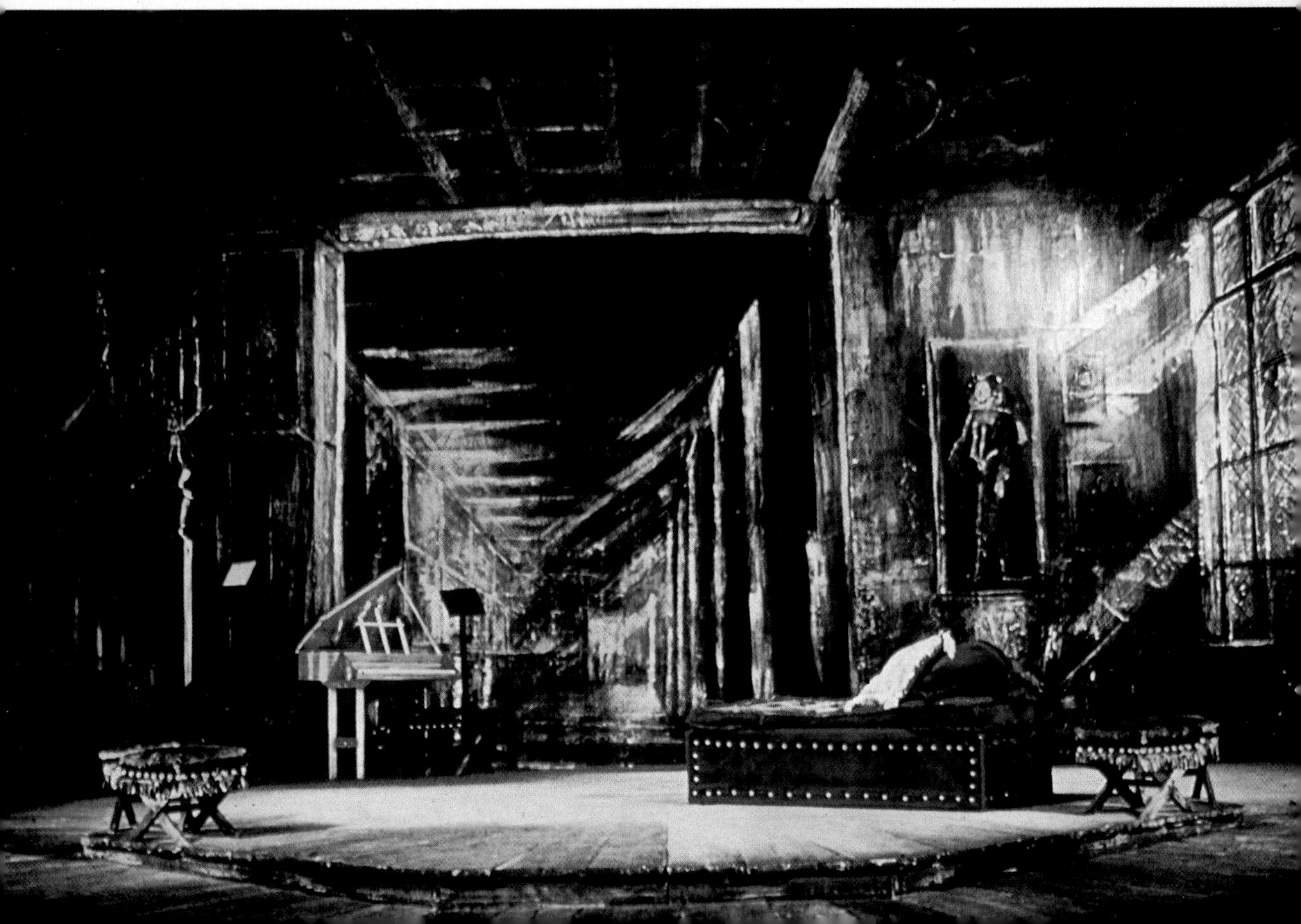

large map in the background was an indication of time and place. Scenic elements, at once solid and stylized, designed by René Allio, combined a suggestion of Gothic with a hint of Le Corbusier. The costumes, alike in colour and material, established the psychology of the characters and their social categories. Visually, the production was a creative achievement of the first order; and its political intention was readily acceptable to the industrial audience of Villeurbanne. But others had proved that Shakespeare played for what he was worth, and undiluted by a Marxist *parti pris,* was equally acceptable to a public which had no belief in the Divine Right of Kings.

2

Just as in France Shakespeare had been brought alive by the translations of two distinguished poets, Pierre-Jean Jouve and Jules Supervielle, so in Italy Ungaretti had translated the Sonnets, and Quasimodo and Montale certain of the plays. The finest directors – Luchino Visconti, Orazio Costa, and Giorgio Strehler – had devoted their talents to the *mise-en-scène.* Copeau's *As You Like It* in the Boboli Gardens had not been forgotten; and it was here that Visconti mobilized his immense *Troilus and Cressida* (1949), putting half the characters on horseback, and contrasting an oriental Troy with the practical and disciplined soldiery of Greece – the heroic and the anti-heroic in striking counterpoint. Less successful was his *As You Like It* in Rome (1951) with costumes and décor by Salvador Dali. The combination of a realist director and a surrealist designer who had turned his back on surrealism, was to get the worst of both conventions. This was the golden age of the Italian cinema, and several talented *cinéastes* were tempted by the visual opportunities of Shakespeare on the stage. In seizing them, Visconti had not omitted a line from *Troilus and Cressida,* but Zeffirelli, as we shall note in due course, was less scrupulous. In 1950 Orazio Costa triumphed with his *Twelfth Night* in Naples, subsequently given in other Italian cities. The comedy was acted, danced, and mimed against a spacious natural background. Certainly Shakespeare *al fresco* in Italy ran fewer risks from the wind and the rain than it did elsewhere.

These productions, however successful, were sporadic. For a consistent effort of interpretation we must turn to Giorgio Strehler and the Piccolo Teatro at Milan. Between 1947 and 1964 the company presented eleven of Shakespeare's plays in its own theatre or elsewhere; Quasimodo's *Tempest* in the Boboli Gardens, Lodovico's *Henry IV* in the amphitheatre at Verona, and his *Twelfth Night* in the Palazzo Grassi at Venice. Of these productions the most significant were Strehler's *Julius Caesar* and *Coriolanus.* The obsession with politics, common to any country recently liberated from fascist rule, was reinforced by the historicist tendency of so much Italian thought. It was confirmed by the experience of partisan resistance, especially in the north of Italy. Strehler had sought to extract a relevance from Shakespeare's historical tetralogy, but he came to find a sharper reference in the two Roman plays. Rather surprisingly, he emphasized the private conflicts in *Julius Caesar* at the expense of the political drama. Here were a group of men, of the same class and much of the same age, divided or allied by temperament and political option. Friends fell apart; the ideals of yesterday were sacrificed to the opportunism of tomorrow. In Italy, as in France, it was the story of a whole generation united in resistance, divided in victory. Strehler avoided the continual movement of his earlier productions,

Opposite: John Stride as Romeo and Joanna Dunham as Juliet in Franco Zeffirelli's *Romeo and Juliet,* Old Vic 1960

Orazio Costa's *Twelfth Night*,
Naples 1950

though the play invited it, and his designer, Damiani, dressed the characters in
a neutral grey.

Between his *Julius Caesar* and his *Coriolanus* Strehler had met Berthold
Brecht. He realized with Brecht that *Coriolanus* was a play about the dialectic
of history, and also about the dialectic of the protagonist's private conscience.
It was a play about politics and also a play about pride. In the first part the
conflict was political; in the second it was personal. The dialectic was also clear
within each opposing camp. Coriolanus finds himself opposed to the patricians,
as the tribunes are opposed to the plebs. But although the victory in the play
goes to the patricians, the sense of history is with the plebs. Coriolanus, whose
sole *raison d'être* is the making of war, is defeated, not only by a mother's
pleading, but because there is no longer a war to make. Aufidius, his adversary
and then his ally, is the sole hero he has left; and only in the sense that he is
murdered by his hero, can his death be described as heroic. In obedience to
Brecht, Strehler gave his audience time to think, dividing the play into twenty-
two scenes and allowing each to register its meaning 'without echoes, colour, or
excessive modulation. Everything was simplified.' Strehler had gone far deeper
than Planchon, though in the same direction. For Brecht, as for Strehler, the
choice of *Coriolanus* was

a mature choice on the part of a man who believes in history and in progress. It is
very easy for such men to choose sympathetic and progressive characters, spokes-
men for a great social ideal. The true task for any reasoning about history is to
discover its hidden conspiracy where the parts are not determined in advance, and
where it may happen that the traitor Coriolanus has right on his side at a certain

[1] Ruggero Jacobbi *Revue d'Histoire du
Théâtre* (January-March 1965) p.92

moment, and that the Roman people do not have it on theirs, particularly when
reason and unreason are concretely at grips among men.[1]

The rehearsals for *Coriolanus* by the Berliner ensemble (1951-2) lasted for a
year. This was the only one of Brecht's Shakespeare productions which merits
consideration as such. The others were adaptations in which economic motives
were given the priority, and the Shakespearian stress on individual destiny
converted into dialectical materialism. In *Measure for Measure* the Duke no
longer presided over a general reconciliation, but over a stratified society in
which the wealthy lived at the expense of the poor, and the nun at the expense of
the prostitute. Brecht did not hesitate to insert parallel scenes to illustrate his
thesis. In *Macbeth* a beggar found sleeping in a corner of the porter's lodging
was accused of theft; and in *Romeo and Juliet* Romeo borrowed money from a
farmer to pay court to Juliet, while Juliet forbade the Nurse to keep an assigna-
tion so that she could remain on the look-out during the lovers' duet. Juliet had
the right to her rhapsody, but the Nurse had not. If anyone had asked how
Romeo would have had the time to borrow money from a farmer between his
ecstatic departure from Capulet's ballroom and his ecstatic leap over Capulet's
orchard wall, or with whom the Nurse could conceivably have had an assigna-
tion, Brecht would have replied that these questions had no relevance for an
'epic' theatre.

In *Coriolanus*, however, he resisted the facility of a *parti pris*. Caius Marcius
was no fascist beast, but a man indispensable to society because of his competence
in war. When the war had been won, and the plebs were organized to claim
their rights, he was no longer indispensable. The servant of the state had
become the servant of his own pride. In only one instance did Brecht twist the

Giorgio Strehler's *Henry VI*,
Piccolo Teatro, Milan, 1965-6

dramatist's intention. Volumnia pleaded, not in the name of the city but in that
of the patricians. If Coriolanus destroyed it, plebs and patricians would perish
together. If he were defeated, the plebs would be victorious; and it was to save
the patricians that he yielded to Volumnia's entreaty. Brecht was haunted by
Shakespeare, and by the Elizabethan theatre which seemed to him the perfect
instrument for the theatre he was himself trying to create. Did he also suspect
that it was inimical to the 'pathos' he abhorred? Without questioning Shakespeare's essential authorship of the works attributed to him, he believed that
many others had had a hand in them – actors as well as poets, and the writers
from whom he took his plots. The plays, too, were the product of an 'ensemble'.
He believed also that Shakespeare's sense of history had transcended, perhaps
unconsciously, the individualistic humanism of his time. Brecht's transposition
of Shakespeare into Marxist terms went far beyond a frivolous gimmickry; it set,
nonetheless, an example which it has been generally disastrous to follow.

In western Germany Gustaf Gründgens inherited something of Jurgen
Fehling's authority, though little of his genius. As Fehling's intendant at the
Deutsches Theater, he sponsored a remarkable production of *The Comedy of
Errors*. When Berlin was divided into two mutually hostile zones of occupation,
he moved to Hamburg and Düsseldorf. His *Hamlet* was much applauded, but
some found it wanting in finesse. Except for an outstanding production of
All's Well that Ends Well in Düsseldorf, conceived as a timeless allegory,
German production of Shakespeare followed traditional patterns. When Peter
Brook's *Measure for Measure* was presented in Berlin, its sobriety passed over
the heads of the audience; they felt they had seen this kind of thing before. His
King Lear – to be presently discussed – woke them up to an enthusiasm greater,
perhaps, than it deserved. For once, those living on the western side of the Wall
welcomed a wind blowing from the east.

We cannot leave the 'popular democracies' without a salute to the great
Hungarian actor, Miklos Gabor. J. C. Trewin wrote of his Hamlet: 'Again and
again, during the night, when Gabor came down towards us on the vast, clear
platform stage Lazló Vamos had provided, it was as if we were meeting for the
first time the figure that had been wrangled about for three and a half centuries.'[1]
Gabor's Hamlet had been two years in preparation. He wore no make-up to
characterize a face deliberately 'uncertain'; people noticed a strange distance

Set design by Adolf Mahuke for
Rolf Schneider's *All's Well that
Ends Well*, Städtische Bühnen,
Dortmund, 1959

[1] *New Hungarian Quarterly* (July-September
1963)
[2] *The Winter's Tale*: IV iv 89-93

Right: Miklos Gabor as Hamlet, Budapest

Gustaf Gründgens and Elizabeth Flickenschildt in *Hamlet*, Schauspielhaus, Düsseldorf, 1949

between the expression of his eyes and the expression of his speech. 'Art itself' he wrote 'is natural so long as it adheres to its own laws.' Shakespeare himself had said much the same thing,[2] and Gabor evidently practised what they both had preached. His Romeo was the eternal adolescent, only maturing after his steel had clashed with Tybalt's. His Iago, however diabolical, was still a man: 'I can't play a demon' he insisted; and the same residual humanity was evident in his Richard III (1969). With the years his acting has grown more economical. A certain resemblance to Josef Kainz may well be more than physical; and he stands with Moissi and Werner Krauss among the few great interpreters of Shakespeare on the European continent during the century of the *régisseur*.

3

In 1947 the governors of the Vic decided to dispense with the triumvirate of Olivier, Richardson, and John Burrell which had given the theatre an international prestige. Hugh Hunt was brought in from Bristol, where the Vic's daughter was now housed in the elegant, eighteenth-century Theatre Royal. He remained as artistic director until 1953, with the Old Vic School and its own triumvirate of Michel Saint-Denis, Glen Byam Shaw, and George Devine feeding him with talent rigorously trained. Michael Redgrave was his leading man, anticipating by eight years – and all of them to the good – the Hamlet at Stratford which we have already discussed. In *Love's Labour Lost*, an exquisite

Above: Michael Redgrave as Berowne in *Love's Labour's Lost*, Old Vic production at the New Theatre 1950

Claire Bloom as Juliet and Athene Seyler as the Nurse in *Romeo and Juliet*, Old Vic 1952

production set among glades and gazebos, Redgrave's Berowne looked forward to his Benedick – as Shakespeare obviously meant it to. Mark Dignam's Holofernes carried, just as clearly, a painful reminiscence of the Stratford Grammar School; and Miles Malleson's Sir Nathaniel – who reminded J. C. Trewin of 'a rabbit nibbling lettuce' – suggested that the local incumbent died many deaths when he saw the local schoolmaster in the front pew.

The company moved back into its own theatre, now restored, in the autumn of 1950, and Peggy Ashcroft into Illyria. On that soil she had a priority which no one then disputed. Glen Byam Shaw had no qualms, and neither had Alec Clunes, about Henry V's Agincourt campaign. Here was the triumph of the 'happy few'; little hint of the long trudge from Harfleur that Peter Hall was to give us later. In 1951 Denis Carey brought *The Two Gentlemen of Verona* from Bristol, with John Neville's Valentine rich in promise; the best production, lyrical and light, of a play too easily overlooked to be given before or since. The brilliance of Guthrie's *Dream* had dulled a little, although when Moira Shearer confronted Oberon in Tanya Moisewitch's moonlit glade it seemed as if Taglioni had stepped into Titania's slippers. The following year produced a Juliet (Claire Bloom) whose surname youth and beauty alike confirmed, and whose Christian name indicated the quality of her performance. Kenneth Tynan reminded those who might quibble about her speaking of the verse that what Shakespeare requires is verse-acting. This summed up the whole doctrine of William Poel, although Tynan was probably unaware of it. Golden voices can easily provoke golden slumbers.

There was a feeling, nevertheless, by 1953 that the Vic had not yet got back into its stride, and many were hoping with A. V. Cookman, the dramatic critic of *The Times*, that 'somehow or other a single, straight, flourishing tradition will emerge'. The promise of this appeared when Michael Benthall was appointed director, with the intention of producing all the plays in the First Folio within five years; and, if possible, within the same décor of triple Palladian arches, set two feet behind the proscenium opening. There were balconies left, right, and centre. This, it was hoped, would make it possible to act the plays in repertory, allowing to each as many performances as it would earn. *Hamlet* was adapted from its début in the Edinburgh Assembly Hall – described by Alan Dent as 'Hamlet at the White City'; indeed it was adapted in more senses than one, for Benthall moved 'To be or not to be' to an earlier and more logical point in the play, and placed the King-Laertes plot immediately following the graveyard scene. The Ghost resembled a skeleton flag with a long blood-stain down its back – hardly the predictable effect of poison; but the courtiers, all in black, coming in from every side to arrest Hamlet, were a sinister reminder that Denmark was indeed a prison. Hamlet's sudden reappearance in the graveyard scene, as he flung open the central grill on 'It is I, Hamlet the Dane', and his half-curtsey to Claudius on 'Farewell – my mother', were striking moments in Richard Burton's performance which was generally slow to find its rhythm. His Falconbridge in *King John* failed, for once, to steal the play from Michael Hordern's King – 'wily, charming, clever, handsome – and haunted'[1] – a welcome change from the traditional cross-breeding of Richard II and Richard III. Fay Compton's Constance – a superb classical actress at last coming into her own – was unforgivably handicapped by the placing of the interval after the Bastard's speech on 'commodity', compelled as she was to burst on to the stage with 'Gone to be married! Gone to swear a peace!' while the audience were shuffling back into their seats. Now, too, doubts arose as to whether the permanent set would last out the length of the Folio.

Benthall's *Coriolanus*, with Fay Compton's urgent and clarion-voiced Volumnia, was described as 'a mighty warming up of Shakespeare's coldest play'.[2] He threw his lights here and there with the selective emphasis of a film camera; wrapped Burton in a scarlet cloak; and put the Volscians into smoky blues and greens, and dark body make-up. (The assumption persists that the Volscians were a different race, not merely a different tribe). The stress was laid on personalities rather than politics; Burton's boyishness excusing his immaturity and the tribunes worth no more than the votes of a turbulent Trade Union. The end of this Coriolanus was only a little less spectacular than Olivier's, as Burton, stabbed in a dozen places, stood motionless and then crashed spread-eagled to the ground, 'a single shaft of lighting catching his scarlet cloak'.[3] Once more it was said that more than mechanics were required to release the magic of *The Tempest* – that 'royal sense of this world, and how it passes away, with a catch at the heart of what is to come'.[4] Not the whole story, maybe, but a good part of it. The catch came when Miranda put her hand to her mouth after Ferdinand's first kiss, but the poetry was thinly distilled; and Prospero was obliged to camouflage the Palladian pillars with island vegetation which he removed before his final speech. Leslie Hurry's imaginative backcloths revealed different parts of the island, although there is every reason, here, to preserve Shakespeare's exceptional unities of time and place.

So the five-year plan got under way, leaving the Palladian pillars behind to the

Michael Redgrave as Hamlet, Old Vic production at the New Theatre 1950

[1] Mary Clarke *Shakespeare at the Old Vic* (1954-5)
[2] Alan Dent
[3] Mary Clarke *Shakespeare at the Old Vic*
[4] Quiller-Couch

John Neville as Richard II,
Old Vic 1954-5

relief of actors and audience alike. *Macbeth* survived its transfer from Edinburgh
less well than *Hamlet*. The dun-coloured plaids, the murky greys and greens,
and the hot red for the Coronation, splashed on the Assembly Hall stage under
Benthall's chiaroscuro lighting, and the whine of the bagpipes, amounted to
what Alan Dent described as 'braid Scots and vera bludy' – although Dover
Wilson was not alone in objecting to the actors' merciless assault upon the ear.
The scream of a dying soldier at the opening; the acclamations of a servile
nobility, heard offstage, on Macduff's line: 'He is already named'; and the
narrow shaft letting in the light through the flinty walls of Dunsinane – were all
imaginative touches. *Love's Labour Lost* could not stand up to the recent memory
of Hugh Hunt's symphony in black and silver; nor did the removal of Christopher
Sly, and a Pedant with pince-nez and gay umbrella, lighten the humours of the
Shrew. John Neville's Richard II grew impressively, adding emotion to melody
in the later scenes where the one had at first been sacrificed to the other. In
Robert Helpmann's *As You Like It* Paul Rogers's Touchstone was compared by
one critic to 'a quietly demented Archbishop'. In Douglas Seale's *Henry IV,
Parts One* and *Two* – the outstanding success of the season – the same versatile
actor's Falstaff reminded Philip Hope-Wallace of a cross between 'a Sickert and
a Rembrandt rabbi'. The balance between Falstaff and Hal was scrupulously
held, Hal speaking his repudiation not *at* Falstaff but over his head. Robert
Hardy, in one of his best performances, always kept himself a little apart, and
always sincere – not least when he was impersonating his father. At the Boars
Head he danced a few paces with Doll Tearsheet, and then stood aside. This
partnership in mischief of Falstaff and Hal was evidently fragile, for Rogers's
Falstaff 'knew, but would not admit to himself, that his affection was not
returned, and his worldly profit precarious'.[1] To eliminate Silence from
Shallow's orchard in a wheelbarrow married comedy to convenience.

By the time that Gielgud and Edith Evans returned to a stage of which they
had long been the Honorary Citizens – as Wolsey and Katharine in Benthall's
Henry VIII (1958) – John Neville, Eric Porter, Paul Rogers, Michael Hordern,
Keith Michel, and Barbara Jefford were among the players whose reputations

[1] J. W. Lambert

were by now assured. Benthall had directed half the plays himself, and the public rewarded him sourly for a beautiful *Cymbeline*. Guthrie called 'a plague on both your houses' in a *Troilus and Cressida* (1956) where Hohenzollern Trojans and Ruritanian Greeks exposed their feet of clay. This production was a field-day of satiric fun, after which the poetry was 'reported missing'. Helpmann's spidery Richard III was another casualty. Psychology can play scurvy tricks with Shakespeare, and here the actor's integrity did not save him. Nastiness of mind and body was not enough, for the splendour of Milton's Satan should occasionally shine through Richard's villainies. This was the world of Webster, where Helpmann had already proved himself at home. He was not less at home in a brave and beautiful production of *Antony and Cleopatra*, with Keith Michell and Margaret Whiting – each younger than their parts required, but allowing the verse to carry them when age and experience seemed likely to let them down. It was an interesting idea to show them dallying as the curtain went up – for Shakespearian curtains still went up in the nineteen-fifties – thus giving extra point to Philo's comment on 'the triple pillar of the world transformed into a strumpet's fool'. Just as Olivier's Richard had made things difficult for Helpmann's Richard, so was his monumental Titus a handicap to Derek Godfrey, and Brook's production an impossible challenge to Walter Hudd. It was cleverly met, however. On birthday night, 23 April

Tyrone Guthrie's *Troilus and Cressida*, Old Vic 1955-6

1957, *Titus Andronicus* and *The Comedy of Errors* were presented in the same bill, and in similar (or occasionally identical) Elizabethan costumes, as they might have been given by a company of strolling players in a great Elizabethan house. The setting remained basically the same, except for the lamps and garlands that indicated the switch from melodrama to farce. Both plays were shortened, *Titus* to an acting time of ninety-five minutes, and *The Comedy of Errors* to an hour. Robert Helpmann once again proved himself a master of comic mime. Kenneth Tynan described him in the small part of Pince 'acting all by himself in the left-hand corner of the stage, and got up like one of the less inhibited members of the Chinese National Theatre'.

Only a fifth season had now to go before Gielgud's lean and arrogant Wolsey, though still hungry for power, and Dame Edith's Katharine – authority still intact in the face of death and humiliation – reminded the authors and actors of the five-year plan of those standards by which they were satisfied to be judged. This was not the end of the Old Vic, as London had known it; but the end was now in sight; for plans for its transformation into the National Theatre were already afoot. In 1960 Franco Zeffirelli directed his popular and controversial *Romeo and Juliet*, where there was more of *mafia* than of magic. Its poetry mumbled or muted, and its romanticism sacrificed to an ungainly realism, the play was reduced to a squalid brawl, and the balcony scene to an awkward

John Stride and Judi Dench in Franco Zeffirelli's *Romeo and Juliet*, Old Vic 1960

scramble. John Stride and Judi Dench (and, later, Joanna Dunham), with youth and sincerity on their side, were helpless before the director's prohibition: 'Verse-speakers will be prosecuted.' The cuts were unforgivable; what sense was left to Romeo's 'Then I defy you, stars!' when the cause of his defiance was omitted? Two of England's most distinguished writers left the auditorium outraged by a foreigner's treatment of the play; and one who might claim to be England's greatest actress held that his production had set back the English theatre thirty years. A good many other people claimed that he had pushed it forward.

Michael Langham's *Midsummer Night's Dream* in the same year steered a nice course between black and white magic, and between Penshurst and the Parthenon. Carl Toms, the designer, had remembered his Tiepolo, and one was left with an impression of Athens seen through late Renaissance eyes. Alec McCowen, with his feline tread and the hushed ecstasy of his speech, was the natural King of these fairies; and of these mortals too, for Oberon has the last word – the magic now distilled to purest white – and very beautifully he spoke it. The lovers' quarrel was a temptation to Langham's itch for incessant movement, and he could hardly be blamed for not resisting it. Nevertheless some *via media* is possible here between a minuet and a rampage. Douglas Campbell's Bottom – an oak-tree struck by moonshine – was quite the bulliest one had seen. One did not expect him to disturb Sir Ralph Richardson's pre-eminence in the part, for that would have been literally asking for the moon. Langham had kept each of the three elements in the play – supernatural, aristocratic, and artisan – firmly in its place. There was all the necessary to and fro, but no trespassing.

Colin Graham's production of *Twelfth Night* in 1961 set one down in the world of Louis Quinze. Scarcely had the curtain risen on Alix Stone's *tableau vivant* of Watteau's *Music Lesson* than a comparison between Shakespearian and Mozartian comedy sprang to mind. The play, essentially Elizabethan though it is, did not suffer from its transplantation. Defying the convention that Malvolio must be tall and thin and pompous, Alec McCowen was small, thin and fussy. There was something almost acrobatic about his avoidance of cliché; and in Malvolio the result was as successful as in Mercutio it had been calamitous. Barbara Jefford's Viola was not quite so touching as Dorothy Tutin's, nor so poetical as Peggy Ashcroft's, and it did not strike so deep as Jean Forbes-Robertson's; but it was a gentle and gallant study, perfectly satisfying in its own right.

The pastel shades of the *dixhuitième* hardly suggested the heavy opulence of *The Merchant of Venice* where it is important to believe in the overdrafts, even though Portia's successful suitor was short of ready cash. But Peter Potter's production (1961) contained some good ideas; the festive opening to set off Antonio's melancholia, Portia and Bassanio left alone for their casket scene, and the glimpse of Tubal escorting Shylock home across the bridge. Robert Harris – a lyrical Oberon in times past, and more recently an endearing Quince – presented a brisk and impassioned Shylock of middle years and obviously sprung from the upper-middle classes of the Venetian ghetto. A sterling honesty is common to all Shakespeare's heroines, and Barbara Leigh-Hunt's Portia never looked like going off the gold standard. In the trial scene she might have been any one of our theatrical Dames receiving an Honorary Doctorate of Law at the Oxford Encaenia. This performance was among the brighter memories of the Old Vic's *intermezzo*; and with it stand Irene Worth's Desdemona and

Maxine Audley's Lady Macbeth – acting as always from her squared shoulder-blades – although both were inadequately partnered. The former played for a balance of strength and submissiveness, the latter for a balance of strength and seduction. Perhaps the stage has seen too many Lady Macbeths; it has not, in my experience, seen one so good.

Peter Potter's *Merchant of Venice*, Old Vic 1960-61

4

Neither in the provinces nor in the West End and other parts of London had Shakespeare been neglected, although attention was increasingly focused on Stratford and the Old Vic. Donald Wolfit ploughed his lonely furrow, giving Valk's Othello an Iago worthy of his steel. It was a misfortune that neither Wolfit's Lear nor his Falstaff could have been seen in a context equally worthy of them. William Devlin, with a voice that belied his slender years, had played a notable Lear before the war, and repeated it under Hugh Hunt at the Embassy in 1947. *Macbeth* defeated Michael Redgrave at the Aldwych in December of the same year, although on paper, so to speak, it should not have done so. Is it the ghost of Shakespeare, shaking the gory locks of Banquo, that warns the best actors away from an almost inevitable Waterloo – even in the Waterloo road? London did not lag behind Stratford in allowing Shakespeare his share in the Festival of Britain. Alec Guinness, with Dr Madariga at one elbow and Frank Hauser at the other, did everything he could to contradict Ophelia's view of Hamlet. His bearded Machiavellian prince contradicted the general opinion just as flatly, and such light as he hoped to throw upon the character was obscured on the opening night by the electricians who mistook their cues. More successful – though less than completely satisfying – was Benthall's *Antony and Cleopatra* at the St James, with Olivier, Vivien Leigh, and a revolving stage. This Antony played down to the scale of his Cleopatra which, though exquisite, was too small. Cleopatra is desirable, but she is also dangerous; seductive but also sublime.

Something like perfection was at hand in Peter Brook's production of *The Winter's Tale* at the Phoenix. Where Barker had seen the resurrection of Hermione as a stage effect consummately managed by a master-craftsman, Brook realized that it held the whole truth of the play – and of Shakespeare's other later plays as well. With Gielgud racing through the metrical counterpoint of Leontes' jealousy and never missing a note, Flora Robson's Paulina blazing like a winter fire, and Diana Wynyard's radiant Hermione, this was a production for the connoisseur. Brook had talked to the cast about Shakespeare's feeling for adventurous journeys and happy returns and the reconciliation of warring opposites. A direct vision had simplified a complicated play, so that the pursuit of Antigonus by a bear did not even raise a laugh, nor the description of Leontes' recognition of his daughter by the four gentlemen a yawn. It was clear that however little Shakespeare may have known about the Greek theatre, he saw the uses of a Messenger.

Beside this splendour other productions were peripheral, though sometimes adventurous. Bernard Miles, an ardent convert to Elizabethan Methodism, had built an Elizabethan stage in the garden of his house in St. John's Wood. All he claimed for it was an approximation to one of those 'gorgeous playing-houses, where the Elizabethan actor would have felt at home'. The richly decorated tiring house beyond the open stage justified his boast, and *The Tempest*, given here in 1951, proved his point. Later he moved city-wards, and in 1953 presented *Macbeth* and *As You Like It* within the portals of the Royal Exchange; and it would not be long before the new Mermaid was established at Puddle Dock. Less happy, but no less adventurous, was Joan Littlewood's *Macbeth* for the Theatre Workshop at Stratford East. Explaining that she wished to 'strip off the "poetical" interpretations which the nineteenth-century sentimentalists had put upon the plays', she contrived that the transcendent verse should be 'slurred, snapped, and barked'[1] by actors in twentieth-century dress. It was asking too much of any Stratford to keep its hands off Shakespeare altogether, however repellent his poetry might appear to its presiding genius. The other Stratfords have all stooped to folly in their time, but they have known better than to allow Miss Littlewood to exercise her undoubted genius at their expense.

Maxine Audley as Lady Macbeth, Old Vic 1961

[1] J. C. Trewin

XV Royal Shakespeare

It is not expected of stage directors that they should 'go through the mill' unless they do so as stage managers. Peter Hall came to an instant authority from the Cambridge Marlowe Society and the elder statesmanship of George Rylands. He was the youngest director ever to be appointed to Stratford. A natural diplomat, he knew what he wanted and was prepared to go the long way round to get it. A natural romantic, he sometimes wondered whether he had the right to be one. From the first he enjoyed the complete confidence of the Stratford Governors, and the company – predominantly young – which he had gathered round him.

His policy was radical. The formation of an ensemble, several of whom would be on long-term contracts; the acquisition of a theatre in London, where they could act in modern plays, and where certain of the Stratford productions could also be shown; and the creation of two companies to make this possible. He was pretty well satisfied with the Stratford stage as he found it, except that he constructed a new false proscenium which effectively framed the background, and slightly altered the shape of the apron so that instead of opening into the audience like a fan, it converged upon it like a wedge. What he lost in space he gained in concentration. He declared war on vocal or emotional self-indulgence, but he had enticed John Barton away from Cambridge to see that the verse was properly spoken. With the firm conviction that experiment was the life-blood of the theatre, he rode free from all established orthodoxies, prepared to make mistakes and to recognize them. He was the reverse of the omnipotent *régisseur*, and the first person plural – never a royal 'we' – was a feature of his ready and articulate pronouncements.

The start was hesitant. He had planned a sequence of comedies to show the variety of meanings Shakespeare had given to the word, and how often they adumbrated serious, and even tragic, themes. Peter Hall had seen the sunshine of *The Two Gentlemen of Verona* throwing its long shadows forward – a play far removed from 'the light and jocund Italianate comedy' of Quiller-Couch's description. But the execution fell short of the idea. A free use of the revolve, continually showing a new face to the isolated fragments of scenery had the effect of breaking up the play instead of pulling it together; and although the speaking was generally good, the company was not deployed at anything like its full strength. It was most unlikely that when Julia set out on what she hoped would be a happy quest, she would have done so in deep mourning. (A hint here of Peter Hall's chronic aversion to colour.) On the other hand the costume and make-up of Sir Eglamour recalled us from the world of Machiavelli to the world of Malory, where the play really belongs. As Lance and Speed, Patrick Wymark and Jack McGowran, admirably contrasted in personality and girth, showed how well they could twist an audience round their little fingers. All in all, one was still able to hear through the entanglements of comedy 'the inly voice of love', and to watch in its earliest functioning the operation of Shakespearian justice.

Patrick Wymark as Lance and Jack McGowran as Speed in Peter Hall's *The Two Gentlemen of Verona*, Royal Shakespeare Theatre, Stratford-upon-Avon, 1960

In John Barton's production of *The Taming of the Shrew* an older and almost forgotten England lived again before one's eyes. Here, unmistakably, was the shrew that Shakespeare drew, tracing its pedigree right down from Chaucer and Langland, and from the *miséricordes* that a curious eye may discover on the choir-stalls of an English or a French cathedral. Having decided to use his revolve, Barton did not overdo the trick. Two faces to Alix Stone's Cotswold inn were enough. Peggy Ashcroft's Katharina made it clear, in a flash of fine acting, that she had fallen in love with Peter O'Toole's Petruchio at first sight. There was tenderness and humour underneath these tantrums and this tyranny, a certain Shakespearian delicacy which the exigencies of farce had not been able to dispel, and which these two performances marvellously disclosed. Jack McGowran's Sly was tactfully faded in and out – very much there at the beginning, and rather touchingly so at the end. The play was over; the actors had changed and were off to their next one-night stand; and McGowran wandered in their wake, ruminating about his wife in Sligo.

It was only too evident that Michael Langham had come from Stratford, Ontario, to direct *The Merchant of Venice* at Stratford-upon-Avon. The circular movement imposed by an open stage, in which instead of going straight up to his opposite number the actor stalks him like a Highland deer, was here pushed to the limits of mannerism on a stage quite unsuited to it. Moreover it unsettled a play whose movement should be steady, and brought its climax to total disaster. The trial scene will not be saved by locomotion; it is in itself so impregnable a piece of theatre that it will save itself if only the director will let it alone. But allow your plaintiff and counsel to wander where they like; let your Magnificoes turn their backs on the Doge in wistful contemplation of the Grand Canal; permit the broken arch from Belmont still to dominate the proceedings; dress your Portia so that she looks less than her normal size, and then set everybody else revolving round her with the motiveless circulation of a clock-work train so that she is only intermittently visible, even in a theatre built for sight-lines – handicap yourself in this way and you have made impossible even the most willing suspension of disbelief. The production was redeemed by certain incidentals – the caskets upheld by three Graces dressed to match; and by Ian Richardson's Prince of Aragon – the last expiring flicker of an effete lineage – preceded by his own portrait which had evidently adorned the Academy at Saragossa, and escorted by a matriarch of 'endless age'. This was to exchange the world of Guardi for the world of Goya. Peter O'Toole's Shylock was a flamboyant and arresting study, robbed of concentration by the St Vitus' dance through which he, too, had to waltz his way. Dorothy Tutin as Portia did everything gracefully, and the most difficult thing of all unforgettably. When she entered for the casket scene with Bassanio, you saw a girl suddenly transformed. The princess of fairy tale had stepped out of her gilded cage into the sunshine of love's reality; and you remembered that look on her face long after criticism had had its say.

Peter Hall's Caroline *Twelfth Night* was a rich symphony in russet, designed by Lila de Nobili. The cavaliers were gathered around Orsino in a panelled hall out of Nash's *English Mansions*, and just as this gave way to the cloud-capped towers of a transitory Adriatic, so these quickly dissolved into an English garden, and Sir Toby Belch enjoying an obviously continental breakfast. Peter Hall was aiming at an injection of melancholy into the comic scenes, and of comedy into the serious ones. But he had pushed the counterpoint to perilous extremes.

Dorothy Tutin as Portia in Michael Langham's *Merchant of Venice*, Royal Shakespeare Theatre, Stratford-upon-Avon, 1960

Opposite: Donald Sinden as Henry and Peggy Ashcroft as Queen Katharine in Trevor Nunn's *Henry VIII*, Royal Shakespeare Theatre, Stratford-upon-Avon, 1969

Feste is *passé*, to be sure, but Max Adrian had borrowed his pathos from a canvas by Georges Rouault. Similarly, in the case of Olivia, the director was reacting against the stately contraltos whom a sudden bereavement has distracted from the organization of the Hunt Ball. But this Olivia would have been incapable of opening a Flower Show. Olivia must, at least, be the competent mistress of a great household; a serious young woman capable of sudden silliness, or – if you prefer – a silly young woman capable of sudden seriousness. To make her incapable of any seriousness whatsoever blunted the impact of Viola on her fantasy. Here the production came near to cutting out its own heart; and that it continued to beat was largely due to Dorothy Tutin's Viola, steering her way to Orsino's bosom, yet not altogether of his element even when her gaze was anchored on him. The minor tactics of the *mise-en-scène* were full of good things; Sebastian and Viola nearly meeting in the street, and the Chaplain's tactful and embarrassed aversion of the head while Sebastian and Olivia were exchanging their first kiss. So, in the end, they all went their separate ways – Antonio to refit his galleys in Cork or Limerick, and Feste to vanish into an eccentric solitude. Instead of landing in Illyria like a leading lady, and not a hair out of place, this Viola had actually clambered ashore as if she were in doubt as to whether she would ever get there. A faint doubt persisted as to whether she would stay.

For the wars and lechery of *Troilus and Cressida* Peter Hall had the assistance of John Barton. Leslie Hurry had designed a bloodshot backcloth, more than a little reminiscent of Graham Sutherland, and in front of it a sort of octagonal boxing ring, strewn with white sand. The idea was audacious since, generally speaking, the last place to which you wish to draw the attention of an audience is the floor of the stage. But here the whiteness of the sand answered the redness of the backcloth, as the satire of the play answers its violence. The effect was that of a no man's land where two wrongs could fight it out to a bloody finish. The directors were under no temptation to turn a Shakespearian battle into a Bolshoi ballet or an American ball game. The playing of different lights through the smoke of a pardonably anachronistic cannon gave a lurid chiaroscuro to the scene, and the slaying of Hector was sinister in its treacherous contrivance. The directors also had the startlingly original idea of letting their actors look like Greeks and Trojans, evidently feeling that the play was so modern that its modernity could look after itself – which it very capably did. Dorothy Tutin's Cressida was a natural and not unsympathetic wanton, failing through weakness rather than perversity; and Eric Porter's Ulysses, magnificently spoken, was a soldier with a brain in his head. When he got home one saw him making short work of Penelope's suitors. Max Adrian's Pandarus had matured in subtlety with the years. His last, decrepit entrance perfectly illustrated the moral decomposition of the play.

In *The Winter's Tale* Peter Wood was able to exploit to their fullest the possibilities of the stage that Peter Hall had redesigned. The false prosceniums came into their own as the scenery shuttled in and out between them; the staging was a classic of production in depth. *The Winter's Tale* begins in time; time passes; and it ends with time redeemed – just on the hither side of eternity. The production matched this progression with the red of passion, the purple of repentance, and the gold of celebration. Eric Porter's phrasing of Leontes was again superb, as he sent the character over the edge – like a man taking a deep dive into damnation. Dame Peggy's Paulina met him with an equal force. Jack

Opposite: Alan Howard as Oberon, Sarah Kestleman as Titania and John Kane as Puck in Peter Brook's *A Midsummer Night's Dream*, Royal Shakespeare Theatre, Stratford-upon-Avon, 1970

McGowran was within his rights in playing Autolycus for slyness rather than for swagger; and the Shepherd and his son – Ian Holm here showing his mettle – conveyed all the delights of sudden luck in a football pool. But neither Perdita nor Florizel could master the music set down for them, and the sheep-shearing scene went badly askew. The masks were ugly, and the tap-dancing and drum beats were too reminiscent of darkest Africa for the peasantry of Elizabethan England – which is what these people really are.

The consistency of style aimed at by the Royal Shakespeare Theatre – as the Stratford playhouse had now been rechristened – was more surely achieved when Peter Hall and his closer associates were in control. This was not easy, for with two theatres on his hands Peter Hall was leading a double life – just as many of his actors were being subjected to a new kind of intensive Shakespearian training, which consisted in going backwards and forwards from London to Stratford as often, and as inconveniently, as possible. If a new director of his own way of thinking was discovered, like Clifford Williams or Trevor Nunn, the results could be brilliant; if an established figure was brought in from outside the chances were no more than even. Michael Langham returned in 1960 for a *Much Ado*, disastrously misconceived. The play is in part high comedy; in part comedy of another kind; and in part serious melodrama. The one thing the play is *not* is farce; yet that is how Langham chose to see it. He put it into early nineteenth-century costume; but where Douglas Seale had suggested a Donizetti libretto which would have jibbed at nothing in Shakespeare's plot, Christopher Plummer's Benedick might have paid court to Elizabeth Bennett – and the rattle of Miss Austen's tea-cups, though they rattle deliciously, does rather lack the Shakespearian resonance. This flight from the Elizabethans – on stages that are doing their best to be Elizabethan – is a curious phenomenon. The production came to grief, like the same director's *Merchant of Venice*, in its *scène à faire*. The plausibility of the Church scene was destroyed by people moving about in circles in a situation, and a setting, which would have frozen them to the ground. Up to this point Christopher Plummer, whose charm, agility, and timing were beyond praise, had more or less held his own. He was lost, however, from the moment he was made to guy his challenge to Claudio; and when the old men rolled up their sleeves, and turned the scene of recrimination into a comic boxing match, the play was down the drain altogether. This was no longer Shakespeare, but *East Lynne* – seen from Western Ontario. The simultaneous décor of iron trellis-work was compared by one critic to a Bavarian beer garden; no one, however, could have enjoyed a mug of Pilsener beside an extension of iron railings which looked like an annexe in search of an architect. The most licentious imagination rebelled at converting it into a police court or a Church.

In happy contrast Michael Elliot's *As You Like It* will be remembered for Vanessa Redgrave's Rosalind, born under a dancing star, and deserving to be remembered for much else besides – the great spreading tree that sometimes flourished in the Forest of Arden and sometimes on Duke Frederick's back lawn. At the end of Part One the Duke was seen blotting himself in despair against the same bark upon which, at the beginning of Part Two, Orlando would hang his verses. The finale celebrated the sanctification of nature by sacrament, the coming together of all kinds and classes of men beneath the shelter of a common benediction. The actual restoration of his crown to the exiled Duke reminded one of Prospero, and Shakespeare's continuity of theme. Max

Adrian's Jaques wore a mask at once voluptuous and melancholy, pale with sensual stings and unbitted lusts, as he wandered off at the end like Marcel Proust retiring to a monastery – for a thumb-nail sketch of Sir Olivier Martext suggested that the Church of England was very insecurely established in the Ardennes. Michael Elliot had looked at the play without squinting. The lighting was beautiful without being fussy; the sunlight fell through dappled leaves; and the birds sang. Earth has not anything to show more fair than a production of this quality at Stratford.

A feature of the Royal Shakespeare style was the emphasis given to the floor of the stage – already noted in *Troilus and Cressida* – and this was pushed to such lengths that in William Gaskill's *Richard III* the royal ladies were made to squat on it during a scene of formal rhetoric. This suggested a picnic at Balmoral with the gentlemen out with the guns; and of course in *Richard III* they are rarely out with anything else. There is no shade of autumn that Edith Evans cannot convey, but the midwinter of Margaret's imprecations is just a little outside her palette. Christopher Plummer's Crookback lacked something both of terror and charm, but it was vividly and variously theatrical. The production went unaffectedly to the heart of the matter with a single pillar, and a few symbolic or heraldic hangings. One only asked – as one was now continually asking – for more colour in the costumes. Peter Hall again used the revolve for *Romeo and Juliet* in Sean Kenny's clever, but too complicated, décor. In the last scene this very nearly involved the production in catastrophe. It was right that we should feel the horror of the Capulets' funeral vault, but the horror should be capable of transfiguration. Death *and* transfiguration is the keynote of the scene; and when the rows of coffins descended like a slot-machine, they threatened to smother more than the finale. They menaced a production which otherwise had held one riveted with emotion. This had been described as 'anti-Zeffirelli', and the contrast was compliment enough. If one could have put the conception and performance of the play inside the Zeffirelli décor, this *Romeo and Juliet* would have fallen little short of perfection. Dorothy Tutin moved like a bird, and the poetry sang when she whispered as well as when she spoke. She was flesh and blood and fourteen years old; yet her rapture lifted her above the earth, and the audience was caught up in its radiant levitation. Dame Edith's Nurse married the tartness of a Bramley to the sweetness of a Cox's orange; Ian Bannen's Mercutio dazzled with its swordsmanship, allowing the poetry and the cynicism an equal sum for their money; and if Max Adrian's Friar Lawrence was a challenge to credibility, this was only because he was so obviously a Jesuit, with the genius of his Order for getting good people out of difficult situations. Peter Hall was right to place the interval *before* Mercutio has been killed; and brave to keep in the Musicians' dialogue with Peter *after* the discovery of Juliet in her death-like coma. Granville-Barker had justified this in theory; it was here justified in performance.

John Schlesinger's brilliant *Timon of Athens,* with Paul Scofield, was to prove exceptional beside the failure of other guest-directors. Nevertheless Zeffirelli's *Othello* was a good deal more persuasive than his *Romeo and Juliet*. He gave one a superb succession of stage pictures. Was this Iago or Baron Corvo slinking out from the shadows of the dank houses on which an uncertain moon reflected the lapping of the canals? The midnight session of the Senate, with its confusion of military and matrimonial business; the sweeping steps of the Cyprian citadel; the Governor's armoury, with Othello and Iago working together at a long table;

the burnished Tintoretto colourings – all this was splendid, though purchased at far too high cost of scene changing. Stratford, having given Zeffirelli his head, should have given him a week of dress rehearsals. A four-hour *Othello* was simply not admissible in that year of grace. Nor is the Othello temperament among the many silver spoons Sir John Gielgud was born with. He gave us more of the Venetian veneer than the Mauretanian depths, more of the music than the man. The disintegration of the character was traced with immense power and excellent variety, but one was never quite convinced that this was happening to Othello. Coleridge's phrase about 'the wretched fishing jealousies of Leontes', with memories of Gielgud's own performance of the part, came recurrently to mind.

In the autumn of 1962 Peter Brook directed his celebrated production of *King Lear*. When this was claimed, in *Crucial Years* – Stratford's manifesto of planning – as 'lucid and Brechtian', one was rather surprised that the theatre's directorate should heap such coals of fire on their own heads. You might as well reassure an audience which is settling down to an evening of Schubert that it is really settling down to an evening of Schoenberg. To watch Peter Brook's mind at work on *Lear* was rather like watching a great surgeon at work on a delicate operation. You were so lost in admiration for the surgeon that you had very little pity for the patient. The director, with Jan Kott[1] at his elbow, had looked at the play through an existentialist microscope, and seen it as a tragedy not of redemption but of despair. The result was belauded by everyone who likes to take their Shakespeare from East Berlin, and resists Aristotelian catharsis. Thus the scene following the blinding of Gloucester, where Cornwall's 'good servants' redeem their master's cruelty, was cut altogether; and so were Edmund's vital words in the last act – 'Some good I mean to do in spite of mine own nature.' Shakespeare having carefully removed Edmund from the scene, Peter Brook as carefully kept him on it, so that Edgar, left alone with the body of his brother, recently reconciled in charity, should be able to lug it off the stage like a slaughtered pig. Shakespeare having carefully brought back the corpses of Goneril and Regan to give point to Edmund's comment – 'Yet Edmund was beloved' – the ultimate flicker of vanity in that insatiable *coureur* – Peter Brook as carefully disobeyed his dramatist's instructions. Strange indeed that he should have missed the irony of the subsequent picture when Lear enters with Cordelia dead in his arms – the old king with his three daughters, as we had seen them at the beginning; only now the three daughters were dead, and the old king was dying.

The deflation of the performance matched the deflation of the play. The opening was so prolonged that one had the impression of an old man deliberately making up his mind instead of recklessly unmaking it. Paul Scofield presented the appearance of majesty – rather like an Old Testament king from the west portal of Chartres – but he was robbed of the height from which *hubris* must fall. Thunder and lightning were demanded, and Scofield could have supplied them, as he was later to supply them in *Timon*. As it was, one only heard a distant rumble, and observed that the glass was falling. The sweeping, symphonic movement of the play was so syncopated that when Lear arrived at his great climactic moments, these were less overwhelming than they should have been. In the later scenes, where there is no excuse for hurry, he had the time to make his effects – and very impressive and original they were. His whole performance matched the iron austerity of the production. If Peter Brook had wished to

[1] *Shakespeare our Contemporary* (1964)

explain to us what was in his mind about *Lear,* then he had admirably succeeded. The significance of his detail held one so riveted – with striking performances of the Fool by Alec McCowen, speaking his lines as if no one had ever spoken them before, of Goneril by Irene Worth, and of Gloucester by Alan Webb – that one hardly knew how slowly the time was passing. One only knew that one was strangely unmoved; and that, no doubt, was the intention. The production enjoyed an international triumph, and among English critics J. W. Lambert was almost alone in voicing a reservation. Yet the comment of a young French student – *'il a transformé Shakespeare en Brecht'* – was echoed by more than one foreign observer.

The Comedy of Errors is so rarely seen that many people must have approached Clifford Williams's production during the same season in a state of Elizabethan innocence. The director seemed to have approached it that way himself. The action flowed with the right pace of hilarious comedy on a simple, sloping platform, built on three levels. Doors were easily imagined, and keys symbolically turned. Here was Elizabethan stagecraft at its best – and so modern in its application that you only noticed its fidelity when you had gone home to bed. It required real imagination to give the right sophistication to slapstick, and a robust body to style. Clifford Williams brought out his equation with a dazzling clarity. John Blatchley's *Measure for Measure* was greatly helped by Tom Fleming in giving the 'Duke of dark corners' the prominence he deserves. This was no remote and philosophical puppeteer, but a sagacious activist putting certain ideas about justice to the test. Marius Goring's Angelo invited our pity and made us feel that, like any other erring mortal, he deserved it. The tortured, frozen mask was perfectly composed; and the sound of the discipline cracking out of the shadows conveyed an interesting hint of masochism. Judi Dench, who played throughout with immense power and intelligence, carried a line which has sunk many a good actress before now, speaking 'More than our brother is our chastity' in an agonized whisper, as if appalled that the truth should be so hard.

In 1963 Peter Brook, with Clifford Williams assisting him, once again came to grips with *The Tempest*. Abdul Farrah's kaleidoscopic cyclorama suggested not so much an island as 'the great globe itself', and this was right because Shakespeare is here concerned with universal things. Lovely and various as were the transformations wrought by the Stratford switchboard on Farrah's designs, Prospero's island was Prospero's universe, spatial and unlocalized; and Raymond Leppard's music recalled the 'sweet sounds that give delight and hurt not'. The placing of the mariners in the cockpit of the forestage was an economical piece of Elizabethanism, and with Tom Fleming's Prospero behind them – a Victorian headmaster steering his course majestically between the Bible and the birch – it effectively showed them in his power. But one missed the swinging, and finally sinking, lantern which had once so vividly illustrated the shipwreck; and the dissolving cyclorama to reveal the galley and its relatively reconciled passengers homeward bound for Milan. There was less of magic than of Maskelyne and Devant in this production, and the comic scenes were excessively laboured. Stephano is a pale shadow of the Porter in *Macbeth*, and not even Touchstone would have recognized Trinculo as a member of Jesters Equity; but there was truth in the observation of a local taxi-driver: 'Bit crude, isn't it?' Phallic gestures were now finding their place in the repertoire of Shakespearian 'business', and the heresy was pretty widespread that on the stage, as in literature,

Tom Fleming as Prospero and Ian Holm as Ariel in Peter Brook's *The Tempest*, Royal Shakespeare Theatre, Stratford-upon-Avon, 1963

you get your effect by putting everything in. It is a pity the devotees of *Lady Chatterley's Lover* do not read Catullus. By contrast Ian Holm's Ariel blazed with an angelic innocence, delivering his great speeches with a slow, unforced gravity which translated the profounder meanings of the play with the clarity of a motet. The 'acknowledgement' of Caliban's emergent humanity by Prospero closed the arc with which, in this almost inaccessible play, Shakespeare had described the human condition and recalled it to its divine appointment.

John Blatchley's *Julius Caesar* illustrated a fault that was becoming endemic at Stratford, and for which Peter Brook's *King Lear* must take some of the blame. It was a good deal too slow. Much of the detail was excellent; a Cicero who might have sipped the port in one of Lord Snow's Combination Rooms; a Lucius who never left off his pyjamas, and had not been licked into even the first sketch of an under-footman. But it was a capital mistake to confine the crowd to the wings, and trust to a sound-track to give the illusion of non-existent numbers – for no Antony can deliver his oration in profile. Meeting the objection that audiences, and actors too, are tired of togas, John Bury, instead of dispensing with them altogether, had reduced their sweep and dimmed their colour, while allowing the current fetish for jackboots and leather to strike an aggressively modern note. He thus got the worst of both wardrobes. Zeffirelli's *Othello* was the expensive high water-mark of scenic Shakespeare at Stratford. The emphasis now lay on starkness, simplicity, and space; and generally speaking, the policy earned artistic as well as economic dividends. But John Bury's set for *Julius Caesar*, though it served the actors well enough with its long slope and bare walls, did not let in enough daylight or moonlight as the case demanded, or suggest the City, which is what the play is really about. When it was suggested to Bury that his décor was inspired by Gordon Craig, he replied: 'Not Craig, but Appia.' It was an excellent décor, but it had been designed for the wrong play. Tom Fleming was a younger Brutus than one is accustomed to see – a political innocent beside Cyril Cusack's worm-eaten Cassius, spitting out his envy with only an occasional overdoing of *staccato*. And since the director had allowed Roy Dotrice's Caesar not only the centre but the four corners of the stage, one could hardly blame the actor for bettering his instruction. All in all, this production left the play wobbling a little uncertainly on its pedestal.

With the Shakespeare Quartercentenary close at hand, Peter Hall's strategy was moving towards its crowning triumph – the production of all the Histories from *Richard II* to *Richard III* in 1964. He had found in John Bury the designer of his heart's desire; he had in John Barton a colleague who combined the affinities of a friend, the erudition of a scholar, the talent of a director, and the mystery of an *éminence grise*; he had discovered another director, no less talented, in Clifford Williams; and he had built a company now greatly strengthened in its middle reaches. He executed the second part of his plan in 1963, with the three parts of *Henry VI* shortened into two plays, entitled *The Wars of the Roses* and *Edward IV*, followed by *Richard III*. A note in the programme threw out a dark hint of pastiche, but few people were able to detect what Barton had taken from Holinshed or what Barton had written in himself. No seams were left showing in the smooth iambics. The Shakespeare of *Henry VI* is not yet conspicuously a great poet, and it was wise to preserve the dramatic proportions and sacrifice the verbal detail. Writing under a dynasty which never felt itself quite secure, Shakespeare may well have found it safer to say in twenty lines what could have been said more succinctly in ten; and the result of stripping away this camouflage was to leave his meaning unmistakable.

A second result was unexpected. *Richard III, as a play,* seemed far less significant than what Peter Hall and John Barton between them had made of its precursors. One found oneself thinking that the most interesting character was the Second Murderer. This was not quite fair on Peggy Ashcroft, who started with a very big handicap in the golfer's understanding of the word. Because she had already built up such a fascinating and formidable figure of Margaret of Anjou, and because one had seen the murder of her husband and her son, one actually looked forward to her subsequent invective. The character emerged as a great tragic creation, with the effect of a restless, unappeased wandering – not merely indignant, but profoundly, incurably unhappy. The actual working out of the story, however, seemed less real and less exciting than the downfall of Duke Humphrey, less moving than the death of Bedford and Talbot, less dramatically persuasive than the ambition of York and the machinations of Warwick, precisely because these characters were more real and involved one more closely in their fate. In the earlier plays Ian Holm's Richard had given the impression of psychotic violence lurking beneath an innocent façade, but when he spoke in soliloquy the façade remained intact. It was not easy to believe in the diabolism; the scale of the performance, initially handicapped by the actor's temperament and physique, was too small and its pitch too low.

The honesty and insight of John Barton's arrangement of the text was matched by Peter Hall's presentation of it. This was no occasion for starved Shakespeare, but none either for turning an historical play into an historical pageant. For once, the Stratford timidity in face of colour seemed justified; in many productions of the Histories coats-of-arms and fine gowns hide all. These plays are a chronicle of calamity, and they illustrate Jan Kott's theory of the *'grand mécanisme de l'histoire'*. Only – and here is Shakespeare's answer to Kott's universal negative – the quest for order must go on. Peter Hall – wiser than Shakespeare after the event – refused to romanticize Richmond. The audience, maybe, would have liked to feel that the *'grand mécanisme'* had ground itself to a standstill, but even Richmond, in the rhetorical flush of victory, threw out a hint that it might start up again. Shakespeare's notion of the good life is articulate in Alexander Iden walking at ease in his Kentish orchard, after promptly despatching the angry young man – alias Jack Cade – who has climbed over the wall. It is a picture more flattering to bourgeois complacency than revolutionary iconoclasm.

John Bury's steely, iron-studded walls, swinging easily into whatever position was required for them; his descending grills; his huge scale map of France filling the background whenever one crossed the Channel; the dusky blues and bronzes of the costumes, relieved by splashes of triumphant gold when the Yorkists were in power; the restrained heraldry – all this was the right pictorial accompaniment to civil strife. The armour clanked, and the broadswords suggested the smithies of their forging. The falling snow was a brilliant illustration of Margaret's collapsing fortunes, and the smoke of Bosworth indicated that artillery was coming into its own; Margaret's mockery of the captured York with a paper crown, after smearing his face with a napkin dipped in his own blood, was a horrifying piece of genuine Elizabethan Grand Guignol; and in the management of Henry's murder by Richard – the assassin physically entwined in his victim's forgiveness – Peter Hall's invention had the glow of pure inspiration which marks the great director. Irony and compassion were here in perfect accord.

Within this secure framework the actors moved at their ease. The right balance was struck between baronial brawling and intelligible speech. These were tough customers and they talked toughly. Roy Dotrice's Bedford, remarkably doubled with his Edward IV; Donald Sinden's crisp and incisive York; Brewster Mason's resourceful Warwick – all made their effective contribution to the Council chamber or the battlefield. Against them stood David Warner's moving portrait of Henry VI. Isolated and incompetent, pathetic but never absurd, he still illuminated the folly of the strife he was unable to quell. One was left thanking him for Eton and King's, and wishing that Shakespeare had found a place for them in the story.[1]

For those who had seen the corpse of Henry V lying in state at the opening of *The Wars of the Roses,* and watched the dissolution of his empire, Agincourt and the dynastic marriage that followed it looked rather less than a happy ending. Everything that happened in *Richard II* and the first sequence of the *Henries* – added to the repertoire in 1964 – asked to be judged in the light of what had already happened, theatrically speaking, in the second. There were certain risks. Would the immaturity of *Henry VI* and *Richard III* stand up to the epic of *Richard II* and *Henry IV*? Would the audience tire of a sombre setting designed, nevertheless, to include Shallow's orchard and Queen Isabella's apricots, the Boars Head as well as the Tower of London, Harfleur as well as Bosworth? Yet the rewards of continuity had been proved in 1951. Bolingbroke, when he throws his shadow forward to the *Henries* becomes a major protagonist; and although Eric Porter mortgaged the latter at a rather high rate of interest, his performance in the second party of *Henry IV* worked a catharsis which the rôle rarely achieves. He secured from the start that the play should not belie its title. That night of the long knives at Pomfret darkened the Council chamber where the long table once more rose so obligingly from its basement; and the pilgrimage to Jerusalem – never to be realized – was emphasized by the gaunt, overhanging crucifix and the toy paladins on the floor. Again, we knew something of what to expect from Hotspur and Hal when the curtain had fallen – though at Stratford it fell no longer – on *Richard II*; and there was nothing we did not know about Northumberland.

David Warner's Richard eschewed even the brittle façade of kingship; no monarch treats a throne as if it were a *chaise longue*. The tricks of delivery, effective in the much shorter part of Henry VI, were here monotonous and out of place. The reality beyond the rhetoric was not achieved by a calculated contempt for the verse. Certain moments were extremely moving, but one missed the 'rash, fierce blaze of riot', and one clamoured for a larger, more lyric, scale. In spite of its excellent detail, the portrait lacked definition. It was too fragmentary and, above all, too faint. The setting again proved its flexibility, as the golden, Gothic foliage threw out a hint of the open country, if not of the open sky. The sense of boot and saddle was refreshing with a Bolingbroke and his levies who had obviously ridden more than half a mile. Paul Hardwick's York gave one the chain-mail in the voice and the cotton-wool in the character, and Roy Dotrice brought off a dazzling double of Gaunt, whose 'royal throne of kings' was allowed to keep all its purple, and a Hotspur who had clearly stolen his accent, tartan, and tam o'shanter in a Border raid. The actor might well have claimed that it was all in the character of Hotspur to assume a tartan when he had it not, and

David Warner as Henry and Peggy Ashcroft as Margaret in *Henry VI*, Royal Shakespeare Theatre, Stratford-upon-Avon, 1964

[1] Henry VI was the founder of Eton and also of King's College, Cambridge

indeed, as *Henry IV* got under weigh, there was more of the madcap in his performance than the brighter half of England's chivalry. But its humour and vitality were irresistible, and its conclusion had the lacerating pathos of the best man who has put himself on the wrong side.

The balance between Falstaff and Hal was nicely held. Hugh Griffiths's particular quality is exorbitance; he burst the society he moved in, as well as larding the earth as he moved along it, and exorbitance is precisely what the two parts of *Henry IV* are about. The movement of this Falstaff's mind had a Celtic rapidity; it struck sparks from the flint on Gadshill and the worm-eaten oak of Eastcheap. The fruity voice was not muffled by an alcoholic senility; and when the shadows came to settle in Part Two, and the truth of mortality pierced the masquerade, Falstaff was allowed his full meed of pathos and seized it with both hands. Something almost recognizable as love went out to meet him from the trollop on his lap, and this was another moment of truth. Yet he had never been so lovable – indeed is Falstaff ever really lovable? – that one could not bear to see him go. Of the four plays in the tetralogy this was the most successful, for Peter Hall had rallied to its autumnal colouring, and Ian Holm as Hal was no shallow hypocrite. Here was a young man suddenly burdened with public responsibility, who could no longer afford the irresponsibilities of the private life. He was also a young man still in the throes of education, and when he had a difficult thing to do he did it clumsily. The action of the community on the individual is generally clumsy, and often cruel. It is no new thing to sympathize with Falstaff in the rejection, but here one also sympathized with Hal. Nor would even this have been possible if the death of Bolingbroke had not been played for more than it is generally considered to be worth. The later humours of the play were safe with the Justice Shallow of Roy Dotrice tottering deliciously on the bench. A whole countryside was contained in it, and the whole pathos – never less than excruciatingly funny – of a life that had been perfectly hollow since the day that Shallow lay with Jane Nightwork and heard the chimes at midnight from Old St Pauls. Here, as the afternoon fell upon the orchard in Gloucester-shire, even John Bury's décor turned its face to the sun.

Henry IV is notoriously unfair to *Henry V*. No sooner have Cantuar and Ely set out on their pedantic exposition than one feels the flagging of creative energy; the effect is only to convince one that the path to Hell is paved with canon lawyers. But these implausibly decorative prelates were attended with such pomp and circumstance that the sole alternative to Henry's assent to their pleading could only have been immediate excommunication. Something had gone very wrong when the most interesting officer in his ragbag of an army was that simple soldier-man, Captain Gower. The almost complete failure of the comedy scenes threw an extra burden on Ian Holm, and on Eric Porter, dressed like a miniature by Nicholas Hilliard and speaking the Prologues with superb clarity and address. Ian Holm's performance grew with the play – an essentially democratic Henry, almost as tattered and mud-bespattered as the 'Old Contemptibles' with whom he marched; discovering his kingship within himself and through his comradeship with other men; a man still deeply thoughtful – still not seeing his way quite clearly – but one who had achieved simplicity, and through resolution was acquiring strength; an anxious Henry, with something of his father's calculation, busying giddy minds with foreign quarrels, but far from giddy himself. The inches were missing, but the voice did not refuse the rhetoric when rhetoric was asked for, and it took the colloquial in its stride. When love brought its crown to conquest, it was the same man that wooed the Princess of France, now completed and perceptibly lightened of care, finding on those sugar lips the satisfaction he had once sought in the stews. The scene was most delicately acted – with all the comedy it demands and none of the vulgarity it sometimes receives – and you had the feeling, as they knelt to receive the Queen's benediction, that Falstaff was not only dead but buried.

With the colour bar in the costumes considerably relaxed, Peter Hall and his associates had done everything possible with *Henry V,* short of creating one or two comedians and borrowing two or three easily imitable accents from the Celtic fringe. Every moment of every play had been squeezed for the last ounce of meaning it contained; the productions were wonderfully explicit. One remembered Hal burning Falstaff's unsettled invoices in the last flickering candle at the Boar's Head, and Fluellen's pocket Tacitus. The speaking was good, except when shouting or *sotto voce* made it difficult to hear and to understand. The pace was deliberate, and occasionally too slow. This was a defect of Peter Hall's principal virtue; the belief that somewhere there is a meaning to be wrested, that everything adds up. Nor was this fidelity incompatible with a personal approach. The plays had been seen as a sequence of *pièces noires,* although they were allowed their moments of *allégresse.* The sun might be setting in Shallow's orchard, but it still shone. A golden backcloth conveyed the brief victorious spring of *Henry V,* and the late medieval Renaissance of *Richard II.* For the rest, however, the gibbets dangled their corpses on Blackheath, and our last glimpse of Shrewsbury was Worcester hanging from the nearest tree. Stratford had celebrated the Quartercentenary of Shakespeare's birth with an Exhibition; this provoked the comment that 'it told one everything one could possibly want to know about Shakespeare, except that he ever for a single moment thought life worth living'.[1] There were times when the Historical sequence appeared to echo this impression; but it was a memorable achievement, and in the future, as in the past, the Royal Shakespeare Theatre would know how to redress the balance.

2

The last word must go to Laurence Olivier. At the National Theatre, of which he was the first director, he produced, in 1963, Peter O'Toole as Hamlet. O'Toole is not a naturally reflective actor. He wore no air of mystery, and he did not, either in voice or mien, suggest a tragic destiny laid upon shoulders incapable of bearing it. Nothing of importance seemed to have happened to him. The technical innocence of his performance showed up in contrast to Michael Redgrave's Claudius. Self-confident and sensual, devious and dignified, here was the plausible sovereign of Elsinore. Matching the baroque sophistication of a revolving décor, he had his feet very firmly in a world that was 'out of joint', thus providing one half of the opposition which should exist between the master of *Real-politik* who is wholly of this world, and his antagonist whose tragedy it is to be divided between this world and the next. Diana Wynyard as Gertrude, morally indolent and physically beautiful, was evidently as satisfied by her second husband as she had been left unsatisfied by her first. But the event of the production was the Ophelia of Rosemary Harris. Far from turning 'hell itself to favour and to prettiness', her mad scene revealed a fury of sexual frustration working on a nature too delicate to sustain the double shock of her father's

[1] Bridges-Adams
[2] *Life Magazine* (1 May 1964)
[3] Ibid
[4] Ibid

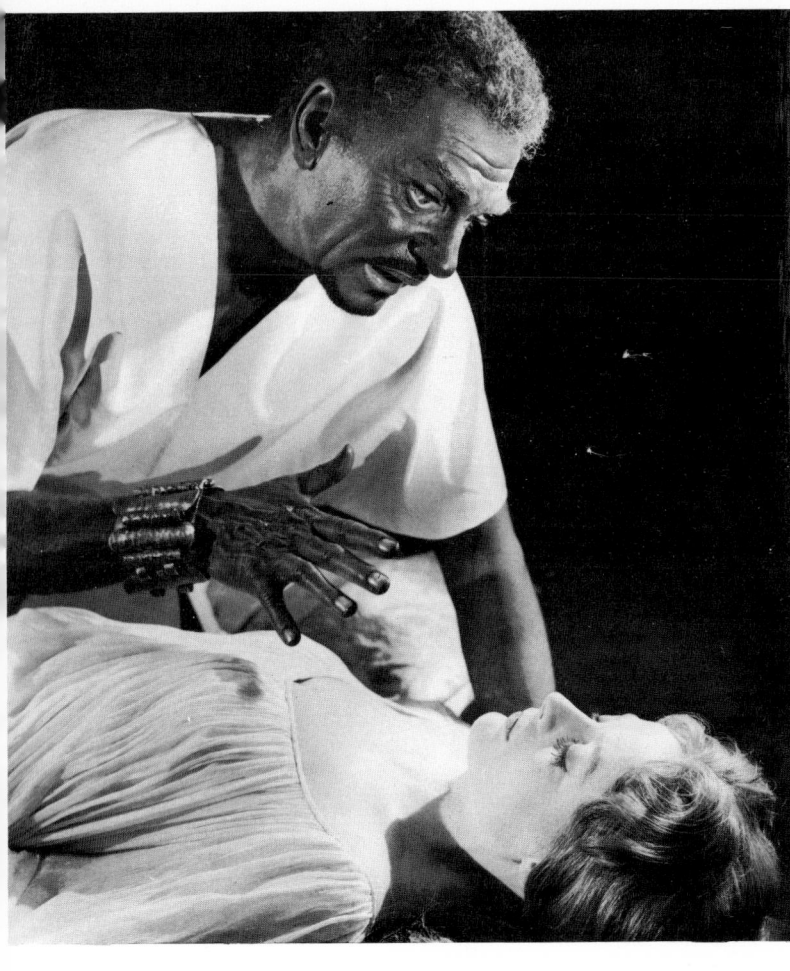

Laurence Olivier as Othello and
Maggie Smith as Desdemona,
National Theatre of Great Britain 1964

death and Hamlet's repudiation. This Ophelia was a tragic contrast and companion to Hamlet himself – the one succumbing to total madness, the other taking refuge in a feigned lunacy, both unhinged, and both defeated in their struggle with unkindly fate.

Olivier had hesitated a long time before attempting Othello. He felt that he lacked the necessary 'blue-black' voice, and now he took much pains in darkening it to the right colour. Having spent, as he admitted, 'a good deal of my early life fighting the lyrical tendencies of my colleagues',[2] and aware that his natural instrument was the trumpet, he was anxious about the strings and the woodwind. He could also be seen sprinting along the sea front at Brighton, loosening still further his always agile limbs. He believed that Othello should be 'very graceful', and walk 'like a soft, black leopard'.[3] Working, as he liked to do, from the outside inwards, he was attracted by the views of T. S. Eliot and F. R. Leavis that a flaw of self-dramatizing egotism and conceit in Othello had led to his downfall. He also decided to present an unmistakable negro, down to the last detail of a remarkable make-up – 'a little tiny touch of lake on the lips, and a lot more brown, and a little mauve'.[4] To this he added an easy, swinging gait. It was a new Othello, and a new Olivier, that took London by storm in the spring of 1964.

Bernard Levin described the performance as 'larger than life, bloodier than

death, and more piteous than pity'; Philip Hope-Wallace wrote of its 'inventiveness, variety, and range, agonizing in the vehemence of anguish'; J. C. Trewin
of its 'bursts of barbaric music and wind-tossed harmonies', comparing it to the
'full, thunder-arched fury of the breaking wave'. One or two people wrote it
off as 'empty virtuosity'; others admitted that it left them unmoved. Certainly
Olivier's conception of the part forbade an easy pathos; he did not present a
wounded simpleton, hardly responsible for his fate. You are moved in a different
way by a man who has in large measure deserved his tragedy than by one who
has scarcely deserved it at all. Naturally a connoisseur of acting took pleasure in
watching and analysing Olivier's spectacular effects; his declared ambition was
'to lead the public towards an appreciation of acting – to watch acting for acting's
sake'.[1] But admiration did not exclude the emotion that any performance of
Othello must excite. The authority was rarely asserted; yet the speech to the
Senate had an easy self-confidence. This Othello knew very well that the state
had need of him in a crisis – and he also knew that Desdemona was 'fast his wife'.
Refusing to regard himself as on trial, he charmingly condescended to an explanation. No one could have been more secure in his universe until it fell about him.
His questioning of Desdemona over the loss of the handkerchief was an angry
imploring, not an angry insistence. The collapse was marked, unforgettably, at
the end of the jealousy scene when he threw away the crucifix hanging round his
neck, and relapsed into the pagan chaos from which baptism had delivered him.
He was now powerless to withstand the atavism of his ancestral past, and we
were spared no horror of psychological and physical disintegration – from the
piercing 'O the pity of it, Iago', when he blotted himself in agony against the
wall, to the dreadful convulsions of the epileptic fit. The final speech was
delivered with Desdemona gathered in his arms; and the act of suicide itself
was a technical feat to admire if one did not choose to be moved by it. Frank
Finlay's Iago was much debated – a small man working a monstrous mischief
from the meanest motives, and Dr Leavis had argued the case for him. Olivier
had once confessed that he had 'no burning desire to go into black-face and have
the stage stolen from me by some young and brilliant Iago'.[2] There was no risk
of anyone stealing the stage from this Othello, but an added dimension would
have been given to the play if Michael Redgrave had been asked to share it.

So the story draws towards its close with an individual performance that took
its place beside the greatest creations of the past, original and controversial as
they had been. I have drawn a faint dotted line after the Quartercentennial
year because this was in itself an occasion for stock-taking. But the door stood
wide open to the future with its triumphs and its freaks and its failures.
Zeffirelli's burlesque of *Much Ado about Nothing* at the National anaesthetized
any sensitive response to his own genius for fantastication. The play has its
côté noir, which was not helped by turning Don John into a half-wit; and where
was the sense in saddling Dogberry – that most obstinately British of Shakespearian constables – with a foreign accent? The director had done his best to
silence Shakespeare, but Shakespeare had the last devastating word – as he
generally does when clever people refuse to speak the speech as it is set down for
them. Peter Hall at Stratford was bent on an existentialist *Hamlet* – and the word
can stand, though it has stood too long – but he wisely refrained from producing
the play in modern dress. He preserved the link between Montaigne's doubt and
Pascal's anguish, and our own, making it quite clear that we were living under
the shadow of Machiavelli and free to decide, according to our political

[1] Ibid
[2] Ibid

sympathies, whether we were also living under the shadow of Macmillan. The production, owing much to John Bury's saturnine imagination, had space and scale and splendour, but it was not obtrusively baroque. Elsinore was not giving itself away so easily.

The action had a merciful immobility. People were allowed to sit at tables and talk without feeling the need to 'break it up' or 'shift the pattern' – although the exciting chase in the dark after the killing of Polonius showed that Peter Hall could move his actors like the wind when he had to. David Warner's movingly mixed-up young Hamlet was all there in Shakespeare's flexible iambics, and he was making things much more difficult for himself when he tried to rearrange the score. But Tony Church's Polonius would have presided over a Cabinet in Downing Street, only the more comic for his ability to do so, and Claudius' curt dismissal of the Court at the climax of the play scene – leaving the hysteria to Hamlet – was particularly impressive. Peter Hall had done here what Bridges-Adams had always dreamt of doing, but never dared to. It was many years since 'Bridges' used to be heard murmuring in the wings 'Speed, speed' when he thought the actors were cerebrating in contempt of the clock. For Peter Hall 'self-indulgence' was the actor's mortal sin, and he might well have applied it to cerebration – for in this instance an exciting effect was spoiled by the ensuing slowness.

The same season (1965) saw John Schlesinger's superb production of *Timon of Athens* striking its contrast between the puppets of Athenian Mayfair, filling their days with emptiness, and the later picture of unaccommodated man discovering, with a stunning irony and symbolism, gold in the cavity which was to be his grave. Paul Scofield had played the earlier scenes with a captivating authority and grace; in the later ones the excess of his misanthropy was the measure of his growth. He had learnt from an emotion, which he could not master, enough to give his outcry a tragic resonance. In this performance of Timon – elegant, electric, and discriminating – Scofield had released a new, though not unsuspected, impetus of passion. The rough sweetness of his voice was beautifully cadenced, and his movements and gestures had the swift emphasis of one who never doubts that tomorrow will take care of itself. When it failed to do so the bass register was at hand to articulate despair and disillusion – and all, as Barker would have said, 'within the framework of the verse'.

Scofield's failure to follow his own example contributed to the failure of *Macbeth* (1967) with which Peter Hall took his leave of the Royal Shakespeare Theatre. Excellently (and theologically) conceived, the production was sadly misbegotten. The accident of illness – for the traditional hoodoo on the play was still to be exorcised – had fatally delayed its momentum. But the Royal Shakespeare, with Trevor Nunn now in charge, had more than one masterpiece in store. Terry Hands's *Pericles* – the stage a canvas on which the actors could execute the calligraphy – gave Ian Richardson a golden opportunity to combine power and finesse. One was left thinking of the very obvious Hamlet that Stratford had allowed to slip through its fingers. In the recognition scene, played with a kind of agonized ecstasy, it was a brilliant touch to make 'the music of the spheres' audible to no one but Pericles and Marina. Trevor Nunn's *Winter's Tale* set the opening scene in Mamillius' nursery, with the hobby-horse in the middle symbolic both of innocence and lust; and the sunstroke of Leontes' obsession was conveyed by a sudden change of lighting – a reminder that in what is described as an 'old tale' we must take its arbitrariness on the chin.

Ronald Pickup as Rosalind in the
all-male *As You Like It*,
National Theatre of Great Britain 1967

Sara Kestleman as Titania and
David Waller as Bottom in
Peter Brook's *A Midsummer Night's
Dream*, Royal Shakespeare Theatre,
Stratford-upon-Avon, 1970

Given the youth and versatility of Judi Dench, the doubling of Hermione and Perdita presented a problem only in the last scene when mother and daughter meet. It was solved by placing Hermione's statue – not, at first, Hermione herself, for Perdita still has some words to speak – on a revolving pedestal. Technically, the solution was water-tight, but one was so busy admiring the sleight of hand that the emotional impact of the scene was a trifle blunted. John Barton's Septembral *Twelfth Night* saw the play through the eyes of Feste. Judi Dench's Viola brought the realities of emotional as well as physical shipwreck into a world where Orsino was reading too much Spenser and Sidney for the good of his soul, and where Olivia had too much money. The humours were given hilarious rein with a Scots Aguecheek trailing his bagpipes, and Donald Sinden's Malvolio towering above his persecutors – a bigger man than they for all his grotesque infatuation – and leaving the right bitterness in the mouth when the play's flight from realism might have seemed too precipitate – like the howling of the gale outside the gilded cage of Orsino's palace with its white trees and contemporary garden seats.

And so – with an appreciative nod at the National's all-male *As You Like It* – we are brought to Olivier's nearly contemporary Shylock; a nineteenth-century Rothschild, speaking faster than anyone else because his mind moved more quickly, and facing his enemies across the mahogany of a Victorian board-room. This was Forsyte country, accurately mapped, but Jonathan Miller should have gone to Hans Andersen for Belmont – for the open door, more significantly than the open stage, sets no limits to the creative imagination, and the genius of Peter Brook was there to fill it. Who could have predicted a *Midsummer Night's Dream* which was applauded as an extravagant invention, but which should more exactly have been seen as a response? For all its breath-taking virtuosity, this left the impression not of a man asking himself what he could do with a play grown too familiar, but of what the play could do with him – stranded as he was, without magical beliefs, in the middle of the twentieth-century. And the magic had been found, far beyond the spinning saucers and Titania's bright-red feather-bed, where Shakespeare had put it and where it must always be rediscovered – in the alchemy of the spoken word.

Select Bibliography

Agate, James *An Anthology* (ed. Herbert von Thal). London and New York 1961.
Brief Chronicles. London 1943.
First Nights. London and New York 1934.
(Ed.) *The English Dramatic Critics: 1660-1932.* London 1932; New York 1958.

Allen, Shirley S. *Samuel Phelps and Sadlers Wells Theatre.* Middletown (Conn.) 1971.

Baring, Maurice *Punch and Judy.* London 1924; facsimile edition New York 1968.

Barker, Felix *The Oliviers.* London 1953.

Barrault, Jean-Louis *Souvenirs pour demain.* Paris 1972.
The Theatre of Jean-Louis Barrault. London 1961.

Beerbohm, Max (Ed.) *Herbert Beerbohm Tree.* London and New York 1920.
Around Theatres. London 1953; New York 1969.

Boaden, James *Memoirs of the Life of John Philip Kemble.* London and New York 1825.
Memoirs of Mrs Siddons. London and New York 1827.

Brasillach, Robert *Animateurs de Théâtre.* Paris 1938.

Brereton, Austen *'H.B.' and Laurence Irving.* London 1922.

Bridges-Adams, W. *Letter Book* (ed. with Memoir by Robert Speaight). Society for Theatre Research 1972.

Brook, Peter *The Empty Space.* London 1968; New York 1969.

Brown, Ivor *Shakespeare Memorial Theatre: 1951-1953.* London 1953.
Shakespeare Memorial Theatre: 1954-1956. London 1956.
Shakespeare Memorial Theatre: 1957-1959. London 1959.
Shakespeare and the Actors. London 1970; New York 1971.

Brown, John Mason *Dramatis Personae.* New York, 1963

Carter, Huntly *The Theatre of Max Reinhardt.* London and New York 1914.

Cibber, Colley *An Apology for the Life of Colley Cibber Written by Himself.* 1740; London 1938.

Clement, Clara E. *Charlotte, Cushman.* London 1882.

Coghill, Nevill *Shakespeare's Professional Skills.* Cambridge 1964.

Cole, Toby and Chinoy, Helen Krich *Directing the Play.* London.

Collins, Herbert F. *Talma: Biography of an Actor.* London and New York 1964.

Craig, E. Gordon *Henry Irving.* London and New York 1930.

Darlington, W. A. *Six Thousand and One Nights.* London 1960.

Davies, Robertson *Twice have the Trumpets Sounded.* Toronto 1954.
Thrice the Brinded Cat hath Mewed. Toronto 1955.

Davies, Robertson and Guthrie, Tyrone *Renown at Stratford.* Toronto 1953.

Davies, Thomas *Dramatic Miscellanies.* London 1785.

Day, M. C. and Trewin, J. C. *The Shakespeare Memorial Theatre.* London 1932.

Disher, M. Wilson *The Last Romantic.* London 1948.

Doran, John *Their Majesties' Servants.* London 1897; New York 1970.

Downer, Alan S. *The Eminent Tragedian: William Charles Macready.* Cambridge (Mass.) 1966.

Farjeon, Herbert *The Shakespearian Scene.* London 1949.

Findlater, Richard *Six Great Actors.* London 1957.
Michael Redgrave, Actor. London 1956.

Forbes-Robertson, Johnston *A Player under Three Reigns.* London and New York 1925.

Gielgud, John *Early Stages.* London 1939.
Stage Directions. London and New York 1963.

Gilder, Rosamund *John Gielgud's Hamlet.* London 1937.

Gourfinkel, Nina *Théâtre russe contemporain.* 1931.

Granville-Barker, H. and Harrison, G. B. *A Companion to Shakespeare Studies.* Cambridge 1934.

Guthrie, Tyrone *On Acting.* London and New York 1971.

Hagarshack, David *Stanislavsky.* 1951.

Hale, Lionel *The Old Vic 1949-50.* London 1950.

Harwood, Ronald *Sir Donald Wolfit.* London 1971.

Hazlitt, William *Dramatic Essays.* London 1895.

Hobson, Harold *Theatre I.* London 1938.
Theatre II. London 1950.
Ralph Richardson (Theatre World Monograph). London 1958.

Holmes, Martin *Shakespeare and his Players.* London 1973.

Houseman, John *Run-Through.* London and New York 1973.

Irving, Laurence *Henry Irving: The Actor and his World.* London and New York 1951.
The Successors. London 1968.

James, Henry *The Scenic Art.* London and New York 1949.

Joseph, Bertram *The Tragic Actor.* London and New York 1959.
Acting Shakespeare. London and New York 1960.

Kemble, Fanny *Records of a Girlhood* (3 vols). London and New York 1879.

Keown, Eric *Peggy Ashcroft* (Theatre World Monograph). London 1955.

Kott, Jan *Shakespeare our Contemporary.* London and New York 1967.

Lamb, Charles *Essays of Elia.*

Lang, Matheson *Mr Wu Looks Back.* London 1940.

Lenormand, H. R. *Les Pitoëff.* Paris 1943.

Lewes, George Henry *On Actors and the Art of Acting.* London and Westport (Conn.) 1875.
Dramatic Essays. London 1896.

Lovat, Laura *Maurice Baring.* London 1947.

McArthy, Desmond *Theatre.* London 1954.

MacLeod, Joseph *The New Soviet Theatre.* London 1943.

Manvell, Roger *Ellen Terry.* London and New York 1968.
Sarah Siddons. London and New York 1970.

Mason, E. Tuckerman *The Othello of Tommaso Salvini.* New York 1890.

Montague, C. E. *Dramatic Values.* London 1910.

Muir, Kenneth and Schoenbaum, S. *A New Companion to Shakespeare Studies.* Cambridge 1971.

Nemirovitch-Danchenko, Vladimir *Myself in the Russian Theatre.* London and New York 1968.

Playfair, Giles *Kean.* London 1950.

Poel, William *Monthly Letters.* London and New York 1929.
Shakespeare in the Theatre. London and New York 1913.

Purdom, C. B. *Granville-Barker.* London and Westport (Conn.) 1955.
Producing Shakespeare. London 1950.
Representative Actors.

Richardson, Joanna *Sarah Bernhardt.* London 1959.

Richter, Hélène *Kainz.* Leipzig and Vienna 1931.

Rosenberg, Marvin *The Masks of Othello.* 1961.

Russell, W. Clark *Representative Actors.* London and New York.

St John, Christopher (Ed.) *Ellen Terry and Bernard Shaw.* London 1931; New York 1945.

Shattuck, Charles H. *The Hamlet of Edwin Booth.* Urbana (Ill.) 1969.

Shaw, G. Bernard *Our Theatres in the Nineties.* London 1932.

Skinner, Otis *Footlights and Spotlights.* 1924.

Speaight, Robert *William Poel and the Elizabethan Revival.* London and Cambridge (Mass.) 1954.

Sprague, A. C. *Shakespeare and the Actors.* Cambridge (Mass.) 1945.
Shakespearian Players and Performances. London and New York 1954.

Sprague, A. C. and Trewin, J. C. *Shakespeare's Plays Today.* London 1970; South Carolina 1971.

Stanislavsky, Constantin *My Life in Art.* London and New York 1924.

Stern, Ernst *My Life, my Stage.* London 1951.

Taylor, A. M. *Next to Shakespeare.* London 1950.

Terry, Ellen *The Story of my Life.* London 1908.

Towse, John R. *Sixty Years at the Theatre.*

New York 1916.
Trewin, J. C. *Shakespeare on the English Stage: 1900-1964.* London and New York 1964.
Benson and the Bensonians. London and New York 1960.
A Play Tonight. London 1952.
John Neville. London 1961.
Peter Brook. London 1971.
Tynan, Kenneth *He that Plays the King.* London 1950.
Curtains. London and New York 1961.
Vandenhoff, George *Dramatic Reminiscences.* London 1860.
Varneke, B. V. *History of the Russian Theatre.* New York 1951.
Watkins, Ronald *Moonlight at the Globe.*

London 1946.
On Producing Shakespeare. London and New York 1950.
Webster, Margaret *Shakespeare Today.* London and Chester Springs (Pa.) 1957.
Wickham, Glynne *Early English Stages Vol. 2.* London 1963; New York 1971.
Wiener, Leo *The Contemporary Drama of Russia.* Boston 1924.
Williams, Harcourt *Four Years at the Old Vic.* New York 1935.
Wilson, J. Dover and Worsley, T. C. *Shakespeare's Histories at Stratford, 1951.* London 1952.
Winter, William *The Wallet of Time.* New York 1913.
Vagrant Memories. New York 1915.

Shakespeare on the Stage. London and New York 1912.
Wood, Roger and Clarke, Mary *Shakespeare at the Old Vic* (5 vols). London 1955-9.
Young, J. C. *The Life of Charles Mayne Young.* 1871.
Young, Stark *Immortal Shadows.* 1948.

Periodicals
Drama
Theatre Arts Monthly, 1916-50.
'Shakespeare en France' *Études anglaises.* April-June 1960. Paris.
Revue d'histoire du théâtre. October-December 1964; January-March 1965. Paris.

Illustration Acknowledgments

Index